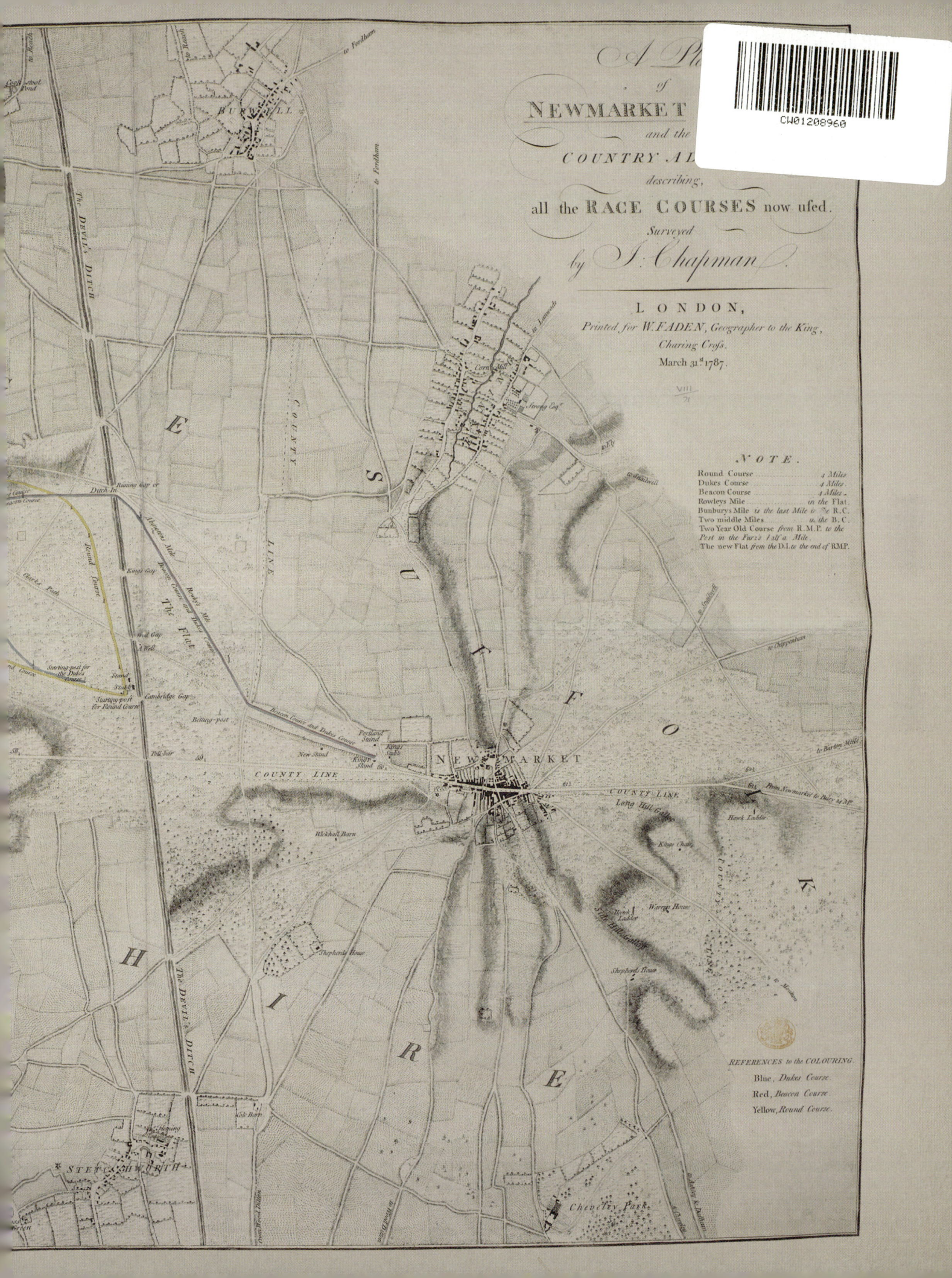

A Plan of NEWMARKET and the COUNTRY ADJACENT describing all the RACE COURSES now used.

Surveyed by J. Chapman

LONDON,
Printed for W. FADEN, Geographer to the King,
Charing Cross.
March 31st 1787.

NOTE.

Round Course .... 4 Miles
Dukes Course .... 4 Miles
Beacon Course .... 4 Miles
Rowleys Mile *is the last Mile in the Flat*
Bunburys Mile *is the last Mile in the R.C.*
Two middle Miles *in the B.C.*
Two Year Old Course *from R.M.P. to the Post in the Furzs half a Mile.*
The new Flat *from the D.I. to the end of R.M.P.*

REFERENCES to the COLOURING.

Blue, *Dukes Course.*
Red, *Beacon Course.*
Yellow, *Round Course.*

THE HEATH & THE HORSE

THE HEATH & THE HORSE

◆◆◆◆

A HISTORY OF RACING AND ART
ON NEWMARKET HEATH

DAVID OLDREY, TIMOTHY COX & RICHARD NASH

PWP

Published in 2016 by Philip Wilson Publishers
an imprint of I.B.Tauris & Co Ltd
London · New York

www.philip-wilson.co.uk

Copyright © David Oldrey, Timothy Cox and Richard Nash 2016

All rights reserved. No part of this publication may be reproduced, stored in a retrieval system or transmitted in any form or by any means, electronic, mechanical, photocopying, recording or otherwise without prior permission of the publishers.

The rights of David Oldrey and Timothy Cox to be identified as authors of this work have been asserted by the authors in accordance with the Copyright, Designs and Patents Act 1988.

ISBN 978 1 78130 023 7

Every attempt has been made to gain permission for the use of the images in this book. Any omissions will be rectified in future editions.

Endpapers: Newmarket Heath surveyed by John Chapman (1787)
Designed by Pippa Kate Bridle

Printed and bound in China by 1010 Printing

FSC — MIX Paper from responsible sources — FSC® C016973 — www.fsc.org

THE JOCKEY CLUB
ESTATES

Contents

Acknowledgements　iv

Foreword by Sir Mark Prescott　vii

Note on Authorship　ix

Introduction　1

PART 1 – Newmarket's Place in Racing History

Chapter 1 (pre-1605)　14

Chapter 2 (1605–1660)　17

Chapter 3 (1660–1714)　25

Chapter 4 (1714–1750)　39

Chapter 5 (1750–1791)　55

Chapter 6 (1791–1863)　89

Chapter 7 (1863–1914)　105

Chapter 8 (1914–1945)　123

Chapter 9 (1945–1980)　137

Chapter 10 (since 1980)　155

PART 2 – Newmarket Heath

I Buildings on the Heath　171

II Layout of Individual Courses on the Heath　200

III Main Races on the Heath　210

IV Newmarket in Wartime　230

V The National Stud　236

VI Topography of the Heath and Its Layout　242

VII Training at Newmarket – Changing Methods for Preparing the Racehorse　250

VIII Holcroft's Memoir of Life in a Newmarket Yard (1758–1760)　262

IX History of the Palace and Its Development as Part of the National Heritage Centre for Horseracing and Sporting Art　266

PART 3 – Early History of the Jockey Club and Its Links to the Collapse and Sudden Recovery of Racing in the Mid-Eighteenth Century

I The Jockey Club before 1750: Politics, Art, and Sport in the Early Formation of the Jockey Club　274

II The Newmarket Bank and the Beginnings of Bookmaking　292

III Comparison Between the Effects at Newmarket and Elsewhere of the Catastrophic Decline of the 1730s and 1740s　296

IV Commentary on Letter by Philo-Hippos of 1752 on Racing's Recovery　301

V Reaction Around 1770 Against Activities at Newmarket　306

VI Acquisition of the Heath by the Jockey Club　311

PART 4 – APPENDICES

Appendix 1　320
Background to Courses on the Heath

Appendix 2　322
Starts, finishes and Distances on the Heath

Appendix 3　326
Leading Newmarket Trainers since 1899

Index　332

Picture Credits　341

Acknowledgements

This book has been several years in the making. Along the way many have encouraged us, helped us to form our views and challenged some of our conclusions. We thank them for all their support and hope they will be satisfied with how we have handled their contributions. While we have unearthed many 'new' bits of evidence about the development of horseracing on Newmarket Heath we expect more to appear as the new technologies allow access to a wider range of sources than ever before.

We would like to thank those who have provided practical help to bring this book to print. It is much appreciated by all three of us.

Sir Mark Prescott and Christopher Foster read the book in an early draft form and added some helpful insights. Sir Mark also wrote the Foreword.

Alan Grundy of the National Horseracing Museum has been tireless in photographing the pictures and objects in private collections and providing high-quality images for the book. His technical skills in taking the original photographs in a variety of unhelpful locations and then preparing them for publication is much appreciated.

Many of the works of art are in private collections and we are grateful to their owners for allowing us to reproduce them here. Martin and the late Gay Slater were very supportive from the start, and we are lucky to be able to show the paintings of the old buildings on Newmarket Heath that were produced by John Flatman, the son of Nat, the great Newmarket jockey. Sir Mark has allowed us to reproduce the picture of *The Heath House String at Exercise* that still hangs in its original place at Heath House and will continue to do so for many years to come.

Lord Halifax, Sir Edward Cazalet and George Winn-Darley have encouraged us to use pictures from their collections. Nick Reed Herbert still has various local images in his private collection, and will recognise many more that he has sold over the years and which appear as illustrations. Both Christie's and Sotheby's have been extremely helpful and supplied many of the necessary images from their old catalogues. Tomasso Brothers kindly permitted us to use the picture of the July Course by Harry Hall.

Much of the work could not have been done without the help of archivists and other researchers. Richard would like to thank the librarians and archivists at the National Archives and the Guildhall Library. We would like also to thank the members of Old Bald Peg, an international group studying the early history of British racing, in particular A. J. Hibbard in Wisconsin, Miodrag Milovanovic in Serbia, William Morgan in Scotland and Tony Byles in Shropshire, Chris Garibaldi and Graham Snelling for access to the archives of the National Horseracing Museum, Vanessa Brett for her help with the Deards Family and Sandra Easom and David Rippington of the Newmarket Local History Society.

Andrew Merriam, Chairman, and William Gittus, Managing Director, of Jockey Club Estates have been enthusiastic supporters of this project. Without their support it would not have come to fruition. We thank them.

Foreword

As a racehorse trainer, I have been lucky enough to train for some of the very best owners. Having only a small stable of 50 boxes to fill, I always say that I have been fortunate never to covet one of my colleague's owners. There is, however, one exception and that is the co-author of this book, David Oldrey.

David is a bachelor, a Form expert, a programme book guru, an owner-breeder of Flat-bred staying horses, a fanatical devotee of accurate sporting historical research, an art aficionado, and an occasional punter. I always felt that these qualities would make him an ideal patron of Heath House – but not a bit of it! In addition to these assets, he is fiercely loyal and has never wavered in his support for the stables of Peter Walwyn and his successor Ralph Beckett, who have trained his horses with consummate skill for over 50 years.

In my annual scrapbook (one completed for each year, for the 45 years that I have trained) I have only ever kept one newspaper editorial. The piece was written by Brough Scott, during the period that Martin Pipe's meteoric rise was rewriting the handbook on how National Hunt horses should be trained – his feats at the time engendering libellous gossip from those trainers less proficient in the art. 'Jealousy has long been Racing's besetting sin', wrote Brough, 'and it demeans us all'.

I always think and hope that I have never been jealous of my peers' success or possessions in whatever field of interest they may operate. However, as an avid sporting book collector, I have found myself fighting the green-eyed monster when contemplating Tim Cox's racing library. A collector for over 40 years, Tim's collection has expanded to such an extent that his house has had to be rebuilt to accommodate it. Affable, precise, self-deprecating and unfailingly generous with his knowledge, his scholarly approach is always accompanied by a good-humoured owlish smile, conveying at all times that nothing is too much trouble in the acquisition and dissemination of Turf history.

While I have never met Professor Nash, the text of the two sections he has contributed make it abundantly clear that he knows a great deal more about the eighteenth-century Jockey Club than that august institution knew about itself.

What good fortune it is, therefore, for all lovers of the Turf, for historians now and in the future, and for all art lovers the world over that David Oldrey and Tim Cox, with the help of Professor Nash, should have combined their 150 years of scholarship into producing this book for the Jockey Club Estates – a labour of love that will satisfy the most discerning and entertain the more casual reader in equal proportions.

It has been my great fortune to be Chairman of the Newmarket Trainers' Heath Committee for over 40 years, and thus to liaise with the Jockey Club over the way in which the Heath is managed. Inevitably, at times, there will have been moments when my training colleagues have doubted the value of my influence, and I have long suspected that my longevity in the position may well have been primarily due to the fact that none of my fellow trainers has relished the thought of undertaking the task themselves. In truth,

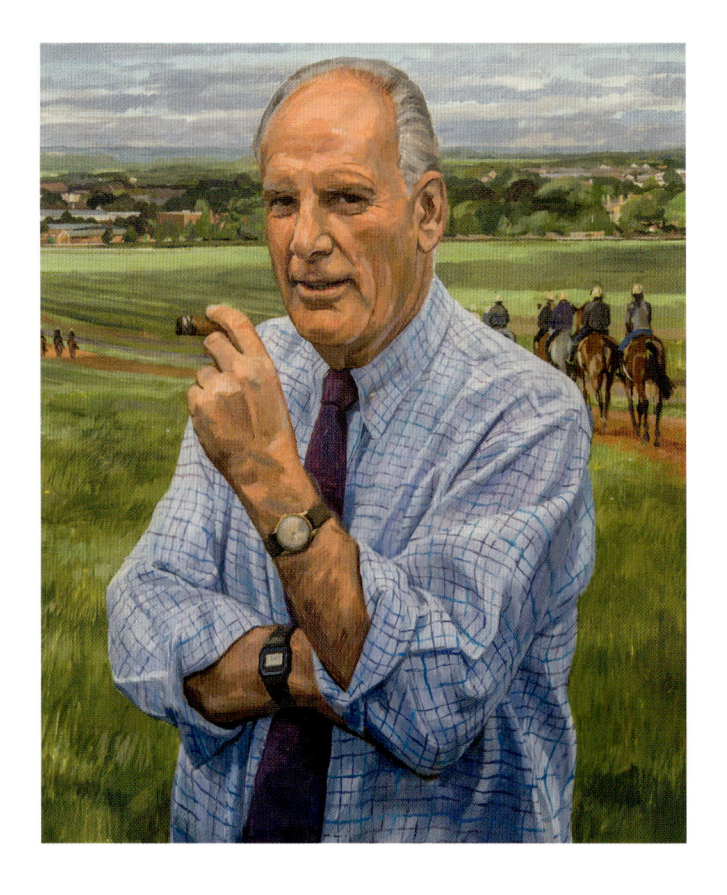

Sir Mark Prescott by Jeff Stultiens (2014)

there may have been times when I have felt that the only two words I have never heard from my contemporaries have been 'thank' and 'you'. Nevertheless, it has in fact been a delight and a privilege to have been part of a period of continual change and development that has enabled the Heath to cope with the varying demands made upon it.

In 1967, when I came to work at Heath House as assistant trainer to Jack Waugh, there were 35 trainers with 750 horses in their care using the Heath every day. Today there are 81 trainers and over 2,500 horses using the same 2,500 acres.

Towards the middle of the nineteenth century, there were more horses trained at Stockbridge than in Newmarket.

Today, no horses are trained at Stockbridge. Yet such was the Jockey Club's influence in those days that in 1851 the new railway line, bored through a tunnel over half a mile in length, was opened to avoid disrupting the hallowed turf. Much later, it was the preservation of the Heath that saved the town from being subsumed by 'over-spill'. Later, the route of the motorway was sent two-and-a-half miles out of its way to go round the Heath, so avoiding a serious attempt to drive straight through the middle. During two World Wars not an acre of the principal gallops was ploughed for the war effort. Only portions of Waterhall and Railway Land succumbed.

Through the last five centuries, the Heath and not the racecourse has been the single most important factor in the town's development – after all, there are over 50 towns that boast a racecourse, but none that has the Heath or anything to compare with it.

It was these gallops that brought the trainers, the staff, the owners and the horses, and with them followed ancillary businesses – veterinarians, saddlers, forage merchants, blacksmiths, sales companies, bloodstock agents, as well, of course, as the development of the surrounding land to accommodate the great studs that now surround the town.

David Oldrey, Tim Cox and Richard Nash chronicle all these developments, with an eye to both fact and anecdote, and all in the context of the art that has lovingly portrayed the central characters – man and beast – as the years rolled by. What a treat lies in store for their readers…

Sir Mark Prescott
Heath House, Newmarket
January 2015

Note on authorship

The division of labour between the co-authors has seen David Oldrey draft the text for all but two sections and Tim Cox conduct the lion's share of the necessary research. Almost throughout the text refers to 'we' but in a few places David's direct involvement in the Jockey Club and other organisations has made the use of 'I' unavoidable. However, the few examples should not be seen as limiting the degree to which the book is a joint and equal collaboration.

The two sections on the Jockey Club prior to 1750 and the Newmarket Bank have been contributed by Richard Nash. His extensive research into the relevant period has been of considerable assistance to his co-authors in their work elsewhere in this book.

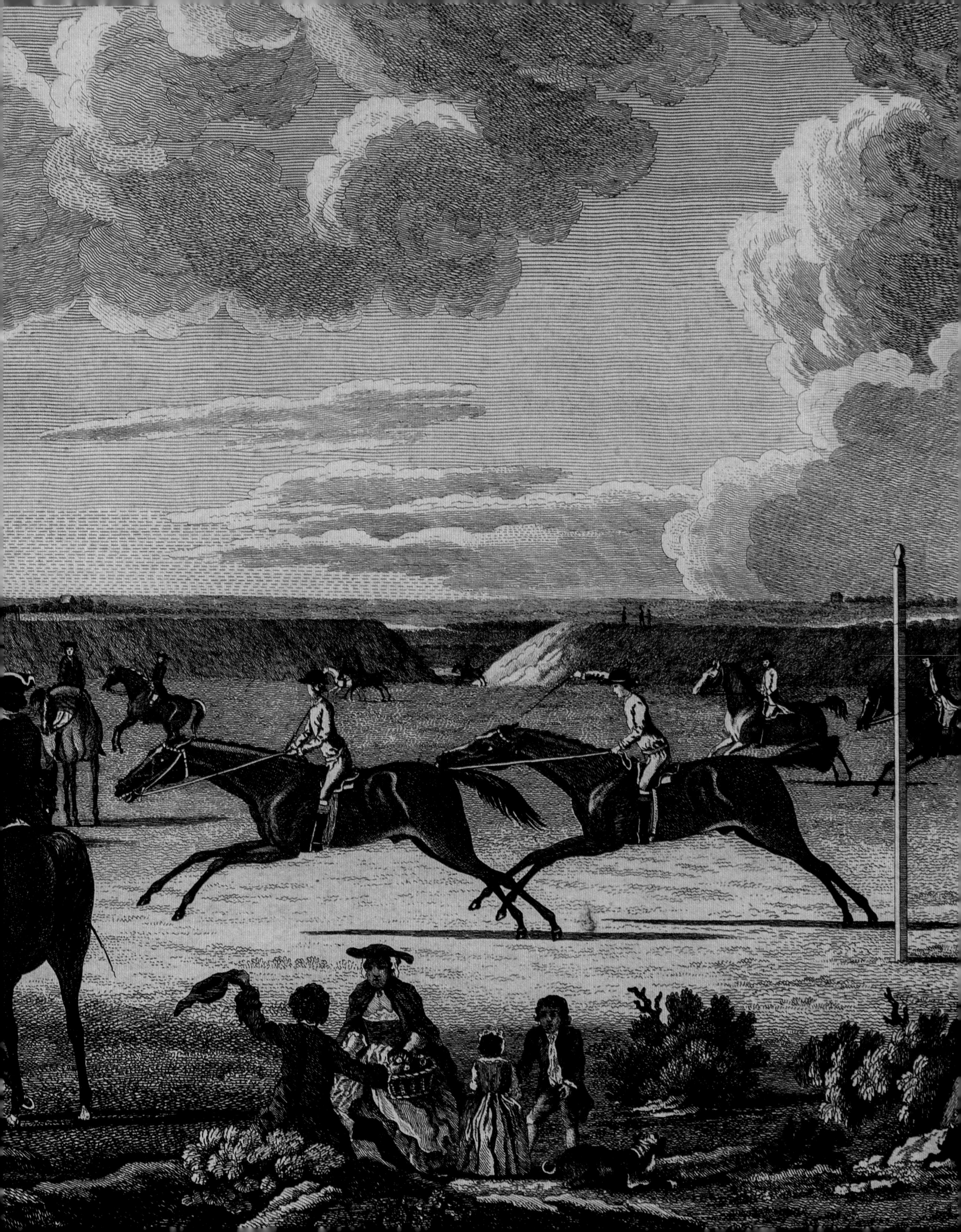

Introduction

Newmarket Heath has been the subject of a good many books since James I arrived there to course hare near Fordham in 1605. However, while some authors have concentrated on the town's many yards and their human and equine inhabitants, others on the Jockey Club, and several more on the crucial links with the Royal Court as being the best ways to tell a remarkable story, no one account has been grounded in the Heath itself, which gave all the rest the chance to play their leading parts in the story of racing.

Spend a fine spring morning watching the glorious spectacle of a thousand or so thoroughbreds stretching their legs on Warren Hill and Racecourse Side (Fig. 1) and you wonder why this should be so. Later in the day the Heath seems almost as attractive in a very different way, as it extends into the distance with hardly a horse in sight (Fig. 2). Equally, the sight of a strong field coming past the Bushes to finish on the Rowley Mile over the same ground that tested their

Engraving of horses approaching the end of the Rowley Mile in a race over the Beacon after T.Smith (1758), detail of Fig. 3

distant ancestors in the seventeenth century should be capable of stirring even the most sluggish of imaginations (Fig. 3). Yet, until now, no book has explained why the Heath has developed in the way it has, from wild heathland to the manicured turf of today.

This is all the more surprising when one realises that the Heath is the site on which a rural pastime has gradually evolved into a global sport based on a new breed of such quality that it has conquered the equine world. Anyway, the Jockey Club and its estates company, as the place's custodians, feel the time is right to fill the gap. The aim is to do so by providing as comprehensive a § as possible both of what has happened on their patch of East Anglia over four centuries and of the wider consequences of these events.

Naturally, telling the story will include all the themes and subjects that fill the earlier works, but we hope we have done sufficient original research to avoid most of the pitfalls caused by errors which have slowly proliferated and then descended uncorrected from one generation to the next (Fig. 4). No doubt we may have fallen into assorted traps

Fig. 1

Engraving of *Warren Hill* after E.F. Burney (1791)

The delights of the Heath in the morning are being experienced by the Prince of Wales and others. The occasion may well be the Prince's visit in early October 1791, only days before the Escape scandal broke. The Prince also appears in Figs. 6 and 57, which shows what an important figure he was during his intermittent bursts of activity on the Turf.

Fig. 2

Warren Hill by James Seymour (*c.*1750)

The two horses have the Heath to themselves as they walk across Warren Hill. Newmarket is on the left with the old racecourse buildings behind. Exning and a distant view of Burwell are in the centre and Ely Cathedral on the horizon to the right.

Fig. 3

Engraving of horses approaching the end of the Rowley Mile in a race over the Beacon, after T. Smith (1758)

Entitled *Finished Horses*, this is the last in a set of six engravings which chronicle the thoroughbred's life from conception to the finished article as a champion. This is April 1756; ahead races Matchem, later to become a great stallion, with Trajan trailing. Matchem thereby became the first fully documented holder of the Whip. Behind Trajan is the Well Gap, and the recently built July Course Stand can be seen peeping over the Ditch; it must have been cold that spring as smoke is rising from the stand's chimneys.

Fig. 4

Undated engraving of the Duke's Stand

This is a good example of past mistakes. The stand was only built in around 1760, but the image has been regularly recycled as representing the days of Charles I. The misleading introduction of figures decked out in suitably archaic clothes explains one way such errors can occur.

too – but hopefully we have managed to correct more of the alarming mistakes of our predecessors than we bequeath to future generations.

Emphasising the central importance of the Heath itself has led us to use as many as possible of the innumerable paintings, prints and photographs which exist to tell its story. It is hard to think of any other place without distinguished buildings which has attracted quite so many competent artists and, in the case of George Stubbs, a genius. From the end of the seventeenth century such works offer a remarkable window to the past through which to study events on the Heath; indeed, they allow real insight into how racing was run in any particular period, and thus are a record of its development. There are also numerous occasions where the link between several works, sometimes by different artists, is useful in trying to unlock the mysteries contained in these old Newmarket scenes. In ten such cases we have thought it useful to group the relevant pictures together, with texts explaining the links; these exercises are called 'Picture Puzzles'. Apart from the ability of these paintings to shed light on the conduct of racing on the Heath, sporting pictures in general provide an extensive commentary on an oddly assorted slice of society, varying from dignified grandees parading about

Fig. 5

Charles Collyer, 2nd Earl of Portmore, watching his string by John Wootton (*c*.1735)

Lord Portmore with Garter star and riband watches three of his horses set off from the King's Stand in the reverse direction to Gimcrack's trial (see Fig. 55). The close similarity between Wootton and Tillemans' concepts of the King's Stables, and the differences from Stubbs, suggests they were rebuilt as part of the many improvements in the 1750s and 1760s.

the countryside in their Garter ribands (Fig. 5), to cartoons of jockeys pulling horses (Fig. 6), and an amusing painting by Seymour of the notoriously lecherous Sir Robert Fagg ogling the local talent (Fig. 7).

◆◆◆◆

The fortunes of Newmarket have gone through some profound swings from peaks under Charles II, George III and Edward VII to deep troughs during the Commonwealth (Fig. 8), the early Hanoverians and the first part of Victoria's reign. Clearly these trends have been quite closely linked to interest in the sport, or lack of it, by the powers that be. Racing overall has also been subject to the same highs and lows, but never to the extreme extent experienced at Newmarket, where the connection between those in national authority and events on the Heath has been the most pronounced.

Fig. 6

Engraving of the supposed pulling of Escape, after Thomas Rowlandson (1791)

The Prince of Wales, seen tapping his nose on the right, watches his jockey, Sam Chifney senior, stopping Escape on 20 October 1791. The next day the horse beat a better field at much extended odds. What really happened can never be known for sure, but the Prince refused to come to Newmarket for the rest of his life after the row which ensued, and his jockey's career was ruined.

As racing has been more or less favoured by the fashionable world, so the town has prospered or stagnated accordingly up to quite recent times. Certainly since World War I the close links of earlier centuries between the town and Westminster have steadily weakened and the days when the Jockey Club could boast numerous MPs (and not infrequently Prime Ministers) among its membership are long gone. Nowadays the regular supplies of money needed to keep the place reasonably prosperous tend to come from abroad (mostly wealth from the oilfields of the Gulf), and such links as remain with Westminster no longer centre on the Jockey Club and the principal owners. These broad trends have usually dictated the history of Newmarket a good deal more decisively than whether this trainer or that jockey was cock of the walk at any particular time.

The first public stand was only completed in 1876 (Fig. 9). Before then the Heath was effectively the preserve of those on horses, in carriages or with right of access to such small buildings as existed. Several different finishes would usually be used in the same afternoon (sometimes even switching from the July Course to the Beacon finish at the top of the town), and there was entrenched opposition to any material change in case it encouraged the public to appear.

Fig. 7

Sir Robert Fagg and the cherry girl by James Seymour (*c*.1735)

The innuendo in the refusal of Sir Robert's proffered coin, dangled purse and aged, broken down but still very evidently entire mount seems plain enough. That he was also a noted miser whose many horses were mainly screws only adds to the picture's assorted inferences. One feels the girl is well advised not to rely on the contents of the purse.

Following the enclosure of racecourses and the consequent chance to charge for entry in the latter part of the nineteenth century, the importance of attracting rather than repelling racegoers has steadily swung things around until they are now at the polar opposite of earlier days. As a consequence, the importance of individual trainers and jockeys as the sport's most apparent public face has also moved in the same direction, and their ups and downs have become far more than mere interesting footnotes to the real history of the Heath.

Ultimately, the effect of all these developments is summed up in the quality of the horses that have been created down the ages from the original mixed bag of seventeenth-century stock. While in the early stages the studs mainly lay far away

Fig. 8

Pen-and-ink caricature of Oliver Cromwell
by Sir Frank Lockwood

While the Lord Protector bred good horses, racing was banned for the latter part of the Commonwealth for fear of Royalist risings. The artist gave this caricature to the Victorian Prime Minster Lord Rosebery and the splendidly contemporary field glasses slung round the Protector's chest surely make the thing.

in Yorkshire, it was primarily due to the Heath's role as a magnet for money that the thoroughbred was eventually created. The new breed, with its occasional champions and the resources behind it, naturally attracted the best talents to exploit fresh opportunities on the Heath, and thereby identify the stock that would continue its development.

Throughout the eighteenth century virtually every really important stallion apart from unraced Arabians turned out on the Heath.

It is also testament to the taste of the main owners of the day that Stubbs first appeared in the 1760s to paint their champions and so build on the legacy of the work of John Wootton, James Seymour and others. Even after he departed the scene after 1799 the story was carried on by Marshall, Herring and then Munnings, and by the development of photography.

◆◆◆◆

By the end of the eighteenth century the relative importance of Newmarket was in decline but it has never lost its position at the heart of the sport. Racing's worldwide spread in the nineteenth century, as well as much increased competition within England, meant Newmarket's relative decline was inevitable – but since 1750, apart from the twenty years around 1850, absolute decline has never taken hold. Indeed, recent history has seen the town's position as the sport's headquarters considerably reinforced by the influx of almost every major organisation dealing directly with the horse itself in terms of breeding, health and sale, plus many of the leading studs and most of the principal stallions. In light of this, the exodus of those organisations dabbling in racing politics, which have mainly migrated to London, hardly seems of great significance.

The creation of the British Horseracing Board (BHB) in 1993 and, a decade or so later, the Jockey Club's transfer of its powers of regulation of the sport plus any remaining responsibility for interaction with the worlds of both betting and Westminster politics, has concentrated the Club's mind quite wonderfully on Newmarket and its other racecourses. As the last antediluvian Steward (if the flood itself is dated 1993) to be left standing as a director of the BHB, I can confirm just how profound has been that change of attitude.

Fig. 9

The Derby Trial by W.H. Hopkins and E. Havell (1884)

St Gatien, ridden by Fred Archer, is depicted in front of the recently erected grandstand on the Rowley Mile, the first there open to the public. The horse belonged to a successful gambler and former stable lad John Hammond, shown here with his daughter on their hacks, and his horse subsequently dead heated for the 1884 Derby without Archer's assistance.

Indeed, not only profound but beneficial too, at least in terms of its racecourses, whatever view you take of the impact of these changes on politics, regulation, race planning in general and the fixture list in particular.

The Club's authority originally took nearly a century to extend much beyond the Heath, and the fact that in many ways things have now come full circle certainly does not feel like too much of a disaster. As the scope of the Jockey Club's activities expanded steadily in all directions from the 1830s onwards, not only were its available talents spread ever more thinly, but assorted conflicts of interest eventually became apparent; these mainly stemmed from controlling so many different racecourses along with having to take care of national race planning and the fixture list. The fact that such conflicts never got out of hand or caused much public disquiet seems good evidence of the genuinely impartial nature of the institution itself. However, it is hard to imagine that things could have continued in such a vein much longer in these more litigious times when appearances often seem to trump reality.

Be that as it may, there were already serious drawbacks, and perhaps the most obvious was the degree to which the

Fig. 10

Flying Childers by James Seymour (*c.*1725)

The accepted champion of the period, which ended with the final emergence of the new breed in Childers' lifetime, is shown in the background beating Lord Drogheda's Chaunter on 22 October 1722. The artist has stressed the ease of his victory by suggesting that the horse is still taking a fierce hold after more than five miles and with only about five furlongs to go up to the King's Stand. Childers immense reputation was largely based on trial matches with no money at stake, as nobody dared challenge him after what happened to Chaunter. Indeed, the first of these was in effect a time trial over the Round Course in 1721, even before the crushing of Chaunter. Here he was timed by the Dukes of Devonshire and Rutland at 6 minutes 48 seconds, figures it would not be easy to beat by much even today, but the use of the Round Course and the relatively contemporary recording of the time by John Pond may well mean it was correct. The other public trial soon after the defeat of Chaunter was against the top class Fox, never beaten in a real race during a long career. Here Childers gave a stone and a beating of some 350 yards, on which note he retired leaving the world satisfied as to his unparalleled excellence.

Club's various businesses were undermanaged. Even the words 'Jockey Club' were omitted from their names to avoid unnecessary stress on potential conflicts of interest while the Club concentrated on its wider governance role. However, where would the National Stud have gone when the Levy Board decided to bail out of breeding had it not been able to deal with the Jockey Club at arm's length rather than facing another bit of the central control structure of the sport? The answer is probably 'into liquidation', and that it has not turned out that way is a good example of what the Club now has to offer racing in general and Newmarket in particular.

The Club certainly cannot claim to have succeeded in passing on its once dominant position in the sport to any one body. No doubt it was inevitable that powers once appropriate to what was in essence an ancient oligarchy should have become widely dissipated in the modern world. However, what it can claim is that its long existence is the principal reason for the survival in such good order of an oasis of several thousand acres of grassland in the middle of East Anglia's arable prairies, some of it unploughed from time immemorial.

Thus the key to producing a worthwhile book has been to bring out the way Newmarket Heath has provided the stage for a very remarkable performance. After first attracting enough grand folk to underwrite the creation of the thoroughbred (Fig. 10) and give the sport an initially rather dubious but just sufficient respectability, it has seen the whole thing go global. Without the Heath and the support it attracted first from the Court and then the Jockey Club, the whole story of racing and the thoroughbred would be entirely different. The scale of things today around the world makes Newmarket Heath as near a sporting equivalent of 'The Valley of the Kings' as can be found, and one that is still in full working order. It is truly a unique place.

◆◆◆◆

In Part 1 we give an outline of the history of racing in this country and Newmarket's place in it from the days long before James I appeared on the Heath. Apart from the opportunity this gives to use the most interesting pictures, it also provides a context for Part 2, which deals with events from the particular standpoint of Newmarket. Part 3 shows evidence of the Jockey Club's existence in the first part of the eighteenth century, before its supposed foundation in the early 1750s. It sets out in more detail an explanation of racing's extraordinary recovery from 1751 onwards and the way in which the ownership of the Heath slowly passed to the Club. Part 4 contains various appendices.

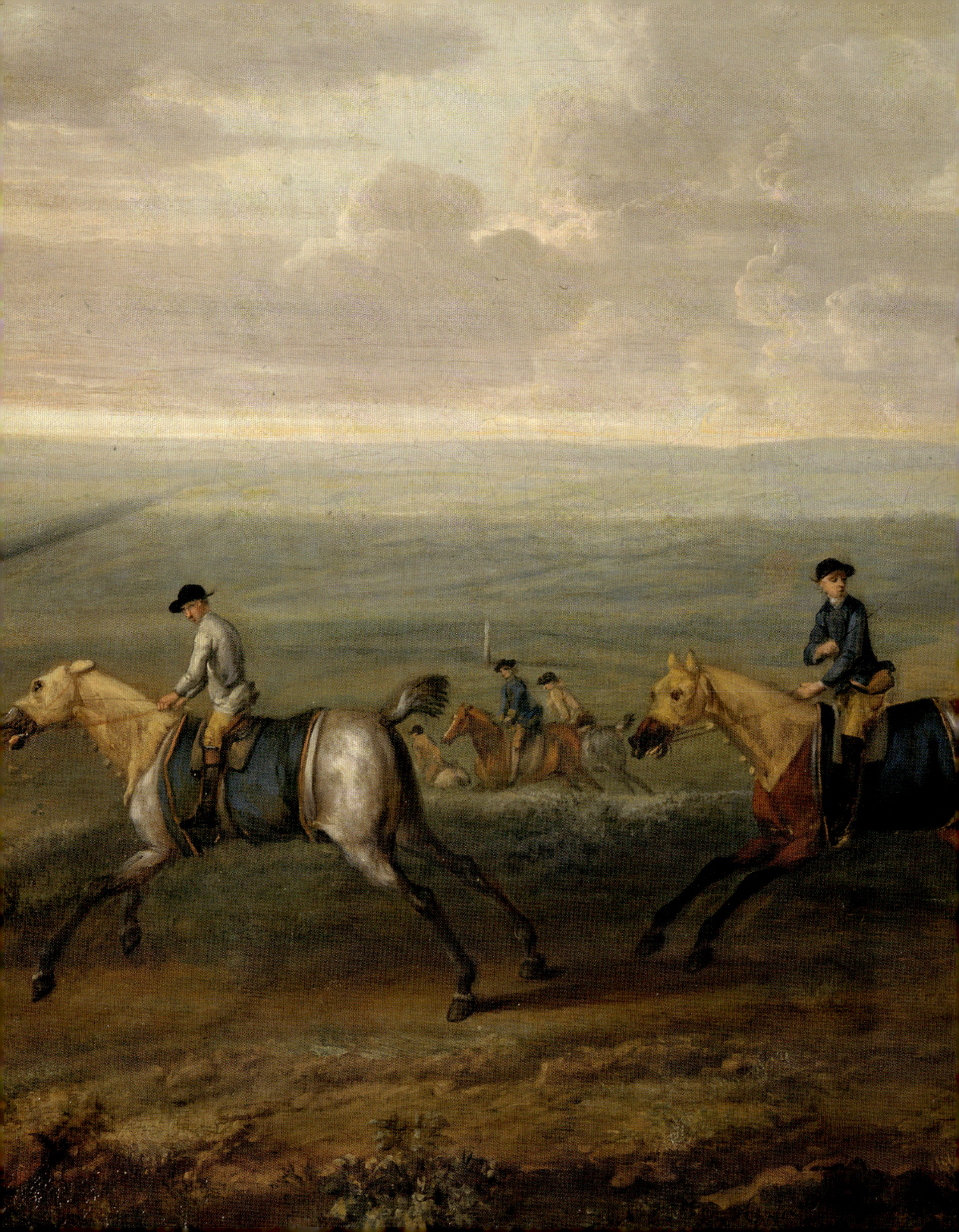

Part One

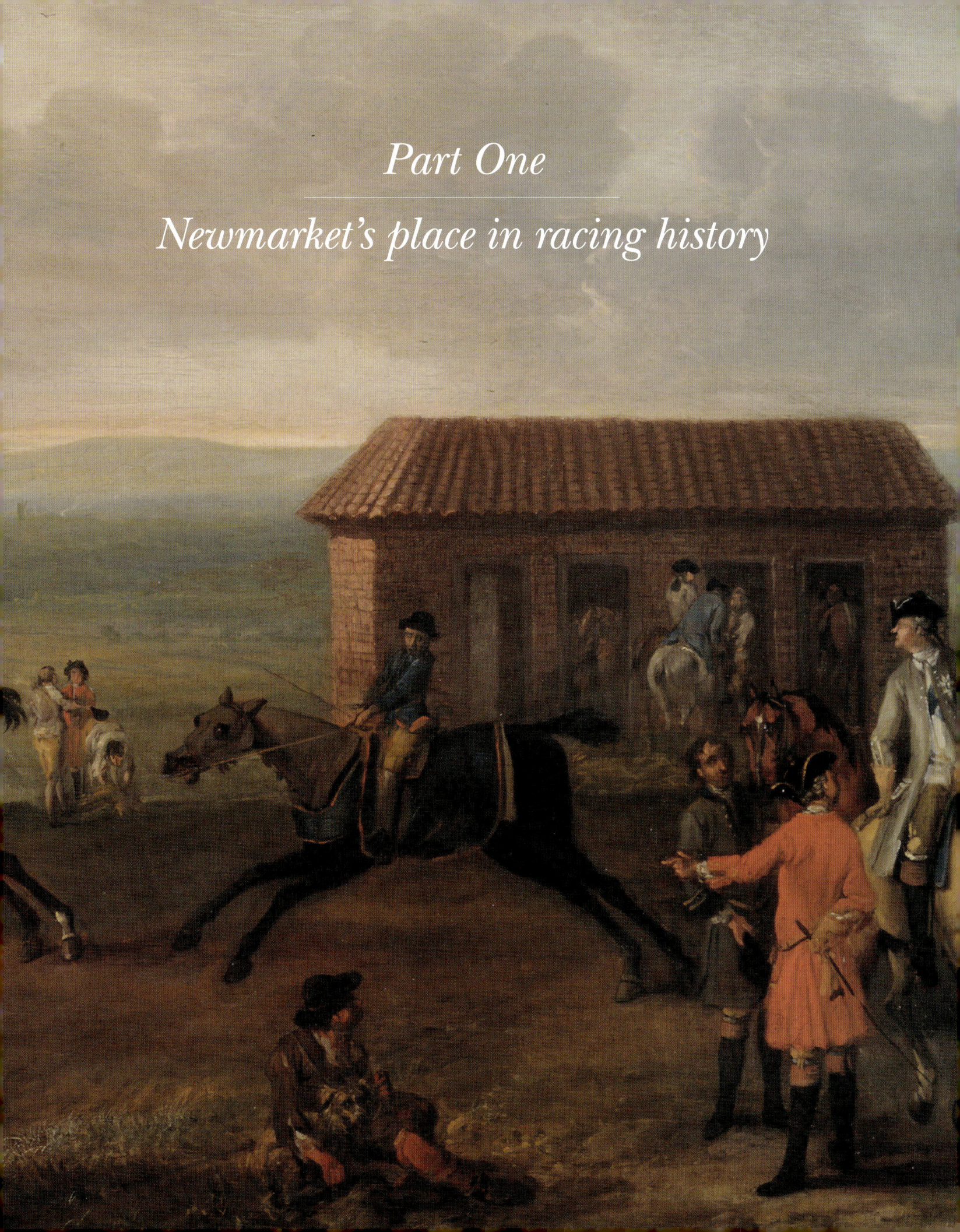

Newmarket's place in racing history

Chapter 1 (pre-1605)

The Sport's Beginnings in Britain before James I Came to Newmarket

In the very unlikely event that there was any racing in this country on an even vaguely organised basis before the Roman conquest of 43AD, no record survives. Elsewhere, the Greeks had started things off, at least in the West, with races both for chariots and later ridden horses included in the programme of the Olympic Games for centuries.

Grounded in those Greek origins, organised racing was popular throughout the Roman world, and records survive of some of the best horses, their pedigrees and numerous victories at Colchester and York. However, no organised sport long survived the loss of the legions in 412. The only link which could exist between those earlier days and the reappearance of organised racing 1,100 years later, in the reign of Henry VIII, would be in the genes of the horses themselves.

There had been earlier imports of better-class horses but things only really began to improve in Henry's day with imports from Italy, Spain and France. Although not purebred Eastern horses, they would have introduced a fair measure of Arabian and Barb genes from North Africa. Slowly the impact of his Royal Studs started to spread in the more settled world of the Tudors, and a horse population of sufficient class to be able to evolve into the thoroughbred through repeated infusions of pure Eastern blood began to emerge.

By the time the last of the Tudors, Elizabeth, was succeeded by the Stuarts in the ungainly form of James I in 1603, the English horse had largely recovered its quite enviable reputation abroad that had been squandered during the Wars of the Roses. It took most of Elizabeth's long and reasonably settled reign to reach that point, as her father's rather vainglorious attempts at warfare undid much of the good achieved by his imports and studs. However, the completion of the process through which the thoroughbred could eventually be considered a separate breed was still over 150 years in the future when the new king first came to Newmarket to hunt hare at Fordham in 1605.

Before James decided that Newmarket was an ideal site for hunting of all sorts, as well as hawking and a little racing to amuse the Court, we know nothing of races on the Heath. Wild theories over the activities of Queen Boadicea and her Iceni, based in their stronghold at Exning, owe their origin to their undoubted adeptness at handling chariots. The truth is that we know little beyond the fact that Newmarket was already a market town before the King arrived. While records exist of who owned the land we cannot know what they did on their rather wild properties beyond the pursuit of assorted quarry.

Nationally, racing had developed on a fair scale, in most cases either in the form of ad hoc meetings linked to the peregrinations of monarchs, or to the annual celebrations of fairs, the original grant of charters, religious festivals or similar events at many towns. A good example of the former type is the well-recorded visit of Queen Elizabeth to Salisbury in 1588, the year of the Armada. The latter class of meeting seems to have been more common in the north and, for obvious reasons, the former nearer London. Such events in Yorkshire always seem to have been pursued with greater zeal than elsewhere, and meetings far from royal habitations or centres of population, chosen presumably for genuinely sporting reasons, such as Hambleton, Bramham and Gatherley Moor, had few southern counterparts in Tudor times.

Probably because these required a class of animal that hardly existed outside the Royal Studs to succeed on its open heaths and moors, the production of horses in Yorkshire was always the province of a wider section of society. Competition there involved many more minor landowners rather than being a largely courtly activity for the aristocracy. While we cannot know for sure, it seems unlikely that anyone made much money out of such sporting competition conducted on a local basis between families, many of whom were closely interrelated. However, the possession of the means to supply horses for the great to amuse themselves was later turned to practical advantage when Newmarket provided a much grander stage for operations after the Civil Wars. Indeed, those events, still half a century away when James first appeared, were an essential element in Yorkshire's long-held dominance, since it was the aftermath of the wars that dispersed the Royal Studs, to a large degree to Yorkshire.

Previous spread: *Charles Collyer, 2nd Earl of Portmore, watching his string* by John Wootton (*c.*1735), detail of Fig. 5.

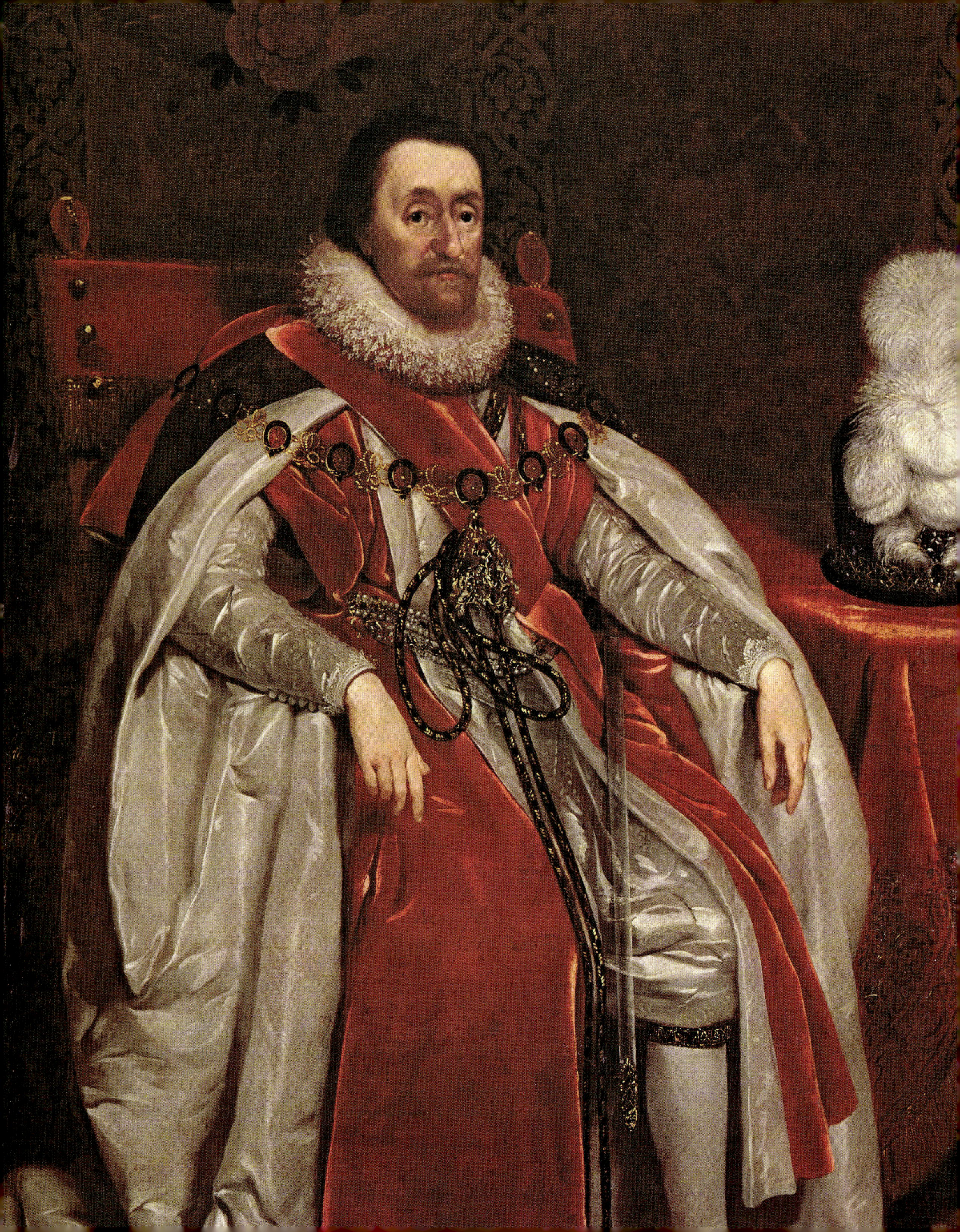

Chapter 2 (1605–1660)

Steady Progress on the Heath until Complete Cessation during the Commonwealth

Prior to James I (Fig. 11) and a sizable part of his Court appearing in February 1605 to hunt, the Heath had long been used for various equine activities. These sometimes took the form of tournaments (going back at least to the fourteenth century) but if any racing was included the fact is not recorded.

Where James and his entourage spent their nights during a visit of some days is unknown, but when he returned in November 1607 it was for several weeks, and something a good deal more substantial than tents would seem to have

Fig. 11

James I by Daniel Mytens (1621)

The King's degree of interest in racing is uncertain and his regular visits to the Heath and his construction of the first Palace were chiefly done in order to hunt. However, there is really no reason why Newmarket would ever have become distinguished from many other small provincial backwaters had he lighted on somewhere else for his twice-yearly expeditions from Whitehall.

been essential in December. Anyway, this visit established a firm pattern of lengthy stays at similarly inhospitable times of the year, and the Griffin Inn began to be transformed into the first royal palace from as early as 1608.

How interested in racing the King may have been is uncertain; he was a notoriously poor horseman, so there is no question of his riding himself in any races. However, like his predecessors, he was keen to improve the breed of horses in his realm and had inherited several studs. While his main sporting interest was certainly hunting (he disapproved of heavy gambling), his courtiers must soon have divined the possibilities of the Heath.

Apart from the demands of the hunting field, the main reason that kings had always involved themselves in horse-breeding was its crucial importance in terms of warfare. As suits of plate armour became reduced to breastplates and helmets for the cavalry, so the speed and quality of the troopers' mounts became of greater importance than their weight-carrying ability. Neither James nor Elizabeth before him indulged in battles they could avoid, and by the time the Civil Wars broke

Fig. 12

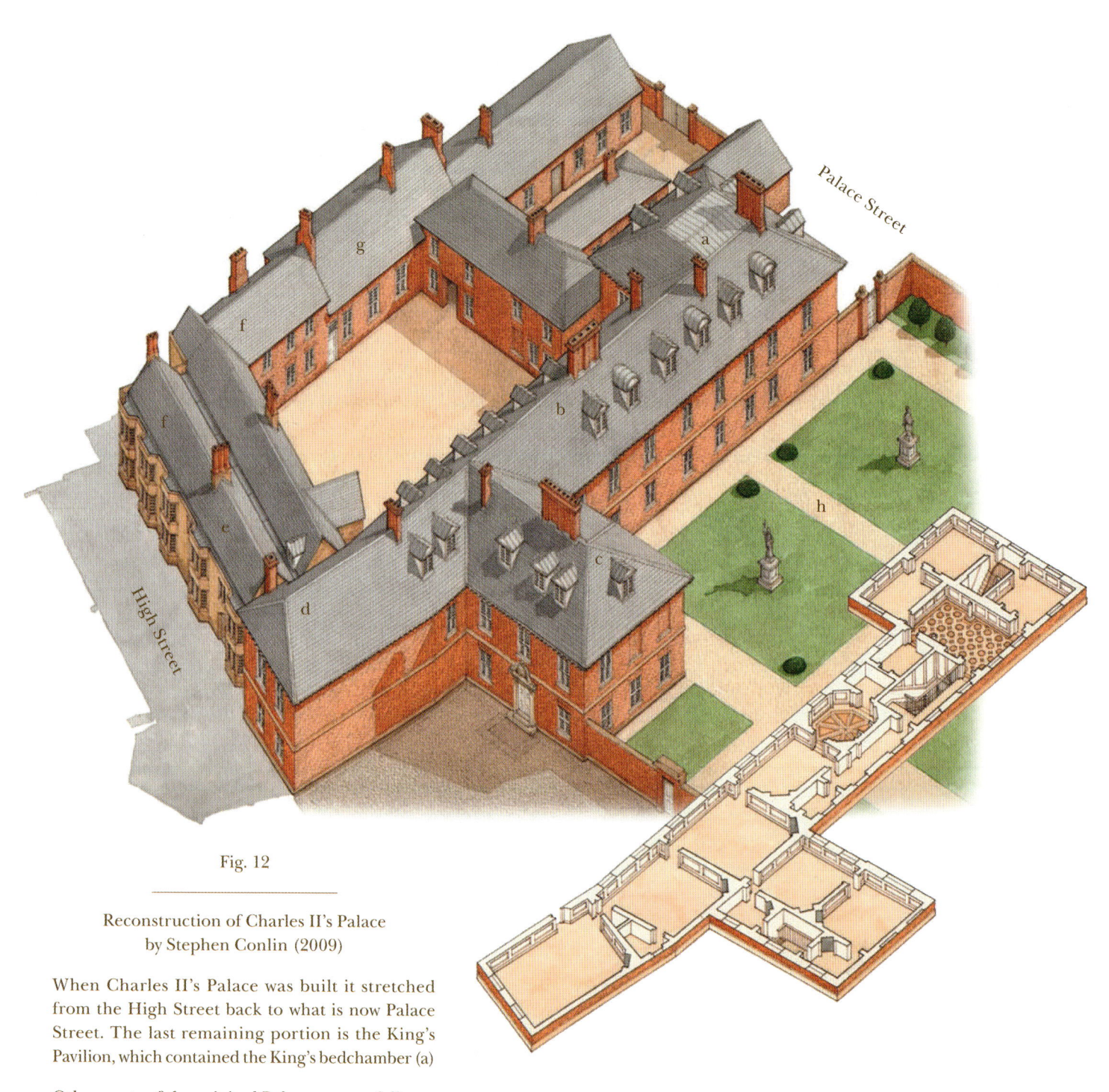

Reconstruction of Charles II's Palace by Stephen Conlin (2009)

When Charles II's Palace was built it stretched from the High Street back to what is now Palace Street. The last remaining portion is the King's Pavilion, which contained the King's bedchamber (a)

Other parts of the original Palace were as follows:
b. The King's Lodgings
c. The Queen's Pavilion
d. The King's Presence Chamber overlooking the High Street
e. The entrance to the Palace
f. Lodgings for the royal family and courtiers
g. Kitchens
h. The royal privy garden

out in 1642 the ability of both sides to find suitable mounts must have been at a peak – which was just as well given the scale of losses that followed. The Cromwellian regime at least made a serious start on filling the gaps.

Due to James's sporting tastes the use of the palace in his day was largely restricted to the period from November to March, and included two visits in most years. Sometimes the Court even held Christmas in the town. The first properly recorded race came as late in the reign as March 1623, when Lord Salisbury won a private contest for two horses, always referred to as a match, involving the Duke of Buckingham (Fig. 13), but we know that the King had already attended another in March 1619. There was a race in the vicinity of Newmarket, in about 1613, which was so well attended that some of the courtiers were forced to slum it in Linton, a mile or so beyond the eight-mile start. No doubt there were a good many more races earlier in the reign, as the appointment of so keen a racing man as Buckingham as Master of the Horse in 1616 seems to confirm. As Master he would have had command of all the Royal Studs. Away from the Heath there is more information of meetings at all sorts of places. Some, like York, Salisbury and Chester, have survived the centuries, albeit usually on slightly different sites.

❖❖❖❖

While the King and his courtiers were always the main importers of Eastern horses to improve the breed, the Heath was certainly not yet the crucial stage in the process of testing the results that it would later become. Indeed, no such stage existed anywhere; the whole concept of breeding racehorses based on the performance of their progenitors simply did not exist until it began to creep in after the Restoration in 1660. While Henry VIII and Elizabeth bred horses on a grand scale at Tutbury, Eltham, Malmesbury and for a time at Hampton Court, the principles on which matings were arranged were very different. Almost the only stallions used were part of the upgrading process

Fig. 13

George, 1st Duke of Buckingham
by Sir Peter Paul Rubens (1625)

Favourite at the Courts of both James I and his son, Buckingham was the leading racing man of the day and a great breeder of horses generally. He has the dubious achievement of owning the first recorded loser on the Heath, when his horse Prince was beaten in a £100 match in March 1623. His stud was of unquestionable quality, and a basis for that of Charles I after he was murdered in Portsmouth in 1628 when about to lead a raid on France.

and imported for this purpose, and there is no reason to suppose that many of the mares had raced. Decisions over matings would have been based largely on make and shape,

Italian riding horses), Jennets (smaller and usually from Spain), or Barbs (from North Africa). All would have carried many Eastern genes, if in a rather impure form; in effect this was why they were imported.

For 150 years from Henry's beginnings breeding would have been an almost entirely hit-and-miss exercise in terms of which stock might happen to breed something fast enough for racing. Furthermore, doing so would have been a secondary aim to producing suitably splendid mounts for the great to hunt with or ride on all manner of occasions. Thus the racecourse represented simply an amusing end in itself for anything which happened to be unusually quick rather than the testing ground for deciding the parents of future generations. Against that background the Heath in its early days was a much less significant place than it became in the eighteenth century. Even today the occasional benighted soul, usually from the betting industry, laments emphasis on the Pattern (an ordered series of races for horses of each type, designed to define the best) rather than their beloved handicaps, so this sort of blinkered view of the sport can at least claim to have ancient origins.

Unlike his father, Charles I (Fig. 14) rode well, and came to Newmarket just as regularly until the war broke out in 1642. Buckingham's murder in 1628 may have removed the sport's strongest supporter, but both the organisation of the Royal Studs and affection for lengthy jaunts to Newmarket hardly changed. The same seems to have been true for interest in racing nationally, and records survive on an occasional basis of meetings in many places.

During the period from Charles's defeat at Naseby in June 1645 to his death, Newmarket Heath figured more dramatically in the broader history of the country than it ever has before or since. However, these events have nothing to do with racing and are covered separately in Part 2. After 1649 Newmarket became a backwater, its palace and similar buildings falling rapidly into decay or being sold off, in

Fig. 14

Charles I by Sir Anthony van Dyck (*c*.1637–8)

Charles continued his father's patronage of the town unabated, but although he was a confident rider himself there is no likelihood he would have deigned to ride in races. His last appearance at Newmarket before the Civil War came in March 1642, when he flatly rejected a parliamentary delegation's petition for joint control of the militia. This soon led to the outbreak of hostilities, and after eventual defeat he returned twice, firstly in 1646, before he was removed to imprisonment in Northamptonshire. His final visit came in June 1647 when, under the control of the army, he lived in some style in his Palace prior to removal to London and eventual execution.

with, no doubt, some crossing between the separate breeds, although this seems to have been rather frowned on. Most of the royal imports were what were called Coursers (large

Fig. 15

Articles of the City Bowl at Salisbury (1654)

If one ignores the fact that the City Bowl has been contested in the form of everything from five-furlong sellers to four-mile heats (in which form both Eclipse and Gimcrack won it), its longevity has no equal for any race in the world run on a recognised racecourse.

some cases simply for building materials. As an unusually well-authenticated example of the early days, the National Horseracing Museum (NHRM) was recently lucky enough to acquire the counterpart deed of March 1654 (Fig. 15) between the City of Salisbury and the local gentry, regularising the already quite ancient arrangements for the City Bowl. The race is still run nearly four centuries later and, apart from gaps arising from various wars, has probably never missed a year. The deed takes one back to the reign of Elizabeth I, as it records the melting down of a gold snaffle, given as a

at each of the intervening mile posts to warn them of the progress of the horses on their way across the plain.

While there is no reason to doubt that there was a race for the City Bowl at Salisbury in 1654, the number taking place during the Commonwealth period was very small. At Newmarket there was one in November 1652; perhaps some others happened, but again there are no details. In fact the Council of State made several fairly vague attempts to stop racing in the years following the King's execution in 1649. Eventually, decisive action was taken when Oliver Cromwell formally took power and orders were issued for recurrent six-monthly bans from July 1654 until the return of the monarchy in 1660 (Fig. 16). This prohibition seems to have arisen from an amalgam of the dislike of racing in principle by the various religious factions that had supported Parliament in the wars and the suspicion of the military that race meetings were potential cover for Cavalier plotting, or even outright rebellion. Thus the Salisbury race (assuming it happened) would have been almost the last run anywhere until the Restoration and so it is sad that no information about it survives.

In Charles I's reign there is an oblique reference to racing in the spring of 1631, suggesting a cup may have been on offer, and rather more extensive ones to happenings early in 1634 at which it seems probable that a gold cup was won by a horse variously described as Bay Turrell or Bay Tarrall – at least we know his colour but not who he belonged to or what exactly happened. His name crops up linked to those of Mackerel, Sweet Lips and others in a song, so maybe they were his victims. Although there is no irrefutable evidence of racing on the Heath in this reign before the 1634 meeting, it seems inconceivable that the Court spent weeks each year (now mainly in March and October) without following earlier practice.

There is no record either of what, if any, stand was in existence before 1660. As explained, the one regularly put forward as dating from these days (Fig. 4) was in fact not built until around 1760. Given that there is evidence of a

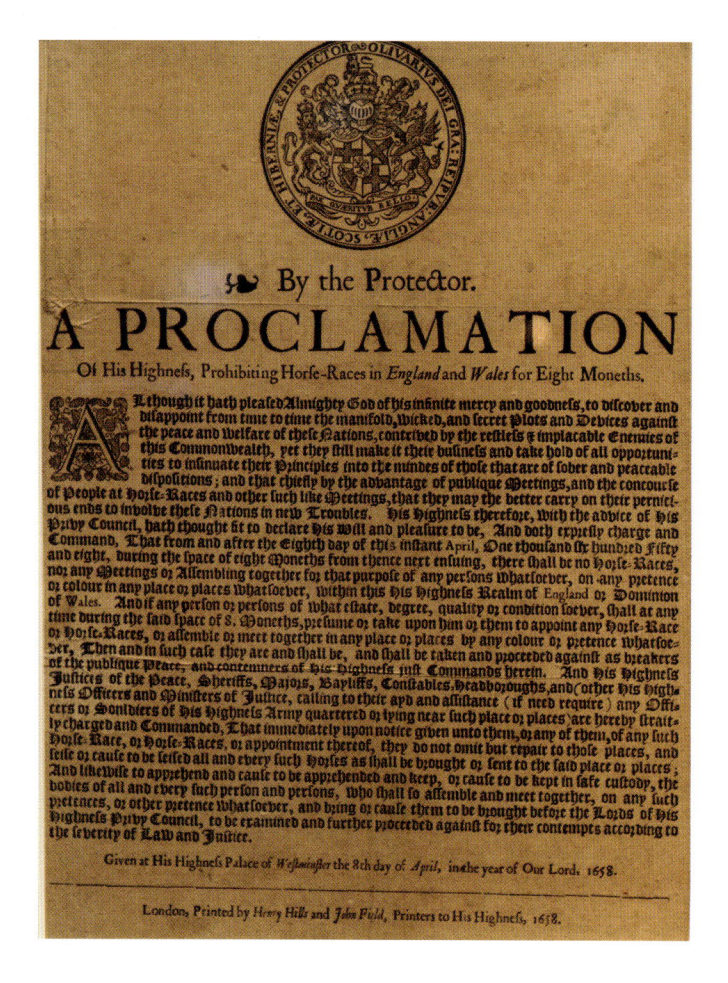

Fig. 16

Ordinance of the Rump Parliament prohibiting racing (1658)

prize by her favourite the Earl of Essex some years before his execution in 1600. The resulting ingot formed a small part of the capital sum of £320, which today still leads to the racecourse receiving the agreed payment of £18 each year from the Corporation, just as was provided in the deed of 1654. Sadly, it is no longer sufficient to pay for the promised 'silver cupp gilte with golde'. However, not all change is for the worse as the modern spectators can at least see the whole race, whereas in 1654 it was necessary to position a musketeer

stand at Croydon in Elizabethan times and numerous records of what were called Hunting Towers (similar in design to the King's Stand at Newmarket), it seems very likely there was such a structure on the Heath. In addition there must surely have been an equivalent to the King's Stables or Rubbing House of later ages, and it may be that the actual buildings survived sufficiently to be worth repairing after the Restoration. As at Salisbury, with its musketeers and presumably fairly straight course over open downland, even in these early days it would seem almost certain that runners on the Heath would have followed the route of the Beacon (the main course until the nineteenth century, running four miles with only two turns of less than 90 degrees each) through the Running Gap. If so, the Heath would have been as dissimilar as possible from the courses used for humbler events at which racing Galloways were scurrying round tight circuits at town festivities.

These differences were more extreme than anything we know today, and would have placed as varied demands on the contestants as can be imagined. Accordingly, it seems reasonable to assume that the breed slowly coalescing in the Royal Studs would have borne little resemblance to the animals providing sport at local gatherings. Thus the complete dispersal of the Royal Studs, ending by 1651 with the largest at Tutbury, must have had an enormous general impact, as over two or three years literally hundreds of high-class horses that had formerly been unavailable were sold, or frequently 'acquired', by a wide variety of people, many in Yorkshire, where the Lord General, Thomas Fairfax, had a splendid stud at Helmsley. The eventual result of this diaspora will have been the broodmares of the next 50 years, available to be upgraded in turn by mating with fresh imports such as real Arabians like the Darley, rather than the less pure strains brought over from Italy and Spain since the days of Henry VIII.

For the reasons set out above, the early books have little to say on how to mate horses; insofar as it is a science, it was still a matter for the future to explore. However, such literature is extremely strong on how horses should be handled at every point of their lives: how best to feed and ride them and how to organise them generally to greatest advantage. Some of the advice verges on the lethal and much of it – like breeding mares in alternate years, only racing horses from six years onwards and covering no more than about twelve mares annually with any stallion – is wonderfully uncommercial. But then what is commercial was hardly the point for a seventeenth-century Court.

◆◆◆◆

Pictures play an important part, in our view, in any properly rounded account of the history of racing in general or the Heath in particular. Sadly, nothing at all has survived before the days of Charles II and precious little even from that crucial period in Newmarket's development. With regard to the days of his father, it seems distinctly unlikely that there was anything to survive. This is ironic when one considers that Peter Paul Rubens was reputedly knighted at Newmarket. Charles also employed Anthony van Dyck as his court painter for many years, but that greatest of connoisseurs did not see fit to instruct either artist to paint anything to do with Newmarket or racing. Both, of course, produced magnificent pictures of horses in portraits of their owners, and Rubens at least painted numerous hunting scenes. The absence of such a commission surely says something about the standing of the sport before the Civil Wars; namely, it represented a minor, subsidiary use of the horse which was fun but certainly not to be treated too seriously.

Thus there are no pictures connected with racing on the Heath before the Restoration, and precious few of it anywhere for another twenty years after that event. What a shame there is no picture by either of these geniuses of Bay Turrall triumphing in his Gold Cup or parading proudly along Palace Street back to his stables.

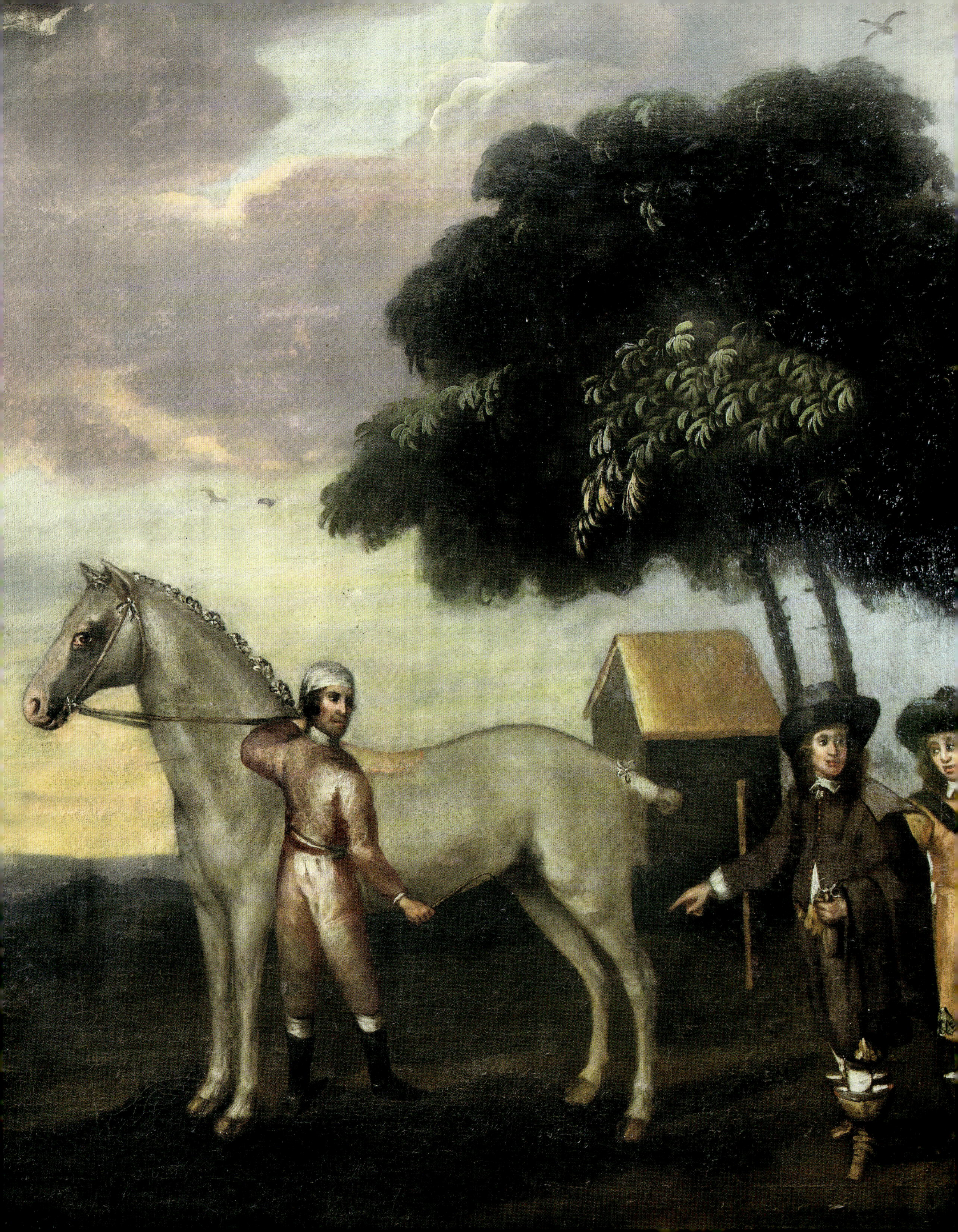

Chapter 3 (1660–1714)

Racing Is Resurrected and the Heath Thrives Centre Stage

After the death of Cromwell in September 1658, his seemingly solid regime collapsed so rapidly that by the end of May 1660 Charles II was restored to his father's throne. Following nearly two decades of the suppression of most forms of entertainment, first by warfare and later due to an all-pervading and rather suffocating worthiness, the frivolous and light-hearted emerged into the sunshine with dramatic suddenness. Along with the theatre, fairs, baiting bears or bulls, dancing round maypoles and jollification in general, racing soon experienced its own renaissance. However severe the shock to the body politic from switching almost overnight from the strictest code of morality the country had ever known to the most lax, it was certainly an unmixed blessing for racing.

Only nine days after his return, Charles II took a decisive step when he appointed James Darcy as Master of the Studs. At first the intention was to begin by recreating the principal stud at Tutbury, but, when it was inspected, it proved to be

Sir John Cotton showing his Mantuan imports to Charles II at Newmarket by an unknown artist (*c.*1670), detail of Fig. 17

in so ruinous a state that Darcy advised that it should be abandoned. Instead it was decided that the new Master would supply the King's needs from his own stud at Sedbury in Yorkshire, providing annually a minimum of six colts for £400 plus a £200 salary. Up to a further six colts would be available for another £400, so the Sedbury stud must already have been pretty extensive. It is rather ironic that much of the Darcy stock traced back to animals 'acquired' originally from the old Royal Studs – if nothing else, Charles was always a realist. Indeed, so realistic was he that the final payments due to James Darcy when he died in 1674 were still outstanding when Charles followed him in 1685, and Darcy's son, also James, was still petitioning succeeding monarchs for payment when Anne came to the throne in 1702.

Darcy's was not the only such appointment, and others were soon made aimed at the restoration of Newmarket. Game had not been preserved and the Palace was in ruins, so no question arose of Charles's early adoption of his father's regular excursions. Indeed, the King did not appear in person until March 1666, and even then his Palace was still not habitable. However, progress in other directions must have been a good deal swifter. Four 'boy ryders' had been

Fig. 17

Sir John Cotton showing his Mantuan imports to Charles II at Newmarket
by an unknown artist (*c.*1670).

This is probably the most important racing picture from the days before better artists like Jan Wyck and John Wootton revolutionised such works and the Arab imports really upgraded horses for racing purposes. The National Horseracing Museum is most fortunate to have been left it by the late Mrs Antrobus having descended in the Cotton family, for whom it was painted some 350 years ago. The few other pictures of the period, such as the Barlow in Fig. 20, underline the point over the coarseness of the little racing galloways of the day.

employed in 1661, and the first race of which there is any record was a match of March 1663 by which the Duke of Richmond relieved the Earl of Suffolk of £100. No doubt others preceded it.

Because studs had been continued on a considerable scale during the Commonwealth (Cromwell himself had some good stock at Dinsdale, again in Yorkshire), the sport could resume with little delay. Indeed, the implications of the spread of the old royal stock into all sorts of hands will probably have meant it rapidly exceeded its pre-war scale. Various records exist of this early resumption but they are naturally fragmentary, as the first national 'form book' would not be created for a further 75 years.

Another important appointment was that of the 2nd Duke of Buckingham (son of James I's favourite) as Master of the Horse. Buckingham now owned the leading stud at Helmsley, originally developed by his father and later handed to Cromwell's commanding officer at Marston Moor and Naseby, Lord Fairfax. Buckingham had prudently married Fairfax's daughter and in 1657 had been given Helmsley and all its stock, including some of the most important foundation mares in the stud book.

Probably at Buckingham's instigation, the King published the articles in 1665 (Fig. 18) for a race on a new course at Newmarket (in addition to the Beacon) to be used in October 1666. This became the basis of what is now called the July Course, to the west of the Devil's Ditch, the enormous earthwork that bisects the Heath (the Ditch forms the background to many of the illustrations and still stands almost unaltered as a witness to the Dark Ages). These articles are usually assumed to contain the first set of rules for the proper conduct of races, but this would seem not to be the case, as many of the clauses are simply repeated from those believed to have been drawn up in the sixteenth century governing the Kiplingcotes race, still run across the Wolds near Market Weighton over four centuries later.

Fig. 18

Articles always assumed to relate to the Newmarket Town Plate (1665)

Sadly this ancient document is in poor condition compared with the even older one from Salisbury in Fig. 15. In fact no race prior to 1720 follows the stipulation in the articles that it should always be run on the second Thursday in October. From that year the Town Plate has an authentic history but whether the articles relate more to a new Royal commitment to the Heath, based on the new Round Course, than a race before 1720 is a moot point.

Anyway, the sport on offer when the King (Fig. 19) returned in March 1666 included no less than six recorded matches, as well as what was called 'A Great Race' over six miles, won by the Earl of Thomond's Thumps. No subsequent meeting had its results so extensively recorded until the 1680s, and in many cases nothing whatever has survived apart from the fact that the Court spent weeks in the town enjoying itself. In one of the early visits the King must have inspected the stock of one of the more important owners, Sir John Cotton of Cheveley Park (Fig. 17).

However, it had certainly not gone unrecorded that the country's reputation as a serious European power had plummeted. Shortly after Thumps was excelling himself on the Heath, the Dutch fleet destroyed much of the English one in the Medway, where it was laid up for want of money. Alexander Pope summed up events with his usual barbed accuracy:

"In days of ease, when now the weary sword
Was sheathed and luxury with Charles restored

Then peers grew proud in horsemanship t'excell
Newmarket's glory rose, as Britain's fell"

While Newmarket's glory certainly was rising, it was not doing so in splendid isolation. For the next eighty years the great majority of top-class horses were being bred by a wide cross-section of the Yorkshire gentry on their various estates in the Vale of York, or northwards towards Richmond. The local rivalry must have been intense, and it is particularly regrettable that so little detail remains until the central meeting of the area settles on the meadows to the north of York at Clifton and Rawcliffe, in 1709. Full details are then available for York, and show that at last mares were being tested on the course, and even the occasional colt succeeded to the degree that it was regarded as a fit rival to the continuing imports as a potential stallion.

During the first twenty years of Charles's reign, the scale of events on the Heath seems to have increased steadily without changing the Court's reliance on stock bought from the north. No Royal Stud was reformed until the middle of the eighteenth century. The King is known to have raced at numerous other courses during his reign (Fig. 20), but the primacy of Newmarket as the place for the Court's regular entertainment did not slacken. While the weeks spent each year in the town required all sorts of

Fig. 19

Charles II by Thomas Hawker (*c.*1680)

Of all English monarchs, Charles II probably had most influence on the development of the sport. His arrival at Newmarket in 1666 for the first time since his father's many visits before the Civil War was a prelude to direct personal involvement as owner, rider and arbitrator of disputes for the rest of his life. A competent jockey with a win recorded as late as 1675, when he was 45, by the time of this picture even his robust constitution looks to have been under real strain. Following the Rye House Plot of 1683 he had decided to abandon the Heath, but his death in 1685 limited any impact.

Chapter 3 (1660–1714)

Fig. 20

Engraving of Charles II racing at Datchet, after Francis Barlow (1687)

Although this is not a scene on the Heath, the King's interest really made Newmarket racing's headquarters, so to show the only authentic depiction of him on a racecourse seems appropriate. It is also the original racing print, showing an event of 10 August 1684, and was published after the King's death, in his memory.

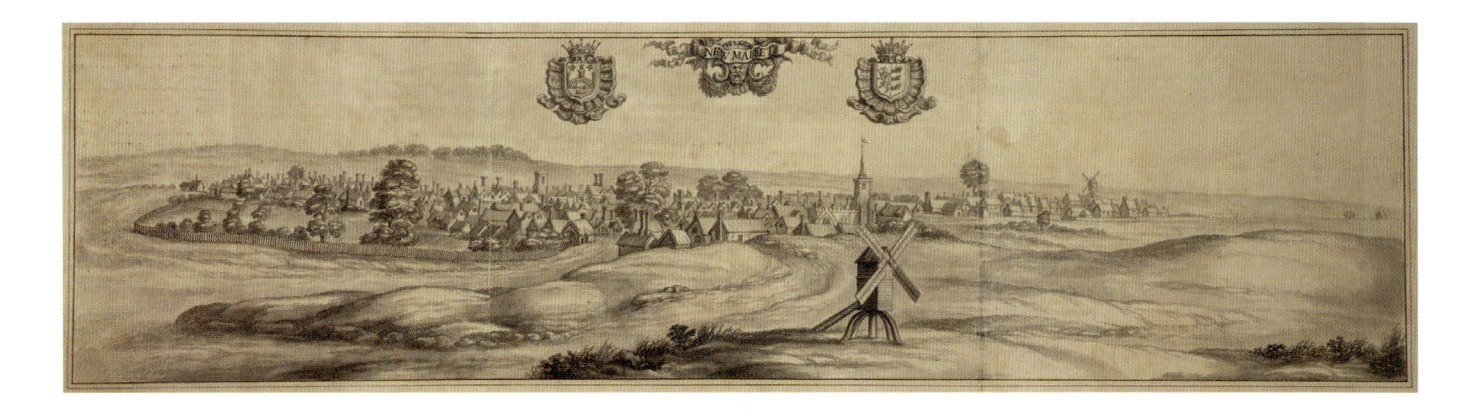

Fig. 21

Engraving of View of Newmarket in 1669

Clearly the town of Newmarket was a good deal grander than would have been the case without the Court's involvement. This shows the scene from Mill Hill with St Mary's on the right and All Saints and the Palace to the left. The print is in the main library in Florence so was presumably collected during the visit of the Grand Duke of Tuscany and Count Magalotti. The racecourse buildings figure close to the right-hand edge.

amusements in addition to racing, it is clear that they were now subsidiary attractions rather than the main focus, as had largely been the case before the war.

In 1669 Count Lorenzo Magalotti came to Newmarket as part of the retinue of Cosimo III, Duke of Tuscany. The Count has left us with an extraordinarily detailed account of what he found on the Heath. Despite his lack of racing knowledge, added to his obsession with reporting the precise nuances of his master's reception by the King on any chance encounter about the town (one suspects Charles found him an awful bore), his account also provides a unique insight into how the court system operated (Fig. 21). It is a sad fact that no Englishman managed anything remotely as informative.

◆◆◆◆

In 1671 the King actually rode the winner of a Plate usually assumed to be that covered by the 1665 Articles (Fig. 18). As a result of his presence it is recorded that he beat three others, including his oldest illegitimate son, the Duke of Monmouth. The King took home a flagon valued at £32 as his prize after a race decided in heats – in this case three. Beating Monmouth was no easy matter as he was an outstanding all-round athlete and a fine rider, with numerous recorded victories over the next decade or so.

Monmouth's racing activities became closely linked to increasing his already considerable popularity in furtherance of his ambition to replace his father's Catholic brother James as the next monarch. Charles would not hear of it, and eventually relations between father and son broke down completely, when in 1682 he had Monmouth dismissed from office as Chancellor of the University of Cambridge. Things became even worse when Monmouth was at least indirectly involved in the Rye House Plot of 1683 aimed at the assassination of both Charles and James on their way back to London from Newmarket after the spring meeting.

The implications of the Rye House Plot for Newmarket's future could have been shattering, and in any case were considerable. The Plot was only frustrated by the fact that a serious fire devastated much of the town to the north of the High Street on the night of 23 March (Fig. 22). As a result, Charles and his brother left early for London and so passed Rye House several days before they were expected by the plotters. Charles had already been toying with the idea of replacing Newmarket as his sporting paradise, and had actually moved its Spring Meeting in 1681 to Burford to coincide with a special session of Parliament he had summoned in Oxford as part of the crisis surrounding the attempt to exclude James from the succession. After the revelation of the Plot he decided to transfer his patronage to the downs near Winchester, and work was started on a grand new palace designed eventually to eliminate further need to use the irredeemably Whiggish Heath.

Fortunately, at least for Newmarket, fate intervened in the form of the King's death in February 1685. His new Palace in Hampshire was never completed after James II's accession, and was long afterwards turned into a barracks. Only a year later, Monmouth's attempt to usurp his uncle failed at Sedgemoor, a defeat that led to the execution of the best jockey the Royal family can ever have produced. Meanwhile racing generally seems to have been on the back burner, and James never visited the town during his three-year reign.

Still, according to Daniel Defoe writing early in the next century, James II did retain an involvement in the sport, and actually constructed an establishment for his horses some miles from Newmarket, near Wandlebury on the Gog Magog Hills. Here Defoe states that he appointed Tregonwell Frampton, whose family had a small estate at Moreton in Dorset, to take overall charge. No record survives of what races took place at Newmarket, or even at Wandlebury, and it may be that the choice of this fresh location followed on the lines set by Charles II's earlier decision to move away from the Heath to Hampshire for largely political reasons. In any case, whatever was in mind was overtaken by events when William of Orange invaded from Holland and James fled into exile in France.

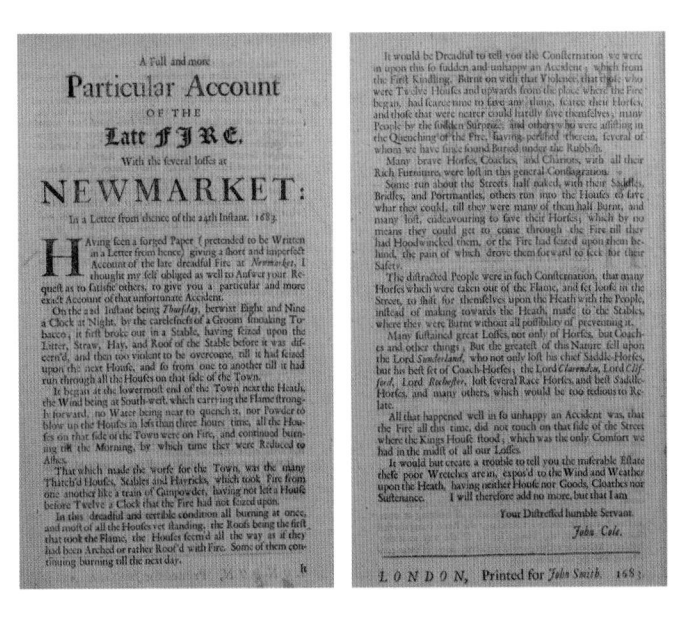

Fig. 22

Newmarket Fire broadside

Charles II had a dramatic influence on the development of racing. From being merely one of many amusing uses of the horse before the wars, it was well on the way to becoming the test bed for improving horses generally by the time of the King's death. Its scale had grown, and at Newmarket Charles had developed the stage from which the thoroughbred would one day spread around the world. Even his notorious liaisons had a profound effect, as the dukedoms of Grafton, Richmond and St Albans were created for sons of Barbara Villiers, Louise de Kérouaille and Nell Gwynn. All three families have played a part in racing history – crucial ones in the first two cases.

Fig. 23

Queen Anne's gold cup for Richmond in 1706

Each of the Royal Plates to 1720 saw the owner awarded a trophy fashioned from 100 Guineas worth of gold. Thereafter, the winner collected his prize in cash. The series had begun with Charles II and blossomed under Anne, only ceasing in 1887 when even their advance to 300 Guineas left staying races of the type traditional in this series unfashionable. Subsequently, the money was laid out on a stallion premium scheme.

An aspect of Charles's contribution we have perhaps unwisely decided to ignore is his remarkable talent for giving rise to innumerable tales of the scandalous activities, of both himself and his Court, during the long sojourns in the town. No doubt many were essentially true, but how to decide which, and quite where repeating them yet again would take one, is not obvious. It seems sufficient to say only that it was the fashion to behave quite outrageously by the standards of almost any age before or since. The result was a vague disapproval of the turf among the more staid elements of society, and something of this view lingers even to this day.

◆◆◆◆

William III may well never have seen a race before he came to the throne after James had fled in 1688, but within a year he went to Newmarket for the October Meeting at a cost of nearly £1,000 to the Exchequer. One of his first acts was to appoint Tregonwell Frampton as his Keeper of the Running Horses, and so effectively as viceroy of the town. Frampton reigned until the 1720s, initially on what is now the site of Heath House, and one must assume King William's rapidly expanding string was trained there in the shadow of Warren Hill rather than in the mews beside the Palace. Clearly any idea of moving things away to Wandlebury disappeared with the Whigs back in charge nationally and the executed Rye House plotters transformed into martyrs to their cause. Such thoughts of moving did not recur for forty years.

The new King seems to have taken to life in Newmarket with rather surprising enthusiasm despite certainly not being a horseman in Charles's tradition. Even the loss of 4,000 Guineas at a sitting at cards during his first visit did not turn him against the place. The first recorded race of the reign only came in October 1695, but many had certainly taken place in the intervening years. Anyway, one that was noted was won by one of the King's horses, and was an important race, being an early King's Plate.

King's Plates, worth 100 Guineas each and with free entry, began under Charles and were an early form of sponsorship. In races run invariably over four miles until well into the nineteenth century, all runners were required to carry 12 stone, so favouring the type that would be useful for the breeding of cavalry mounts. In effect these races, run at level weights and open to major winners, were the first attempt at what has become the Pattern, today and provide

Fig. 24

A grey Arabian thought to be the Taffolet Barb
by Jan Wyck (1686)

The most important horse returned here after the withdrawal from the Tangiers colony in the early 1680s was the Taffolet. Wyck is known to have worked for the family involved with the horse, so it is likely to be him and it certainly appears to be Tangiers in the background. The differences between Barbs and Arabians could be considerable, but the former term really meant an animal from North Africa descended from Arab stock – quality usually depended on how many generations had elapsed since arrival in North Africa, and this horse shows none of the traditional coarseness of the true Barb.

further reason to be grateful to Charles. By Queen Anne's day the prize was always a gold cup; the one she awarded at Richmond in 1706 was sold in 2001 for £223,750 (Fig. 23).

◆◆◆◆

Throughout the political turmoil of the seventeenth century horses continued to be imported, some with purer Eastern pedigrees than in earlier periods; a factor in this improvement was the acquisition of Tangiers, a prime source

Fig. 25

The Byerley Turk with the Golden Horn in the background
by John Wootton (*c*.1730)

One of the three Eastern horses from which the thoroughbred descends in the male line. The artist has again emphasised his origins in the groom and the background. Unlike Seymour (Figs. 12 and 32), Wootton always tended to accentuate the Arabian traits in his subjects, whether pure bred or English for several generations, as a form of compliment. Certainly a huge element of Eastern genes was essential in the early days.

of North African horses. When the colony was abandoned in the early 1680s numerous horses came back with returning soldiers (Fig. 24). At much the same time, the Byerley Turk (Fig. 25) was probably captured from the Turks at either the battle of Vienna (1683) or Buda (1686). He certainly came

Fig. 26

The Darley Arabian at his owner's stud at Aldby in Yorkshire

This life-sized picture by a naïve and unknown artist still hangs at Aldby, and is the only contemporary image of the sire of Flying Childers. The horse was imported from Aleppo in 1704, arriving at Portsmouth on 2nd June via Kinsale. A delay in Ireland had arisen as the Ipswich, which had brought him from Syria, had to await a naval escort during the year of Blenheim. The picture has been decried by those who believe so important an influence must have looked more like a Wootton horse (Figs. 25 and 30). However, there is no doubt it is authentic, and that all more florid portrayals are subsequent reworkings of this image 'suitably' embellished. If you compare the animal with the pictures of Childers (Figs. 12 and 32), he looks a far more plausible father than the great majority of Arabians.

Chapter 3 (1660–1714)

into the possession of an English cavalry officer, Captain Robert Byerley, who famously rode him at the Battle of the Boyne in 1690, where William III frustrated James II's attempt to recover the throne. Later Byerley retired the horse to stud at Goldsborough Hall, near Knaresborough, North Yorkshire, where he died in 1706. It has recently been calculated that 4.8 per cent of the genetic material in the average thoroughbred today is derived from this horse.

Even more crucial was the better-documented import of the Darley Arabian (Fig. 26) from Aleppo in 1704, to stand eventually at the Darley family stud at Aldby, near York, as in his case the calculated contribution is 7.5 per cent. The Darley had been foaled in 1700 and died relatively young (although some records wrongly indicate that he lived until 30), though before doing so he sired the brothers Flying and Bartlet's Childers. However, their stories fall into the next reign.

Although by 1714 the thoroughbred certainly did not exist as a separate breed, crossing home-bred stock with pure-bred Arabians like the Darley started to produce brilliant racehorses, and things were beginning to change. It was no longer essential to use imported stallions, as the later career of the outstanding racehorse Bay Bolton (Fig. 27) demonstrated. Foaled in 1705, the horse was bred at Lowthorpe, and sold midway through his fine career by his breeder to the Duke of Bolton. Not reliably recorded as being defeated on the course (there is some doubt whether he may have lost a race to Windham), he was later the champion stallion several times around 1730, although precise details of his achievements on the course or at stud are no longer calculable from the patchy records available. Nevertheless, he was the first racehorse of such eminence fully to reproduce his success as a stallion in the face of imported opposition, though even he failed to set up a long-lasting male line, despite living to 31.

♦♦♦♦

Fig. 27

Engraving of Bay Bolton, after James Seymour (1755)

Foaled in Yorkshire in 1705, this was the first really successful stallion whose ancestors seem to have been bred in England for several generations. He had some major victories on the Heath before retiring to stud at Bolton Hall in his home county, where he died in 1736. The prints in this set of twelve are indicative of the snobbish age in which they were created: two of the owners had no coats-of-arms, so the plates were etched including entirely imaginary ones.

Queen Anne and her husband were both enthusiastic supporters of racing, and she inherited not only William's throne in 1702, after he had suffered a fatal fall from his horse, but also his bloodstock, the Palace at Newmarket and Tregonwell Frampton. By now usually known as Governor Frampton, this cantankerous misogynist ruled Newmarket with the proverbial rod of iron. This was probably just as well in the absence of any other authority between the departure of King Charles and the appearance of the Jockey Club.

Fig. 28

Engraving of Tregonwell Frampton in old age, after John Wootton (1791)

Published more than sixty years after Frampton's death, this print still sold in large numbers – indicative of what an important figure the subject had been in his day. He was the various monarchs' effective viceroy on the Heath from the death of Charles II to his own demise in 1728. He had been a success in that role, and his death ushered in a dark age on the Heath. The text set out the slanderous accusation over the gelding of Dragon, so giving it far wider currency than would otherwise have been the case in relation to a story that only appeared in print for the first time in the 1750s. His autocratic disposition seems to have run in the family as his estate at Moreton in Dorset eventually passed to the Squire Frampton largely responsible for the transposition of the Tolpuddle Martyrs.

Frampton was almost as fruitful a source of legend as King Charles had been, and a particularly implausible one appears in the lengthy text below Fig. 28. This claims that he had once killed a horse named Dragon by having him gelded in order to qualify him for the betting coup he landed the following day. Had such a thing been attempted it would have been about the most foolish speculation in racing history, which might well have killed the horse and would almost certainly have cost Frampton the bet. The fact the story comes with the authority of Doctor Johnson hardly gives it much credence, in view of the famous Dictionary's definition of a fetlock as being the knee of a horse.

Another inaccuracy arising from Frampton's remarkable career was the date of his death, which most racing historians, following their predecessors, have placed in 1727. In fact he died in 1728. The error must have arisen from the practice of referring to the early months of the calendar year as though spliced to its predecessor. Accordingly, his death was specified at the time as happening in March 1727/28 – hence the misunderstanding.

One story that certainly has a kernel of truth is indicative of the way links were slowly beginning to appear between the sport's heartlands in Yorkshire and the Heath, following the sale of stock to the Court. During the Queen's reign a northern champion in Merlin (there is doubt which of the Merlins was involved) was brought to Newmarket for a great match, and defeated an unnamed horse of Frampton's. Supposedly the latter had been outwitted by Sir William Strickland's trainer, a member of the Hesseltine dynasty of trainers and jockeys and one of the earliest of either profession not to be entirely anonymous. This he was said to have achieved by arranging a covert trial of the horses and juggling with the weights carried. All we really know is that the Yorkshire contingent won so much money that a long ballad was composed in celebration, which has survived.

After her husband Prince George's death in 1708, the Queen, by now grossly obese due to dropsy, ceased to visit the town, and instead fully earned her place in racing history by having Ascot laid out on the edge of Windsor Great Park in 1711. Thus six of our seven main flat racing courses (Newmarket, Epsom, York, Doncaster, Chester and Ascot) already existed three centuries ago, even if the two in Yorkshire shifted to different sites after Queen Anne's days. As the seventh at Goodwood has now chalked up over two centuries itself, those who accuse racing of being innately conservative do seem to have a point.

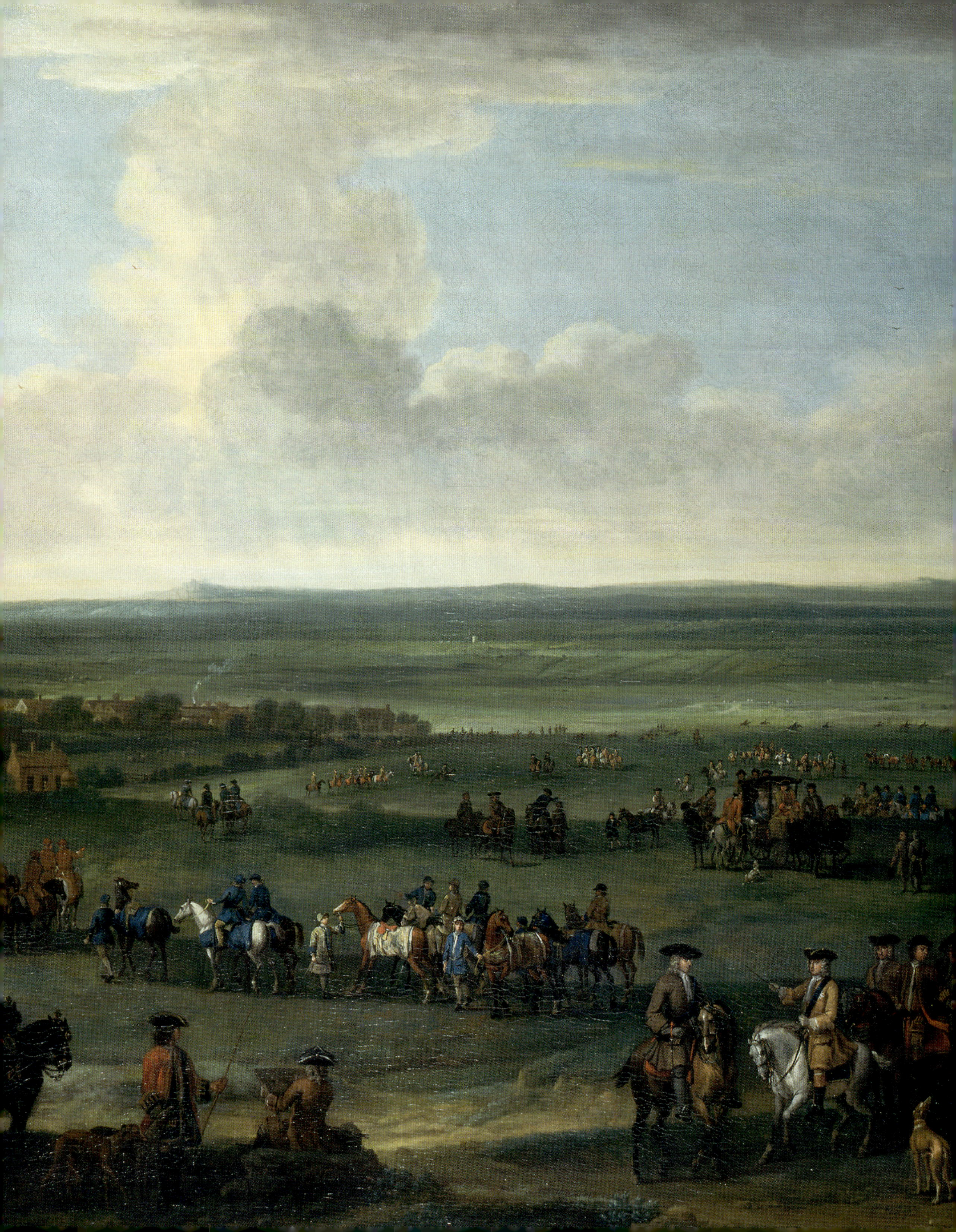

Chapter 4 (1714–1750)

The Sport Declines, Especially at Newmarket, as Fraud Proliferates without Central Authority

Inevitably, this chapter repeats assorted details adduced by Richard Nash in Part 3 to show the existence of an earlier version of the Jockey Club; such details from the late 1730s and 1740s are also crucial components in this section, as it tries to explain racing's near collapse in the years running up to 1751. Before decay set in here, there is interesting external evidence supporting the case Richard makes for an earlier Jockey Club at one of the turf's earliest outposts in Colonial America. In South Carolina, along with New York, Maryland and Virginia (the states which first introduced racing as anything beyond local scurries for half-bred horses), a group actually calling itself the Jockey Club had organised a racecourse in Charleston by 1734. By the 1750s the Club's leader was Edward Fenwick, from the Northumbrian family which owned Matchem (Fig. 3), and Charleston racecourse was actually called New Market. Did the name and concept of a Jockey Club running racing on the principal course originate in Colonial America to be imported here along with the name in 1751, or was the idea exported along with the early English stock like Bulle Rock? Surely the odds are overwhelmingly in favour of the latter proposition. Further support can be derived from events in Ireland in 1747. Although never called the Jockey Club, a rough equivalent has been identified by Tony Sweeney. Forerunner of the Turf Club, it was initiated by a Yorkshireman, Sir Marmaduke Wyvill, also a leading racing figure here who was at the time part of the set-up in Dublin Castle.

Richard Nash explains the antecedents of the reformed and reinvigorated Jockey Club – it may have been a much less effective body that he identifies, but it is hard to imagine events from 1751 taking the shape they did had there been no base on which to rebuild rather than create an institution. In the early days after the replacement of the Stuart dynasty by the Hanoverians, racing did not seem to be particularly threatened. Both George I and George II came to Newmarket and at least affected some interest (Fig. 29). Yet this seems largely to have been a matter of seeking popular support by appearing more English than either was by blood or disposition. As became endemic in the new dynasty, each

George I at Newmarket in 1717 by John Wootton (probably 1717), detail of Fig. 29

Fig. 29

George I at Newmarket in 1717 by John Wootton (probably 1717)

The scene is on the lower part of Warren Hill, with the King on the grey to the right and Frampton looking out of a coach, while Wootton himself sketches things in the centre. The main features in the town are as usual the two church towers and the Palace, in those days stretching from Palace Street through to the High Street.

Fig. 30

The Godolphin Arabian by John Wootton (1731)

This fine Wootton shows the last great Arabian stallion as a very young horse soon after import. If his forelegs had really resembled Wootton's depiction of them it is as well he never raced. However, his success as a stallion was immense, and the genetic contribution he made to the thoroughbred exceeds that of any other horse.

generation detested the one before – a feeling which was usually mutual. Anyway, once safely on his throne George II must have felt he had made his point sufficiently without the need to while away his time in Suffolk. Indeed, his only involvement thereafter came from his continued support for the Royal Plates, no doubt in the interests of his cavalry rather than his popularity.

Until Tregonwell Frampton died, within a year of George I, things had seemed to go rather well on the Heath. In that year racing in general took a major step forward with the publication of the first national record of results. John Cheny's calendar remained in print until his death during the production of the 1750 volume, and the work was continued by assorted followers until the Weatherbys took over in 1773. Without Cheny's work and the numerous pedigrees he collated, our knowledge of racing's history and the accuracy of the General Stud Book when it first came out in 1791 would have been badly impacted. The extent to which Cheny was operating on behalf of the earlier version

Williams seems to have started the Match Book on its behalf in October 1718, and as the links between Calendars and Match Book seem clear enough, it is quite likely that Cheny was operating in conjunction with it from 1727.

Meanwhile, the breed itself was developing steadily even if its pedigrees were patchily recorded before 1791. In 1730 the last of the great Eastern stallions, the Godolphin Arabian, arrived (Fig. 30). Contrary to the general perception of the Darley's superior role due to his virtual monopoly of tail-male descent via Eclipse, in fact the Godolphin made the largest genetic contribution of all, at 14.6 per cent. The horse had been a present from the Bey of Tunis to France, and was imported here by Edward Coke of Derbyshire. On Coke's early death he passed to Francis, 2nd Earl of Godolphin (Fig. 31), whose stud near Babraham thereby got an animal whose career exceeded all expectations, which at the outset had been rather limited. By the time he died in 1753 further imports, which were still quite common, were tending to degrade the stock rather than improve it in terms of racing ability. Accordingly, it seems fair to consider the thoroughbred to be a genuinely separate breed from that date.

◆◆◆◆

If the breed continued to prosper after Frampton died in 1728, racing most certainly did not. Indeed, things began to go steadily down hill in the 1730s despite well-meaning efforts to check the slide. Eventually it became so bad that in 1742 only four races were run on the Heath, and three of them were 100 Guineas Royal Plates, leaving only a single sweepstakes paid for by subscribers all year and worth a miserable 52 Guineas to the winner.

The decline in racing's fortunes following the death of Frampton and the loss of royal involvement can be traced to the failure to find owners to replace the likes of the Dukes of Bolton, Wharton and Somerset when they lost interest,

Fig. 31

Francis, 2nd Earl of Godolphin, English School (*c.*1740)

Born in 1678 he raced as Lord Ryalton in his father's lifetime and inherited his position in 1712 among the leading aristocratic figures in the town. In 1733 he also inherited the great mare Roxana on the death of Edward Coke, and bought an even more important horse in the Godolphin Arabian (Fig. 30) from Roger Williams, also a Coke beneficiary, and keeper of the Coffee House which was the Jockey Club's first London home. Roxana's last foal, by the Godolphin, was the important stallion Cade. Based largely on the success of his Arabian, he raced with great success until retiring soon after the horse died in 1753. Godolphin himself lived on at Babraham to 1766, and by good luck his detailed private studbook has survived.

of the Jockey Club identified by Richard Nash is uncertain but his successors like John Pond, Reginald Heber and finally the Weatherbys certainly were after he died. As Roger

lost too much money or simply died; the two factors of royal disinterest and the failure to find new recruits are probably closely linked. By 1750 the only serious players to have emerged and stayed the course were the Earls of Portmore (Fig. 5) and Gower. What eventually made the changes from 1750 so remarkable and then sustained them was the appearance in rapid succession of Lords Rockingham and March, Sir Richard Grosvenor, Richard Vernon and Jenison Shafto, who were the main owners for the rest of the century. When their impact was combined with the return of royal interest in the figure of the Duke of Cumberland, spectacular recovery became possible.

The collapse in racing's fortunes over the period preceding 1742 was truly remarkable. In 1722 the Frankel of the day, Flying Childers, won no less than 1,000 Guineas for the Duke of Devonshire in his match with Lord Drogheda's Chaunter. That year there were 33 races at Newmarket (excluding walk-overs and forfeited matches) and eleven were worth 200 Guineas or more. One carried the astronomical stake of 3,000 Guineas – poor Lord Drogheda lost that one too, to Thomas Panton senior, soon to succeed Frampton as the King's representative on the Heath. While Panton was not seemingly a great success in that role at least he showed some of his predecessor's notorious shrewdness over this match, as his horse would have had no chance if asked to take on Chaunter.

It would seem unfair to blame the problems of the 1730s and 1740s on Thomas Panton senior (Fig. 33). Considerable confusion has long reigned over his activities and indeed, even his identity, as it has become accepted by racing historians that he died in 1750. In fact he remained formally 'Keeper of the Running Horses' until he actually died in 1782, aged 84. Thus the reality was that he held office longer even than Frampton, who had only been appointed when the place was created in 1693. On Panton's demise the office was abolished, and in any case had for a long time been little more than an excuse to pay him £600 a year. Given that he was a major owner from the days when he had the outstanding mare Molly as a very young man in the early 1720s (her only defeat was when dropping dead in a match in 1723), the £600 was hardly of much consequence, and with no royal string merely a sinecure.

Fortunately the artist's father decided to commission a monumental portrait of the great horse Childers by the young James Seymour (Fig. 10). It is a splendid representation which includes his defeat of Chaunter in the background and considerable detail of the last part of the Beacon, with the town and racecourse buildings separated at the time by a tall white fence. Attendance to see the great horse seems pitifully small, but correspondingly grand in showing what one can assume to be the ducal coach, with its liveried postillions in the Devonshire straw, evidently able to ignore any restrictions implied by the rails on the right which normally barred entrance onto the course to wheeled traffic. The jockey's straw colours, as opposed to the blue normal in portraits of Childers (Fig. 32), will presumably have arisen because Chaunter's owner, Lord Drogheda, always used the same blue, and Devonshire must have adopted the straw of his liveried servants for the day to avoid confusion. It is interesting that in the 3rd Duke's lifetime, on the only four occasions when colours were noted in the Match Book, on three he used blue and once red, but never the straw that was formally registered by the family for the first time in 1762, during the 4th Duke's reign.

◆◆◆◆

By 1750 things on the Heath had improved very little since the depths of 1742, and the rest of the country had done rather worse than Newmarket. The reasons for the crash elsewhere were very different, and stemmed largely from an Act of Parliament of 1740 rather than the loss of support of the Court. The 1740 Act prohibited any race being run for less than £50 and as most were worth far less the effect on the minor meetings was catastrophic. It is clear that the

Fig. 32

Flying Childers by James Seymour (*c.*1740)

Accepted in his day and for long afterwards as the finest racehorse of them all, Flying Childers is also the best example of how far breeding had advanced before the thoroughbred was created around the time he died in 1741. He was the son of a pure Arabian, and due to the horse's reputation Seymour reworked the image many times based on the Chatsworth portrait (Fig. 10) before his death in 1752. It gives a fair impression of the combination of strength and class he represented. With his short back, long legs and excellent shoulder it is easy to imagine his fabled length of stride which misled his owner and the Duke of Rutland into calculating he could reach the speed of a mile a minute. As they tried to do this by timing a single stride as he passed them, measuring the distance between the hoof marks and multiplying the result, the fact they got things so wrong should not cast a shadow over their clocking over the whole Round Course.

Chapter 4 (1714–1750)

recent short-lived introduction of tariffs by the Horsemen's Group had the effect of downgrading many programmes quite seriously, but the impact of that particular wheeze never began to approach the havoc wrought by Parliament, seemingly egged on by the Newmarket grandees, in 1740; both interventions well demonstrate the law of unintended consequences.

The year before the Act was passed there were 145 different courses staging racing on the mainland and a total of 157 separate meetings. Only Lincoln staged three fixtures but as two of them were single matches its three-fixture, status was a fluke and one can see how widely racing was spread even if prize money was often as low as £10. Parliament, however, decided this was most unsatisfactory and that their Act was necessary 'to restrain and prevent the excessive increase in horse races', which it considered had led to 'excessive and deceitful gambling'.

In reaching this conclusion Parliament seems to have been guided by the principal figures at Newmarket, led by the Duke of Bolton and Lord Godolphin. They had all foregathered at the former's house at Hackwood Park in Hampshire in August 1739 and decided that racing would be improved by suppressing the smaller meetings, at which they thought scenes of lawlessness discredited the sport.

No doubt they were right but, however worthy their intentions, the impact of the Act (from some of whose provisions they thoughtfully had Newmarket exempted) had implications far beyond the wishes of any supporter of the sport. By 1741, in place of 145 courses, there were only 56, and they staged just 60 fixtures. While the likes of Newmarket, Epsom and York were able to rake up the necessary £50, they too put on much smaller programmes due to the general lack of confidence, and the lesser tracks largely shut up shop. Those that survived were reduced to running single races on each of one or two days. Even run in heats the sport must have been so poor that it was as well the meetings were over so soon.

Fig. 33

Thomas Panton (1698–1782)
by Thomas Gainsborough (1772)

Panton became a prominent figure on the Heath when he raced a famous mare called Molly in the early 1720s. Based on his quite sizable string, by the time Frampton died in 1728 the new king, George II, decided to appoint him as the second and final 'Keeper of the Running Horses' in that year. This created a storm of protest from Lord Godolphin (Fig. 31) and others. They met to debate this and other issues in 1729, but things soon settled down and Panton continued to collect his £600 annually for doing nothing in particular until he died in 1782, after which the sinecure was abolished. Always with a decent-sized string himself, Panton was owner of some very useful horses at times, and he and later his son lived in a large house between those of the Duke of Queensberry and Richard Vernon on the left of the hill as you leave the town en route to the racecourse. Looking at Gainsborough's revealing portrait, one appreciates why Horace Walpole was tempted into likening this leading figure in the sport to 'a disreputable horse jockey'.

◆◆◆◆

As already mentioned, a topic also dealt with in Part 3 is the degree to which the Hackwood meeting really demonstrated that the Jockey Club existed some years before its supposed foundation date of 1750. In this context it is important to note that much the same thing had happened in 1729 when a similar group of Newmarket grandees had also met at Hackwood to decide how to react to the new King's decision to appoint Thomas Panton senior (Fig. 33) to replace the recently deceased Frampton as the Keeper of the Running Horses. As there is no evidence that the King had any running horses this was really the equivalent of nominating a viceroy, and it seems that the other major owners were not happy with what had happened. As Panton was only 30 it may be this upset them. Apart from that fact what else may really have provoked the meeting is not clear, though it does not seem to have been an objection to Panton as an individual as he had close links with most of them and Devonshire in particular. However, the published purpose of this earlier meeting had been to decide whether to respond by removing their strings from such royal involvement at Newmarket and effectively relocating the Heath to Wandlebury, just as James II had considered doing forty years before. The place now belonged to Francis, 2nd Lord Godolphin (Fig. 31), who was soon to acquire the eponymous Arabian for his stud on the estate. How near those who attended the meeting came to effecting a move is unknown, but in the event nothing actually happened. Meanwhile, although Newmarket was left undisturbed, a change was to take place soon afterwards at York, when in 1731 the racecourse made its final move from the north of the city to the Knavesmire on the west.

It is relevant that there is a sprinkling of references in the press between 1729 and 1743 to something actually called 'the Jockey Club' and to 'the noblemen and gentlemen' who were said to belong to it. They seem to point to a foundation date before 1729 and to be linked to the beginning of proper records with the opening of the Match Book in October 1718 and the first Hackwood meeting. With no further references from 1743 until the dramatic events of April 1751 (covered in the next chapter and in part 3), perhaps the Club was effectively moribund during the years of racing's slump after the 1740 Act. Maybe the members were feeling a degree of collective guilt over what they had engendered – if not, one can only feel that they should have.

In so far as racing was still going on in the 1740s it seems that it was reliant on individuals and families to take entries, collect forfeits and pay out prize money for each course. Sometimes they appear to have decided to keep it for themselves, and things occasionally ended in the law courts. At Newmarket the Deards family played an honourable and much undervalued role in acting almost as forerunners of the Weatherbys. The family were jewellers based in Fleet Street but attended various meetings around southern England in the course of trade. Since the days of Queen Anne they had organised a coffee house in Newmarket, much on the lines of the later Jockey Club Rooms. They continued to function in the town for several generations and had clear links to the later Jockey Club after 1750, acting as stakeholders and even as judges on the racecourse. Indeed, it is suggested in Part 3 that the family probably ran the Club's new Coffee Room after it opened in 1753.

Further evidence of an earlier history of the Jockey Club is linked to the name of Roger Williams, who ran an important coffee house in London for over 25 years. Known simply as Williams Coffee House it was latterly at 86 St James's Street. When Williams died in 1747 he was referred to as being 'Clerk to the Races' at Newmarket, and Number 86 seems to have been the London hub of racing activity, with entries accepted and calendars sold. In 1731 it was noted in the press that he had placed a painting of a horse 'in the Jockey Club Rooms' in his coffee house. Overall the picture seems to emerge of a largely social institution which made occasional forays into the governance of racing in general and Newmarket in particular but without making any coherent effort to provide central control. Its members were served in various ways, in terms of ensuring their racing continued on the Heath post Frampton, by people who made their real living out of supplying luxury goods or hospitality in London or elsewhere.

Apart from substantial London figures like the Deards family, the Ponds and Roger Williams, a closely-knit group of local families in Newmarket provided all sorts of services to the sport and the Jockey Club both before and after the 1751 watershed. We are lucky that the early registers at All Saints have survived, although sadly those for the other half of the town at St Mary's have disappeared. A good example of the information they contain relates to the Buckle family, for in 1707 Samuel had married Elizabeth Harrison. Her father was keeping the Match Book records before 1751 (presumably having taken over from Roger Williams, unless he had acted as his local representative) but soon after that date relinquished the role to Buckle. By the late 1750s Samuel had been succeeded in office by John Deards, owner of the original Coffee House in the High Street as well as his large shop in London. Samuel's son John was a saddler in the town but his chief claim to fame was as the father of the great jockey Frank Buckle (Fig. 57), who was born in 1766. Long before Frank brought the name Buckle to national prominence family weddings were being witnessed by people like William Tuting, last Keeper of the Match Book and publisher of the Calendar before the advent of the Weatherbys. Racing Newmarket is still quite a small world, but certainly not to the degree that was true in the eighteenth century when the sport really was the place's sole raison d'être. The shock to these local families of the almost complete collapse of the 1740s must have been truly traumatic.

◆◆◆◆

The most successful innovation in terms of the racing programmes from the early days of the century apart from the Royal Plates had been the idea of funding races by persuading major owners to promise to subscribe an agreed sum for several years, anything from £3 to £10. In return they could have a runner in any year if they had something suitable. Almost all races were still being run over four miles but the age fixed for each of these race's entrants varied, as did conditions over who needed to have bred the horse in order to qualify. Such races were usually both better-class and more valuable, and appeared at several improbable places like Wallasey in the Wirral and Quainton in Buckinghamshire. However, by 1734 Newmarket had collared the lot, and its Wallasey Stakes and Great Stakes (ex Quainton) were the biggest prizes of the year on the Heath. Both races were funded in five-year cycles ending in 1739 but, with confidence at a very low ebb, insufficient subscribers could be found to renew them. This left a yawning gap not filled until the 1750s.

Racing has to thank an initiative developed during discussions at the York August meeting of 1750 for the first steps in its recovery.

◆◆◆◆

The period covered by this chapter saw the beginnings of racing as a subject for artists on more than a very occasional basis. Until John Wootton, Peter Tillemans, and later James Seymour and assorted followers produced quality pictures of racing, such as existed were chance offerings from foreigners like Jan Wyck. Tillemans died in 1734, and Wootton rather lost interest in the new school they had largely created after the 1730s. One must assume there ceased to be as much money in it, as the popularity of racing rapidly declined leaving only Francis Sartorius to begin his career as about Seymour's only rival. However, during the 1740s really only Seymour was painting racing scenes of great interest, and was unlucky enough to die in early 1752 at exactly the point when he might have made some serious money out of the dramatic upswing in interest in racing that followed.

Fig. 34

Drawing of the Round Course by Jan Wyck (late 1660s)

Wyck arrived in England aged about 21 in 1666. This would seem to be an early work. It suggests, firstly, that the Round Course began as a tight circuit of no more than a mile and, secondly, that the Ditch between the Cambridge and Well Gaps was being used as a carriage stand from which to watch the races. While there is no written evidence that either was so, the second, and more implausible proposition is supported by the fact that the top of the Ditch between these two points has been removed to make it broader and the surface still shows evidence of a form of hardcore.

Fig. 35

Waiting to start on the Round Course by Peter Tillemans (*c.*1720)

Even if the Wyck in Fig. 34 is correct, the Round Course can only have resembled Chester very briefly, and soon became a single circuit of nearly four miles starting and finishing at the post with a flag on it. In the background is the Ditch with the relevant Rubbing House near the post.

Fig. 36

Grey horse leaping a sheep around the end of the Rowley Mile
by James Seymour

It has not yet proved possible to tie this remarkable event to a recorded occasion, but something of the sort must always have been a risk, as sheep were used as substitutes for gang mowers.

Perhaps the fact that Seymour continued to paint racing scenes meant that he had little alternative. Unlike his two main predecessors, he was essentially a racing man who only took to painting horses professionally because he understood them better than anything else and needed the money after his father's business failed. We are lucky that he did because, although by no means as good a painter as Wyck (who had died in 1702), Wootton or Tillemans, his horses seem a good bit more plausible, owing less to fashion or artistic conventions than to what he must have seen in front of him.

All these artists produced highly informative pictures of the Heath from which one can know very precisely how things were being organised in their day. Good examples of topographical paintings by four of them are illustrated here (Figs. 34, 35, 36 and 37) while others by Wootton appear elsewhere, such as Fig. 29. In the case of the Seymour (Fig. 36), which shows a runner jumping an errant sheep while racing on the Beacon, the artist must have been the first responsible for depicting a horse on the Heath with no feet on the ground.

By 1750 racing as a national sport had declined to such a degree that a dispassionate observer might well have wondered if it had a future. Maybe York's initiative over its 'Great Subscription' could have been recognised as the green shoots of recovery that it proved to be, but it would have taken a congenital optimist to have done so at the time. As the next chapter shows, the real catalyst for the sudden switch from decline to truly dramatic advance must actually have looked like yet another disaster to those assembled on the Heath on 11 April 1751. That almost forgotten event is surely as good evidence as you could get of how hard it is to foresee the future impact of anything at the time it happens, whether it be an act of parliament, a tariff initiative or, in this case, a crime.

PICTURE PUZZLE 1: IDENTIFICATION OF RACE AND COURSE

This splendid Wootton (Fig. 37) has always been known to depict a race at Newmarket, but which race and on what part of the Heath it took place had been unclear. By repute the figure with the Garter riband in the foreground was Frederick, Prince of Wales, heir to the throne after his father succeeded in 1727 as George II. In fact this belief is wrong, as Frederick was only seventeen years old in October 1724 when the race took place. Probably the principal figure is Charles, 6th Duke of Somerset and usually known as 'The Proud Duke' for very good reason, who owned the winner. The rather full face is similar to that in his portraits, although his depiction is too small to be confident. His winner was Grey Windham, who is in fourth position at this early stage in the race.

The scene is the Round Course, originally ordained by Charles II, and the precision with which Wootton has taken care to align correctly all the landmarks by which the site can be identified is only equalled by his depictions of other runnings of the same race in earlier years – his other scenes from this spot employ the same formula but include different horses and people to reflect different races. In the distance to the right is Warren Hill with the town and buildings at the Beacon finish, together with its railed section, visible over or through the Cambridge Gap in the Ditch. On the near side of the Ditch the building is the Rubbing House for the Round Course, which stood just across the track from the present stands at the finish on the July Course. The flag among a crowd of people shows where the race had started and will soon finish after the horses have covered nearly four miles. To this point the field has come about a mile to turn right round the post in the foreground. Before that they will have had to diverge slightly to leave the smaller post on their right, from which point the mounted spectators are hurrying off to see the later stages of the race.

In essence the runners have traversed one side of a diamond which will be completed when they come into a final mile more or less up the present July Course straight, running parallel to the Ditch, to finish at the flag. The other gaps you can see in the Ditch are the small Well Gap in the middle and the broader King's Gap to the left of the canvas. The race is identifiable with confidence from the colours of both the horses' coats and the jockeys' silks. Leading is the Duke of Bolton's Sloven, known to be a dark-brown-going-on-black, with his jockey in the correct colours of the Duke. Third here is Miss Hen in Thomas Panton's silks (eventually only finishing fourth), followed by the winner in the suitably regal Somerset scarlet. Bringing up the rear are the Duke of Rutland's Bonny Boy with the jockey in his blue and Sir Richard Grosvenor's Shag, who was still last three miles later. The owners' silks for the other four runners are not recorded but we do know two of the horses were bay, which fits well enough although it is hardly significant as identification. However, a field as large as nine was a considerable rarity at the time. For five of the owners' colours to fit, two confirmed by their horses' coats, and with nothing whatever out of line, there is really no doubt that this is the race depicted by Wootton. It was called the Noblemen's and Gentlemen's Contribution Stakes and was one of the highlights of the Newmarket season and probably had been since 1709, although early records are scarce.

Picture Puzzle 1

Fig. 37

A race on the Round Course by John Wootton (probably 1724)

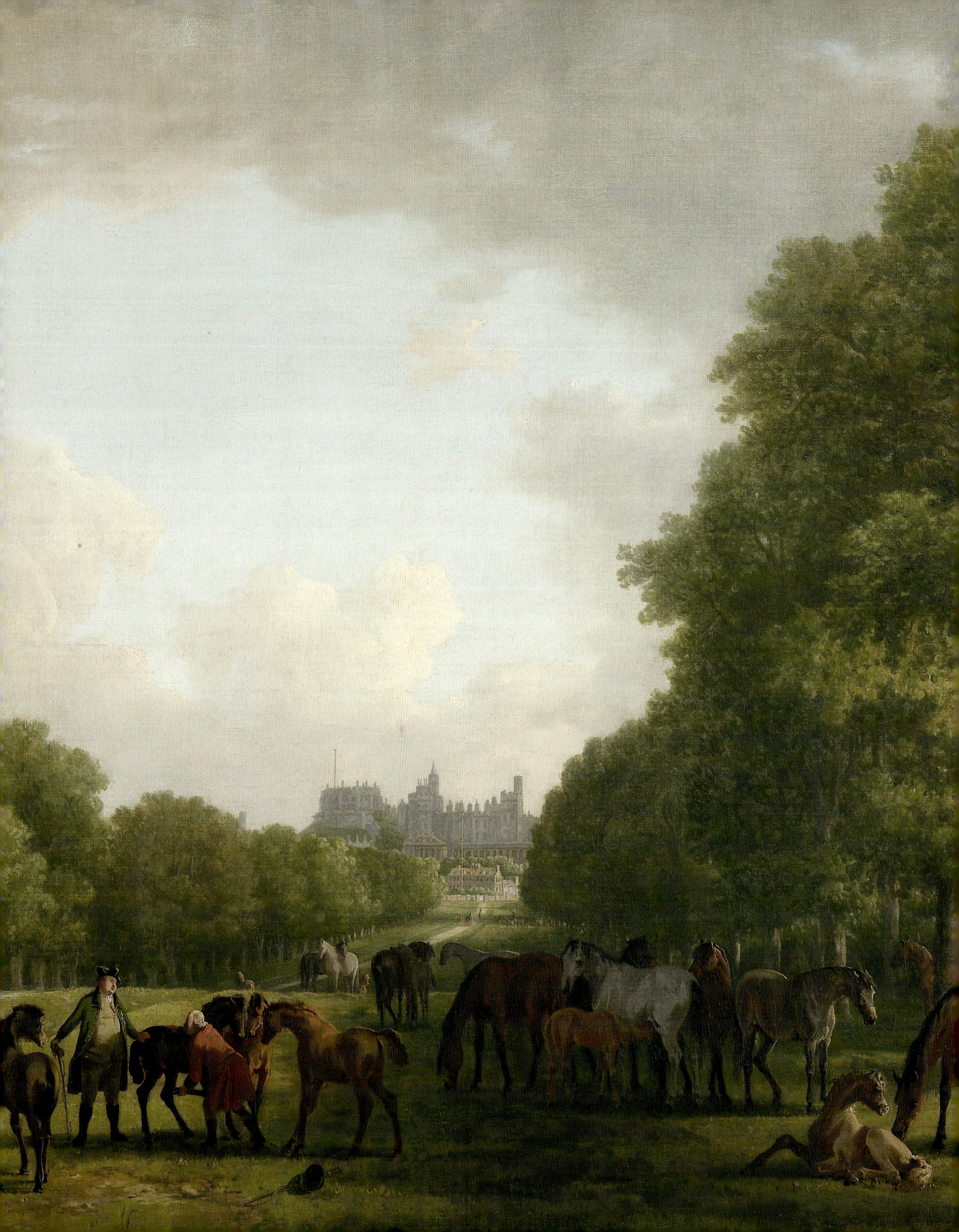

Chapter 5 (1750–1791)

A Golden Age as the Jockey Club Finally Takes Control on the Heath and the Thoroughbred Emerges as a Separate Breed

The events at York in 1750 covered elsewhere and also those at Newmarket only eight months later seem to us to have been ignored in racing histories to an extraordinary degree as both are so pivotal to the way the sport switched suddenly from decline to an unprecedented degree of growth. Part 3 adds more of the detailed evidence; accordingly not all is repeated in this chapter, and assertions made should only be accepted as facts to the extent that in conjunction with Part 3 they are shown to be so.

Much of the trouble for racing in the 1740s stemmed from all the villainies that the 1740 Act was supposed to suppress becoming concentrated onto a smaller stage. With no central authority or method of control, short of resorting to the law courts, it is hardly surprising that disenchantment with the sport was so widespread. However, what happened on 11 April 1751 in a Royal Plate at Newmarket was so outrageous that the result was to

The Duke of Cumberland inspecting his stud by Sawrey Gilpin and William Marlow, detail of Fig. 39

galvanise whatever remained of the earlier Jockey Club of Bolton and Godolphin into taking control of events on the Heath and turning the place into an equivalent of the Pole Star by which the rest of the sport would be guided, though not yet controlled.

The story begins seven years earlier, when George Prentice of Barrow Hedges in Banstead near Epsom started his career as an owner by buying two good northern horses, Crazy from Miss Dolly Routh and Moorcock from John Hutton. Crazy by Flying Childers had won his three races that year for Miss Routh, ending with a win in the only race run at York on the fourth day of the August Meeting, 9 August 1744. Moorcock by Blacklegs, who had been bought by Prentice after an unlucky defeat at Durham where he fell, won the only race on the following day. Given the form and pedigrees of these horses they would have cost a considerable amount.

The fact that the five-day York meeting, the main one in the north and the only one on the Knavesmire all year, had only one race each day tells you all you need to know about the state of the turf in the 1740s.

During 1745 Prentice unwisely sold Moorcock, after two honourable defeats at Newmarket, as he later became a top-class horse for Lord Portmore, while Crazy lost his form after two quick wins. It was not a good start for Prentice, and thereafter his string of anything up to seven achieved very little, and he must have been losing heavily until he found the money to buy a different Blacklegs by Blaze for 250 Guineas and Trimmer by Hobgoblin who may well have cost more. Again, both came from Yorkshire.

Trimmer had won his only race, the King's Plate at Lichfield, for Mr Dutton, having been bred by Lord Godolphin. He was a half brother to an important stallion in Blank and a full brother to another useful one in Shakespeare, but was himself already a gelding. While Prentice was again rather unlucky with Blacklegs, who broke down after a good victory, Trimmer seemed like a harbinger of better times. He began by winning 135 Guineas at Newmarket but then, to general surprise, was last of four in the King's Plate at Lewes with Noble third. As Noble had been behind him in third at Newmarket, alarm bells should no doubt have been ringing and matters would not have been improved when less than two weeks later Trimmer won the King's Plate at Canterbury beating Stump, who had won the Lewes race. At least the season ended as it should have when Trimmer also won the King's Plate at Newmarket in October, beating Stump again and the future stallion Crab (incidentally, not the great stallion of that name from whom almost all grey horses derive their colour, but a son).

Perhaps events at Lewes should have made people wary but it seems that they did not. On the fateful 11 April 1751, again at Newmarket, the horse began (and indeed, ended) his season in the King's Plate run on the Round Course. In a field of five, including Stump and Crab, Trimmer ran so badly in the first heat he was beaten a distance, or more than 240 yards, and so was eliminated from the later heats, causing everyone to lose their money. The inevitable conclusion was that the horse had been pulled. The whole performance was said to have 'caused much surprise and speculation among the spectators' and one can imagine that may be something of an understatement following such blatant skulduggery. In view of what happened next it is perhaps ironic that an announcement had appeared in the press in the previous November to the effect that the Duke of Cumberland had leased Mr Prentice's house and stabling in Banstead as his base for hunting on the Downs.

What happened next day was a resurrection of the October Stakes, followed by an evening of tumultuous riot, and in very short order thereafter, unprecedented changes in the way racing was conducted at Newmarket and beyond. On 12 April, the day following the King's Plate, Articles were drawn up for a 20 Guineas Subscription to be run over the Beacon course every October from 1752 to 1756, for five-year-olds, carrying 8st. 7lb. While this subscription was headed by the senior figures of the earlier Jockey Club like Lords Godolphin, Gower and Portmore many of the subscribers came from a younger generation.

Later that night, with tempers probably still frayed after the Trimmer debacle, an incident broke out in the Hazard Room at the Palace that rapidly escalated into violence, spilling out of Deards's Coffee House into the High Street, where the riotous crowd swelled to over a hundred, with the object of their fury, one James Fletcher of Lancashire, subjected to a severe beating, horsewhipping, and 'the discipline of the horse pond'.

This saga began at about nine o' clock at night, when John St Leger (brother of the Anthony St Leger, for whom the classic would later be named) was playing Hazard in company with (among others) John Healy, a merchant; Edward Bigland, a wine merchant; and Augustus Hervey, second son of the Earl of Bristol. We know from his diary that Hervey, at least, had been losing heavily during the meeting, and had lost especially on Trimmer, 'by a supposed trick... Mr. Prentice was suspected in this...' James Fletcher, of Bury, in Lancashire, entered the Hazard room from the Coffee Room, making some gesture of acquaintance or familiarity with one of the group which was strongly resented. Words were exchanged, and quickly escalated to blows. Fletcher was beaten, and a crowd of 'upwards of thirty and more whose names are as yet unknown', apparently led by St Leger and Bigland, forcibly expelled him from the building, bleeding profusely from the nose and cuts to the face. During this action Bigland was heard to yell, 'Damn him, it is Fletcher the pickpocket. He gave a bet against me at the Cockpit. It does not signify what you do to him!'

Not long after, Fletcher, accompanied by friends, returned to the Coffee Room, seeking his hat and wig which he had lost in the melee. St Leger and company took the return as an act of defiance. Now at the head of a group numbering 'upwards of forty and more', St Leger led his party against Fletcher and his companions, demanding Fletcher get down on his knees and beg pardon for his presumption. Fletcher refused, and again the larger party resorted to force, this time including the use of horsewhips, with which Fletcher was beaten out of the building a second time. During this encounter, Bigland was heard to shout 'Kill him. Kill him. Kill him. [He is a gam]bler, thief and a pickpocket'.

Once out of the building, however, the assault did not end, but escalated yet again. The crowd of those 'whose names are as yet unknown' swelled to upwards of 100 and more, as Fletcher was beaten and dragged to the nearby horse pond, which lay in the middle of the High Street east of what is now the Rutland Arms. From here to its conclusion, the mob is now led by, in addition to the four already mentioned, Peregrine Bertie, Duke of Ancaster, and Alexander Montgomerie, Earl of Eglinton, with others such as Lord March and Richard Vernon involved. Forced to his knees to beg pardon of St Leger, Fletcher continued to be beaten before being dragged repeatedly through the horse pond for at least half an hour and finally dumped, unconscious and near death, on the ground. He was, from there, carried to 'a nearby coffeehouse', where he was tended to, but it was another six days before he fully recovered his senses.

Before Fletcher had fully recovered in Newmarket, the more influential of the rioters, together with other key owners, had returned to London and, perhaps led by wiser old hands like Devonshire and Godolphin, set the revitalised Club on a very different and more fruitful path in bringing things under control than lynch law.

Influential racing figures attended a dinner on 16 April at the Star and Garter in Pall Mall to celebrate the Duke of Cumberland's birthday the day before. Cumberland, the younger son of George II and a national hero after Culloden, had never seemed interested in racing but was a notorious gambler, and so would have moved in the same circles as the remaining Newmarket grandees. That same day it had been reported that Prentice had been 'excluded from being concerned in subscribing to plates at Newmarket' in order to prevent his 'wicked designs'. After that a rash of notices appeared in the press over the next few weeks from some twenty racecourses stating that entries for Trimmer or in some cases any of Mr Prentice's horses would not be accepted. While nobody apart from the various landowners would have had the right in law to warn anybody off the Heath that is in effect what had been done, and Newmarket's leadership in such matters could hardly have been more clearly established.

Even as the Jockey Club mobilized to exclude Prentice and all horses that had been owned by him at the time of the Newmarket Meeting, stories were inserted in the newspapers, putting the best possible face on the riot at Newmarket, as a necessary disciplining of 'sharpers'. Fletcher, however, sought remedy at law, by bringing a prosecution before the Court of King's Bench in Westminster. His case was heard in June and informations were issued for the six individuals named above, including Ancaster and Eglinton, to stand trial at the next assizes in Bury St Edmunds before the Lord Chief Justice. An exactly contemporary case that April of assault and ducking in a horse pond for witchcraft that resulted in the death of a woman, and the near death of her husband, resulted in the death penalty for the individual at the head of that mob, so the stakes were not trivial. But the assizes came and went without trial, as presumably Fletcher was bought off and did not pursue his prosecution. In August, sworn affidavits were published by a lawyer, denying any connection to the Fletcher prosecution – an indication that some serious pressure was being exerted to stop proceedings. And through it all, during the summer, one race meeting after another fell in line with the exclusion of all horses that had been owned by Prentice at the time of the last Newmarket meeting. Moreover, a story appeared alleging that Prentice's jockeys, William Moody and John Gillum had purchased horses on Prentice's behalf with a design to circumvent the exclusion. That such a story even appeared demonstrates how seriously the exclusion was taken, but the ensuing public exchange, in which the new owner had to justify and document his independence from any connection to Prentice, makes it clear that the Jockey Club was taking a new approach to racing at Newmarket and beyond.

We only have the details of events in April 1751 due to the extensive researches of Richard Nash. They seem to us to illuminate a crucial period for both the Turf and the Club, a period that had the effect of pulling the latter together to form a cohesive body capable of running things on the Heath and, eventually, nationally for some 250 years. It seems fair to assume that the looming prospect of facing the Lord Chief Justice from the dock had brought the younger bloods to their senses over how best to respond to the likes of Mr Prentice.

◆◆◆◆

Following the victory over Prentice and his 'wicked designs', three more notices were published that Autumn showing how quickly measures to regulate things, at least at Newmarket, were being put in place. On 2 November it was announced that every 'Noblemen and Gentlemen that keeps stables at Newmarket' should put up 100 Guineas for a race the following April, and even those who did not have a runner on the day should pay 50 Guineas. Crucially the details were to be agreed 'in the first Jockey Club [meeting] that shall be in December'.

This was followed on 19 November with the announcement that 'the first Weekly Meeting will be held on Thursday, as usual, at the Star and Garter in Pall-mall'. As the notice was addressed to the 'Noblemen and Gentlemen of the Society call'd the Jockey Club', it seems that there had been a tradition of weekly meetings on Thursdays during the winter, presumably when Parliament was sitting. The piece imply place in 1750 and perhaps for years, before the catalyst of Mr Prentice's misbehaviour turned them into something much more than social evenings.

At the 5 February 1752 meeting, articles were drawn up for a subscription stakes whereby owners would agree to a five-year annual 100 Guineas subscription to run horses of their own breed, in the tradition of the Wallasey and Great Stakes. This plan, however, was only 'perfected' in the next month by a slight alteration in terms that not only expanded the scope and scale of the event, but effectively brought racing at Newmarket back under a form of royal patronage. This is best recorded in a fascinating public letter signed Philo-Hippos dated 5 March 1752, the full text of which is printed in Part 3. We also know from the calendars established by John Cheny's successors John Pond and Reginald Heber (now in competition for Jockey Club support) that it had been decided to follow York's lead and start a long-term fund to support a major race. The main difference was that instead of the stingy tenner paid annually, as was the plan in Yorkshire, the Newmarket grandees fixed their subscription at 100 Guineas, also settling it for seven years, as had their northern counterparts.

The subscription list of twelve for what they called initially, with a marked lack of imagination, the 1,200 Guineas Stakes, included three dukes headed by Cumberland, three marquises, five earls and a lone commoner in Mr Thomas Duncombe, an antecedent of the future earls of Feversham. What is much more important than the grandeur of the subscribers is the fact that several of them were in the same position as the Duke of Cumberland himself in never having had a runner, much less a stud. While the conditions for the new race specified five-year-olds (if aged as we treat horses from 1 January rather than then at 1 May), they also stated that subscribers must have bred their contestants and fixed the first running for 1757. As those with no studs in March 1752 would otherwise be in an impossible position it was agreed that for the 1757 running the horses could be bought, but must be homebred from 1758.

During 1750, five of the twelve subscribers did not run even a single horse and two others had only one representative. The fact that at least six were without studs and yet were prepared to make long-term commitments to race homebred stock against established operators like Lord Godolphin is extraordinary. It was a remarkable vote of confidence in the future recovery of racing, and surely a statement of intent to make that recovery happen.

One of the twelve subscribers to the new race was the Marquis of Granby, the general after whom so many pubs were named, the heir to the non-racing 3rd Duke of Rutland. Indeed, Granby himself had only the occasional runner before 1752, but in 1750 his wife inherited Cheveley Park and the lease of the Palace as heir to the Duke of Somerset. In 1752 he opened the Long Room in the Palace to members of the Jockey Club and particular friends, which extremely convenient arrangement continued for years, probably until he died in 1770. It is impossible to prove but seems logical to assume that the decision to greatly extend the facilities in the High Street taken in 1771 arose because of the loss of the Long Room, where one of the treasures was the Seymour of Flying Childers (Fig. 10). This splendid picture seems to have been commissioned by the artist's father and only came to the Long Room following the second of its recorded sales in 1757. After the arrangement allowing access ceased the painting was removed to Chatsworth, where it still hangs.

When Lord Granby first made the Long Room available in 1752, a newspaper reported that he did so to ensure that members had sufficient privacy from 'gamblers and other idle people'. No doubt Lord Granby had in mind the likes of Mr Fletcher. The offer of such a facility together with the construction of the semi-public Coffee Room, the extensive festivities allied to the great cricket match (see Part 3) and the inauguration of the new race within a matter of a few months in 1751 and early 1752 accumulate to show just what effort was being made to turn things around on the Heath.

◆◆◆◆

Who should be credited with the idea of using the Duke's standing to front an organisation such as the Jockey Club with the aim of controlling abuses and enabling racing to prosper will surely never be known. Probably events owed more to chance than inspiration, after common revulsion at the doings of Mr Prentice had brought things to a head. The two most plausible candidates are the Earl of March and Ruglen, and Mr Richard Vernon. Both were young men who lived in Newmarket and cut great figures on the Turf for the rest of the century. Both rode well themselves, and Vernon also oversaw his large string trained for him by various people in his yard just to the west of the Avenue near the Rooms. March lived even closer to the Heath on the site of what is now Queensberry House with his yard across the road in the now derelict Queensbury Lodge.

March, later 4th Duke of Queensberry (Fig. 38) probably played the crucial part in initiating the scheme for the 'Great Stakes', and several of his famous and ingenious gambling

Fig. 38

Engraving of the 4th Duke of Queensberry
(formerly known as the Earl of March and Ruglen),
after R. Dighton (1796)

Infamous as the duke became in later life (he still had fourteen years to go after this caricature and did not mend his ways), the turf owes him a lot. His remarkable ingenuity in winning extraordinary bets demonstrated something more than mere cunning, and it is easy to see how such a fertile mind would have been very effective around 1750 in stirring Newmarket out of its long torpor. Had he not been so notorious he might well have got a lot more credit for his early efforts as jockey, cricketer and principal resident owner in Newmarket in the 1750s.

plots date from the period 1750–1752 as mentioned in Part 3. Immensely rich and with the best of connections he had yet to acquire much of the infamy of his later years and is perhaps the most closely involved of the subscribers in all the events of the day on the Heath. However, Richard Vernon is not far behind him in that respect. Recently retired from the army, he took up racing with remarkable success and won the first race the Club put on for its members in April 1752, although not a subscriber to the Great Stakes. Well born and a Whig MP for 36 years, he moved in the right circles, was a first-class jockey and a brilliant gambler, who used these skills to turn a very small fortune into a large one, which he retained until his death in 1800. Thus the sudden recovery at Newmarket could not have suited him better and he made full use of the times; even if he did not direct events, it seems likely he had as much to do with them as anyone. Along with Jenison Shafto, whose background was very similar, the pair had almost usurped the position of the former leaders on the Heath, such as Devonshire and Godolphin, by the time Shafto died in 1771. Their success as gamblers was legendary and their strings the largest in Newmarket, until more traditional grandees like Grosvenor and the Prince of Wales really arrived on the scene.

The remarkable change in the climate for the sport can be most graphically shown by the growth in the number and value of races. In 1751 the Heath saw only twenty-one run, worth under £1,600 to their winners. Yet only two decades later, in 1771, there were 169 worth over £51,000. Things were also improving elsewhere, but to nothing approaching the same extent. The rest of mainland Britain saw the quantity of races rise from 172 annually to 303 and values nearly double from under £12,000 to almost £23,000.

Thus Newmarket's share of national racing rose from 11 per cent to 36 per cent in terms of races and from 15 per cent to a staggering 70 per cent in money. At least in terms of cash, its leadership was seemingly verging on monopoly. While correct, these figures must be seen in the context of

Chapter 5 (1750–1791)

Fig. 39

The Duke of Cumberland inspecting his stud
by Sawrey Gilpin and William Marlow

The Duke's remarkable success once he was persuaded to become involved in breeding at the time the Jockey Club was re-formed to handle the Prentice scandal, really has no equal. To have bred both Eclipse and Herod in the thirteen years left to him is extraordinary. Here he is shown in Windsor Great Park where he was Ranger, with his stud groom in his livery coat of scarlet and green.

the huge matches being made on the Heath, which tend to exaggerate the position. Obviously a match for 1,000 Guineas is as much a bet as prize money. However, outside Royal Plates there was precious little added money anywhere and in principle a sweepstake on such terms is really identical except that more people are involved. Anyhow, in 1771, even if you exclude the matches, Newmarket still provided marginally more money (at over £18,000) to winners than the rest of the country combined.

In 1765 there had been an outcry over the prodigious betting on the match between Gimcrack and Ascham, and it is instructive that activities at Newmarket had now become such a byword for excess that Philip Parsons even published a two-volume satirical study in 1771. Called 'Newmarket, or an Essay on the Turf' (see Part 3), it pokes fun at everyone involved and their inflated ideas of their own importance. Similar books nowadays are more likely to deal with Premier League footballers or Russian oligarchs than happenings in rural Suffolk, despite the scale of modern Newmarket, backed by foreign money.

Perversely, racing really has a good deal for which to thank George Prentice. Not that it ever did him much good, as Trimmer had to be sold to Ireland to get a race (he was quite successful) and in 1767 his owner set an important legal precedent when a debt of £1,290 owed in England was successfully pleaded in France and resulted in Prentice being locked up in Dunkirk. While it is a most improper sentiment for a former Jockey Club Steward to express after nearly a decade as that institution's equivalent to the Director of Public Prosecutions, I cannot help feeling rather sorry for Mr Prentice. Wicked he certainly was, but the fates really do seem to have thrown the book at him. History does not record what happened next, but one fears that his future after incarceration in Dunkirk's debtors' prison is likely to have been pretty bleak if he even survived the experience.

◆◆◆◆

After the Godolphin died the contribution of the Eastern horse to the formation of the thoroughbred was complete. His sons and grandsons made far better stallions than any horse which could be imported, to the extent that his influence dominates proceedings far beyond the end of this chapter in 1791. Indeed, from 1752 to 1822 only five horses which were not his direct male-line descendants took the stallion championship, and then for a total of only nine years as against his sixty-two. That things have changed so dramatically since, with the last time one of his line triumphed as long ago as 1964 (and previously on only one other occasion since 1857), does seem strange. Nowadays the Darley Arabian, through his great great grandson Eclipse has established a virtual monopoly of tail-male descent worldwide.

The fact that the subscribers to the 1,200 Guineas had to breed their own stock more or less brought to an end the Yorkshire monopoly of the production of potentially high-class animals. Only two of the magnates involved were Yorkshiremen, and about half were southern based. The Duke of Cumberland's (Fig. 39) remarkably quick success as a breeder was very largely a result of his purchases in the north. Cypron, dam in 1758 of the great stallion Herod, was bought by him unraced in 1756 from the stud of Sir William St Quintin of Scampston, along with her first two foals, later good winners for him. He also acquired Marske from Mr John Hutton, and used him to cover another purchase in Spiletta, bred by Sir Robert Eden at Durham. The result of that mating was the legendary Eclipse, though sadly the Duke died on 31 October 1765 when he was still a yearling. On 23 December, when the stud in Windsor Great Park at which he was bred was sold by John Pond (perhaps the son of the publisher of the Calendar in succession to John Cheny, but could have been the man himself if still alive), Eclipse was bought by Mr William Wildman (Fig. 40), a grazier and wholesale butcher. Put into training near Epsom, by early 1769 a half share in him had passed to the remarkable Dennis O'Kelly (Fig. 41) who bought the balance by the end of the year as well as taking over Wildman's scarlet colours, those

Chapter 5 (1750–1791)

Fig. 40

William Wildman with Eclipse and his sons John and James
by George Stubbs (probably 1769)

Mr Wildman's horses were trained at Mickleham but among the few he ran at Newmarket were Gimcrack (Fig. 49) and Eclipse (Fig. 50). He is supposed to have paid only £30 for the tiny Gimcrack and the annotated sale catalogue of 1765 – when he bought Eclipse as a yearling – shows 45 Guineas rather than the usually accepted figure of 75 Guineas. As he sold the latter for 1,750 Guineas in two tranches, and Gimcrack for a figure variously reported at 800 and 1,500 Guineas, he seems to have been as good a dealer as befits someone made rich by success as a grazier and wholesale butcher. He also had good taste in pictures; when he died in 1784 he owned at least a dozen Stubbs canvases, several of which, like this one and the portrait of Gimcrack, he had commissioned.

Fig. 41

Turfites by Thomas Rowlandson (*c.*1775)

The man with the military pigtail holding forth on the left is Dennis O'Kelly, owner of Eclipse and successively Captain, Major and Colonel in the Militia by purchase. He is being inspected suspiciously by a grandee and his equally dubious dog. The grandee might be Lord Grosvenor.

depicted by Stubbs on Gimcrack five years before (Fig. 49). O'Kelly then commissioned Stubbs to paint Eclipse (Fig. 50) on the same spot but facing in the opposite direction. The involvement of these two commoners really signalled the beginning of the end of the virtual monopoly of good-class stock by the sort of landed families that had bred them in Yorkshire and raced them at Newmarket. The change cannot truly be said to have had a beginning or an end, but if an event has to be marked out as a turning point it is perhaps the purchase of Eclipse.

Unraced until five, he was unbeaten in eighteen races spread over two seasons, although he was so good that on eight occasions no opponent bothered to turn out. As a stallion O'Kelly stood him at Epsom and then at Edgware after he bought the former home of the Dukes of Chandos there just before both of them died, in 1787 and 1789, the horse outliving his owner. The remarkable success of the O'Kelly string was almost entirely based on Eclipse's stock, and left him a rich man by the time he died. Despite his success at stud the horse was never champion stallion due largely to the value of the matches made at Newmarket for the progeny of the local champions Herod and Highflyer; but, as already mentioned, things look very different today in the matter of sire lines.

Over the forty-two years covered by this chapter the programme of races used to test horses and amuse spectators changed in a way that had never happened before. Eclipse's career followed the old pattern fairly exactly in that only two of his eighteen races were run over less than four miles, and none below two. His slightly older contemporary, Herod (Fig. 54), ran all his ten races at four miles but the next champion, the latter's son Highflyer (Fig. 42), raced below four miles on three of his twelve appearances. Next in line as perennial leading sire came Highflyer's son Sir Peter Teazle, and he turned out over as little as a mile, won the Derby at a mile and a half and in all ran six of thirteen races below four miles. By 1791 versatility counted, but the ability to stay four miles certainly did too. Indeed, the almost unbroken reign as champion stallion of Herod, Highflyer and Sir Peter Teazle from 1777 to 1809 was based to a considerable degree on their ability to pass on stamina to their stock. Eclipse's line tended to show more speed, and perhaps this had something to do with the increasing dominance of his descendants as race distances shortened, although his influence would by that time have had only a very speculative effect.

As distances reduced so did the ages of the participants. The new pattern was really set when the St Leger (1776), the Oaks (1779) and the Derby (1780) were introduced for three-year-olds. Although all were initiated by Jockey Club members none was run at Newmarket, which is a fair example of the spreading influence of the Club even though it did not aspire to run things directly away from the Heath. The first two-year-old ran in 1769 (and won, surprisingly as he was the son of an Arabian), and the oldest race for this age group which survives today is the July Stakes, run at Newmarket since 1786.

Fig. 42

Highflyer's feet made into candlesticks

Along with Flying Childers and Eclipse, this horse has the right to be considered the best of the eighteenth century. Bred by Sir Charles Bunbury and raced by Lord Bolingbroke in the name of a friend, as his owner was by then insolvent, he had to be sold to Richard Tattersall, founder of the auctioneers. His unbeaten career was followed by a reign of thirteen stallion championships in fourteen years, before his death aged 19 in 1793.

Until the eighteenth century there had been very little organised racing in the modern sense outside the British Isles. The first horse to have much impact elsewhere was Bulle Rock by the Darley Arabian, who was exported from England to Virginia in 1730 and became a successful sire there in old age. In France racing began after a fashion under Louis XIV as a Court entertainment, but petered out when he died in 1715, and only really restarted under the ill-fated Louis XVI when all things English became fashionable after the end of the Seven Years War. Initially things were based largely on horses sent across the Channel, trained and ridden by expatriates, and again were closely linked to the Court. Such export markets as they opened up undoubtedly had a bearing on the way racing in this country expanded so dramatically in the years after 1750, but it was inevitably a one-way trade until well into the nineteenth century.

◆◆◆◆

During the latter part of the eighteenth century, the way in which betting on horses was conducted was beginning to shift. To some degree there must always have been professional betting men who did not own horses but simply made (or lost) a living by gambling on those of other people. However, up to this period betting on any scale was largely a matter of owners and others wagering against those they knew who happened to have different opinions. That this was not always so is shown by Richard Nash's researches, as at least in Newmarket something much nearer to the activities of a modern bookmaker already existed in the form of the Newmarket Bank as early as the 1730s. Details of this remarkable institution appear in Part 3. These activities foreshadow the more practical arrangement of professionals acting as early bookmakers taking bets on all, or most, of the runners, which began to become the usual way of doing business. An amusing print of the period dated 1791 says it all (Fig. 43). The 'Deep One', looking suitably poker-faced, and holding his 'List of the Horses', is eyeing the clearly over-confident and better-dressed 'Knowing One', who stands holding his little betting book with pencil at the ready. Somehow one would not give much for the chances of the latter coming out on top in this encounter.

Another important change is the great increase in information that has come down to us about the professionals actively involved with the horses. Before 1750 we occasionally know the names of trainers and jockeys, but usually very little about them as people, and few of those painted by Wootton or

Fig. 43

Engraving of *A Deep One and a Knowing One* (1791)

This comment on the early days of the betting ring was published in April of the same year that the Escape scandal erupted in October. The social nuances of the relationship between the lantern-jawed betting man and his smug-looking customer seem clear enough and rather well done, even if the artist is unknown.

Gimcrack at Four-Mile Stables by George Stubbs (1765), detail of Fig. 49

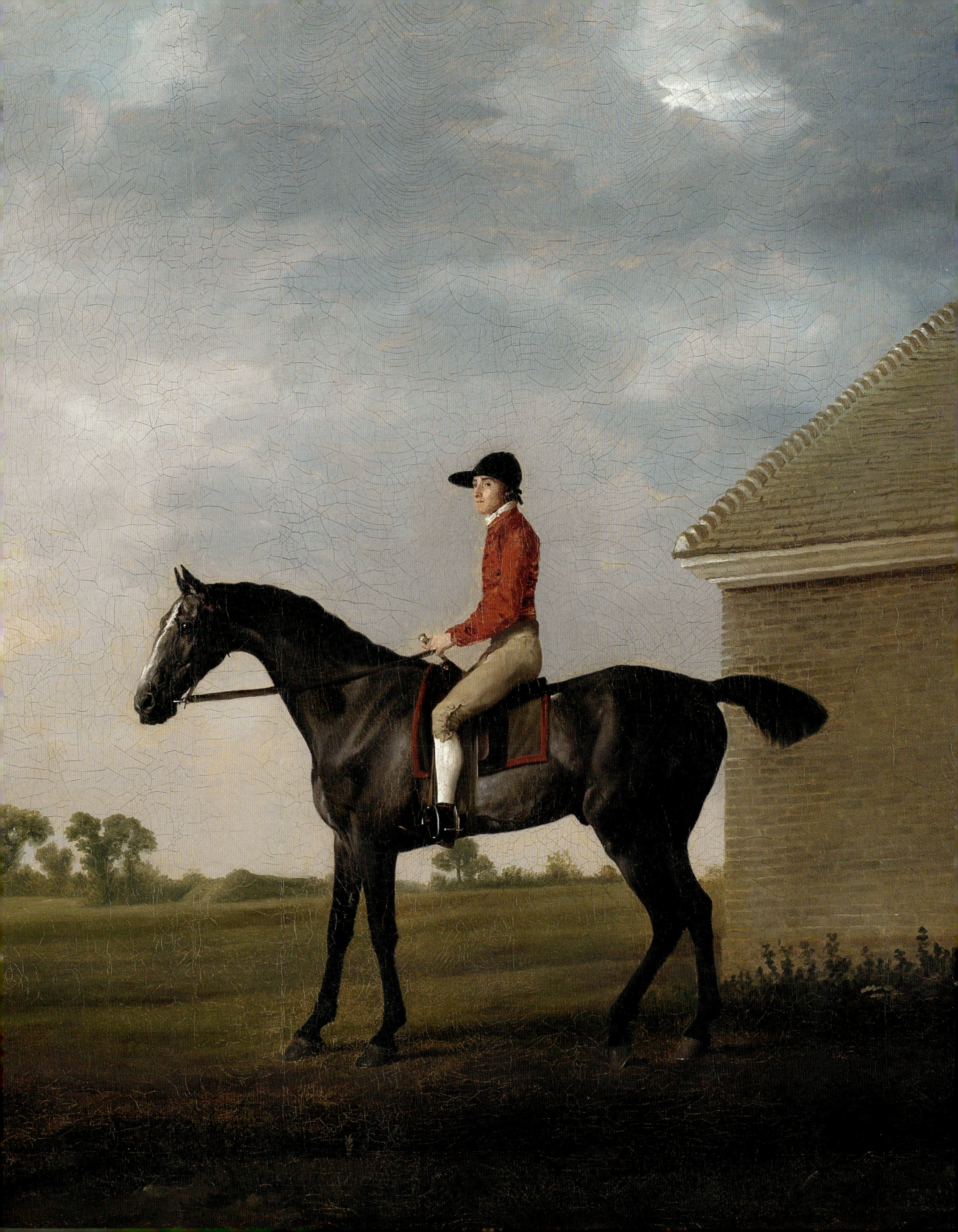

Fig. 44

Engraving of *Bay Malton beating Gimcrack*, after Francis Sartorius (1765)

As is not unusual with Sartorius, the background is rearranged to suit the 350 yards between the King's and Duke's Stands is foreshortened to little more than fifty. The artist has also stressed Gimcrack's lack of size by portraying Malton as well over 16 hands, which he certainly was not. However, he has incorporated the owners riding in with their champions beautifully. Bolingbroke looks in a state of shock as he points to Gimcrack, while Rockingham shows the quiet dignity (and perhaps self-satisfaction) suitable to the current Prime Minister.

Seymour even have names. Usually referred to as training or riding grooms, to mark them out from the army of grooms in general, they mostly worked for one employer as part of his racing establishment. If you could not afford to race on that scale you would not really have been too welcome at Newmarket, and in all probability would not have wanted to be there anyway as more than a spectator. As had long been true, the hunting fraternity around the country would have provided many of the runners drawn from the best class horses in their yards at the surviving minor meetings. The whole set up would somewhat have resembled our arrangements for point-to-points but without fences, as steeplechasing was very largely a nineteenth-century development.

Perhaps the best known of the early jockeys was John Singleton, whose main employer was the Marquis of Rockingham, one of the twelve subscribers to the 1,200 Guineas in 1751 at the start of his career. Singleton had been one of the main northern jockeys long before that, but transferred to Newmarket each year to ride and to train the Marquis's horses during the summer before returning to Yorkshire for their big meetings at York and Doncaster, taking a large group of Wentworth horses with him to Thixendale. Perhaps their greatest triumph came when Bay Malton defeated the previously unbeaten Gimcrack in a famous match in October 1765. A revealing print (Fig. 44), shows both owners but not Singleton. However, Stubbs depicts the horse's usual rider on Bay Malton galloping up towards the Beacon finish (Fig. 52).

The fortuitous appearance of George Stubbs to depict the Newmarket scene in the 1760s as it was approaching the zenith of this golden age resulted in the finest racing pictures ever painted, including one of Gimcrack at the Beacon start (Fig. 49). Another also shows Gimcrack (Fig. 55) approaching the Beacon finish as part of a trial, probably in preparation for one of his earlier matches, a famous victory over Thomas Panton's Ascham in July 1765. In the foreground the horse is being dried off after his work and is surveyed by an appreciative John Pratt, at this point early in his great career as jockey and later trainer. Records of Pratt's feats in the saddle are incomplete, as often no details of who rode are known, but as a trainer in Newmarket he turned out four winners of the Derby and no less than seven of the Oaks. Most were for the 1st Earl Grosvenor (Fig. 45), who was the largest owner of all after Jenison Shafto died in 1771. Eventually the cost of ownership began to gnaw at the foundations of even his fortune, and in the final decade before he died in 1802 his participation was on a rather more restrained – if still considerable – scale. One of Stubbs's biggest patrons, Grosvenor is presumed to have once owned the Jockey Club's version of Gimcrack's trial, having bought the horse himself in 1769.

Two other important events in racing at this period were the foundation of the firms of Tattersalls in 1766 and Weatherbys some five years later. As Europe's principal bloodstock auctioneers and racing's secretariat respectively, both are still central to the sport's future nearly 250 years later. Tattersalls began on the edge of Lord Grosvenor's London estate near Hyde Park Corner, and provided the Jockey Club with its London base for many years before finally being consolidated in the present sales paddocks at Newmarket, when the main yearling sales were shifted there from Doncaster in 1958. Weatherbys has gone in the other direction, spending most of the intervening period in London, in all sorts of shared accommodation with the Jockey Club, until in an age of easier communications transferring to its present headquarters in Wellingborough.

In 1773 Weatherbys took over the production of the annual Calendar in controversial circumstances during which their rival lost the edition he had printed and was effectively put out of business. The precise details of events are not clear but what seems quite obvious is that the Jockey Club was delighted to unite this aspect of its affairs in the hands of its official Keeper of the Match Book, James Weatherby, who thus combined the various roles of its earlier servants like Roger Williams and the Deards family.

In 1791 this consolidation was completed when Weatherbys brought out the first edition of its General Stud Book (GSB) in a format that still exists almost unchanged today. Unlike the Calendar, the Jockey Club never owned the GSB, which is still Weatherbys' property and forms the natural basis for every other stud book in the world, of which there are now 70 dealing with the thoroughbred. Weatherbys carried pedigrees back when they could to the seventeenth century but some flaws in the fifth edition of

Fig. 45

Richard, 1st Earl Grosvenor, after Benjamin West (c.1771)

His uncle owned one of the runners in Fig. 37 in 1724, his great grandson became a duke and owned Ormonde (Fig. 74) and Flying Fox (Fig. 81) while Arkle belonged to the wife of that Duke of Westminster's grandson. Lord Grosvenor himself occupied Hare Park as well as Oxcroft Farm at Balsham, where he kept his numerous stallions. Indeed, he had the largest string of all in the later decades of the eighteenth century and won three Derbys and five runnings of the Oaks, although neither race existed for half his time on the Turf. Even that level of success did not stop him losing a reported £300,000 through racing by the time he died in 1802.

Fig. 46

Engraving of *Escape*, after J.N. Sartorius (1792)

This good example of the work of the younger Sartorius shows what a handsome horse caused all the trouble. The print was published only four months after the race, which ended Escape's career as he joined his father as a stallion at Highflyer Hall. He had won ten of his fifteen races, beating Grey Diomed (Fig. 65) on the four occasions they met and he carried huge weights unsuccessfully in the first two races for the Ascot Oatlands. He was not a success at stud.

Volume One, published as long ago as 1891, have since been revealed as private stud books of earlier days have come to light and DNA analysis has amalgamated or split some lines of tail-female descent. However, in the latter cases the analysis can usually only prove something is wrong but not replace it with the right answer, and deciding which early record to trust is also a risky business, so a sixth edition of Volume One seems very improbable.

◆◆◆◆

While truly remarkable progress in the regulation of the sport had been achieved over the previous four decades, racing at Newmarket was about to be hit by a spectacular row with long-term implications in the Escape Scandal of October 1791. This related to the running of the Prince of Wales's good horse Escape (Fig. 46), a son of Highflyer. The Prince (George IV from 1820) had first come to Newmarket in 1784. His string swiftly multiplied, but his habit of spending more than he could afford soon brought things to a halt and his twenty-four different runners in 1786 were succeeded by only one the following year. Parliament having been persuaded to bail him out, he returned with renewed vigour in 1788 and by 1791 his string of thirty-nine horses which ran during that season exceeded his near rivals Lord Grosvenor, with thirty-two runners, and the young Duke of Bedford, with thirty.

The Royal jockey, Sam Chifney senior, seen here on Baronet (Fig. 56), enjoyed a splendid reputation for skill but a somewhat tarnished one for trustworthiness. In addition he was by no means popular with the Prince's racing manager Warwick Lake. On 20 October, in a race over the two-mile Ditch In course, their best horse, Escape, put up a lamentable display, finishing last of four to horses which were certainly very useful but not good enough to prevent him starting at 2-to-1 on. Chifney claimed the horse was very short of work, and expressed no surprise when next day, over the four-mile Beacon, Escape beat five animals of much the same class as the day before. Warwick Lake and the royal trainer Frank Neale were not amused – nor was any one else, particularly as Lord Grosvenor's Skylark, having been second in the earlier race, was well behind Escape in third, the latter being now 4-to-1 instead of odds on.

As with Trimmer forty years before, there is a strong whiff of singed fingers about the general reaction, but this time a great deal less certainty over what had really happened. In addition, with the heir to the throne involved it would clearly need a far more measured assertion of authority to do anything about it and, for better or worse in this case, that authority now existed in the form of the Jockey Club. The leading light in the Club from his appointment as a Steward in 1768 had been Sir Charles Bunbury of neighbouring Great Barton. Bunbury (Figs. 47 and 48) was an extremely successful owner and breeder, if on a much smaller scale than the likes of the Prince and Grosvenor. A man of strong character, Bunbury was the last person to turn a blind eye to the events of 20 October. Eventually, the stewards, consisting of Bunbury, the younger Thomas Panton and Ralph Dutton, decided that Chifney had pulled the horse. Panton had continued with his father's string (indeed, they may have been partners) after the latter's death in 1782, but did not succeed to his office as 'Keeper of the Running Horses', as the post was now abolished. However, he was quite an important figure in his own right and played a prominent part in persuading a seemingly very grudging William Pitt to drop his proposed tax on racehorses in 1784. Had the tax gone through, several of the principal owners threatened to abandon the turf, so foreshadowing similar threats of more recent times.

Debating so long afterwards whether Chifney had cheated and, if so, who knew, is surely fruitless, but the Prince's reaction was thunderous when he was told nobody would race against him if he retained Chifney. His string was put up for sale, and he refused to come to Newmarket again, although after a gap he did start racing elsewhere and even ran a few on the Heath, although in his absence. The Palace stayed leased to the Rutlands until eventually sold by Queen Victoria.

The scandal reverberated for years and produced assorted cartoons and caricatures like the Rowlandsons (of Figs. 6 and 48). The first is merely coarse, but the second brilliantly satirises all involved (bar Chifney), including the institution of the Jockey Club itself. Chifney fared little better than George Prentice, and his fine career was at an end. The Prince generously maintained his 200 Guineas retainer as a pension, but Chifney seems to have sold the right to receive it for a capital sum. When this disappeared in a venture with Mr Latchford for the production of the famous Chifney bit, which left £350 owing, Latchford had him committed to the Fleet debtors' prison, where he died in 1807.

Fig. 47

Sir Charles Bunbury, print by W. Humphrey (1800)

Bunbury bred good horses for many years at his estate of Great Barton near Newmarket. From 1768 to 1818 he was consistently re-elected as junior steward of the Club when the system automatically landed you in the top spot after two years. In practice he acted as if he was senior steward most of the time until 1818, when it was agreed he would remain a permanent junior for life. He died in 1821. Member of Parliament for Mildenhall for nearly half a century, he was briefly Chief Secretary in Ireland under Rockingham. Bunbury raced famous horses in Diomed (winner of the first Derby) and Eleanor (first filly to win both Derby and Oaks) but sold an even better animal in Highflyer (Fig. 42) unraced.

Fig. 48

Undated engraving of *'The Jockey Club, or Newmarket Meeting'*
by Thomas Rowlandson

Here Rowlandson pokes fun at the whole Escape scandal of 1791 in general and the Jockey Club in particular. Centre stage the Prince of Wales is holding forth while a malevolent Sir Charles Bunbury (Fig. 47) takes notes behind his back. Also present in the foreground are the Duke of Queensberry (Fig. 38), looking very much the aging roué he was, Lord Egremont and the Duke of Bedford, appearing rather unconcerned, with his hands on his hips.

An original Rowlandson is in the Halifax Collection where the image is reversed with Queensberry on the left and with various subtle differences in the pictures hanging in the background.

Chapter 5 (1750–1791)

◆◆◆◆

Not only is the whole Escape saga a sad coda to perhaps the greatest period in the Heath's history, but other things apart from the war conspired to bring this to an abrupt halt. The main owners of the period such as March (later Duke of Queensberry), Grosvenor, Vernon, Shafto and Rockingham were getting too old or were dead, and their natural replacements like the Prince and Bedford, who died young, failed to fill the gaps. Allied to more than two decades of war, racing generally declined from its peak of prosperity and in the case of Newmarket that decline, with one short interlude, ran for three-quarters of a century even if things recovered strongly elsewhere in the country after 1815. Apart from a false dawn in the 1820s, the town remained in a depressed state until changes for the better began in the 1860s, in the heyday of Admiral Rous.

It is a wry comment on racing as a way of life at this time that while the stories of Prentice and Chifney end in debtors, prison, Dennis O'Kelly spent five years in the Fleet before bouncing back to die in possession of a ducal palace and about the best horse of all time. Meanwhile the fortunes of the more typical large owners were equally varied, with the likes of Rockingham and Grosvenor losing immense sums from their even more immense incomes, at the same time as their shrewder contemporaries such as Richard Vernon and Jenison Shafto were playing Newmarket like a wrongly programmed slot machine to which they had the key. Perhaps these extremes of fate and fortune were part of the sport's appeal.

If Stubbs caught to perfection the timeless qualities and seemingly Augustan tranquillity of the place as the grandees liked to think of it, that was only part of the story. It was just these pretensions at which Philip Parsons aimed his jibes in 1771 and which stimulated Horace Walpole and Alexander Pope so often to the heights of sarcasm.

The odd man out in all of this was the remarkable Dennis O'Kelly. After all, Eclipse was bred at Windsor, trained at Epsom and stood as a stallion there and in Edgware, of all places, only seeing the Heath twice, for the Spring and Autumn meetings of 1770. His owner may have been the ultimate outsider but his nephew and heir, Andrew O'Kelly, was eventually elected to the Jockey Club. However, once there he signally failed to follow the example of his uncle, or Vernon and Shafto, being a good deal better at spending than getting, like so many of his contemporaries on the Heath.

PICTURE PUZZLE 2: IDENTIFICATION OF COLOURS

A crucial part is played in the identification of most racing scenes and their people or horses by the owners' silks. Whether reflected in the jackets of their jockeys or as browbands, horse or human clothing, the colours can be a great help but also quite often a trap for the unwary. Until 1762 no formal effort was made to regularise the use of colours, but naturally different owners had favourites and when they appear often enough in early pictures a pattern emerges. However, owners chopped and changed quite frequently, for instance when failure to do so would have seen the same ones carried in a particular match. Occasional written evidence also appears from 1718 in the early Newmarket race records. In 1762 one of the re-formed Jockey Club's early actions was to publish a list of those that would in future be used by nineteen of the major owners on the Heath. At that stage black caps were almost de rigueur, and this resulted in the only mention of headgear being if something else was to be used instead. Over the next century or so things expanded only slowly, and even major owners who restricted their activities to the north were ignored for many years. Accordingly, using colours for the purposes of identification can be a surprisingly complex business with eighteenth-century pictures.

An interesting example of this complexity arises over the colours carried by the legendary Eclipse. Bred by the Duke of Cumberland, he had been sold in 1765 after his breeder's death to William Wildman, a Londoner who made his money in various parts of the meat trade. Soon after his first race at Epsom in May 1769 Wildman sold half the horse to the notorious Dennis O'Kelly for 650 Guineas but he continued to run in Wildman's name for the rest of 1769. Neither was at that stage grand enough in the context of Newmarket to have registered colours, and O'Kelly was yet to have a runner anywhere, although he did start with four horses in his own name in 1769 – one of which won three races. On the other hand, Wildman had run horses for years – for instance, in 1768 he had eight, which was quite a big string for the period, and four won that season. They were trained for him at Mickleham near Epsom, and as O'Kelly also started there there may well have been links apart from the partnership in Eclipse.

Wildman was one of Stubbs' earliest and best patrons, and at the start of the 1765 season had owned another famous horse in Gimcrack. On 9 April that horse won his only race in Wildman's name over the Round Course before his canny owner sold him (allegedly for 1,500 Guineas) to Lord Bolingbroke. Stubbs was commissioned to paint Gimcrack for Wildman, and the glorious result shows the little grey ridden by Lord Bolingbroke's jockey John Pratt beside the Four-Mile Stables at the Beacon start (Fig. 49). It seems odd that this site was chosen, as it is about a mile away from the nearest point on the Round Course where he had won; superficially, it is even more odd that Pratt rides here, as the records report that Wildman put up Ben Johnson on 9 April. However, they also confirm that Johnson rode the race in red silks and not in the Bolingbroke black ones. Thus it seems clear that when Wildman had to borrow the horse back for Stubbs to paint him Bolingbroke also lent his jockey, by now the horse's regular rider. In the circumstances it is hardly surprising that William Wildman was not fussed by Stubbs basing the portrait on his sketch (Fig. 158) of the wrong background. The result was eventually sold after Wildman's death for £17 6s and is now in the Fitzwilliam.

About the end of 1769 O'Kelly bought out Wildman's half-share in Eclipse for 1,100 Guineas and when he came to Newmarket for the first time to run a match against Bucephalus in April 1770 he owned 100 per cent of the horse. Confusion sometimes arises because he appears in the records of this win as being Wildman's. That happened because the match in question had been made in Wildman's name, and O'Kelly would have taken over the rights to it along with the horse but it was still nominally Wildman's match. Probably the match stake of 600 Guineas was always down to the more speculative O'Kelly.

Stubbs was commissioned again to work his magic after the race (Fig. 50). He had already painted the horse the year before for Wildman (Fig. 40) and as he used the sketch (Fig. 158) for the background in this new picture he could well have done it in his London studio. Here Sam Merriott is arrayed in what are now the O'Kelly silks, taken over from his partner along with the horse. We know Stubbs was working for O'Kelly this time, as the painting descended in his family until it was sold to the USA in the 1920s. The earlier one of him with Wildman and his two sons under an oak tree went the same way to the Woodward Collection (Fig. 40).

Anyone who wondered what colours Wildman used for the last fifteen years of his life, during which he continued to race on a fair scale, got their answer in November 2000, when the Stubbs of Euston came on the market dated 1774 (Fig. 51). Despite never making it to the official list (O'Kelly registered scarlet with a black cap from 1776), Wildman seems to have gone even further upmarket in his choice of all crimson. Very splendid they look too on another grey horse.

Picture Puzzle 2

Fig. 49

Gimcrack at Four-Mile Stables by George Stubbs (1765)

Fig. 50

Eclipse at Four-Mile Stables by George Stubbs (1770)

Picture Puzzle 2

Fig. 51

Euston by George Stubbs (1774)

PICTURE PUZZLE 3: IDENTIFICATION OF HORSES

Fig. 52 shows Lord Rockingham's Bay Malton striding up towards the finish on the Beacon, ridden by his usual jockey and trainer, John Singleton. It seems reasonable to assume he is racing, and the rails show that he has already turned out of the Rowley Mile – only the last part of the Beacon had rails. In this case the absence of a crowd proves nothing, as this would have been true of much of the last few furlongs in the 1760s. The picture is of added interest, as no other Stubbs depicts a race rather than its preliminaries or aftermath.

When the second picture by Francis Sartorius (Fig. 53) was last sold, the four horses were unidentified. As can be seen by comparison with the Stubbs, the horse on the left is again Bay Malton with Lord Rockingham's green on his browband. On 21 April 1767, Malton beat the future great stallion Herod with Turf third and Ascham fourth, in a race with 2,000 Guineas at stake. In each case the other browbands from left to right of black, green and pink conform to the owners' silks, and the horses' coats and markings (or lack of them) tally precisely. There can be no doubt Sartorius has shown these fine horses being set right behind the King's Stables on the Heath after their famous race.

However, the main point of this puzzle is not this relatively minor work and the horses depicted but the third picture, the fine Stubbs of a horse apparently out of training but still looking extremely fit (Fig. 54). For many years it has been an anonymous animal, interesting only as a painting. However, if you compare him with the great Herod (the third from the left in the Sartorius) you see a very similar horse. Again looking surprisingly immature for a nine-year-old and still just as startled, with teeth bared as in all pictures of Herod, he surveys what one can only feel is the same exceptionally tall groom. The latter's rather arrogant stance is virtually identical, while his livery on the Heath is much the same colour as his garb here; it is a pity Sartorius did not see fit to finish his face. Within a month Herod had won his final race for 1,000 Guineas against Ascham, and retired to Sir John Moore's stud near Newmarket, where he immediately started covering mares – perhaps it is not surprising Stubbs found him looking rather startled. No doubt Moore would have wanted a portrait of his champion, only acquired a year earlier on the death of the Duke of Cumberland. The fact Herod is known to have had a small star as his only marking apart from his black legs is another factor in

this identification. So too is the extraordinary emphasis Stubbs has laid on the arteries in the horse's head. In 1766, when again racing against Malton at York, 'a blood vessel burst in his head when running the last mile, and he was taken dangerously ill'. Given that he is now regarded as the primary progenitor of bleeding in thoroughbreds after his remarkable career at stud, it has become the most notorious disaster of its kind ever to happen to a horse. The background of the Stubbs is broadly consonant with that of Moore's stud at Nether Hall, but with the artist's favoured addition of a big spread of water. Unusually for this part of East Anglia there is actually an area of water there called Bartonsmere, presumably that at the bottom left of the painting, in broadly the right place in relation to Nether Hall, but the ocean in the background is entirely imaginary.

The great expert on the work of Stubbs, the late Judy Egerton, thought that stylistically the painting looked like an even earlier work and felt the groom's awkward stance pointed in that direction. However, the remarkable similarity to the Sartorius groom would seem to address at least the latter aspect adequately, and to a degree they are really the same point.

Picture Puzzle 3

Fig. 52

Bay Malton and John Singleton by George Stubbs (1770)

Fig. 53

Bay Malton, Turf Herod and Ascham by Francis Sartorius (1767)

Picture Puzzle 3

Fig. 54

Herod by George Stubbs (probably 1767)

PICTURE PUZZLE 4: IDENTIFICATION OF OCCASION

It has always been clear that this great Stubbs of 1765 (Fig. 55) was based on his sketch (Fig. 157) of the Beacon finish. However, attempts to link the occasion to any of the many races Gimcrack won on that course always foundered because the colours of the jockeys and the horses chasing him home do not fit. As the horse was both bought and sold later by Frederick, 2nd Viscount Bolingbroke, in 1765, during which he had carried that notorious figure's appropriately black silks, the field is limited to the four races he ran for him after his win for Wildman (Fig. 49). Since in each of the four he had only one opponent it follows that this is none of them. Indeed, there can only be two explanations of the occasion: either it is a formal trial with jockeys up or Stubbs was commissioned to paint an imaginary frieze as a background for his second portrait that year of the splendid little grey.

Surely anything so whimsical as the latter theory is effectively disqualified by the fact the picture was commissioned by Bolingbroke; it descended in his family until 1943. The only basis for such a proposition would be if any element in the picture showed the alternative of a formal trial to be unsound. Instead of that being the case, the reverse is true, and several factors make it clear that it was not a race – imaginary or otherwise – and so it was indeed, a trial.

Had this been supposed to be a race Stubbs could hardly have avoided including a few people, apart from the jockeys and grooms, however strong his antipathy to crowd scenes. Per contra the Club's rules at the period actually forbade any outsiders attending formal trials, for the purpose of which the Heath was booked in advance; hence no doubt the fact the shadows show it was well into the afternoon rather than a morning scene, as might be expected for work. Given Stubbs's unique talent for investing his Newmarket scenes with a timeless pastoral dignity, as a compromise between a patron wanting action and an artist objecting to disrupting the ambience with crowds a trial seems the obvious answer. This is confirmed by two other regulations of the day. The first prohibited any trials from including the horses of more than one owner unless the fact it would do so was declared in advance, and in this case there are three sets of colours. Secondly, running two horses in a race was also forbidden due to the danger of the rider of one acting the part of a 'spoiler' in the days of 'Cross and Jostle', when interference was permitted along the lines of riding opponents off in polo today.

Against all this it hardly seems necessary to prove the point further by reference to the closed white shutters on the top floor of the King's Stand, which swung down on hinges when a race was taking place (Fig. 66). It would seem to us absurd to suggest that the fact that they are closed in all of the five Stubbs portraits which include the King's Stand indicates an adherence to the original sketch rather than a desire to show that no race was involved. It is interesting that the artist recognised that the white paint of the early pictures had been replaced by brown by the 1790s (Figs. 56 and 67), so he clearly did view the stand in later years rather than just relying on his old sketch.

The identities of the horses chasing Gimcrack at a respectful distance are inevitably less clear-cut, and it is hard to deduce which of his matches is the reason for the trial. The first time he won for Bolingbroke came in early May, when he beat Thomas Panton's Rocket for 1,000 Guineas. At first sight, perhaps, a trial soon after purchase for the owner to see what he had bought would make sense, but this appears the wrong assumption here due to the grey bringing up the rear. He carries Lord Grosvenor's yellow silks, and the only grey he raced that year, Cardinal Puff, was not bought by him until after a win on the same day Gimcrack had beaten Rocket. Therefore the trial seems to have been one organised in advance of the match for a further 1,000 Guineas against Ascham (Fig. 53) on 10 July.

If the pinning down of the occasion is accepted, the second horse in the white silks of Richard Vernon is very probably his chesnut horse Cheshire Dick. This animal had also won at the same early May meeting when racing for Grosvenor, who had then sold him to Vernon – dealing of this sort between major owners was a feature of the period. In third place is probably Boreas, a bay of Grosvenor's all year which had also shown he was in good form, and thus suitable trial tackle, by winning one of the eighteen races at the May meeting.

The second version of this picture belongs to the Jockey Club, and presumably came to it after being put on the market by Lord Grosvenor's son in 1812, en route to the Club's Victorian father-figure, Admiral Henry Rous. Probably Lord Grosvenor won a fortune over the Ascham match by using the information gleaned from such a trial, as the betting was on sufficient scale that it caused some finger-wagging in the London papers. Either for that reason or because he eventually bought

Picture Puzzle 4

Fig. 55

Gimcrack's Trial by George Stubbs (1765)

(Enlarged on pp. 84–5)

Gimcrack himself in 1769, he wanted his version of the picture, and in any case he commissioned another from Stubbs of the horse at his stud after his career on the Heath ended in 1771.

The jockey is again John Pratt, although he looks shorter on the ground here than when mounted on Gimcrack (Fig. 49), but as the latter was really a pony at 14 hands (4ft 8in at the shoulder) that is hardly surprising. Less certain is the identity of the rather grand groom holding Gimcrack. Perhaps he is the trainer of the horse, but a comparison with the Stubbs 1768 portrait of Otho, now in the collection of the BSAT, suggests he is that horse's rider John Larkin. In fact, Larkin did also train horses in Newmarket, but in 1765 he was probably involved as a result of acting as assistant to his father, James, out at Six Mile Bottom, where he had Grosvenor's string.

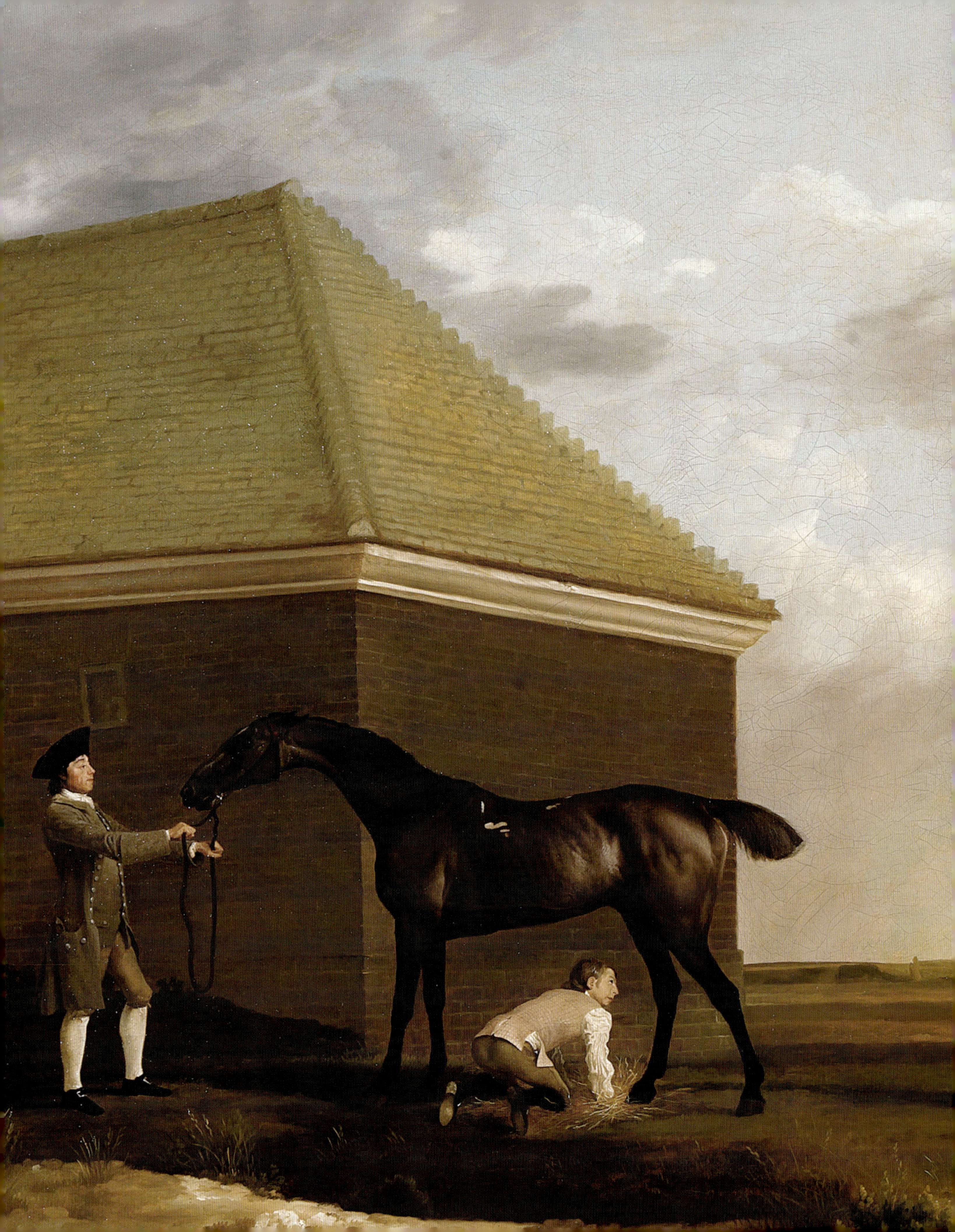

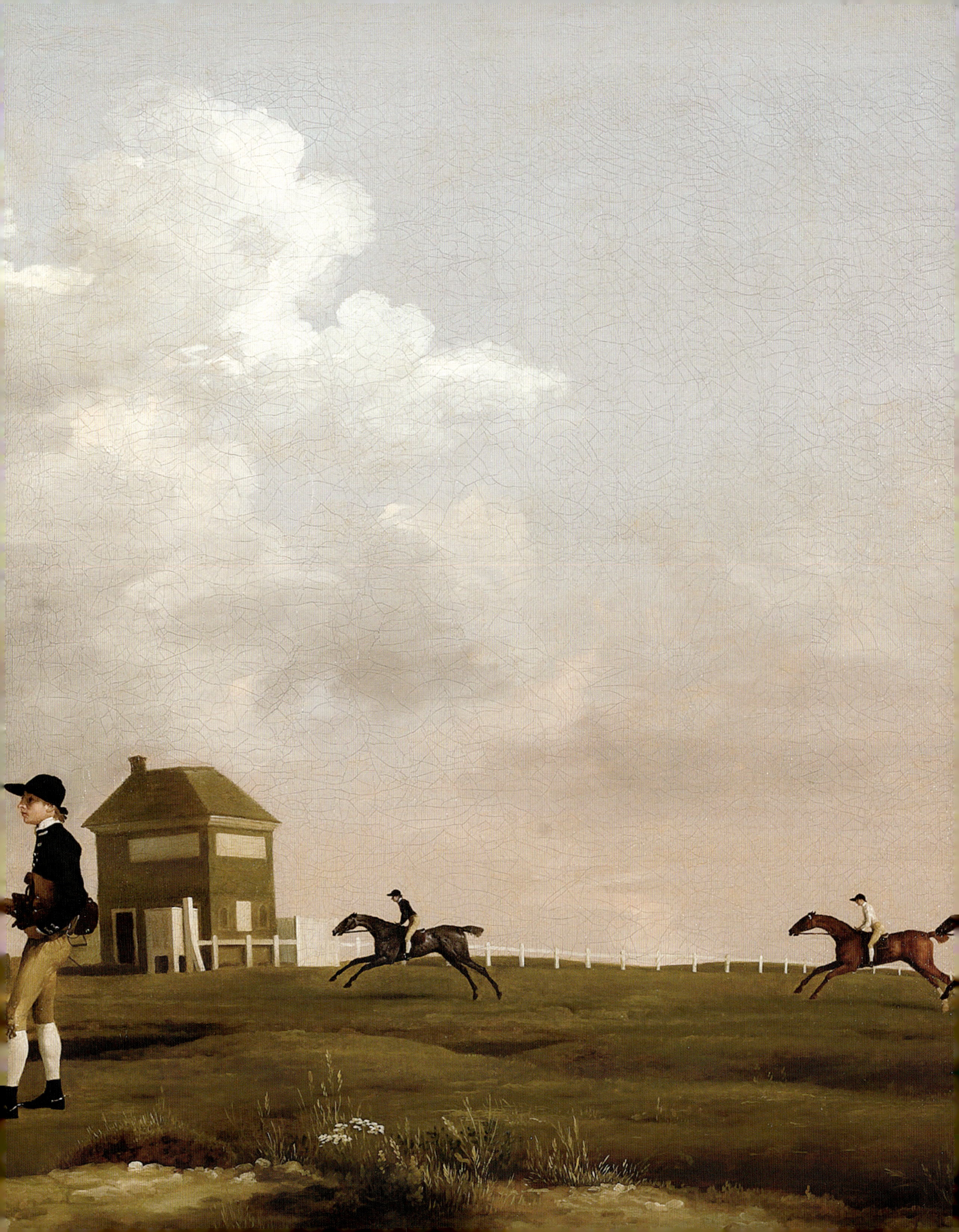

PICTURE PUZZLE 5: IDENTIFICATION OF OCCASION AND THE ACTION OF THE HORSE

There are three versions of this first attempt by any artist to depict a horse at the point in his action when no foot is on the ground. The prime one was painted by Stubbs in 1791 for the owner of Baronet, the Prince of Wales, and is still in the Royal Collection. This version (Fig. 56) is also dated that year and went to the jockey, Sam Chifney senior, before passing between various branches of his family, until being bought by the 5th Earl of Rosebery from a descendant in 1898. It has passed since then by descent to the Earl of Halifax, and hangs in his collection at Garrowby. The last version was done in order to produce the print in the Turf Gallery series issued in February 1794, and is now in the US. As always with Stubbs, but almost never with any other artist, the shutters on the stand are closed and the horse is here shown at much the same strange angle as Gimcrack (Fig. 55), moving almost parallel to the winning line on the Beacon. As neither horse was competing in a race, the fact that both are shown well past the finishing line and at an angle which suggests they would not have crossed it at any point between the winning posts on opposite sides of the course is discussed further in connection with the later masterpiece of the unsaddled Hambletonian (Fig. 67).

The first recognition that all horses leave the ground when cantering or galloping had come in July 1791, when the founder of the Royal Veterinary College, Mon. Charles Vial de St Bel, published his dissection of Eclipse, who had died in 1789. It seems reasonable to assume that this discovery inspired Stubbs to try to depict the new position when he produced this work later in the year, following Baronet's only appearance on the Heath, when he won the King's Plate on 6 October. The picture exerted prodigious influence on later artists such as Marshall (Fig. 167) and Herring – before the fact that the true critical moment comes when all four feet are gathered under the animal rather than extended was revealed by the arrival of photography, soon followed by the Muybridge experiments.

That Baronet is not racing is confirmed by the fact that his only win on the Heath had taken place on the Round Course on the far side of the Ditch, nearly two miles away. In any case, the way Chifney is looking the viewer in the eye strongly suggests he is showing off his mount's paces and his own legendary skills as a horseman to an audience standing in front of the King's Stables. As the Prince was in Newmarket for the races that week, it does not seem fanciful to imagine him as the principal viewer. Whether Stubbs would have come to Newmarket to paint Baronet is very doubtful, but the fact he has noted correctly that the shutters on the stand (white when he last painted them some twenty years before) have changed to brown seems to show that he had seen them anew at some point.

Baronet was not a local horse, and presumably returned to the Prince's other stables near Ascot after this single excursion to Newmarket. Accordingly, it must be more likely that Stubbs would have found it easier to get there from his London home than to travel to the Heath. After all, no one could know in advance whether any particular occasion would be a triumph or disaster, and one doubts whether Stubbs ever turned up on the off-chance rather than being commissioned after the event to produce his great Newmarket portraits, usually necessitating a visit to wherever the horse might then be.

Picture Puzzle 5

Fig. 56

Baronet by George Stubbs (1791)

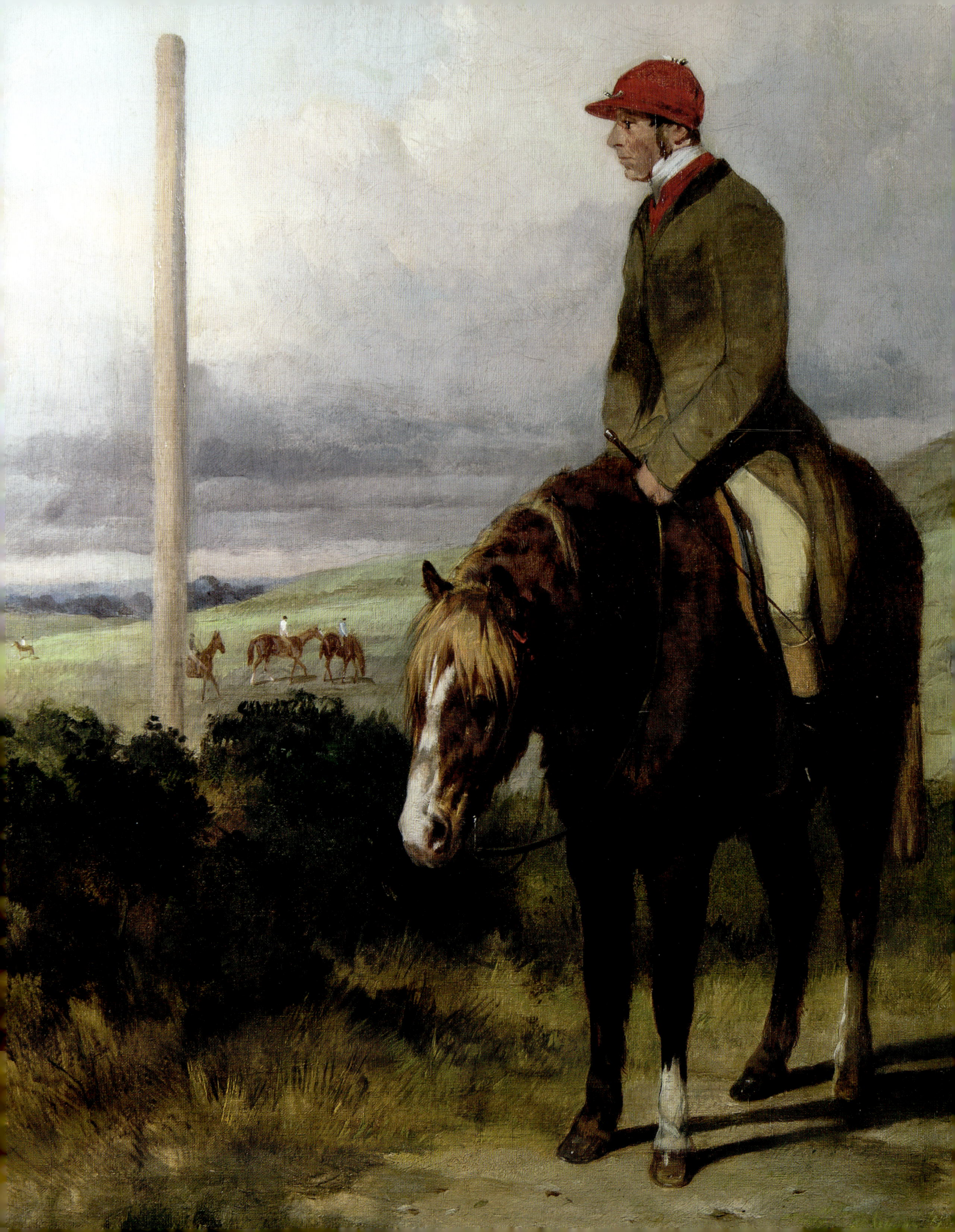

Chapter 6 (1791–1863)

Slow Progress Followed by Collapse in the Fortunes of the Heath from the 1830s

It is no accident that, covering seventy-two years, this chapter encompasses the longest period in the Heath's racing history. While elsewhere the sport prospered, attracting a much wider cross-section of the rapidly expanding population, Newmarket in contrast endured something resembling a private ice age for much of the time. Superficially, this is difficult to understand, as during this period racing and the Jockey Club saw probably the three most dominant personalities ever involved and at the height of their influence in Sir Charles Bunbury, until his death in 1821, Lord George Bentinck in the 1830s and 1840s, and Admiral Rous, very active in all sorts of roles from 1835, and effectively in charge of events from around 1850 until he died in 1877. While nationally so much changed for the better, and the Jockey Club steadily acquired powers little short of dictatorial, things at Newmarket deteriorated so badly from the mid-1830s that by the 1850s the universal view seems to have been that the Heath was no place to train decent horses, and the Club was almost broke. Indeed, no horse trained there won the Derby between Orlando in 1844, by courtesy of the law courts, and Macaroni in 1863.

Nat Flatman by Harry Hall (*c*.1850), detail of Fig. 60

This strange course of events had a good deal to do with the personalities and interests of the only so-called dictators to have held sway since the days of Charles II and Tregonwell Frampton. Both of these two had been essentially Newmarket figures in the context of racing, and the town had prospered as a consequence. That was still the case for most of Bunbury's long reign ,but by the time of the Escape Scandal in 1791 the Club's influence on and interest in events elsewhere was rapidly increasing. However, largely as a result of Bunbury's devotion both to the Heath and the affairs of the Club, Newmarket continued to maintain its position within the sport, albeit during the difficult times of the Napoleonic Wars and their aftermath, and despite its being a low period for bloodstock by comparison with the glory days of Eclipse, Highflyer and Hambletonian as the breed adjusted to the new approach to racing a good deal less speedily than the programmes themselves.

The fact that things locally continued to be reasonably successful until the 1830s cannot be attributed solely to Bunbury, as it was a period when Newmarket produced a flowering of talent in both trainers and jockeys which helped sustain its position. Indeed, the skill of the main trainers in the town from 1791 onwards was, as it always

The Heath and the Horse

Fig. 57

Robert Robson and Frank Buckle by Ben Marshall (probably 1802)

This fine sketch is almost the only image of the great trainer of thirty-four classic winners between 1793 and 1827. His usual jockey was Frank Buckle, whose comparable career saw twenty-seven classic winners ridden between 1792 and their shared final victory in the 1827 1,000 Guineas. Here Marshall is celebrating their win in the 1802 Oaks for Mr John Wastell with Scotia. Traditionally this picture has been supposed to include Mr Wastell, but as he was 66 at the time, and much too grand to be depicted folding rugs, one of the central figures must have been Robson's head lad.

Frank Buckle was the son of a Newmarket saddler, and started as a boy in Richard Vernon's yard. He was also related to the Samuel Buckle who looked after the Match Book for the Jockey Club after 1751. He was the dominant Newmarket jockey before the arrival on the scene of Sam Chifney junior (Fig. 58) and Jem Robinson (Fig. 59) and he carried on with considerable success until aged 65.

has been since, one of the most decisive factors in the town's prosperity.

The most influential trainer of the day was certainly Robert Robson (Fig. 57), and it is a pity we know so little of him beyond his remarkable achievements. Between 1793 and 1827 he won no fewer than thirty-four Classics, and it seems safe to say that had the 2,000 Guineas begun before 1809 and the 1,000 Guineas in 1814 he would comfortably have exceeded the forty of his only real rival later in the century, John Scott of Malton. As Scott's total included no less than sixteen St Legers, whereas Robson never deigned to walk his champions up the Great North Road, his feat is all the more remarkable.

Robson deserves to be far better remembered than he is and one would have thought he would have merited a major race on the Heath or some sort of memorial in the town if the understandable reluctance of sponsors to link such names with their own had not prevented this. Apart from his twenty-two triumphs for the 3rd and 4th Dukes of Grafton, he also won classics for seven other owners, and was the first person to succeed on a grand scale as a public trainer rather than as a private training groom. On top of that, he revolutionised the way horses were trained by abandoning the rather barbarous tradition of long work in very heavy clothing followed by scraping the abundant sweat from the often infuriated beast, a procedure reminiscent of a Turkish bath. An aspect of his success for the Graftons was the fact that the 4th Duke's half-brother, the Reverend Lord Henry Fitzroy, had an enviable reputation for organising things brilliantly both at the stud and on the Heath for his father and his brother.

Not only Robson, but Dixon Boyce, John Pratt (Gimcrack's jockey), Frank Neale (Escape's trainer) and Richard Prince got into double figures in terms of Classics won by their stables without taking a single St Leger between them. It was a great period for Newmarket trainers, and while it lasted the town prospered despite the poisoning of several of Prince's

Fig. 58

The Chifney brothers (Sam, junior and Will) with Zinganee
by Ben Marshall (*c*.1830)

This picture, seemingly finished by a hand other than Marshall's, probably suffered that fate following the artist's death in 1834. The Chifneys' collapse ushered in a bad run for the Heath until the 1860s. Sam continued to ride with considerable success, but Will abandoned the sport completely after a fine career as a trainer, including the outstanding Priam, which for a time the brothers also owned.

Fig. 59

James Robinson on Matilda by J.F. Herring Senior (1829)

Probably the best jockey of the first half of the nineteenth century, Jem Robinson only won the St Leger once apart from his 1827 victory on Matilda. In all he rode twenty-four classic winners including fourteen at Newmarket, where he was particularly effective in matches. He was notably honest in an age when some riders took a very different approach. Like Buckle (Fig. 57), he was a Newmarket man by birth.

string by Daniel Dawson in 1809– a crime which resulted in Dawson's death on the gallows outside Cambridge gaol. The betting man who had put him up to it seems to have been rather sharper at avoiding the consequences.

Meanwhile the local jockeys played their part, with Pratt succeeded by Sam Chifney, Frank Buckle (Fig. 57) and the former's son Sam junior (Fig. 58), and James Robinson (Fig. 59). Buckle was the holder of the record for Classic wins until Lester Piggott overtook his mark of twenty-seven. However, since Robson's day the success of the town has always depended far more on its chief employers, the trainers, than their most important employees for its relative standing. After Will Chifney (also Fig. 58), Sam junior's brother, went broke while still the town's leading trainer in 1833 and the Heath's reputation hit a real snake (as opposed to Bunbury's long ladder), the place slid back to a position much inferior to its standing in 1791. If the later trainers were rather moderate, luckily the jockeys, Nat Flatman (w 60) and George Fordham (Fig. 61), kept the flag flying with at least twenty-five championships up to the time of Fordham's last one in 1871.

◆◆◆◆

Fig. 60

Fig. 61

Nat Flatman by Harry Hall (*c.*1850)

George Fordham by Harry Hall (*c.*1865)

Officially champion jockey from 1846 to 1852, Flatman had in fact reigned for several years before such records were properly maintained. Fine rider that he was, it could not be said he was quite in the class of his predecessors like James Robinson (Fig. 59) or those who followed him like George Fordham (Fig. 61) and Fred Archer (Figs. 73, 74 and 75). Able to ride very light, and particularly honest, he dominated throughout what was really a far from inspiring period in terms of jockeyship.

After fourteen championships it is perhaps not too surprising that Fordham had his supporters as the best jockey, even after Fred Archer burst on to the scene. His sixteen classic wins compared with Flatman's ten and, like Sir Gordon Richards in the next century, both achieved more in terms of the number rather than the quality of their victories. Both Fordham and Richards had to wait until the end of their careers for their single Derby victory, and if Flatman's came quicker it was due to the disqualification of Running Rein.

Over the whole period 1791–1863 the number of races run fell from 234 to 230, but the Heath's share of the national programme had crashed from 41 per cent to 16 per cent by 1863 (if one includes all the new steeplechases being run the drop is even sharper). Given the tiny field sizes so common in those days, and the absence of watering, there was really no bar to running as many races as desired over the various separate courses at Newmarket. Indeed, the only limiting factors would have been the availability of horses and money and by 1853, when things were at their lowest point, both were in extremely short supply on the Heath.

As a consequence, in July 1853 the tradesmen of the town appealed to the Jockey Club for the inevitable cut in the Spring programme to be achieved by chopping out the Second Spring entirely rather than docking a day from each of the three meetings. The Club eventually agreed and the meeting was dropped from 1856 until happier times allowed its restoration in 1870. The need to do something had been very clear, as the 198 races of 1853 saw forty-one with only two runners and many of the rest with only three or four. Such matches were certainly not the great ones of the heyday of the eighteenth century, when Hambletonian beat Diamond (Fig. 66 and 68) with 3,000 Guineas put up by each side; instead, in 1853 the biggest sum risked by the more parsimonious Victorian owners was no more than £200.

◆◆◆◆

The turf's next important leader after the death of Bunbury was Lord George Bentinck (Fig. 62 and 183). He has often been unfairly traduced by racing historians persuaded by the spiteful references to him by William Day (whom he rightly had warned off) and Charles Greville (his cousin, who seems to have cheated him and was certainly rather more than sharp on occasion) and by his own notorious arrogance. Bentinck certainly cut corners by the standards of today, but those of the early Victorian turf were very different, and nothing he is credibly accused of doing amounted to dishonesty in contemporary terms. His relationship with the Jockey Club was almost as unfriendly as it was with the aforementioned racing historians, despite his father being the 4th Duke of Portland and owner of much of Racecourse Side on the Heath, and the Club's principal benefactor. Indeed, in February 1842 he had rebuked the Club so severely in the *Morning Post* over its handling of the bankruptcy of Mr Gurney that he even deigned to offer a very lukewarm apology, so tepid it can hardly have improved matters, at the next meeting. It is not generally realised that, as opposed to being its long-term dictator of legend, Bentinck was not even elected a Steward until July 1845. Prior to that date the remarkable influence he exerted was almost in spite of the institution rather than through it. No doubt such influence was a combination of force of personality, innumerable connections via parentage and politics, and the fact that he raced by far the largest string in the country.

Bentinck's huge string was trained for some years by John Day of Danebury in Hampshire, and when he fell out badly with the whole family over the handling of his great filly Crucifix, his horses returned to Goodwood to be trained by John Kent. At Goodwood Bentinck was largely responsible for improving the racecourse and its programmes to the point that the meeting briefly attained a status hardly matched anywhere else, but he is also remembered for introducing assorted changes in the way in which all meetings were organised. His innovations, such as flag starts, parades, properly identified paddocks and saddling arrangements, as well as general presentation, were so successful that they became standard practice. All this greatly enhanced his influence around the country without really endearing him to the somewhat comatose Jockey Club that existed after the death of Bunbury.

The 1840s were rather similar to the 1740s in terms of widespread dishonesty and, in particular, the pulling of horses to fix races. Even worse, and on a par with Mr Prenctice's efforts of 1751, were the events of 1844, when the four-year-old Maccabeus turned out as a ringer for the three-year-old Running Rein to win the Derby. There had been similar accusations after earlier Derbys, although nothing had come of such investigations as were instituted, but this time Bentinck decided to take matters into his own hands. Initially at his own expense, he successfully prosecuted the connections of the winner, and eventually all the gory details of the fraud were exposed in court. Presumably shamed by these events, the Club promptly elected him as a Steward, in which post he remained very active despite both selling his entire stud at Goodwood in July 1846 and turning his talents to politics. In this other role he led the majority of his fellow Conservative MPs in their defeat of Sir Robert Peel's government over its volte-face regarding the repeal of the Corn Laws, but subsequently gave up the leadership when he could not persuade his followers to take a more generous view of the plight of the Irish during the Potato Famine. After such an active life it hardly seems surprising that he dropped dead of a heart attack, aged just forty-six, when walking across his father's estate at Welbeck in September 1848.

Even extreme arrogance sometimes has its good points. After the Running Rein verdict in the High Court the sport had been so delighted with Bentinck's efforts that a large testimonial fund was spontaneously raised for him, partly in recognition of the fact that he would have been badly out of pocket over the costs. This he declined to accept, and the money was eventually used to set up the Bentinck Benevolent Fund 'for the benefit of the widows and children of deserving trainers and jockeys'. It is now amalgamated with several other Jockey Club funds in Racing Welfare, and the 'deserving' can still benefit from it, and it is probably a good deal easier to fulfil the qualifications nowadays than it would have been in the 'hungry forties' of the nineteenth century.

Whatever the Club's members may have thought of Bentinck before 1844, their successors were later delighted to have been given a 'memento mori' of their sometime irritant and

Fig. 62

Engraving of *Lord George Bentinck* after J.C. Wilson (*c*.1840)

A younger son of the 4th Duke of Portland, Bentinck's immense influence on the Turf was essentially personal rather than via the Jockey Club, which he regarded as largely ineffective. Apart from racing the largest string in the country, the changes in the organisation of meetings he introduced at Goodwood and elsewhere much improved the sport. Even more important was his exposure of the fraud which saw the 1844 Derby won by a four-year-old. In 1846 he sold his entire stud to concentrate on politics but combined this with acting as a Steward of the Club for the first time until the summer of 1848, only months before his death in September at just 46.

more recent hero in the form of a fine painting by John Ferneley (Fig. 183). Done in 1849, it records Bentinck's last visit to Newmarket for the Guineas meeting of 1848, and shows him with his great friend the Earl of Glasgow inspecting the latter's string of, by Bentinck's high standards, extremely poor horses. His had been a very ambivalent relationship with the Club, and in respect of Newmarket itself there seems very little that can be said in its favour. All Bentinck's influence had been in favour of Goodwood, as well as racing in general and its conduct nationally, rather than the interests of Newmarket Heath, and that seems to have been the direction in which the Club was also moving, and indeed, had been since Bunbury's days.

Perhaps the crucial switch of emphasis in a process that had first really arisen over the Prentice Affair, and been accelerated by the formidable figure of Bunbury after the Escape Scandal, came on 1 November 1831. On that day a preface was added to the 'Rules and Orders of the Jockey Club', stating that they only applied to Newmarket unless any other racecourse decided it wished to adopt them. No appeals would be entertained against local decisions from courses which did not comply. The result was that everyone fell into line rather than accept pariah status. By this nicely thought out sleight-of-hand the necessary degree of central control became available, even if it had been inadequately applied before the Running Rein Scandal.

By the middle of the century the breed seems to have adjusted to the necessary degree to produce more champions suited to the way racing now took place after the relative dearth of such horses in the first three decades of the century before Priam. Some exceptional horses such as The Flying Dutchman and the first Triple Crown winner West Australian appeared, as if to celebrate the Bentinck improvements, but all had in common the fact that they were not trained at Newmarket. Both these champions were from Yorkshire and most other good horses were either trained there or on the downs in Berkshire or Hampshire. Indeed, the last great horses trained on the Heath up to the 1860s had been Priam (foaled 1827) and Bay Middleton (foaled in 1833). West Australian's three Classics contributed to his trainer John Scott's record total of 40, accumulated at a rate that the whole of Newmarket put together could not match after the collapse of the Chifney dynasty. Until Mathew Dawson arrived in the town in 1866, if there had been any real talent in the training ranks it would have been made conspicuous by its rarity. In any event, with far fewer horses paying Heath Tax and the Club's finances in a very poor way, the condition of the Heath itself was adding to the problems of the town.

◆◆◆◆

Fortunately talent did eventually make itself evident within the Club in the formidable figure of Admiral Henry Rous (Fig. 63 and 194), who began to fill the void which had existed locally since Bunbury's days. Like Bentinck, the younger son of an important racing peer (Lord Stradbroke) and, like Bunbury, a native of Suffolk, Rous slowly began to sort out the Club's finances and build on the reputation which it had rather undeservedly acquired after the successful prosecution of the Running Rein case. Although he had been active ever since he retired from the Navy in 1837, he did not really emerge as a dominant figure until after Bentinck's death. However, Rous had been a steward from 1838 to 1840, and over the years had acquired an unrivalled knowledge of the technicalities of racing, in terms of its rules and the rather arcane science of handicapping. Added to the bluff exterior and forceful personality that befitted a retired sea captain, his administrative skills really helped Newmarket to begin to change for the better and regain lost ground by the close of this period. Yet the Admiral was also by nature deeply reactionary, and as a result sometimes acted as a brake on long overdue change at Newmarket, as evidenced by his resistance to combining finishes at the same winning post because he feared it might encourage too many pedestrian spectators.

In many ways the sport on the Heath must still have left the impression of a semi-private gathering laid on by the Club primarily for its members' entertainment. If the races themselves were better organised, there was still very little effort to attract the public by anything as dramatic as building a grandstand for their accommodation. All that existed were little structures to which they were not admitted, most of which had been built in the eighteenth century. To race at Newmarket you still needed a horse or the right to bring your carriage onto the Heath. As several finishes as much as a mile or more apart might be used on the same afternoon, you needed to be either mounted or very dedicated to enjoy yourself. Nevertheless, the Admiral's efforts did provide a sounder basis for change which could be developed with surprising speed once things really began to move on the Heath in the 1870s.

◆◆◆◆

One of the biggest changes which affected racing everywhere was the introduction of the horsebox by Bentinck in 1836 to take his St Leger candidate Elis (Fig. 64) from Goodwood to Doncaster in three days, rather than the normal fifteen it would have taken on foot. Soon to be followed by the expanding network of railways in the 1840s and 1850s, the possibility of moving horses around the country and enabling far larger crowds to attend had a dramatic impact on the quality of the sport. The feat of Mr Christopher Wilson's Champion in winning both the Derby and St Leger of 1800 had not been repeated until Surplice, ironically bred by Bentinck but sold as a yearling, won both races in 1848. Yet that was achieved seventeen more times by the end of the century – as a good a guide as you can get of the enormous effect on racing of the new ease of movement.

A comparable change stems from the huge expansion of sources that contribute to our knowledge of the people involved in the sport. The *Sporting Magazine's* existence began in 1792 and ended in 1870; together with the main sources of information on northern racing, William Pick and John Orton (the latter high-handedly removed from office at York by Bentinck), we know far more of the backgrounds and personalities of the main players. At Newmarket, the best source is the unique combination of the brush of Ben Marshall in depicting the more important locals until the mid-1830s, allied to the illuminating articles he wrote as 'Observator' for The *Sporting Magazine*. From this point on there is far more information available about the main figures than could be included in a small library, much less a single book.

After the death of George Stubbs in 1806, the leading equine artist was indeed, Ben Marshall, who lived near the town from 1812 to 1825. Even after he moved to London he kept his house in the area, and was a close friend of the main trainers and jockeys such as the Chifneys and Robinson. James Ward, who painted only one Newmarket picture (Fig. 68) based on a Stubbs drawing, was his best early rival, but drifted off into a wide variety of other subjects well before Marshall left the town. In his later years Marshall's chief rival was J.F. Herring senior, and he too abandoned Newmarket for London in the early 1830s when things began to decline fast and presumably commissions tended to dry up. It is a clear sign of the times that all Stubbs's pictures set on a racecourse, and most of Marshall's, depict the Heath, but the large majority of Herring's show winners represented at Epsom, Doncaster and elsewhere. Most racing Ferneleys show the same trend away from Newmarket, and the picture of Bentinck on the Heath in 1848 (Fig. 183) is an exception. The Cooper family did a great deal of work for the Dukes of Grafton, but otherwise most of the racing scenes are of other places, and from about 1850 probably a majority of decent Newmarket scenes are the work of Harry Hall, even if he was no Herring, much less a Stubbs. He lived in the town, and when Herring deserted the turf in favour of farmyard scenes he could view in his own backyard in Meopham in Kent, Hall had the field almost to himself well into the period covered by the next chapter.

Fig. 63

Captain the Hon. Henry Rous by Sir George Hayter (*c.*1830)

Promoted by seniority to Admiral in 1852, having retired from active service in 1837, his only rival as a servant of the Jockey Club was Sir Charles Bunbury. A Steward from 1859 to his death in 1877, Rous was instrumental in both sorting out the Club's finances and in handicapping most of the important races for even longer. His codification of the previously vague weight-for-age arrangements and his 'Laws and Practice of Horse Racing' of 1850 had untold influence on the way the sport developed.

Fig. 64

Elis and The Drummer at Lichfield by Abraham Cooper (1836)

The St Leger winner is shown en route to Doncaster with his travelling companion leaving their box at Lichfield. Elis is ridden by his trainer, John Day, and the man with the pony is his head man John Doe. The colours are those of Lord Lichfield, which were often carried by Lord George Bentinck's runners before he registered his own pale blue ones in 1838.

If little changed at Newmarket until the 1860s, across the country the effect of the dramatic expansion in the number of fixtures and the size of the crowds attending were instrumental in creating the betting industry. This happened despite assorted efforts by Whitehall to stem the tide. Bookmakers on and off the course had arrived and, for better or worse, racing has had to accommodate itself to their presence on a major scale ever since.

PICTURE PUZZLE 6:
MISUNDERSTANDINGS ARISING FROM THE ALTERATIONS TO THE BEACON COURSE IN THE 1780s

In or just before 1786, a new stand was constructed at the Beacon finish directly across the course from the ancient King's Stand. It was painted by J.N. Sartorius as the background for a 1790 match (Fig. 65), but had been built at least three years earlier as it appears in the maps of John Bodger and of John Chapman of 1787. Several things changed as a result of the construction of the new stand. This is confirmed by Bodger's publicity for his effort, which specifies that it is an accurate account of all the changes to the courses and fixtures 'since the several alterations'. These alterations seem to be based on a Club meeting of December 1785 about changes to fixtures, and the fact that two people saw fit to compete by producing the first new maps for twenty years points firmly to a 1786 date for the Portland Stand. The changes include:

1. The old bank, painted by Stubbs in 1765 (Fig. 157), running up to the north winning post, was removed.

2. The course was broadened by moving the post quite near to the new building (Fig. 65) instead of leaving it stranded out on the Heath (Fig. 157). It was embedded in the usual mound, designed to stop horses colliding with such obstacles.

The roadway from Reach was relocated behind the Portland Stand, as is evident from Chapman's map of the town done in the same year. Chapman's Heath map may well record things before the stand is actually in use and the old position of post and track have yet to be altered, and would make no sense once it was in operation; the Bodger map of 1787 shows the road behind the stand.

All this naturally raises the question of why Stubbs should show the bank still in position a decade later when he painted the unsaddled Hambletonian after his 3,000 Guineas match with Diamond on 25 March 1799 (Fig. 67). This is the life-sized picture that led to a bitter dispute between the artist and his patron, Sir Harry Vane-Tempest, over the 300 Guineas fee, which was eventually resolved in court in 1801 with victory for Stubbs. Sadly no record of the pleadings survives, and it has always puzzled people why Vane-Tempest should have sought to reject by far the finest work of Stubbs's old age. Maybe he was irritated by the monumental image including features that had disappeared years before and which excluded the new stand. As this stood only about 150 yards away from the old one, it should have appeared unless completely obscured by one of Hambletonian's attendants. If so, that in itself might have been a source of friction, and as the gap from the stables to the old stand was only slightly smaller than that between the two stands it must have lain well within the scope of the canvas.

Given that Stubbs was the most meticulous artist imaginable over such details, surely the only conclusion is that he mistakenly thought he could still rely on the old sketch and simply did not know that things had changed. Assuming the commission followed the triumphant match, Stubbs probably constructed his sublime images of the exhausted horse and his attendants either by going to Yorkshire, where Hambletonian was trained and won his other races or, as a result of the mountain visiting Mohammed, in his studio in Somerset Street near Covent Garden. *The Manchester Mercury* of 2 April 1799 recorded that Vane-Tempest intended to indulge his notorious vanity by riding the champion as a hack, and for this purpose 'is coming up to town'. If Hambletonian ever did put in an appearance in Rotten Row, a visit to Covent Garden seems the most likely answer. The horse did not run again until winning at Doncaster in September, so an interlude as a hack is perfectly possible.

Whatever may have caused the dispute, behind it presumably lay Stubbs's failure to complete the commission with a companion piece showing the two horses in the finish. A drawing thought to be a study for it was exhibited at the Royal Academy in 1800, and it has always been supposed that James Ward's painting of 1819 (Fig. 68), which now hangs with the Stubbs at Mount Stewart in Northern Ireland, is based on it. While the drawing has disappeared it is known that Ward bought several lots at Stubbs's studio sale in 1807, and that his purchases included Fig. 157 from 1765, so he was always liable to fall into the same trap as the master over the layout of the course in 1799. Indeed, he made things a good deal worse by relegating the bank to the far distance up against the old Duke's Stand and showing the contestants running almost literally parallel to the finishing line. Although Ward painted a good many racehorses, none of the pictures offers any evidence that he ever visited the Heath, by this time in decline following the Escape affair, and this fine painting provides every reason to think he had never seen it. Indeed, the image of the two horses is so good one cannot help feeling Ward's painting was directly inspired by Stubbs's drawing.

In summary, one begins to have some twinges of sympathy for Sir Harry Vane-Tempest, even if his fit of pique deprived us of Stubbs's only picture of a race in progress apart from that of Bay Malton in lonely state (Fig. 52). Had he painted it, it would he really have followed the course chosen by Ward of basing his depiction of such an animated scene entirely on a drawing, which may well not have included either people or stand? Having only the drawing, the Stubbs of Hambletonian and the 1765 sketch (Fig. 157) poor Ward would have had no realistic chance of combining them to create a wholly successful version of the finish. As Ward's only other attempt at the portrayal of a finish on his own account is a disaster, this may well be a faithful copy of the central images of the race from the drawing.

What things actually looked like appears in the print after J.N. Sartorius of the two horses passing the King's Stand (Fig. 66) on an entirely realistic racing line. Anyway, however much Stubbs preferred a rural idyll to such intemperate excitement, it is hard to think he would have rejected reality entirely had he ever painted the finish of a race, certainly if done on a scale to match Fig. 67. Apart from anything else, the dramatic impact of the contrast between even a moderately realistic finish and Hambletonian in lonely state would have been very striking on this scale. That contrast would have been accurate on 25 March 1799, as all the later races that day finished elsewhere on the Heath, so the horse and his two attendants would have been left to their own devices by this stage in the proceedings, while the crowds migrated to see the next race, finishing in the dip on the Rowley Mile.

Fig. 65

Engraving of *Grey Diomed beating Traveller* with the Duke of Portland Stand in the background, after J.N. Sartorius (1790)

Picture Puzzle 6

Fig. 66

Engraving of *Hambletonian beating Diamond* as they finished at the King's Stand on the other side of the Beacon course, after J.N. Sartorius (1800)

The Heath and the Horse

Fig. 67

Hambletonian after his match with Diamond by George Stubbs (1800), showing the bank in the distance although it had been removed by 1786

Picture Puzzle 6

Fig. 68

Hambletonian beating Diamond by James Ward (1819), probably based on a Stubbs sketch preparatory to a companion piece to Fig. 67, with the bank now removed further west to a site it had never occupied

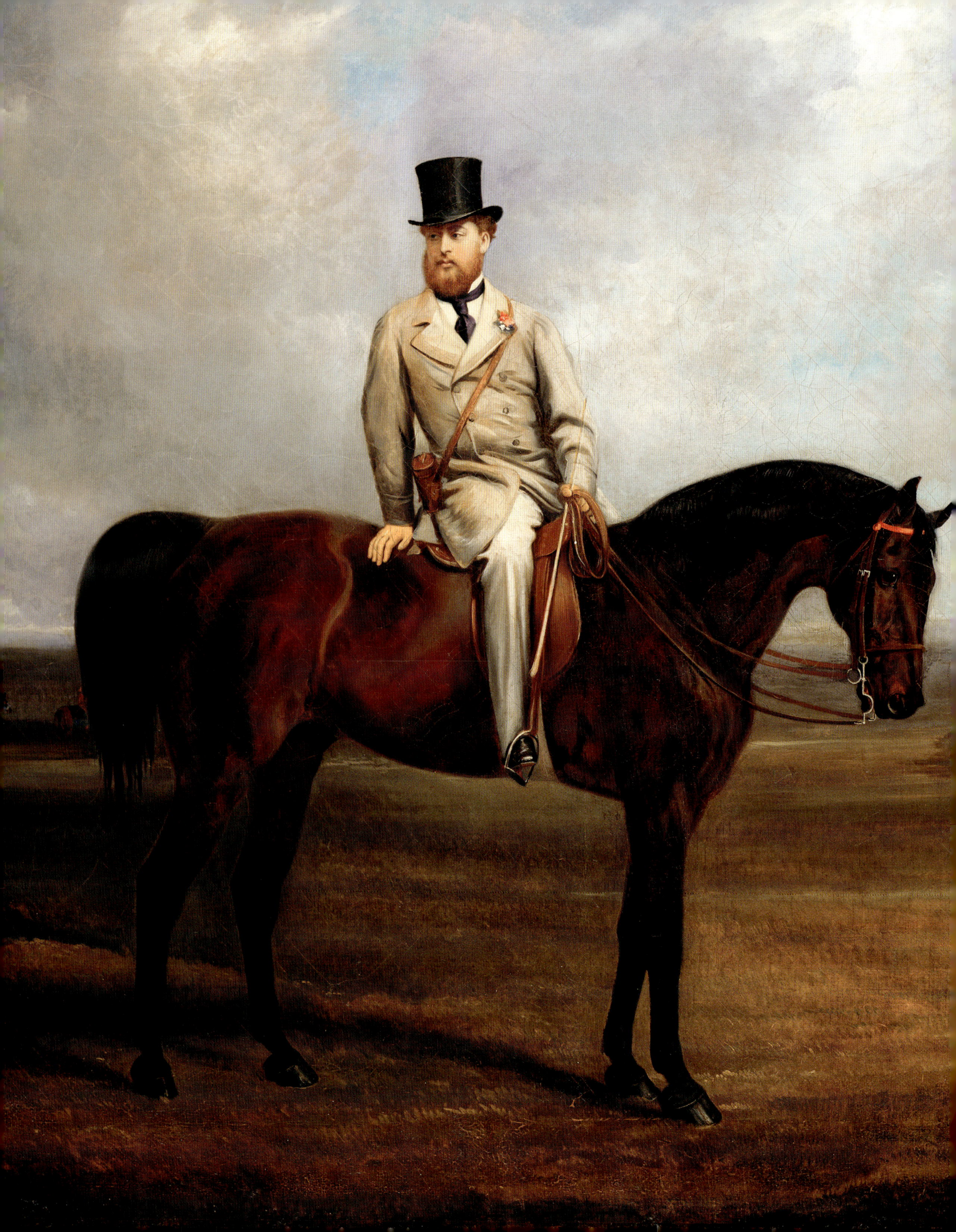

Chapter 7 (1863–1914)

A Period of Unbroken Progress as the Breed Improves and Racing Spreads around the World

It comes as something of a relief to turn from three decades of decline at Newmarket, lasting from the Chifneys' crash to Macaroni's Derby of 1863, to a Heath basking in its late Victorian and Edwardian glory. During the earlier dark age, the town's real claim to being central to racing was that it remained the Jockey Club's base. In that sense alone was it 'Headquarters', as in no other way could such a claim really be sustained. While the corner had actually been turned a few years before, it would have taken a pretty acute observer to have read the rather limited signs in the 1850s of an upward trend with over half a century to run.

The first indication that things on the Heath might improve began to show in the early 1850s with the increasing influence of Admiral Rous. After years of procrastination the town finally got its railway in 1851, when the Club agreed a route based on a tunnel under Warren Hill; one alternative would have placed the station out at Wickhambrook and others would have severely compromised the Heath itself. Being linked to the national network was obviously indispensable if the town was ever again to thrive as a training centre.

Edward, Prince of Wales, detail of Fig. 76

Rous's competence shows clearly in the way the Club's lamentable finances began to improve steadily in the 1850s. This meant that it could begin to buy small but crucial pieces of the Heath as they became available, essential if the gallops were to match those of the Wiltshire downs and Yorkshire. Admittedly these purchases led to most un-Victorian borrowings, which it took a fair time to repay, but in general it is clear from the Club's minutes that things were on the mend. As early in the process as 1858, Rous called a special meeting to consider a 'Proposal for the amelioration of Newmarket Race Course', more details of which appear in Part 2.

It falls outside the scope of this book to go far into the details of the Jockey Club's control (or sometimes lack of it) of the sport nationally, where the effects on the Heath are indirect. In general the Club made very ineffective use of its position until stimulated to produce a proper set of rules in 1858; these replaced the vague eighteenth-century efforts of John Pond, which had theoretically been extended everywhere by the 1830s. Action in 1858 seems to have arisen largely as a response to a highly critical letter received from a member the year before, complaining of the failure to warn off undesirable elements. As it came

Fig. 69

Mathew Dawson (c.1870)

The picture was probably taken soon after he came to Heath House in Newmarket from Berkshire as a well-established trainer. His arrival in 1866 was as good a sign as any that fashion was turning back towards the town after a bleak thirty years. Eventually little behind Robson with twenty-eight classics to his name, he appears as a much older man with the last of them in 1895, in Fig. 79. By then he had left Heath House to train on a smaller scale at Exning, where he died in 1898. His best horse was the great St Simon (Figs. 72 and 73). The latter picture was sold for £75 on his death but, most appropriately, has now found its way back to the walls of Heath House.

from the 14th Earl of Derby, during a gap between two periods when he was Prime Minister, that he got a proper response is not surprising.

Another event of considerable long-term consequence was the arrival in the town of the Rothschilds, in the portly form of Baron Meyer de Rothschild in 1856. Some three years after James Godding of Palace House had at last broken the town's Derby hoodoo, in 1863, the Baron bought the place and soon set up his own very competent trainer, Joseph Hayhoe, across Palace Street. The Rothschilds and to a lesser degree the Hayhoe family had considerable influence on the town's fortunes, and as early as 1871 their season was so successful it became known as 'the Baron's Year'.

Equally important turned out to be the win of a Malton-trained filly in the Oaks only two days after Macaroni's Derby. In this case the win marked the finish of the seemingly endless triumphs of the yard of John Scott, who won no more Classics before his death in 1871. Queen Bertha's Oaks was the second of no less than nineteen Classics won by the 6th Lord Falmouth (Fig. 70) and, more to the point in this context, all but one of the other seventeen came after Falmouth had moved his string to the rising Newmarket star, Mathew Dawson.

◆◆◆◆

The arrival of Dawson in 1866 (Fig. 69) really did mark the turning of the tide, as it came after a successful twenty years in the north and on the downs, and his willingness to move to Newmarket is a firm indication of the way the town's stock was rising. His previous downland base was about to suffer a separate eclipse when the powerful Danebury yard of old John Day of Crucifix fame began to collapse. This disaster was attributable in considerable degree to the Day family's handling of the hot favourite for the 1868 Derby, Lady Elizabeth, followed by the way Admiral Rous hounded the Days over the whole sorry business. In terms of the impact on the relative position of Newmarket it was almost the Escape Scandal of 1791 in reverse.

◆◆◆◆

The appearance of the remarkable Captain James Machell (Fig. 71) in 1863 also had long-term significance. Machell set up a major yard at Bedford Lodge to which his talents attracted a succession of rich (at least initially) owners to fund things until the end of the century. His background was too grand in those days for him to train in his own name but in effect he combined that role with managing his owners' strings, and profited greatly from backing them too.

Perhaps the event which had most influence on Newmarket's revival was the return to England of Tom Jennings to train an initially small string for the leading French owner Count Frédéric de Lagrange. Even before Bulle Rock was sent to America in 1730, horses of the improved breed being created here had been sold to France and stock regularly passed to and fro from Ireland. However, apart from Ireland, nothing was coming back to balance the steadily increasing export trade to all parts of the world, but good class horse populations were beginning to develop elsewhere, especially in France. To considerable, if unwarranted, surprise the Count sent over Monarque to win the 1857 Goodwood Cup and in 1861 opened up at Phantom House on the Fordham Road where he installed Tom Jennings, brother of Henry, his French-based trainer. The success of their home-bred stock was immediate and Fille de l'Air's Oaks of 1864 was soon followed by Monarque's son Gladiateur taking the Triple Crown itself in 1866. Apart from the period of the Franco-Prussian War and its aftermath the Count's success, often in partnership with an expatriate London banker, Monsieur Charles Lefevre, continued until shortly before his death in 1883. Thus the scene was effectively set for Newmarket's renaissance.

Even before the American invasion of the early twentieth century several major owners set up here, such as James

Fig. 70

Evelyn, 6th Viscount Falmouth (1819–1889)

For nearly twenty years before his sudden departure from racing in 1884 Lord Falmouth was the most important owner of the day. After winning an Oaks in 1863 with John Scott he switched to Mathew Dawson just before Scott's death, and began a long series of triumphs with Kingcraft's Derby in 1870. All the subsequent victories were with horses trained at Heath House and most were home-bred at Mereworth in Kent and ridden by Fred Archer (Fig. 74 and 75). After dark and probably unfair rumours involving Archer's riding when only third in the 1883 Derby, both stud and stable were sold off during 1884. The fifty-five animals from Mereworth realised over 75,000 Guineas and 24 in training 35,000 Guineas. We do not know whether Falmouth believed the rumours or was so disgusted by the whole thing he lost interest. Apart from the fact that the sale included both the Derby and Oaks winners only weeks before Epsom, the purchasers made bad bargains, and in general Falmouth seems too have timed his departure pretty well.

Fig. 71

Undated drawing of *James Machell* by Finch Mason (*c*.1880)

Captain James Machell's racing career began when he was soldiering in Ireland in the early 1860s. After early success on the Turf he resigned his commission and began training his own horses at Kennett outside Newmarket. A coup in 1864 provided the funds to set up on the Bury Road at Bedford Cottage, with George Bloss holding the licence. As quickly as 1867 the stable won its first Derby with Hermit, and later added two more including with Isinglass (Fig. 77), by which time James Jewitt was the nominal trainer. Machell also owned three Grand National winners, but they were trained elsewhere. Never an amiable figure and dangerous to cross, Mason seems to have caught these qualities better than a likeness of his mount.

Keene and his son Foxhall, also the name of his best horse, and Richard Ten Broek. Such people usually seem to have gravitated to Newmarket as opposed to other training centres almost automatically, and thoroughly deserved the much warmer welcome they received than that given to some of those who followed twenty years later. Occasional imports of horses such as the great Carbine and people like Alfred Cox and Sir Daniel Cooper from Australia did the turf nothing but good, and this internationalisation of racing represented a wonderful dividend following more than a century of one-way export trade. When you consider the degree to which the prosperity of the town and its Heath are grounded in foreign money today, the arrival of Tom Jennings senior at Phantom House in 1861 has cast a very long shadow indeed,. From these rather promising circumstances it is hardly surprising that Newmarket rapidly recovered its place in the racing firmament. In the north, however, precisely the reverse happened, and from Pretender's Derby of 1869 to this day only one horse trained north of the Trent, Dante in 1945, has won the Derby. Considering that no less than ten did so during the three decades of easier travel up to Pretender's year, this change of fortune needs more explanation than the favourable turn of events at Newmarket.

The damaging effect of the long depression in farming from the early 1870s was more than balanced nationally by the vastly increased prosperity of the other sections of society. However, in the north these were usually based in towns and cities with a strongly nonconformist background and little taste for the pleasures of the turf. Thus the new prosperity brought little benefit to the sport in the north, and certainly by no means enough to replace the now impoverished landowners who had been its bedrock, especially in Yorkshire, from the earliest days.

The exception to these general rules proved to be the great estates of the grander aristocracy where mines and towns would often more than replace farm rents as a source of income. All this played well for the Heath, as such grandees might well be members of the Jockey Club, and anyway by now they largely thought in national rather than local terms. Thus they could accept the idea of having their horses in Suffolk or Berkshire while they continued to live on their piece of Yorkshire where they bred their stock. It is instructive that, in the thirty years up to Pretender's win,

Fig. 72

St Simon by A.L. Townshend (1884/5)

By far the best horse trained by Mathew Dawson, St Simon won all his nine races, including the Ascot Gold Cup by 20 lengths at three years old. This picture was painted for Robert Vyner, owner of perhaps Dawson's next best, Minting. Unable to compete in most of the best races due to his entries being cancelled on the death of his breeder, Prince Batthyany, his later career as a stallion was the most successful since Stockwell's and saw him champion nine times.

only four Derbys went to peers or their foreign equivalents but for the same period after the figure was 15.

Without the same nonconformist traditions to contend with and with the City of London being a major advantage, southern trainers prospered as those in the north declined. Towards the end of the century another factor that had a similar effect was the huge influx of wealth from the Empire, in particular from the mines on the Rand, a fair proportion of which found its way into the pockets of southern trainers via the Joels, Wernhers and others who became long-term supporters of racing. When you add the fact that the cost of producing and training horses must always reflect the level of agricultural wages, the value of land and the price of its produce, it is not surprising things played into the hands of Newmarket and the south in general. With all such costs and values restrained by the long agricultural depression and incomes from other sources vastly increased, the future for the fashionable southern trainers was set fair. Apart from the main Newmarket stables these were the Darlings of Beckhampton, the Taylors of Manton and John Porter at nearby Kingsclere, and it was their yards that were to provide most of the Heath's opposition until the Second World War.

These trends were helped by the fact that racing was slowly becoming organised on a national basis, with Newmarket's standards being more properly enforced. However, it seems the major advance represented by another new set of rules in 1877 was at least partly stimulated, as in 1858, by the threat of action from Parliament. In this case it was not an aggrieved friend like Lord Derby but a hard line opponent of gambling in the form of a Glasgow MP, George Anderson. The new rules required a minimum of £300 in prize money to be added to every day's racing, with not less than £100 in total going to each winner. Just as in 1740 the effect was to shut down most of the riotous gatherings that passed for race meetings, as they could not afford to fund such prizes, but this still failed to satisfy Mr Anderson, as he managed to get an Act through in 1879 which ensured there would be no backsliding. The licensing of jockeys, trainers and eventually even racecourses, followed by the end of the century. Obviously this affected Newmarket too, but to a much lesser degree than elsewhere as what was happening was the formal extension nationally of what had already applied more or less effectively on the Heath for well over a century.

The major increase in the money being put into the sport had the same effect as it had from the 1750s, and indeed, would again from about 1980 – namely, the horse population improved to a marked degree. In the 1880s, two of the greatest champions the breed had yet seen in St Simon (1881) (Figs. 72 and 73) and Ormonde (1883) (Fig. 74) graced the

Fig. 73

Heath House string at exercise by A.L. Townshend (1884/5)

This picture confirms that not all late Victorian racing pictures were dull even if most are pretty mediocre. St Simon with Charlie Fordham is watched by Fred Archer on his hack, and Mathew Dawson with Heath House in the background. The painting still hangs in the house, for which it was commissioned. Although the building itself has been reconstructed several times it is on the site of Tregonwell Frampton's seventeenth-century yard. Nobody seems too concerned about the protection of their heads in the event of an accident.

Fig. 74

Ormonde at Epsom with Fred Archer and John Porter by Emil Adam (1886)

Unbeaten in sixteen races including the 1886 Triple Crown, Fred Archer rode Ormonde until his suicide that autumn bar two occasions, when Mat Dawson's superior claim saw George Barrett on the champion. Both times Archer was second for Dawson on Minting in the 2,000 Guineas and Melton in the Hardwicke. Ormonde became a roarer at four, and as a result was sold abroad by the Duke of Westminster for fear of the effect on his progeny, but he got one very good horse before he went in the Duke's Orme.

turf, and the latter's claims were conclusively proved by his victims in the Guineas and Derby: Minting and The Bard – themselves having real claims to the status of champions. People were uncertain at the time which was the better of these two great horses, and that still seems the sensible view to take. If St Simon had never had such rivals to defeat, his victories were even easier and at stud he ruled as champion on nine occasions, whereas Ormonde, relative to his ability, was a failure who only got one really top-class horse, Orme.

Both these unbeaten champions were fortunate to be trained respectively by masters in Mathew Dawson at Heath House and John Porter in Berkshire. In addition they shared in Fred Archer (Fig. 75) the best jockey of the day in most of their races, although St Simon was sometimes ridden by Charlie Wood and Ormonde by Tom Cannon and George Barrett (Fig. 87) – all good jockeys in an age which produced more than usual. If Archer was certainly the best in the latter stages of his great career before it ended in the tragedy of his suicide in 1886, in his early days he had in George Fordham (Fig. 61) a rival who some argued was at least his equal. Fordham had succeeded Nat Flatman (Fig. 60) as the perennial champion jockey, and reigned from 1855 to 1871 with only three gaps, and then rode on well into the days of Archer's supremacy, which lasted from 1874 to 1886.

Fig. 75

A pastel of *Fred Archer* by OWS (1888)

Son of a trainer and brother of another, Fred Archer's only serious rival for fame as a sportsman in the late nineteenth century was probably W.G. Grace. Born in 1857, he was apprenticed to Mat Dawson (Fig. 69) aged only eleven, soon after the great trainer had switched to Newmarket. Starting out as a jockey weighing out at under five stone, by the end of his career he could not get below 8 stone 7lbs and, standing nearly 5ft 9ins, to do that equated to starvation. After his wife Helen, Dawson's niece, died in childbirth in 1884, depressed and ill he shot himself in 1886. Between 1874 and that year he had ridden an astonishing 21 winners from the 65 classics run, and in all chalked up 2,748 winners from 8,004 rides, an unparalleled 34.3 per cent.

Fig. 76

Edward, Prince of Wales (later King Edward VII) (1841–1910)

Beginning in 1877, the first decade of his career mainly involved Jumping and he retained his affection for racing over fences. Indeed, he is still the only man to win both the Triple Crown on the Flat with Diamond Jubilee (Fig. 82) and the Grand National with Ambush, both in 1900. He was also leading owner for the only time that year, but went close when winning both the Derby and a second classic with Persimmon (Fig. 80) in 1896 and Minoru in 1909. The latter was leased, but his other two Epsom winners were both bred from the great mare Perdita II and all three were trained for him at Newmarket by Richard Marsh.

After Archer died things became much less certain and only Tom Cannon's son Mornington and Frank Wootton managed sequences of any length before 1914. Apart from the Cannons the others back to Flatman were based in Newmarket, but things began to change on the Heath with the retirement of Dawson, soon followed by the death of Machell. Slowly the balance of power in the racing world began to swing back towards Manton, Beckhampton and Kingsclere, despite the retirement in 1905 of John Porter ,who decided to devote his time thereafter to developing

Fig. 77

Isinglass (Triple Crown 1893) ridden by Tommy Loates with trainer James Jewitt

Fig. 78

Ladas (Derby and 2000 Guineas 1894) ridden by Jack Watts

Fig. 79

Sir Visto (Derby and St Leger 1895) ridden by Sam Loates, with trainer Mathew Dawson

Fig. 80

Persimmon (Derby and St Leger 1896) ridden by Jack Watts, with trainer Richard Marsh

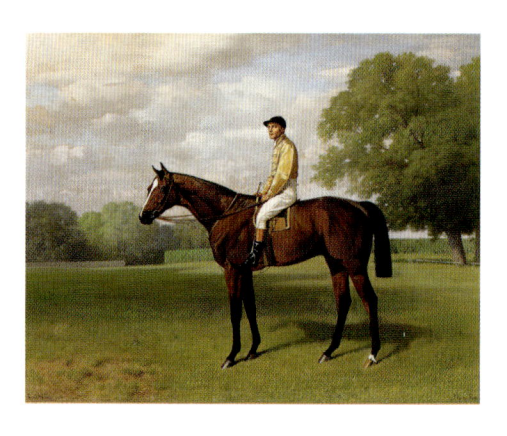

Fig. 81

Flying Fox (Triple Crown 1899) ridden by Mornington Cannon

Fig. 82

Diamond Jubilee (Triple Crown 1900) ridden by Herbert Jones

Fig. 83

Rock Sand (Triple Crown 1903)
ridden by Danny Maher

Fig. 84

St Amant (Derby and 2000 Guineas
1904) ridden by Kempton Cannon

Fig. 85

Cicero (Derby and 2000 Guineas 1905)
with Danny Maher and stable lad

Fig. 86

Spearmint (Derby 1906)
ridden by Danny Maher

Pictures by Emil Adam illustrating the introduction of the American
seat around 1900, from the Jockey Club Dining Room

Tod Sloan's arrival in the autumn of 1897 was too late to affect much in that year. However, his remarkable success during 1898 had demonstrated for all to see that horses improved by several pounds ridden in the American style. The champion jockey from 1894 to 1897, Mornington Cannon was not prepared to go far enough in adapting his style, and simply retired early in the next century. The young Herbert Jones on Diamond Jubilee in 1900 only got the ride because the horse was unmanageable by other people, but it seems he was not yet ready to adopt the new seat on this unruly animal. Thereafter, Cannon's brother Kempton faced reality in 1904 – Danny Maher was an American who did not have to change anything in order to conform with what was now universal practice on the Flat. The pictures are all by Emil Adam, and it became a tradition for Club members winning the Derby to present such paintings, greatly to the benefit of the dining room in Newmarket, where all now hang.

Fig. 87

La Flèche at the Cambridgeshire start by Emil Adam (1892)

Ridden here by George Barrett, Archer's successor as John Porter's jockey, this daughter of St Simon won twelve of her first thirteen races, including the Cambridgeshire as hot favourite. Her only defeat in the Derby was when Barrett came far too late and just failed to catch an inferior rival. Later she beat Orme in the St Leger. The building in the background is the last survivor of the Heath's many Rubbing Houses and its only significant use in recent times was by Sir Alfred Munnings.

Newbury racecourse. It seems safe to say that Porter's feat of training three winners of the Triple Crown will never be equalled; apart from Alec Taylor junior, with two, nobody else has managed more than one, and Taylor's brace were wartime races all run at Newmarket.

Newmarket did score one important point in competition with Porter when the Prince of Wales (Fig. 76) decided to move his relatively small string of eight horses from Kingsclere to the care of Richard Marsh (Fig. 80) at Egerton House before the 1893 season. Included among them was the top class Florizel II, soon to be followed by the Derby winners Persimmon (Fig. 80) and Diamond Jubilee (Fig. 82), all three out of Perdita II. Full details of the ructions that led to the Prince moving his string never properly emerged, but seem to have related to ill feeling between Lord Marcus Beresford and the Duke of Westminster or his entourage. The former managed for both the future king and Baron Maurice de Hirsch, who owned the brilliant filly La Flèche (Fig. 87). The 1892 season at Kingsclere had revolved around her and the Duke's Orme, with their meeting in the St Leger being the source of much trouble in the yard. Although Orme was odds on La Flèche won, and the rest is history, even if its details go unrecorded. Thus Marsh got La Flèche too, but so far as the Prince was concerned, the fact Newmarket was so much closer to Sandringham was a happy by-product of a row in which he had no direct part. With another Derby winner in Minoru in 1909, Newmarket had more reason to celebrate the involvement of a second heir to the throne than it had over that of the future George IV.

◆◆◆◆

Steeplechasing, in the literal sense, across natural country, goes back to the eighteenth century, but was only tamed to the degree of being staged on racecourses on any scale from the 1830s. Captain Machell rode some winners for himself when soldiering in Ireland and later, in the space of four years, three of his horses won Grand Nationals in the 1870s, but they were trained for him in Lincolnshire rather than at Bedford Lodge. The future royal trainer, Richard Marsh, learnt to ride on the Flat and went on to become a good jockey and trainer over fences. Training under both codes for the Duke of Hamilton, he operated from what is now Lordship Stud before eventually graduating to Egerton House, where jumpers would not have been thought appropriate. In general, the relationship between Newmarket and Jumping can be described as being a little distant.

In fact, until near the end of the nineteenth century, the relationship was very distant indeed,. The National Hunt Committee had been formed in 1866 on the lines of the Club to provide Jumping with a regulatory function. While it always included some Jockey Club members, the Committee only arrived on the scene at all because the Club had refused to take Jumping under its wing, and in 1884 overtures for amalgamation were politely but firmly rejected. Eventually this union did happen but not until 1968, and in 1890 Joe Cannon was even arraigned by the Jockey Club's Agent Mr Gardner for desecrating the Heath by exercising his hurdlers there. In the end it was decided that what was considered a 'bona fide' Flat racer would be redefined to include dual-purpose horses, and all was well for Joe Cannon.

Things seem to have changed for the better at around the time Mr Cecil Marriott was appointed Agent in 1895, which was just as well since he remained in distinctly autocratic control of the Heath until 1945. In 1893 a National Hunt course was laid out on the edge of Colonel Harry McCalmont's huge Cheveley Park estate. While it proved rather successful and staged the National Hunt meeting itself in 1897 in the days before it settled at Cheltenham, when the Colonel went off to the Boer War, it lapsed between 1899 and 1903, and finally ceased operations in 1905. However, its grandstand (Fig. 88), long ago converted into some cottages and the hostel for visiting stable staff, can still be seen on the Links.

While always keeping a foothold on the Heath, Jumping has never approached centre stage, and nowadays, with All Weather racing in every month, it has really been pushed further towards the wings in Newmarket. Therefore it seems ironic that the Jockey Club owns a far bigger slice of the principal National Hunt courses like Cheltenham, Aintree, Sandown and Haydock than it does exclusively Flat courses. Accordingly, its ownership of the public gallops at Lambourn, acquired in 2006 and considerably improved since, is particularly appropriate.

Fig. 88

Jumping at Newmarket in November 1895

The stand on the Links has been converted into housing as the meeting only lasted until 1905. However, an inspection today shows it is quite clearly still the same basic structure, and the present racecourse office at Westfield House nestles among the trees in the distance.

♦♦♦♦

The art of jockeyship changed suddenly and more radically than ever before or since with the arrival of Tod Sloan in the Autumn of 1897 (Fig. 89), bringing with him evidence that horses run faster ridden in the American style with much shorter stirrup leathers which has the effect of balancing the jockey's weight over the horse's withers. In three seasons the old ideas were swept away and jockeys either adapted or retired leaving the way clear for younger men or, in the case of the Reiff brothers, Danny Maher and others, American jockeys.

Fig. 89

Tommy v Toddy at Newmarket after G.D. Giles (1898)

This is really a caricature of the riding styles of Tommy Loates, champion jockey in 1893, and the American Tod Sloan, rather than a picture of a race. The sympathies of the artist in the year during which things were still debateable seem clear enough, but results soon showed that by far the more effective method was Sloan's.

The eleven paintings of Derby winners by Emil Adam in the dining room at the Jockey Club Rooms in Newmarket perfectly demonstrate this change. On page 112 appear the six of the seven who won up to 1900, all ridden by jockeys using the old English seat; the missing winner is the picture of Ormonde with Fred Archer up (Fig. 74). Opposite, on page 113, are four later winners from the period between 1903 and 1906. They show three horses ridden in the new style (more or less successfully in the case of St Amant) and Danny Maher surveying Cicero before mounting; as he is the man on both Rock Sand and Spearmint we do not need Adam's brush to tell us how he will look once aboard Lord Rosebery's winner of 1905.

The American invasion of Britain not only consisted of jockeys but also some important owners (several of whom

Fig. 90

Euphrates with trainer and jockey by William Webb (1825)

There are numerous paintings and prints showing how often alcohol was used to stimulate horses in the early days but these dry up with the more reticent Victorians. Presumably that was a matter of what was thought seemly to depict rather than what actually happened before the ban of 1904. Here the trainer W. Dilly is clearly about to encourage John Mytton's horse with a good swig, and he did not even have the excuse of heat racing as Dilly always avoided them with Euphrates.

Fig. 91

Edward, 17th Earl of Derby (1865–1948)

An immensely popular figure, the 17th Earl's public services as minister, ambassador and uncrowned King of Lancashire (quite apart from his successes on the turf) explained that popularity. In the affairs of the Club and Newmarket in general he seems to have been rather reactionary, but nobody appears to have been particularly bothered. His triumphs as both owner and breeder have never been exceeded in terms of classic winners and only equalled numerically by the 4th Duke of Grafton in less competitive days. The influence of the many stallions bred at Knowsley and his Newmarket studs spread worldwide following training at Stanley House; no other establishment in this country has achieved more in that direction.

Hon. George Lambton (1860–1945)

After considerable success as an amateur rider Lambton took out a licence to train in 1892, and soon afterwards was appointed by Lord Derby. From then until 1908 that meant acting for the 16th Earl as he rebuilt the family stud at Knowsley, after a long gap since the days of the 14th Earl, thrice Prime Minister, in 1869. It was indeed, a family operation, as the 17th Earl really instigated the revival for his father and their string was trained or managed by Lambton until the connection ceased rather abruptly in 1933. From 1926 to 1930 his role had been as manager, while Frank Butters (Fig. 98) held the licence. Champion trainer three times and the leader on the Heath on a further twelve occasions, Lambton continued on a smaller scale until he died in 1945. He was succeeded at Kremlin House by his son Teddy, but the days of such horses as the Stanley House champions like Swynford, Phalaris, Pharos and Hyperion were not to be repeated.

stayed for the longer term), a few trainers (who went home quite rapidly in most cases) and, unfortunately, the habit of doping horses to make them run faster. All this came about primarily because state after state in the US decided to limit gambling by banning racing, much in the same spirit that alcohol was tackled in the 1920s. The doping of horses to improve their performances had been a very widespread practice in America long before the invasion and, naturally, the American trainers who migrated here continued to use dope, mainly cocaine, as it was not against the rules. Stopping other people's horses over here by all sorts of improper methods is, sadly, almost as old as racing itself, and naturally illegal, but up to then the technique for getting your own to go quicker was limited to administering a generous swig of whisky. Sporting prints sometimes include the evidence in the form of the relevant bottles (Figs. 90 and 128).

Over the first years of the new century, doping became so widespread and its effects sometimes so obvious that campaigners called for action. George Lambton (Fig. 91), probably the most talented of the younger Newmarket trainers, decided to do something about it in 1903, according to his fascinating but not entirely reliable autobiography. As his brother was the 4th Earl of Durham (Fig. 92) and one of the most influential members of the Jockey Club, he was well placed to do so. He states that he tested the effects of dope on six horses between Folkestone's win on 23 September 1903 at Pontefract and Cheers's victory on 18 November at Derby. All but one was successful, the single loser came second and in each case what was afoot was made known in advance. In fact the Club had approved a new rule banning the practice on 30 September but it was not to apply until 1904. Therefore this famous experiment was only to confirm the dramatic effect of such treatment and provide a justification for the new rule. Sadly, when America eventually removed its racing ban, nothing on the lines of the prohibition of the use of artificial stimulants was introduced and relatively little has changed over a century later, leaving the States extremely isolated and

Fig. 92

John, 3rd Earl of Durham (1855–1928)

Although he bred and raced horses for fifty years, resulting in 1927 in his greatest success with Beam's Oaks, it was not as an owner that Lord Durham made his major contribution. A Steward for five periods of three years each, his influence on events either side of 1900 was exceptional. It began in December 1887, when his speech at the Gimcrack Dinner needled a former Senior Steward, Sir George Chetwynd, into suing for libel based on accusations of cheating. Sir George nominally won but received a farthing in place of the claimed £20,000, and his activities were stopped in their tracks. His jockey, Charlie Wood, was warned off, and in conjunction with Cecil Marriott (Fig. 103) Durham effectively reorganised the Heath, and even made the first attempt at a Tote monopoly in 1902. However, he failed to persuade opponents of betting to help in his endeavours, although claiming that they would represent at least a relatively benign result.

paying a considerable price in terms of the widespread distrust of the form underpinning its horses' pedigrees. A less essential move to protect the integrity of the breed came in 1913 when the Club passed the highly controversial 'Jersey Act' designed to exclude horses from the General Stud Book where there were gaps in their descent from the foundation stock. The Act was made effective back to 1909 as the GSB is only published every fourth year. It was (and still is) regarded in America as a sort of trade protection and it is certainly true that it was principally its stock over which doubts arose. Eventually so many good races were being won by horses excluded from the GSB (usually due to the presence in their pedigrees of the great stallion Lexington) that the Act was repealed in 1949. The terms of entry into the stud books around the world were then brought into line with each other.

Even if today things in America seem to be moving slowly in the right direction, where real doubt is beginning to be evident over the wisdom of artificially improving performance by suppressing pain or replacing absent courage, these are still threats about which it is dangerous to be complacent. I remember being quietly canvassed by a prominent administrator, back in the days after the Jockey Club had ceded governance but regulated the sport, over the advantages in commercial terms of the American approach to drug administration. As nothing came of it, presumably he found few takers for his ideas, but whenever something which is damaging in the longer term offers short-term commercial advantage, danger lurks.

◆◆◆◆

Equally anonymous should remain a conversation with a genuinely expert breeder some 25 years ago which raised a somewhat similar threat in terms of our racing programmes. He foresaw breeders eventually being forced to conform to the dreary American stereotype of restricting almost all race distances to little more than one mile. His reasoning was that such concentration was producing a specialised

Comparison between race programmes with respect to the distance of races

	1876*		1913*		1994	
	Races	%	Races	%	Races	%
Races of four furlongs or less	269	14.1	0	0	0	0
Other races under a mile	1,053	55.2	1,115	53.0	1,918	49.2
All races under one mile	1,322	69.3	1,115	53.0	1,918	49.2
Races of one mile	258	13.5	319	15.2	638	16.4
All races of a mile or less	1,580	82.9	1,434	68.2	2,556	65.6
Longer races under two miles	239	12.5	562	26.7	1,207	30.9
All races under two miles	1,819	95.4	1,996	94.9	3,763	96.5
Two miles or more	88	4.6	108	5.1	138	3.5
All races	1,907	100.0	2,104	100.0	3,901	100.0

*Races in Ireland included

gene pool which would make American horses unbeatable over such distances and force the rest of us to follow suit. Against the background of Sadler's Wells, Galileo, Montjeu and Frankel that threat seems to have receded too, but complacency is again out of order as we got ourselves into just such a position quite unnecessarily in the late nineteenth century, as the table in page 120 shows.

Contrary to what one would imagine, racing programmes in the late Victorian period showed a lack of variety or imagination that even the poorest All Weather cards avoid today. The bias in favour of short races for very moderate horses, which are naturally the easiest to fill, was far more marked then than it is now, There were virtually no races for fillies or mares below the highest class and surprisingly few beyond 10 furlongs, for the great majority of horses. Had our Edwardian forefathers not grasped the nettle it must be quite likely that our programmes today would be as lacking in variety with respect to distances as those in the States. Indeed, it has taken repeated efforts on a rather patchy basis to check that form of narrow commercialism and the threat can never be eliminated. How bad things got is well exemplified by the position in 1876, during the last full year of Admiral Rous's life, when contrasted with the final completed season before the First World War. Despite several bumps along the way, not too much has changed overall since 1913, and the comparable figures for 1994, after the last national review in 1993, are also included. Hopefully it will not be too long to the next review, as average distances have certainly slipped again since then.

◆◆◆◆

The results of the late Admiral's prudent handling of the Club's resources really paid off when the entire Exning Estate was put up for auction in 1881. Negotiations having failed to result in an agreed price for the whole 2,500 acres, the position of the Jockey Club was by now sound enough to bid £190,000, mainly funded by an insurance company in return for interest at 4 per cent. Details of the transaction appear in Part 3, including subsequent sales of surplus parts. With the racecourse now making a useful profit after the building of its first proper grandstand in 1876 (the earlier Private Stand following the 1858 proposals also proving a money spinner) the loan was repaid by 1895. The stand's builder, Sir John Astley, also founded the town's first effort to provide staff recreation with the Astley Club; reformed as the New Astley in 1893, it moved to its present site in 1976.

During the nineteenth century the use of the area around the town for breeding horses increased. Details are not readily available but even by the outbreak of the First World War the studs around Newmarket will still have been producing a smaller share of the horse population than is the case today when the great majority of the important stallions are located in the vicinity. The fact that the land around Newmarket is by no means the best for the rearing of horses matters much less nowadays, when so much more is understood about how to tend the paddocks and remedy any deficiencies.

◆◆◆◆

The success of Newmarket in the period 1863–1914 had at least one unfortunate side-effect: Victorian building largely removed from the town most traces of its Georgian and Stuart days, and virtually nothing remains from before the coming of the racehorse except St Mary's Church. Some of the late nineteenth-century houses are rather splendid examples of that period and the work of Sir Albert Richardson on the Jockey Club Rooms and Tattersalls Sales Pavilion provide fine examples of twentieth-century neoclassicism. It is also fair to say that some of the old yards in the town have considerable charm and a few, like Palace House itself, have parts surviving from its Stuart days. However, the town's architecture taken as a whole is hardly worthy of the timeless Heath which encircles it.

1886

Chapter 8 (1914–1945)

High Class Racing is Restricted to the Heath in Both World Wars

The effect of the two World Wars was to thrust the town forward each time to the point that it became the crucial link between racing's past and its future. Accordingly, things that might ordinarily have been little more than local issues became for a while of real importance in the long struggle to keep racing going during war time.

Even prior to 1914 the lead up to the First World War had an effect, when in 1911 major military manoeuvres were decreed, covering many square miles between the town and Cambridge. While the details of this are interesting and show the value of the close links which a cooperative Jockey Club could still have through its contacts with Westminster, military matters are better dealt with in Part 2. As the war dragged on, those contacts became increasingly important and in 1917 proved sufficient to overturn a complete ban on racing, which had lasted from April to July that year.

There is little evidence that warning signs like manoeuvres led to any planning as to how to react when the sky did fall in on 4 August 1914, and a ban was imposed. While a meeting at Brighton which began on the 4th was allowed to continue for two more days there were no others until 28 August, largely due to the railways being turned over to transporting troops. On 13 August a notice was issued that racing would resume on the basis that no advance warning need be given or indeed, any reason announced for a cancellation. However, once things were restarted at Gatwick a majority of the expected fixtures did take place for the remainder of the year, including the Leger meeting at Doncaster and the three usual autumn ones on the Heath.

Fig. 93

Archibald, 5th Earl of Rosebery (1847–1929) by J.E. Millais

Unlike Lord Durham, in this instance the subject's major contribution was via his horses rather than racing administration which, as a sometime Prime Minister, he seems to have regarded with a fair degree of disdain. However, his political standing played a crucial part in keeping racing going in the First World War. Breeder of each of his three Derby winners, he also developed some important families carried on by his son.

On 16 September the Club met at Derby House off Oxford Street, its base for the whole war, and the first signs of dissent appeared over the propriety of continuing to race at all. Although all twenty-five members present favoured the current arrangements, three written objections to continuance were received. A reasonably normal fixture list was prepared for 1915 but doubts over the policy were reinforced when the 6th Duke of Portland, owner of St Simon, wrote to *The Times* suggesting that racing at such socially high-profile meetings as Epsom and Ascot should be cancelled. On 16 March he summoned a special meeting of the Club to reconsider the whole question, but undermined any support he might have had by failing to put in an appearance. In the end the Stewards' policy was carried by 34 to 1. The one seems to have been a former Steward, Mr F.W. Lambton, as he interrupted a speech by the former Prime Minister, the 5th Earl of Rosebery (Fig. 93). When the latter rhetorically asked if anyone could possibly think racing really impeded the war effort Mr Lambton said that he did. To this Lord Rosebery observed that Lambton was always 'somewhat distinguished for singularity', and continued urbanely to develop his case.

While the Duke and Mr Lambton had been defeated in March, public pressure was being cranked up although based on arguments a good deal weaker than theirs might have been, and on 19 May the government asked the Stewards to cancel all racing apart from that on the Heath 'for the duration of the War'. Although it was only a request the Stewards must have been wise to accede to it, and duly did as asked after the Windsor meeting ended on 22 May. No doubt as a reward for good behaviour five extra meetings were allowed at Newmarket and in the end the two courses on the Heath saw forty-five cards in 1915. In one area at least, previous standards were maintained as not one was allowed to take place on a Saturday.

With many older horses and most geldings acquired as officers' chargers or cavalry remounts, racing could not have continued anyway at former levels. The Derby was run on the July Course and a substitute for the Leger on the Rowley Mile, which allowed Pommern to be granted a somewhat tawdry Triple Crown. Indeed, at the insistence of the Doncaster Race Committee it would not even have the words St. Leger in its title and the race was run as the September Stakes until 1918. Their successors took a more generous line during the Second World War. On 23 January 1916 the Club sent a deputation headed by the Senior Steward, Captain Harry Greer (Fig. 94), a leading breeder in Ireland, to seek extra fixtures. A total of twenty-two was permitted in addition to those on the Heath, the last of these at Newbury on 12 August 1916, and none was held north of Newmarket where again all five classics were divided between the two courses.

Racing always seems to attract a variety of enemies whether in the form of Victorian opponents of gambling or Animal Rights extremists and their more moderate fellow travellers of today. Certainly the war gave a broad selection of these a real field day early in 1917 when the government was persuaded to ask that no fixtures should be put on apart from those at Newmarket. This was bad enough but it also led to a view throughout the sport that the Club was being too reasonable in its dealings with a government easily swayed by bogus statistics over the number of horses in training and their collective capacity to eat oats on a scale able to undermine the war effort. However, worse was to follow when on 29 April, after only the Craven meeting had been held, the Club was forced to cancel all racing on the Heath. This was considered so utterly unreasonable that a special meeting was hurriedly convened to decide what to do.

On 14 May a Club delegation was sent to Downing Street headed by a former occupant, Lord Rosebery. While nothing concrete was achieved, it was invited to return a month later and did so on 18 June, after which government, giving every appearance of disarray, allowed forty meetings with a better

Fig. 94

(Left) Sir Henry Greer (1855–1934)

Retiring from the Army in 1890, Harry Greer devoted most of the rest of his life to racing and breeding. His best buy for himself was the outstanding stallion Gallinule for only £1,000, who sired the great Pretty Polly. Considerable success as a breeder in his native Ireland was followed by wins with other horses in the 2000 Guineas and St Leger, while Greer himself became a highly effective Steward of the Jockey Club in 1908. Reappointed in a hurry in 1914 as Senior Steward to fill a gap caused by illness, his arrival to cover the first part of the War proved a lucky break. Following the gift of the National Stud in 1916 he was the obvious person to manage it, which he did almost to his death with a good deal more success than many expected. Having shut down his own operation at Brownstown, the Aga Khan persuaded him to get his breeding venture running with remarkably speedy results, and Sir Harry even found time to be a Free State senator.

(Right) Mohamed, Aga Khan III (1877–1957)

Having succeeded his father as Aga Khan aged only eight, he developed an interest in racing in India as a young man. Eventually Colonel Hall Walker (Fig. 177) really fired his enthusiasm but it was not until 1921 that he launched out here. George Lambton (Fig. 91) had no room for more horses but agreed to buy the early yearlings to be trained by Dick Dawson in Berkshire. After falling out with his trainer in 1931, most of the Aga's horses went to Frank Butters (Fig. 98) in Newmarket. Success continued unabated for the rest of his life, during which he won five Derbys among sixteen English classics. Butters was eventually followed by Marcus Marsh and the Aga's various trainers gained him thirteen owners' titles (Butters landed nine, Dawson three and Marsh the other).

geographical spread than at any time since 1914. Various face-saving caveats were attached limiting the number of horses in training to 1,200, on pain of forfeiting part of their daily oat ration, but racing had effectively won the day and was never again so threatened until the next War broke out. Thus things were able to begin again with three days on the July Course from the 14th of the next month. Like Pommern in 1915 and Gainsborough in the final year of the War, Gay Crusader took an all-Newmarket Triple Crown for Manton winning his Derby on the later than usual date of 31 July.

Apart from its ability to summon aid from such luminaries as Lord Rosebery, Lord Derby (Fig. 91) was a member of the Cabinet, and in Captain Greer and the 8th Earl of Jersey the wartime Senior Stewards were probably the best the Club found in the first part of the twentieth century. Later to become Sir Henry, apart from his other activities he also served as a Senator in the Irish Free State.

◆◆◆◆

It had been thought politic as well as patriotic to allow the Royal Flying Corps to take over part of the Rowley Mile stands and 250 acres beside the course to its east for a school to train officers to fly. Perhaps surprisingly, this was agreed on the far from onerous basis that no flying would take place on racedays and necessary parts of the stands like the weighing room would be vacated by the airmen so that the course could be used. Things went on in 1918 much as the year before had ended but with a few more courses used, although none was allowed more than a single meeting, and with 43 cards the Heath staged some two-thirds of the national programme. There might have been more but the Club's Agent, Cecil Marriott, refused any extra that autumn or in 1919, due to his need for all available hands to get in the harvests, having only half the staff, and nearly twice the area under plough, as well as the air force's continued use of the stands in 1918.

Jumping continued on a limited scale during the war, and when Aintree ceased to be available after 1915 a Grand National was run at Gatwick for three years. To a degree, Jumping seems to have fallen beneath the radar of racing's opponents, which was just as well since the defence of keeping things going for the long-term good of the breed could hardly have been used as an argument.

In general it seems fair to say that the Jockey Club had rather a good war. So too did its Agent – he was formally thanked and told to expect a long-overdue pay rise. It seems extraordinary, but as a consequence of keeping racing going the number of foals being produced fell only 14 per cent from the 1914 crop. In part this was no doubt due to the older mares which had been culled being replaced by fillies which had never been trained. The fact that racing had continued in Ireland with fewer restrictions will have affected the percentage given the joint stud book, but the statistics are still surprising:

	Live foals registered
1913	3,349
1914	3,505
1915	3,687
1916	3,689
1917	3,463
1918	3,179
1919	3,019
1920	3,102

Partly as a result, and also because there had been far fewer sales of stallions than were to happen in the next war, the quality of the horse population hardly seemed to fall. Race times continued to improve decade by decade as they had done since those for the Derby were first recorded in the mid-nineteenth century. The only decade which has shown any deterioration was that immediately following the Second World War, when the impact on the quality of the horse population was far more marked, as explained in the next chapter.

Fig. 95

Phalaris (1913) by Polymelus out of Bromus

Against any expectation, this fine sprinter became the dominant classic sire of the period, judged on his distant posterity. Only champion twice himself he died at 18, but you have to go back to 1974 to find a year when one of his male line descendants did not top the list. With fourteen horses winning since then, his domination resembles that of his distant ancestor Eclipse. Bred and raced by Lord Derby and trained by George Lambton (Fig. 91), his opportunities were limited by the First World War. However, it was clear he was best up to seven furlongs and although he won at ten it was a poor race with three runners.

◆◆◆◆

The most important classic sire of the 1920s was not one of the three wartime Triple Crown winners but Lord Derby's Phalaris (Fig. 95), who had been the best sprinter of the period despite a grand classic pedigree; his later triumphs as a stallion emphasised the growing importance of Newmarket studs. Perhaps his main rival was Blandford, an early product of the National Stud in the days before it was relocated to Dorset from Ireland in 1943.

The fact the Club's finances were healthy became particularly important when the McCalmont family decided to sell the 8,000 acre Cheveley Park Estate soon after the Allixes had sold Bunbury Farm (the area enclosed by the old Round Course originally called Boundary Farm), in 1919. Both purchases and similar matters are dealt with in detail in Part 3, and were followed at five-year intervals by the reconstruction of the Rowley Mile and July Course stands. With the Limekilns and adjacent areas such as Railway Land acquired from the Tharp family of Chippenham and the Rooms reconstructed

Fig. 96

Gavin, Lord Hamilton of Dalzell (1872–1952)

Elected to the Club in 1908, the 2nd Lord Hamilton's importance was solely as one of its more effective administrators, as his few horses were of no consequence. His two main contributions to the sport were as the accepted father of the Tote and an effective decade in charge at Ascot, including the difficult years of the Second World War.

in the mid-1930s, the Club gives the appearance of turning inwards to concentrate on its own affairs between the wars. Probably its most effective Senior Steward was Lord Hamilton of Dalzell (Fig. 96), who was mainly responsible for the foundation of the Tote after a series of battles in the 1920s.

One wonders what his ghost must be thinking of recent events leading to its sale to a firm of bookmakers.

At the same period Lord Derby and others became exercised about the state of the Heath and the antagonism between the autocratic Agent Cecil Marriott and many of the trainers, which certainly shows itself in the Club minutes of the day. For instance, Lord Lonsdale, in his support of the Agent, was moved to say that if he was not rude to trainers he doubted he was worth anything, and Lord Durham observed that he would rather trust Marriott's judgement in preference to that of any three members of the Club which, considering his audience, was rather less than tactful. The part played in all this by the Hon. George Lambton, Durham's brother and Derby's trainer, is opaque. Anyway, the net result was that Lord Derby never got the Committee of Enquiry into the condition of the gallops and general conduct of things on the Heath which he sought, and was eventually content in 1927 to second Lord Durham's vote of thanks to Mr Marriott for the successful completion of the Rowley Mile works.

Meanwhile, the battles between trainers on the Heath and those on the downland swung in either direction with Manton and Beckhampton seeming – if anything – to gain the upper hand until Alec Taylor junior's retirement in 1927. His successor at Manton, Joe Lawson, who had been Taylor's travelling head lad and later assistant, rather lost his momentum there after a good start and in 1948 he eventually switched sides by exchanging the downs for Newmarket and ended his days in a blaze of glory at Carlburg on the Bury Road with Never Say Die's Derby and St Leger double of 1954.

By the 1930s Newmarket had regained the lead with horses such as Hyperion (Fig. 97) trained by George Lambton for Lord Derby, Bahram trained by Frank Butters (Fig. 98), for the Aga Khan, and Blue Peter (Fig. 99) by Jack Jarvis (Fig. 100), for the 6th Earl of Rosebery (Fig. 101). Neither Steve Donoghue, champion jockey from 1914 to

Fig. 97

Hyperion (1930) by Gainsborough out of Selene

Few would have imagined that Lord Derby's most influential stallion would turn out to be the sprinter Phalaris (Fig. 95) rather than this easy winner of the 1933 Derby and St Leger. For years the issue was in doubt, as Hyperion topped the list six times, but nowadays his line is struggling in this country – whereas Phalaris via Northern Dancer rules the roost worldwide. Under 15.2 hands on Derby Day and an immense character, Hyperion was a public favourite. Many ascribed his failure to train on at 4 to George Lambton (Fig. 91), leaving Stanley House after his three-year-old season.

1923, nor his successor Gordon Richards who reigned from 1925 to 1953 with only three gaps, was Newmarket-based. Perhaps the best genuinely local jockey was Harry Wragg (Fig. 102), who filled the 1941 gap in Gordon's reign and later became a more successful trainer in the town than any comparable jockey since John Pratt, who had ridden Gimcrack. If the net extended nationally only old John Day achieved the same on both fronts, so it seems such a talent arrives about once a century on the Flat, even if it is more common in Jumping. The Heath had a purple patch in the 1920s with regard to Jumping. From 1923 to 1929, five of the seven winners of the Grand National were trained there, three by the Leader family. How extraordinary that was is best demonstrated by the fact that since then the nearest thing to a Newmarket victory was Oxo's win in 1959 for Willie Stephenson, of nearby Royston. Thus it was hardly a local issue when Jumping was entirely shut down from March 1942 to January 1945 in the Second World War.

◆◆◆◆

For both the Club and Newmarket in general, the years between the wars represented consolidation rather than dramatic progress. The same was really true of racing nationally, although a good deal more was being achieved abroad, especially in America and France, as well as from lesser bases in numerous other places. However, when the Second World War broke out on 3 September 1939, both the Club's finances and the Heath were in good order and few people would have questioned that Britain still had the strongest horse population. It was as well that this was so; six years later things had regressed badly on all fronts in the aftermath of the long conflict.

As in 1914, the immediate reaction was to cancel all racing, and none took place from 2 September until a card on the Heath on 18 October, when the Cambridgeshire was staged in two divisions, with 27 runners in each. A second meeting was put on in November and a few other cards staged at Newbury, Thirsk, Stockton and Manchester before the season ended on 18 November. The Leger meeting was lost and with it the expected match between Blue Peter and the French champion Pharis II, who had already been shipped over and would have run if the race had been reprogrammed. An extensive fixture list was provisionally issued for 1940 with the Derby pencilled in for Newbury.

Until after the evacuation of Dunkirk, things went as had been planned, but with Newbury no longer available the

Fig. 98

Frank Butters (1878–1957)

Born in Austria, Butters trained there or in Italy until taking over Lord Derby's string in 1926. He did well, winning the championship twice, but in 1930 George Lambton was restored to office after five years as manager, to save money during the slump. Having lost one of the two best strings in the country, Butters took over the other for the Aga Khan (94) and won six more trainers' titles before being forced to retire in 1949, having been knocked off his bicycle by a lorry outside his yard at Fitzroy House.

Bahram (1932) by Blandford out of Friar's Daughter by A.G. Haigh

Trained on the Heath by Frank Butters for the Aga Khan (Fig. 94) Bahram won the 1935 Triple Crown. Unbeaten in nine races, he shares an unblemished record with Ormonde alone among the 15 colts who won Triple Crowns. Good as this handsome horse was, he may have been flattered by that comparison as his opposition was weak and he tended to do no more than necessary. Sold to the USA in 1940, after a reasonably promising start he was moved on again to the Argentine rather prematurely, and overall was hardly the success expected before his death in 1956.

Fig. 99

Blue Peter (1936) by Fairway out of Fancy Free by A.G. Haigh

A sighting shot followed by a good second in the Middle Park was a prelude to four wins at 3, including the 2000 Guineas, Derby and Eclipse. But for the outbreak of war Blue Peter would have had his chance at the Triple Crown, but the St Leger was never run, and in any case the French champion Pharis II would have been a serious danger. Trained for Lord Rosebery (Fig. 101) by Jack Jarvis (Fig. 100), he retired to Mentmore, where he was not a great success, having got the Derby winner Ocean Swell in his first crop.

Fig. 100

Sir Jack Jarvis (1887–1968)

A member of one of the Newmarket training dynasties active since the early nineteenth century and still in evidence today, Jack Jarvis was light enough to start out as a successful apprentice. After riding Hackler's Pride to land a coup carrying 6st 10lbs in the 1903 Cambridgeshire, he eventually moved on to Jumping until taking out a trainer's licence in 1914. After the war he rented what would remain his base for the rest of his life at Park Lodge, where he soon won a 2000 Guineas for Lord Rosebery, (Fig. 93) in 1923. His Derby winners for the next Earl (Fig. 101) came in 1939 and 1943, and his long career saw three championships and a further season as the leader on the Heath.

Fig. 101

Harry, 6th Earl of Rosebery (1882–1974)

Among all the grandees of the twentieth century turf Lord Rosebery (the figure looking through his field glasses) probably had the most complete grasp of the many facets of racing and its organisation. Unlike his father, he excelled at several sports and had three seasons as captain of a good Surrey eleven before concentrating on racing for his final sixty years. Given the stud at Mentmore by his father as their extremely prickly relationship mellowed, he was elected to the Club in 1924, and as a Steward for the first time in 1929. His first major success came in the 1931 St Leger and his last in the 1971 Oaks, with his only championship in 1939 via Blue Peter (Fig. 99). However, his main contribution to racing was the impact of his famously forceful personality on a Jockey Club often in need of goading into action.

Fig. 102

Harry Wragg (1902–1985)

Champion jockey in 1941, Wragg retired in 1946 to train with great success at Abingdon Place on the Bury Road until his son Geoffrey took over in 1982. He rode thirteen classic winners in this country and trained six more only needing an Oaks for a full set in both roles, a feat never yet achieved. Although he got very close on occasion he was never top trainer nationally, but overall came nearer to replicating his high status as a jockey than anyone since John Day. At Newmarket you would need to go back to John Pratt in the eighteenth century (Figs. 49 and 55) to find an equal. As might be expected. he was also an excellent tutor of apprentices.

Derby was run on the July Course on 12 June, with the Oaks the next day. It was a close call for both races in terms of the continuance of an unbroken sequence since their foundation, as after a few cards during the next week everything was cancelled until Ripon raced on 14 September. While the campaign that might confidently have been expected, based largely on the impropriety of any form of public amusement, got under way it is not clear that the government actually took any steps in response. Indeed, it seems that a combination of the practical difficulties allied to a degree of sympathy with the objectors' point of view while the country was in such dire straits led to the suspension. However, as things settled down into some sort of pattern the resumption of racing was announced in early August with a small programme of fixtures, all on courses north of Newmarket rather than south as in the First World War, with a St Leger of sorts run at Thirsk on 23 November 1940.

In 1941 racing continued on a more extensive basis than in the previous year with fixtures south of Newmarket limited to Newbury and Salisbury. The Heath's share of thirteen meetings of two days each, all run on Wednesdays and Thursdays, formed a smaller proportion as there were fifty-three meetings sanctioned on eleven other courses in the north and midlands plus the two in the south. The Leger went to the wrong county at Manchester but at least was run in the right month.

What seemed likely to be a very important initiative came with the setting up of the Racing Reorganisation Committee under the 6th Earl of Ilchester in October 1941 to consider the future of the sport after the war. It eventually delivered a report of considerable wisdom in April 1943 advocating policies which now seem rather visionary but which had to be abandoned after 1945 when a less benevolent government than Lord Ilchester had presumably envisaged was in power. However, some of the key recommendations have, to a degree, come about by routes he could never have foreseen. In particular his ideas on racecourse ownership in a form conducive to investment in the sport have been at least partially fulfilled as Jockey Club Racecourses (JCR) now distributes over a third of the national prize fund.

It is ironic that Lord Hamilton of Dalzell's seemingly successful efforts to construct an alternative to bookmaking in the Tote have hardly turned out as once seemed likely. On the other hand, Lord Ilchester, who had often deputised for Lord Hamilton when the latter was Senior Steward, would probably be rather pleased if he could peruse today's JCR accounts. The irony is underlined by the fact that the company he formed to pursue his scheme was actually registered as Jockey Club Racecourses, but had been wound up in 1947 when it seemed to serve no purpose.

In the 1942 season racing was formally regionalised for any but the top races based at Pontefract, Salisbury, Stockton and Windsor, in addition to Newmarket. There were fifteen meetings on the July Course of two days each and both the Derby and an autumn card were allowed to take place on Saturdays. In all, eighty cards were staged around the country's five active tracks and George VI's victories in four of the five Classics with Sun Chariot and Big Game must surely have been influential in preventing a repeat of the perverse 1917 decision to shut the whole show down. Both horses were products of the National Stud and were leased to the King for their racing careers. Trained for him at Beckhampton by Fred Darling, they later became good producers themselves though in that role were far surpassed by the one-year-younger Nasrullah whose wayward temperament probably prevented his trainer Frank Butters from sweeping the board with him in 1943. Nasrullah was by one of the best stallions of the day, the Italian import Nearco, and Sun Chariot was a daughter of the other, Hyperion. The fact that both spent their entire stallion careers at Newmarket studs is good evidence of the town's standing. However, Nasrullah escaped to America via Ireland and it really took until the 1970s before the damage to the breed started to be repaired through the importation into Ireland, and later this country, of the progeny of Nearco's grandson Northern Dancer.

With the tide of the war beginning to turn Ascot was added to the fixture list in 1943 but the Heath's quota was reduced to twelve with three of them cut to a single day. Overall, the total number of meetings nationwide was down to only 67, with all five Classics again run at Newmarket plus, for some inscrutable reason, the Gold Cup – although Ascot raced only three days later.

With the war now seemingly sure to end in victory very little changed in 1944 with one additional card only and no changes at all in the racecourses used or the regional scheme adopted to reduce transport requirements. The Leger stayed on the Heath, as did the Gold Cup. When victory actually arrived in 1945 several more courses were added to the list, of which York and the Rowley Mile were by far the most important. As discussed, the latter had been occupied by the RAF throughout the war. At York the Leger returned to the North only to be won by the Newmarket-trained Chamosaire in the absence of the northern champion Dante who was already well on the way to total blindness.

During the Second World War the Jockey Club failed to find leaders of quite the quality it had first time round. From 1939 to 1945 there were five Senior Stewards with only Lord Sefton providing the continuity of a reign of more than a single year. It was perhaps as well that the government under Churchill, a Club member himself when a leading owner after the war, was a good deal more supportive when the inevitable attacks came, this time aimed more at the consumption of petrol than oats. After 1941 transporting horses by rail was banned completely if they were going to race meetings but permitted if they were being taken to the ports, largely for sale to America. It is hardly surprising that the quality of the horse population plunged.

◆◆◆◆

The return of peace in Europe saw the end of Marriott's fifty-year reign as Agent on the Heath. He had continued to hold the fort with considerable success during the war in the expectation of being succeeded by his son. However, when news of his son's death during the fall of Singapore eventually became known, Marriott – by now aged 75 – retired in July 1945. The Newmarket trainers recognised his enormous contribution with a suitably immense salver and he continued to live at Portland Lodge on the edge of the Heath to which he had devoted his life for a further two years. As he admitted when presented with his salver (Fig. 103), 'my rule has been autocratic and at times impossible' but that undoubted truth hardly diminished his achievements. The Club gave him a pension of £1,500 as well as the use of Portland Lodge until his wife too died in the 1950s. When he joined the rather like-minded Tregonwell Frampton in one of the town's churches (St Mary's in his case), the Club had a whip round for his memorial which Lord Rosebery unveiled in 1948. Despite his achievements one suspects that a twenty-first-century Agent who followed his example in all its particulars would be lucky if the local trainers gave him a set of plated teaspoons.

By the time of the 1945 Leger the regional restrictions had been lifted at all levels. Attendances briefly rocketed to unrecorded heights, on courses that must in some cases have verged on the derelict, to watch the French win one major race after another as the weakness of the British horse population became painfully obvious. But all that is a subject for the next chapter. It encompasses a world which begins with tax rates sometimes well over 100 per cent, and a government which could hardly be expected to worry much about the interests of the Jockey Club or its Heath, and which saw both become almost depressed areas over the next 20 years.

Chapter 8 (1914–1945)

Fig. 103

Cecil Marriott's presentation on 21 September 1945

The Newmarket Trainers' Federation, presided over at the time by Jack Jarvis (Fig. 100), presented this splendid salver to Mr Marriott to mark his half-century in charge of the Heath. A few of his antagonists are conspicuous by their absence, which in the case of George Lambton (Fig. 91) is explained by the fact he had died on 23 July. Fortunately, the evidence that all had been forgiven is provided by his signature on the salver, added only days before his death.

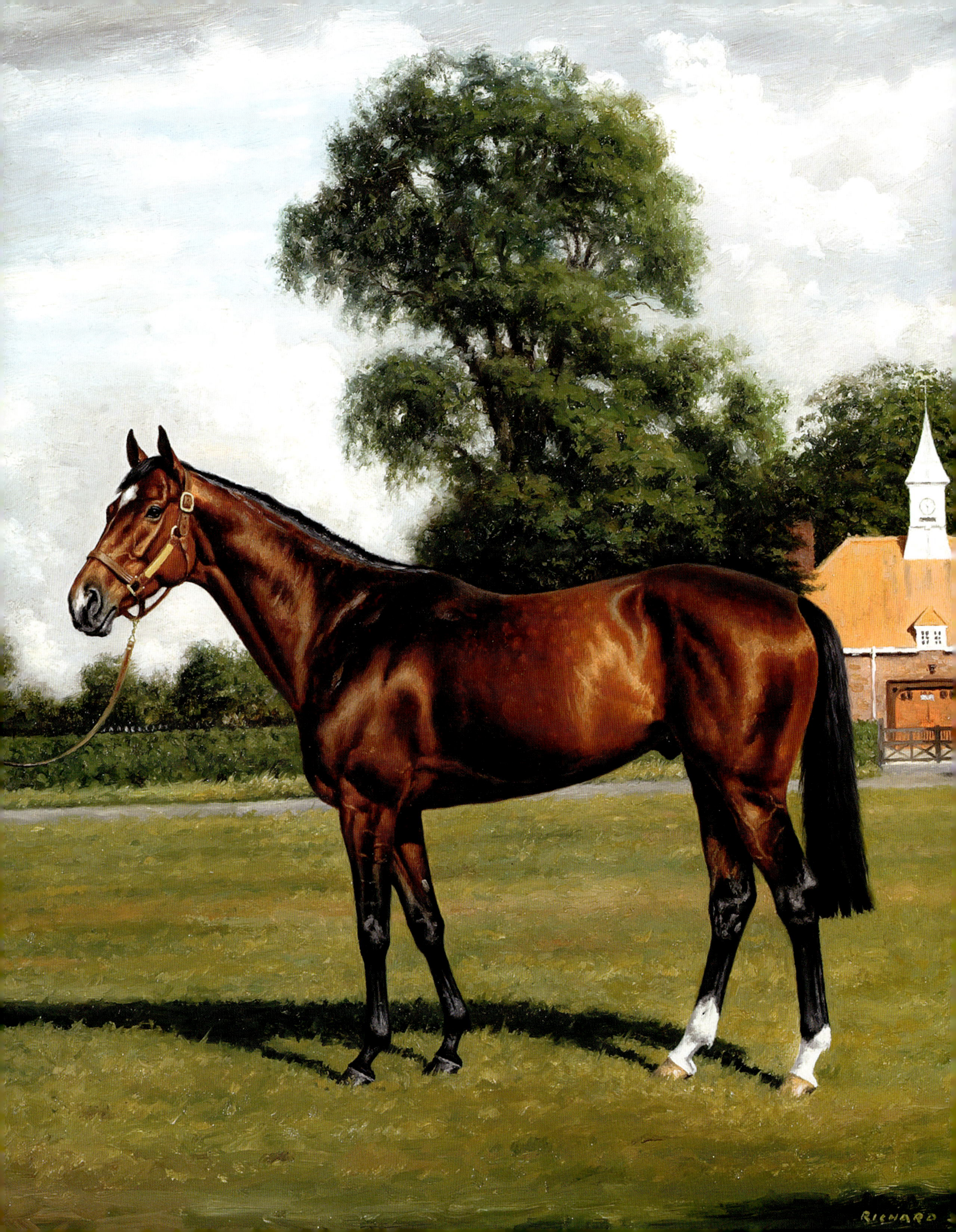

Chapter 9 (1945–1980)

Recovery from the Second World War Is Slow in a Conservative Newmarket

Newmarket had certainly played the leading role in the sport during the War but found it increasingly difficult to keep its end up once peace returned. There were several reasons for this which were peculiar to the town itself, as well as the effect of the difficulties racing faced throughout the country arising from shortages of everything, particularly money in the hands of its pre-war supporters, and the drastic reduction in the quality of the horse population.

Perhaps the local problems which cast the longest shadows were the steady deterioration in the Club's finances and the increasing average age of the leading trainers. Leaving finances aside for a moment and dealing first with trainers, by far the most important addition to the ranks came when Noel Murless (Fig. 104) moved from Beckhampton, where he had succeeded Fred Darling in 1948, to take over at Warren Place for the 1953 season after Sam Armstrong had moved to St Gatien in the town. However, Murless was already an established figure well into his forties and he joined Captain Cecil Boyd-Rochfort (Fig. 105) and Jack Jarvis (Fig. 100), all three eventually knighted, in a relatively ageing and perhaps rather old-fashioned band of leaders on the Heath. Only when they retired around 1970 did their far younger successors, Henry Cecil, Michael Stoute and Mark Prescott, come rapidly to the fore. The arrival of these

Royal Palace (1964) by R. Stone Reeves, detail of Fig. 109

Fig. 104

Sir Noel Murless (1910–1987)

Having begun in a yard of one member of the Hartigan family, Murless acted as an assistant to another both here and in Ireland to learn the trade. After taking out a licence in Yorkshire in 1935 he succeeded Fred Darling at Beckhampton in 1948, before moving on to Warren Place for the 1953 season. There he became the pre-eminent classic trainer of the next quarter century winning nineteen before he retired in 1976 to be followed in both his yard and his pre-eminence by his son-in-law Henry Cecil (Fig. 114). Nine times the national champion and top of the list on the Heath for a further three years he also had considerable success as a breeder, including producing his wife Gwen's Caergwrle to win the 1968 1000 Guineas.

Aureole with owner and trainer by Sir Alfred Munnings

Fig. 105

Aureole (1950) by Hyperion out of Angelola

Bred by her father and raced by the Queen, Aureole's attempt to win the Coronation Derby was only thwarted by the outstanding Pinza (Fig. 108). Having won the Acomb first time out both the Middle Park and 2000 Guineas showed he needed further. Third favourite for the Derby after a win in the Lingfield Derby Trial, Pinza proved four lengths the better at Epsom and by three for the King George. Aureole's season ended with a disappointing third in a Leger for which he was hot favourite but his final season, by which time his fiery temperament was under better control, ended with wins in the Coronation Cup, Hardwicke and King George. At stud he was a fine sire of stayers and champion in both 1960 and 1961, largely due to his Derby winner St Paddy. In this painting his trainer is flanked by Sir Humphrey de Trafford and the horse's usual jockey Eph Smith.

Captain Sir Cecil Boyd-Rochfort (1887–1983)

After the First World War Boyd-Rochfort was well taught by a particularly shrewd trainer in Atty Persse and launched out with his own licence in 1921. Based at Freemason Lodge during his long career, he did not retire until 1968. His 13 classics included no less than six St Legers and he was always particularly good with stayers, while also showing the advantages of his early lessons from Persse in the number of his well-supported triumphs in major handicaps. Followed for only a season at Freemason by his stepson and assistant Henry Cecil (Fig. 114) before the place was sold, he was leading trainer five times between 1937 and 1958, plus heading the Newmarket list in another three years. In this picture he is the very tall figure beside the Queen.

Fig. 106

Queen Elizabeth II

This picture shows the presentation of the Ascot Gold Cup in 2013 following the victory of the Queen's filly, Estimate, trained for her on the Heath by Sir Michael Stoute (Fig. 115). The Queen's unwavering support for the turf during her long reign has been of immense benefit. Nothing comparable has happened since the days of Charles II, and in his case Oliver Cromwell as well as death at only 55 compressed things into twenty years. In the early part of the reign the Royal string was split between Freemason Lodge for those bred at Sandringham and Warren Place for horses leased from the National Stud. When it ceased keeping mares and Sir Cecil retired, operations gravitated to Berkshire and Wiltshire with a period when only William Huntingdon trained in Newmarket, so continuing the local link. Since 1999 much of the string has returned to the Heath to be trained by Sir Michael Stoute joined by Michael Bell in 2009 and now William Haggas for the first time in 2014. The Queen was champion owner in both 1954 and 1957 – no one else alive today topped the list before the 1980s. Her five classic wins have been via the fillies Carrozza, Highclere and Dunfermline, plus Pall Mall in the 2000 Guineas. Only a Derby is still needed to complete a nap hand.

Fig. 107

Fig. 108

Meld (1952) by Alycidon out of Daily Double by R. Anscomb

Sir Gordon Richards on Pinza (1950) by R. Anscomb

Winner of the fillies' version of the Triple Crown when trained for Lady Zia Wernher by Cecil Boyd-Rochfort (Fig. 105), Meld had the unique distinction of making the owner champion on the only two occasions she headed the list. This she did in her classic year of 1955, and repeated in 1966 when her son Charlottown won the Derby. Defeat in her first race when 20 to 1 by a horse of the Queen's from the same yard was her only loss, and when her racing days ended with victory in the St Leger she had coughed on the morning of the race and was very sick indeed, next day. At stud she bred some useful horses apart from Charlottown producing her last live foal in 1973. However, she lived on to 33 and is thought to have been the longest-lived classic winner of them all.

Sir Gordon was not a Newmarket jockey but after a career which saw him crowned champion 26 times between 1925 and 1953 his only Derby came on this local horse in the latter year. This seems a good opportunity to include a picture of the rider of more British winners (4870) than anyone else has yet managed, even if his 14 classics do not rank in the Top Ten. Pinza was trained by Norman Bertie at Green Lodge and was outstanding at three when he won all his races with ease before breaking down after the King George. Bred by Sir Gordon's old master Fred Darling, he was the first of Sir Victor Sassoon's four Derby winners in only eight years. However, Pinza was not a success at his stud out at Woodditton where the horse lived to 27 without ever making the Top Ten in the stallions' list.

new trainers had the effect of quickly lightening what had become a distinctly conservative, perhaps almost oppressive, atmosphere which had probably had a real part to play in the bitterness of the 1975 strike of stable lads in the town.

◆◆◆◆

However conservative Newmarket may have become in the years after the war, it did not prevent some major successes being achieved, initially by both Cecil Boyd-Rochfort in the 1950s and then by Noel Murless. In 1953 Aureole (Fig. 105), trained by Boyd-Rochfort, was second to another Newmarket horse, Pinza, in the Coronation week Derby, and the following year won the King George VI and Queen Elizabeth Stakes for the new Queen Elizabeth II (Fig. 106) en route to twice becoming champion stallion. Boyd-Rochfort also trained outstanding horses in Alcide and the 1959 Derby winner Parthia, for Sir Humphrey de Trafford, as well as the great filly Meld (Fig. 107). Winner of three classics in 1955 for Lady Zia Wernher, Meld not only produced a Derby winner but also lived to the great age of 33, so becoming Matchem's only serious rival among outstanding horses in terms of longevity. In beating Aureole, Pinza was just in time to provide Sir Gordon Richards (Fig. 108) with his only Derby at the twenty-eighth attempt in the year before injury caused him to switch to training. Pinza was trained by Norman Bertie for Sir Victor Sassoon, and two of that owner's other three Derby winners were handled by Murless, including the outstanding Crepello who won in 1957 ridden by Lester Piggott (Fig. 118).

Such triumphs apart, the trend of events in the period covered by this chapter are graphically illustrated by its Derby winners. In the twenty years between Dante's last win for the north in 1945 and Meld's son Charlottown scoring in 1966, foreign-trained horses won no less than half the renewals. As Newmarket chalked up nine of the remainder (all ten if you include that trained at neighbouring Royston), the weakness of internal competition seems clear enough. Between the old guard's last hurrah with Royal Palace in 1967 (Fig. 109) and the first victory of the next generation of Newmarket trainers, when Harry Wragg's son Geoff won in 1982, the Heath managed not a single Derby triumph. Apart from six more foreign winners, all eight home wins were credited to trainers on the Berkshire or Sussex downs, so Newmarket's relative weakness was all too clear.

❖❖❖❖

If the influence of the major trainers had been of increasing importance in the fortunes of the Heath since the war that is certainly not to say that the Jockey Club itself had ceased to be

Fig. 109

Royal Palace (1964) by Ballymoss out of Crystal Palace by R. Stone Reeves

Bred by his owner Mr Jim Joel and trained for him by Noel Murless, Royal Palace's appearance on the scene ushered in a spate of three-year-old champions who graced the turf from 1967 to 1971. He beat the only one he met, in the form of Sir Ivor in the 1968 Eclipse, and only lost twice–first time out, and when beaten in the Champion Stakes after a difficult preparation interrupted by the injury that cost him his chance of the Triple Crown, a prize he certainly deserved. The Royal Lodge at 2 followed by the 2000 Guineas and Derby preceded a clean sweep of the Coronation Cup, Prince of Wales, Eclipse and King George, to end his career in a race in which he actually broke down about a furlong out. At stud he did not achieve a lot apart from siring the Queen's outstanding dual classic winner Dunfermline.

significant. However, the dwindling of its reserves in the 1950s and early 1960s did restrict the command of events locally. Yet, for considerably longer than that it gave the impression of an institution in danger of spreading its available talents too thinly over too many fields as the sport's demands on it steadily increased both nationally and internationally.

During the war not too much prize money had been needed, costs were much reduced and the Club's finances fared surprising well; after it ended the huge crowds attracted to racing everywhere kept things on an even keel despite the country's problems. However, by the early 1950s, occasional losses started arising as the crowds melted away (indeed, losses were habitual in the Rooms), the reserves were too slender, while both the stands and the Heath were in need of considerable investment. In such circumstances Marriott's replacement as Clerk and Agent, Major Hugh Gorton, hardly had a fair chance and after he died it was found that the Heath was in such a bad way and the farm equipment so run down that his successor in 1953, Colonel Nicol Gray, must have wondered why he took the job. Part of the problem was that the cost to the Club of regulating the sport was by no means being covered by the charges levied on owners, racecourses and others.

The position became quite serious with regular losses of around £10,000 to £15,000 against a background of diminishing reserves and a fifteen year backlog in capital expenditure, and a distinctly troubled meeting was summoned. There Lord Rosebery questioned the whole basis on which things were being conducted in financial terms. It seems that no proper separation existed between public and private functions, or matters at Newmarket as against those in London and elsewhere, and even the treatment of capital expenditure in the accounts was archaic. A year later, in April 1955, leading accountants Cooper Brothers, headed by a future member in Sir Henry Benson (later Lord Benson), were employed to produce a detailed report which turned out to contain an extremely wide-ranging series of recommendations, described by Lord Rosebery as 'brilliant'. He even went on to express 'qualms' over the fact that, having been an accountant in his youth, he had not demanded such a report himself when in office as a Steward.

Anyway, he got an Implementation Committee set up, whose reports caused a good deal of controversy before the main principle of complete separation of everything at Newmarket from the regulatory and administrative function in London, still to be controlled by Weatherbys, was agreed. Part of the rationale for the division was Coopers' calculation that Newmarket operations had been subsidising racing generally (by something over £10,000 annually) for years without anyone knowing.

◆◆◆◆

Two initiatives intended to make things better on the Heath were debated in 1954, but neither got immediate acceptance. The first was to introduce Saturday fixtures on the July Course which was rejected on the seemingly eccentric grounds that any potential crowds would be going to the seaside, presumably because people usually started their holidays on Saturdays. The second was to blame poor attendance on the difficulty of watching sport on the Heath due to the ancient layout of the courses. The answer proposed was to introduce a round course in front of the Rowley Mile stands. In opposition to the idea Marriott was quoted by Lord Ilchester as saying that this would disrupt the gallops and others feared, rather less cogently, that people would be able to avoid paying for entry by watching racing from the Cambridge Road or the top of the Ditch. Neither seems a likely vantage point for freeloaders, as this photograph (Fig. 110) of the finish of the 2,000 Guineas of 1951 shows you could get a lot closer to the action on the Rowley mile for nothing. Given the apparent scale of non-payment the shortage of funds was hardly surprising.

Eventually, opposition was overcome on both fronts – beginning with a toe dipped in the water when a single Saturday was allowed in August 1955, which I recall enjoying greatly. Enough other people must have been waylaid en route to the seaside for the experiment to be deemed a success, and in early May 1958 a Saturday was added to the Guineas Meeting on the Rowley Mile. This became a double first when the main race was run on a new round course. Details of the

Fig. 110

Finish of the 1951 2,000 Guineas

A moderate Guineas that year was won by the enormous Ki Ming, who stood 17 hands. Indeed, the three-year-old colts were so moderate that he actually started favourite for the Derby although a son of the sprinter Ballyogan and naturally did not last beyond Tattenham Corner. The picture seems a graphic illustration of things at Newmarket, with the freeloaders (one of whom was your co-author) a good deal more numerous than those lining the rails in Members' across the course.

unhappy life of this course appear in Part 2; perhaps the new course's promoters should have been forewarned by the fact that both earlier efforts to start a round course on the Flat had ended in ignominious failure and, in this case, history repeated itself in 1973. However, the Saturday experiment, allied to Coopers' recommendations, played a large part in turning round the Club's finances. The improvement was helped in 1959 when a Committee chaired by Mr Jim Philipps, aided by the trainers Jack Clayton and Noel Murless plus the leading handicapper Geoffrey Freer, reviewed both Newmarket's fixtures and its programmes. With the new Levy system in the offing, the Committee reported in 1960 and then became transformed into a permanent grouping, initially consisting of Lords Sefton and Howard de Walden plus Mr Jakie Astor. Over the years it changed by degrees into the Race Planning Committee, which was transferred along with its staff to the British Horseracing Board (BHB) in 1993, by which time it had largely forgotten its distinguished ancestry.

◆◆◆◆

While not limited to Newmarket or the Club, the crucial importance of the protracted debate that ended in the setting up of the Levy Board needs covering, as it has affected the fortunes of racing ever since. One of the most persistent stories about what happened is the theory that the Club turned down the offer of a Tote monopoly because some influential members, in particular Lord Rosebery, liked to bet with the bookies. However, a study of the papers and minutes shows any such theory has no substance – it is a myth.

What actually happened followed a debate on betting legislation in the Commons in March 1956, and then one in the Lords in June, on motions involving respectively Mr Jakie Astor and his elder brother Lord Astor. In May the Club formed a committee with extremely wide representation including not only organisations like the Racehorse Owners and Thoroughbred Breeders Associations but also the Tote and the Bookmakers Protection Association. Its purpose was to try and hammer out an agreement with the Home Office for an acceptable way ahead. Yet by November the Home Secretary, Major Gwilym Lloyd George, would offer only a scheme for an off-course monopoly for cash-only bets in new Tote offices designed to regulate illegal street business and thereby stop serious corruption. However, the offer excluded on-course activity as well as credit bets by telephone and the popular cash trade through the post. No form of levy was on offer – just the highly speculative profits of a partial monopoly for the Tote. The Senior Steward, the Club's most ardent Tote monopolist Lord Willoughby de Broke, concluded his remarks at the Club's Winter Meeting by saying that he rejected the proposal and hoped that 'the great majority of racing organisations in the country will feel bound to oppose [it] by every means in their power'.

One need only consider this offer to see how unattractive it must have seemed in 1956. Nothing would accrue from any racing turnover like credit and course bets – the only business being conducted within the law in the mid 1950s, indeed, all that would be gained was the very dubious value of the turnover in new and untried betting shops that would have to trade at Tote odds against a combination of credit, on-course, postal and any remaining street business, all being conducted at fixed odds. As good a judge as William Hill refused to open shops for years after 1961, so it was not easy to foresee their success even betting at fixed odds, much less without that attraction. The Tote did test the water in the mid-1960s and the City accountants I worked for at the time acted for it and sent me to check out one of its north London offices where results were particularly bad. To say that business was in short supply would be a gross understatement – the place was virtually deserted and eventually the Tote had to admit defeat and bail out of betting shops until the law changed in the 1970s to allow them to offer fixed odds as well as pool bets.

Patently, such a strange monopoly offering only Tote odds against such competition would have been most unlikely to achieve the government's principal aim of abolishing extensive street betting. Equally clearly, such arrangements would have posed no problem to the mythical culprits in the Club – it is hard to imagine Lord Rosebery and the others who liked a bet as potential patrons of the new cash-only offices. Accordingly, their supposed selfishness cannot in reality have been the reason for the 1956 proposals being found unacceptable. All the same, little happened except talk until after the 1959 General Election. Then a new and more realistic Home Secretary in Mr R.A. Butler put through the 1960 Betting and Gaming Act, which led to racing gaining the proceeds of a Levy but without the offer of any form of monopoly. It is true that some Club members opposed acceptance of a Levy as against pressing for a monopoly. However, the majority view was that continued intransigence was very unlikely to persuade the new government, with its large majority, to give way and one can only think they were very probably right in that opinion. But the facts have never got in the way of the groundless view that the Club refused a proffered Tote monopoly in a meaningful form.

◆◆◆◆

If the arrival of the Levy system did begin steadily to improve racing's finances across the country in the 1960s, such changes were many years overdue and took several more to work much magic. The impact of the war on the quality of the horse population was little short of catastrophic and those beginning to take an interest in the sport after it ended probably had no conception of how badly things had been affected. I for one certainly had no idea that my early heroes had feet of clay when compared with the likes of Hyperion, Bahram and Blue Peter. Yet, in retrospect, the scale of the sales abroad of much of the best stock during and after the war could only have been expected to have such an effect. However, it might be more accurate to say that although Pinza, Meld and the few real champions may have stood comparison with their predecessors, the general standard of their opposition certainly did not.

The easiest way to assess what had happened is to contrast the times for the Derby and the Oaks, run over the same course at Epsom, during the relevant parts of the twentieth century. To be meaningful such conclusions cannot start before the American seat arrived with Tod Sloan or continue after the watering of the course was introduced in the mid-1960s. The period between has therefore been split into five decades: one before the First World War, two in the lull between the Wars, and finally two more after 1945. Times for the last decade from 2003 have been added for interest but are not comparable for the reasons stated in the next paragraph. The figures tell the story with remarkable clarity. They have been calculated on the basis it is best to omit the three slowest times in each decade to allow for anything up to a maximum of that number of races run on slow ground – as indeed, happened in the 1920s. Thus the averages struck contrast the seven fastest winning times in each decade, all of which were run on good or faster ground. In considering the results it should be appreciated that a second equals about six lengths, or a little under twenty yards.

The fact the Oaks times follow those of the Derby so precisely, at a respectful distance of about thirty yards, goes some way to validating the story told by these calculations. As can be seen, Classic performance seems to reach a plateau between the wars, at a level not previously attained. However, it plunges after the Second World War before slowly recovering over the next twenty years, though still leaving it well short of its pre-War peak. Any later comparisons are of much less value for several reasons, of which the most important is likely to be the impact of irrigation eliminating the several occasions in each decade when the Epsom going on chalk would naturally be firm or even hard. Other factors, such as improved training

Average times of winners of the Derby and the Oaks

Decade	Derby	Oaks	Differences
1905–1914	2 mins 37.6 secs	2 mins 38.9 secs	1.3 secs
1919–1928	2 mins 35.5 secs	2 mins 37.0 secs	1.5 secs
1930–1939	2 mins 35.5 secs	2 mins 37.1 secs	1.6 secs
1946–1955	2 mins 37.5 secs	2 mins 39.2 secs	1.7 secs
1956–1965	2 mins 36.5 secs	2 mins 38.6 secs	2.1 secs
2003–2012	2 mins 33.8 secs	2 mins 35.4 secs	1.6 secs

and veterinary regimes and electric timing, point in different directions, and how they all balance out is guesswork. However, the chances are they do more or less equate, and that the considerable recent improvement is largely the result of the immense investment in bloodstock of the past thirty years, involving the reintroduction of the bloodlines lost after 1939 and improved further in the USA before their return. Thus the history of events on the Heath and in the sport nationally since the Second World War can be seen as a slow but very remarkable recovery from a catastrophe. Those whose racing lives began at the bottom around 1950 and have stayed to see Frankel can count themselves very lucky, even if the level of competition nowadays does make it an awful lot harder to breed or own a decent winner.

◆◆◆◆

A series of five champions in as many seasons around 1970 showed that the sport really had recovered its pre-war quality in the UK, even if three were bred in America and belonged to US nationals, and two went back there as stallions. From 1967 to 1971 Royal Palace, Sir Ivor, Nijinsky, Brigadier Gerard and Mill Reef won four 2,000 Guineas, four Derbys and four King Georges. As a group they probably represented champions not equalled since the days of Ormonde, St Simon, Minting, and others over 80 years before. It is surely instructive that Royal Palace and Brigadier Gerard, the two bred in England, had only one distant line of American blood between them in five generations and both failed badly to live up to expectations at stud, whereas the three imports all succeeded as stallions, in the case of Mill Reef as the mainstay of the National Stud. Indeed, it now seems highly unlikely that a horse with a pedigree free of any US-bred ancestor will ever again reach the heights of Royal Palace, the only one among the five to be trained on a Heath that was still some way from regaining its pre-War status, despite the eminence of his trainer Noel Murless.

If we try to pinpoint the year when things began to take a

Fig. 111

Major-General Sir Randle Feilden (1904–1981)

After a distinguished career as a soldier, including being Field Marshal Montgomery's quartermaster general, Feilden's retirement began with running the NAAFI and progressed to the affairs of racing. Elected to the Club in 1949 and wisely made a Steward almost immediately, he did not retire to the backbenches until 1973 after 14 years in office, eight as chairman of the new Turf Board. His reforms aimed at promoting efficiency and staff welfare generally were legion and even Lord Wigg was almost fulsome in his praise after he died. The Turf Board was the start of the process which led to democratisation in 1993, also seeing the Jockey Club and National Hunt Committee fused together long before that in 1968. Sir Randle's few horses were not as distinguished as their owner, and were usually trained for him at Newmarket by John Oxley.

decisive turn for the better nationally it would probably be 1960, although locally it must be somewhat later. Apart from the belated decision to introduce overnight declarations for the following year, a spate of doping led to wholesale revision of racing's archaic approach to controlling this problem and, as already mentioned and – more important than either – the Betting and Gaming Act passed into law. This was followed by the Peppiatt Committee's recommendation that racing should indeed, receive a material contribution from all off-course betting. Sadly, the Committee decided that equity would be achieved with not much more than a third of the Club's proposal of £3 million annually and although the difference between the two views has narrowed somewhat in percentage terms since then it has never got near to disappearing. However, at least Sir Leslie Peppiatt's new principle found its way into another Act which eventually set up the Levy Board under Field Marshal Lord Harding in 1961. Without the total raised for the sport by the Board over the next half century, which must by now be well over £2 billion, it is hard to imagine how impoverished our racing would be today and how squalid its racecourses, but quite easy to think of much of the Heath under the plough.

◆◆◆◆

The conduct of matters on the Heath seems broadly to have reflected the views of its owners, but there is no doubt that things were becoming better managed and the Club's finances mended steadily through the 1960s. Part of the reason was certainly the solid impact of General Sir Randle Feilden (Fig. 111), who was much more often than not a Steward from 1952 to 1973. An early triumph after a long dispute with distinctly unhelpful authorities came in 1964 when it was agreed that the Newmarket bypass would eventually be sited north and west of the town. It seems to have been quite a close-run thing, and the alternatives were extremely unpalatable being based on roundabouts and cutting through the town itself. The Club was jubilant and the temporary Agent, Pat Firth, warmly congratulated.

Fig. 112

John, 9th Lord Howard de Walden (1912–1999)

Lord Howard's father began on the grand scale, buying the horses of Colonel Harry McCalmont when the owner of Isinglass died suddenly in 1902. After succeeding in 1946, his son's first notable horse was Sanlinea, third in the 1950 St Leger, and others like Amerigo and Oncidium plus some splendid fillies followed at fairly regular intervals, most bred at Plantation Stud or in Yorkshire under the watchful eyes of Bunty Scrope and then Leslie Harrison. Starting with Jack Waugh, followed by Noel Murless and Henry Cecil, most were trained on the Heath. Success reached a peak either side of 1980 with Kris (14 wins from 16 races), Slip Anchor (Derby), Diesis and Grand Lodge, trained by William Jarvis. A Steward for nine years, Lord Howard's influence as one of the last traditional family operations was both considerable and regularly exerted in the direction of involving more of the racing world in its administration. It seems symptomatic of the changing times that no peer has owned a Derby winner since Slip Anchor in 1985.

Steadily the Club became more open to change, including trying harder than it is usually given credit for to democratise the administration of the sport, by creating and giving some responsibility to various new bodies rather than trying to democratise itself. Over the years Lord Howard de Walden

(Fig. 112), in office for nine years either side of 1970, was a prominent influence and others too did a good deal of spadework in advance of the decisive changes under Lord Hartington, now Duke of Devonshire, which saw the creation of the British Horseracing Board in 1993.

◆◆◆◆

Through the 1960s and early 1970s Jumping's flag on the Heath was kept flying very largely by Harry Thomson Jones. Meanwhile, Jumping was the source of a major event in 1963 quite outside the scope of the Jockey Club's activities, which has since had huge implications both for it and the Heath. For many years Cheltenham had been run by entirely well-meaning but not very business-like enthusiasts and the stands had fallen badly behind the times. Threatened by a takeover by property interests, two equally enthusiastic but much more efficient people, Johnny Henderson and Ruby Holland-Martin, plus a few friends, bought the place for £240,000. In 1964 they formed a company named Racecourse Holdings Trust (RHT) and thereby created a structure which could obtain the necessary commercial loans or various forms of support, largely grants in the early days, from the new Levy Board. Wincanton was added in 1966 and Market Rasen the following year when long leases were also taken on the council-owned courses at Nottingham and Warwick so that by the time the National Hunt Committee was amalgamated with by the Jockey Club in December 1968 RHT operated five Jumping or dual purpose tracks while the Club ran Newmarket entirely separately.

◆◆◆◆

In 1967 Lord Harding was succeeded at the Levy Board by a far less benign bedfellow for the Club when the former Labour Cabinet Minister Lord Wigg was appointed Chairman. Almost throughout his time in charge, which lasted until 1972, relations with the Club were dreadful as he sought to use the power of the Board's income to dominate proceedings rather than using it, as Lord Harding had, to help those already in charge to run things better. As ever, there are two views about battles of this sort and several good things did come out of it for the Club when the dust settled under his successors Sir Stanley Raymond and Sir Desmond Plummer (later Lord Plummer). However, any such by-products were certainly not in the mind of George Wigg.

Right from the start, Lord Wigg took the logical view that making grants to racecourses was a bad policy and making loans at low or nil interest, which had to be repaid and so could be recycled, was the better approach. But his appearance threatened the plan agreed in outline by his predecessor for adapting the Rowley Mile Stands largely based on a grant from the Board like the one already being so usefully employed at Cheltenham. Proposals for such a scheme had been launched in 1964 costing a very ambitious £2.5 million. However, in 1968 the Club wisely decided to settle somewhat hurriedly for what turned out to be a brilliant alternative, largely inspired by the Duke of Norfolk (Fig. 113) and needing only £680,000, before any hopes of a grant evaporated (again the details appear in Part 2). Lord Wigg obtained what he must have regarded as his pound of flesh by insisting that the Club grant the Board a 999 year peppercorn lease on the present site of the National Stud, in place of one of 99 years at £5,000, as part payment for his grant so that he could move the remainder of the stud from a temporary home at West Grinstead. Heaven knows what his reaction would be if he knew that the Jockey Club would not only retrieve the last 962 years of the lease in 2008 but also acquire his treasured stud assets too when the Levy Board eventually decided, very rightly, that it was not in racing's interests for it to continue to finance what was at the time a loss-making stud.

Another of the many clashes came over further finance for the RHT racecourses, mainly Cheltenham. Here Lord Wigg overreached himself in 1970, when dealing with people like Johnny Henderson and the RHT Chairman Jim Philipps, by

Chapter 9 (1945–1980)

Fig. 113

Bernard, 16th Duke of Norfolk (1908–1975)

With little prior interest in racing the duke was elected to the Club in 1933 and over the next forty years not only accumulated vast experience but became probably General Feilden's only serious rival as a competent and industrious administrator. However, he certainly did not share the general's progressive views and his epic public battle with Lord Wigg is the stuff of legends. He chaired the Norfolk Committee in the 1960s, which led to the introduction of the Pattern and was a most effective Representative at Ascot from 1945 to 1972. His own string and stud, based at Arundel in later years and run in conjunction with his formidable duchess, had numerous successes but produced no classic winners, so that Ragstone's win in the 1974 Ascot Gold Cup seemed almost a consolation prize.

demanding that they transfer the whole RHT share capital to the Levy Board in return for it guaranteeing the large commercial loans the company had in place. Instead, with RHT shares virtually given to the Jockey Club, it agreed to take over all the guarantees basing them on its whole Newmarket estate, thus effectively linking the Heath to RHT for the first time. Eventually, in 1975, following the recommendation of a committee chaired by Major Michael Wyatt, the company which owned the racecourses on the Heath, Newmarket Racecourses Trust, was transferred to RHT in return for its unissued capital of £200, which meant it represented 10 per cent of the whole racecourses group. There is no doubt that the battles with George Wigg sharpened up the Club generally and the amalgamation with the NH Committee turned out to be no bad thing either, especially on the regulatory front, where the leading lights in its Disciplinary Committee have far more often than not come with Jumping pedigrees.

Yet another result of the Wigg years was the decision to seek the protection of a Royal Charter which was granted in 1970 and theoretically enshrined the Club's roles in perpetuity. In practice the roles changed, firstly when the governance of the sport passed to the BHB and again in 2007, when the role of regulator finally passed to its successor the British Horseracing Authority (BHA). What can never change is the fact the Club has a statutory duty to use its assets in what it reasonably considers are the interests of racing and under no circumstances to pay dividends to its members or alienate assets. The result is that all the RHT racecourses (now numbering fifteen if you regard Newmarket as two) must be operated in the interests of the sport, which is partially reflected in the relative generosity of their contributions to prize money.

After he left the Levy Board in 1972 Lord Wigg continued to be a thorn in various sides (including now that of the Levy Board as well as the Club) by taking the chair of BOLA, then the betting shop owners' trade body, so it would be untrue to say there was any sort of rapprochement. Indeed, his 1972 departure was marked in an appropriately prickly manner when the Club's olive branch of a formal dinner to mark five years in office was rejected by the putative guest of honour. The response to that was equally unyielding when it was decided not to convert honorary membership of the Rooms while in office into a lifetime right.

◆◆◆◆

Fig. 114

Sir Henry Cecil (1943–2013)

Stepson and son-in-law respectively of trainers Cecil Boyd-Rochfort (Fig. 105) and Noel Murless (Fig. 104), both were also knighted in recognition of great training careers, Henry Cecil followed in their wake aged only 26 after several years as assistant at Freemason Lodge. His first season in 1969 produced an Eclipse via Wolver Hollow so when his stepfather sold the yard he had a rather sounder basis than might have been expected for transfer to Marriott Stables, named for the Heath's great autocrat. When Murless retired, transfer to the much grander Warren Place was fully justified in 1977 with his first trainers' championship in the bag. Any attempt to detail his roller-coaster ride of the next 35 years, which eventually saw Cecil back at the top of the tree with the great Frankel (Fig. 123), a further nine championships and a grand total of 25 English classics despite some dramatic upsets, would be impractical. Suffice it to say that when he died he was probably the most universally popular figure in the sport and the attendance at his memorial service almost filled Ely Cathedral.

During the 1970s RHT prospered. Colonel Tommy Wallis remained its first managing director until 1989, serving four chairmen with great success. Those following Jim Philipps were Tom Blackwell until 1973 and then Jocelyn Hambro and finally the founder himself after Johnny Henderson retired from Cazenoves in 1982. Profits of about £100,000 at the start of the 1970s had grown towards a million by the end of the decade and, as is always the case, could have been a good deal higher in the short term if prize money was not regarded as part of the company's raison d'être rather than just another expense.

From 1964 the Heath itself had been run by Robert Fellowes in succession as Agent only to Colonel Nicol Gray, who had doubled as Clerk of the Course as well in the Marriott tradition until 1962. In the office of Clerk he was succeeded on a temporary basis by the retired senior handicapper Geoffrey Freer until Pat Firth took over in 1964, and since then the jobs have never been combined. In 1974 Captain Nick Lees followed him on the racecourses and the chapter ends on a more optimistic note than it began with the Heath and racecourses all in decent order and the town generally recovering well from the sorry days of the lads' strike only five years before. By 1980 the two yards that were to dominate Newmarket until the Godolphin operation appointed a private trainer in 1995 had come to the fore with Henry Cecil (Fig. 114) in second place on the national list and Michael Stoute (Fig. 115) in fourth. Also in the top ten were Robert Armstrong, having succeeded Sam at St Gatien, and Bruce Hobbs at the Palace House stables. Tom Jones, having largely abandoned Jumping, was training the early purchases of three of the four Maktoum brothers at Green Lodge on The Severals in the days before they appointed private trainers, a decision that would have immense significance when that policy started in the 1990s.

Easily the most successful jockey after Gordon Richards switched to training following an accident at Sandown in 1954 was Lester Piggott (Fig. 118). Son of a trainer with a Grand National winner to his credit and grandson of a jockey who rode three, Piggott for long lived in the town as its most famous citizen since Fred Archer. He moved there on his marriage in 1960 having ridden for the town's leading yard at Warren Place from 1955. Champion jockey on eleven occasions, he took Frank Buckle's crown as the most successful Classic jockey of all by the time he finally retired in 1995 with thirty victories, and even Gordon only narrowly held on to his as the rider of most winners in this country. In 1966 he caused general consternation by insisting on riding the Oaks favourite, Valoris, to victory for Vincent O'Brien rather than the Murless-trained Varinia, who came third. After months during which hot air had been widely circulated, the breach became permanent when Piggott (again correctly) opted for Pieces of Eight over Hill Rise in the Champion Stakes. While he lost the ride on Royal Palace as a consequence, those on Sir Ivor and Nijinsky for O'Brien yet again were more than ample compensation. His only Newmarket rival was Doug Smith, who was champion for five seasons in the late 1950s before taking up training, initially with considerable success, in 1968. Indeed, after Sir Jack Jarvis died suddenly that December Smith took on a second yard in Park Lodge where he trained the Rosebery horses for three years and won him an Oaks in 1969 with Sleeping Partner. However it was not an arrangement fated to last, and after the 1971 season the horses crossed the road to join Bruce Hobbs at Palace House until their owner died in 1974.

◆◆◆◆

Fig. 115

Sir Michael Stoute

Fig. 116

Saeed bin Suroor

Fig. 117

John Gosden

Current Newmarket trainers who have taken the championship

With the death of Sir Henry Cecil in 2013, there are only three trainers based in Newmarket who have headed the national list – Sir Michael Stoute on nine occasions, Saeed bin Suroor four times, and John Gosden in 2012. Only the latter had a British racing background, his father having trained at Lewes where he turned out Aggressor to beat Petite Etoile in a famous running of the King George in 1960. Bin Suroor is from Dubai, and has for two decades been the principal trainer to the Godolphin operation while Sir Michael hailed from Barbados via Yorkshire before setting up in a small Newmarket yard in 1972. His speedy success saw him ensconced in Beech Hurst on the Bury Road for 1973 and it remains his base, now much extended, while his fifteen classics is the highest number for a current British trainer. Bin Suroor is not far behind him on twelve, while Golden Horn recently brought the Gosden figure to eight.

Fig. 118

Fig. 119

Lester Piggott

Probably the racing figure with the highest public profile in the last half century, the notoriously taciturn Piggott's prominence was certainly not the result of courting publicity. Bred to the sport for generations on both sides of his family he was a star from 1950, when, while still an apprentice aged 15, he rode 52 winners. He remained a winner due to his uncanny skill in the saddle until he finally retired in 1994. Champion jockey from 1964 to 1971 and on three other occasions, despite his exceptional height and consequent problems with his weight, his talent and his problems were both reminiscent of Fred Archer (Fig. 75). After retiring to train in 1984 his very public problems with the Inland Revenue saw a return to the saddle from 1991 to 1994 which added another classic winner to the 29 he had amassed first time round, to overtake Frank Buckle's (Fig. 57) previous record of 27. His total of nine Derbys has never been approached– nobody else has exceeded six. Despite his weight, Piggott's 4,493 winners in this country almost overtook the 4,870 of Sir Gordon Richards and he won many more abroad.

Steve Cauthen

Champion jockey in the years 1984, 1985 and 1987 when riding for Warren Place, Cauthen had earlier been brought over by Robert Sangster and promptly won the 1979 2000 Guineas. He transferred from his native USA on the back of a Triple Crown series on Affirmed, but took a little time to adjust his style to British racecourses. When he did his judgement of pace was recognised as masterly and he rode here with great success until increasing weight problems brought things to an end in 1992. His must have been the finest talent to be imported from America since Danny Maher in the early years of the twentieth century and he was equally as popular as his predecessor with those for whom he rode, both personally and professionally. Like Piggott, he came of a racing family.

The Jockey Club had faced many difficulties, with distinctly varied levels of success in solving them, since the war. While the prosperity of RHT did underpin its efforts as both governing and regulatory authority, some fairly obvious conflicts of interest were beginning to arise between its various roles. The fact that, post-Wigg, they never caused anything much beyond some minor sniping can be taken as a compliment to the membership's justifiable reputation for trying to do its best for the sport on an impartial basis. However, duties and responsibilities had become so broad that wiser heads within that membership seem to have grasped by 1980 that things could not continue indefinitely without more pairs of hands, from more varied backgrounds, on the levers of power. Clearly the choice would lie between altering either the Club's roles or its whole approach to electing members, or a combination of the two.

Attention from 1976 to 1980 tended to be dominated by the events surrounding Lord Rothschild's Royal Commission on Gambling. The Club accepted from the outset that it would be fruitless to press for a Tote monopoly allied to a full-scale statutory authority to run racing on the lines originally proposed by another important report from Sir Henry Benson in the 1960s. However, the clamour arising from several of the major racing organisations for a representative organisation with not only the functions of the Club but those also of the Levy Board included, seems to have rather muddied the waters. Matters were made a good deal worse in 1977 when the Economist Intelligence Unit, which had been commissioned jointly by the Club, the Tote, the Racehorse Owners' Association and the Racecourse Association, as well as the pressure group BRIC, to universal horror, reported in an unambiguously unhelpful way. That racing's case for much increased support from betting was poorly made on this occasion must presumably have been a factor in that disaster. Pained reactions within the Club included Lord Willoughby de Broke, always a strident Tote monopolist, being moved to observe at a meeting to discuss the report that 'the authors do not even know which end the oats go in at' and Lord Howard de Walden successfully defused the considerable potential for acrimony by remarking 'I obviously stand rebuked' by the outcome. Nobody seemed in the least inclined to rebuke him after such a generous concession to wounded pride.

After lengthy cogitation the Commission itself reported in more helpful terms than expected in July 1978. However, its key recommendation in support of a central authority which included the Levy Board was ultimately rejected by the government, with the upshot that what resulted was not really an authority at all. Instead, what eventually was created was a much better-constructed talking shop in the Horseracing Advisory Council than earlier groups with such unattractive acronyms as RILC and BRIC.

In his valediction as Senior Steward in June 1979 Lord Howard was moved to advise the Club to be 'magnanimous in victory' by which he meant that it should try to put together something that worked, rather than treat events as a licence to continue much as before. Given the demands of all this activity on the Stewards it was surely as well that the Heath and the Club's other racecourses were in good hands. Indeed, one begins to see the future in the recognition of the need to rely more on high quality professional management both at RHT and racecourse level in addition to that so long provided to the Stewards in their wider political and regulatory roles by Weatherbys.

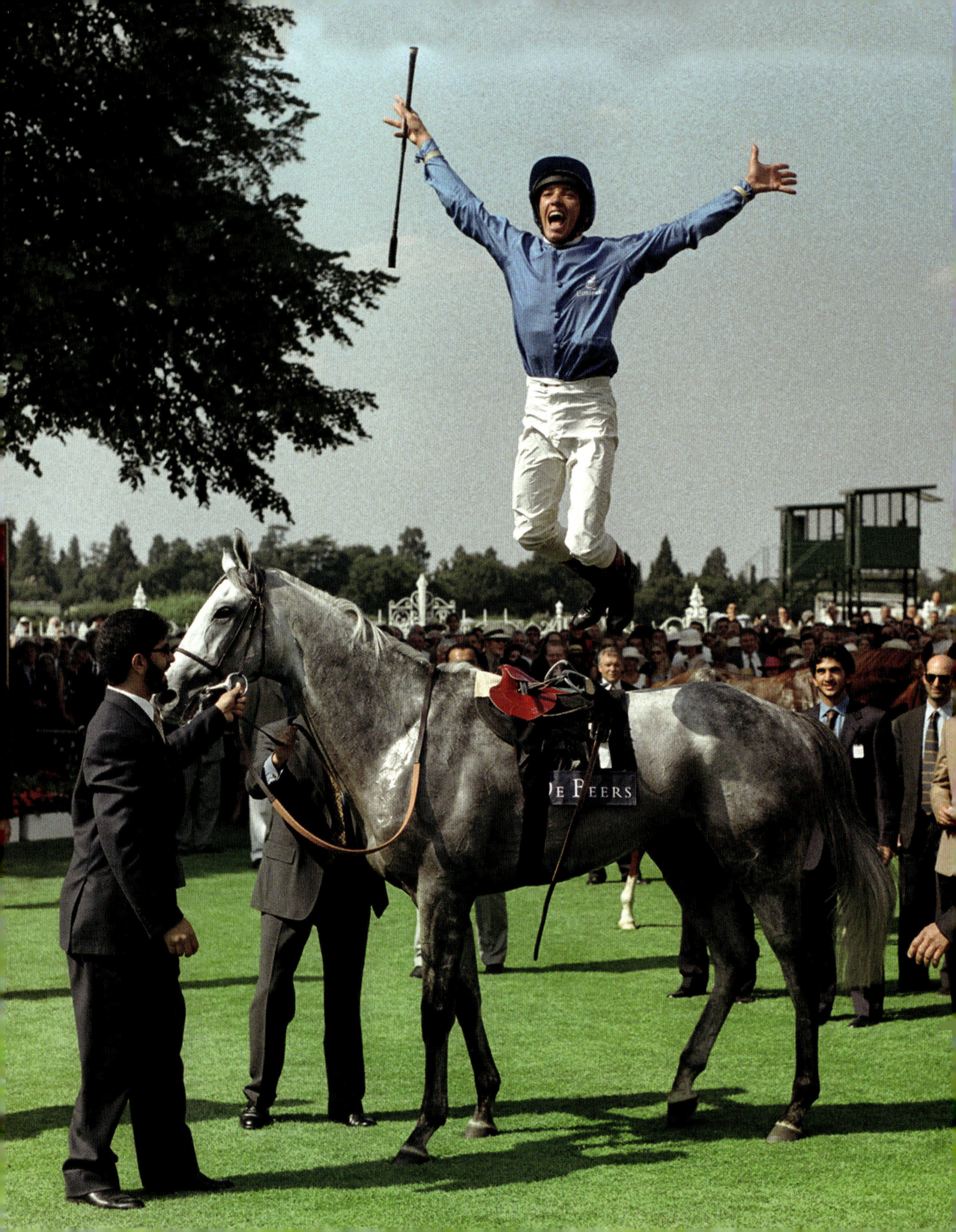
De Beers

Chapter 10 (Since 1980)

Progress Based on Foreign Investment Despite Recurrent Funding Crises

Writing the final chapter on any subject with such a long history and a continuing future poses some obvious problems. First, it is easier to be honest but unkind about people who have long since disappeared from the scene; secondly, and far more important, is the fact that the story of this phase of the Heath is not a history at all but a comment on current affairs. Therefore it is the job of someone in the future to give the period since 1980 any historical context; all we can do here is to note the events which seem important and try to view these in the context of the passage of time since James I settled on an insignificant market town in East Anglia as the place for his rural entertainment.

Daylami (1994) by Doyoun out of Daltawa after winning the 1999 King George VI and Queen Elizabeth Stakes at Ascot. Owned by Godolphin, trained by Saeed Bin Suroor and ridden by an exuberant Frankie Dettori, he seems splendidly imperturbable. Bred by the Aga Khan this subject seems an appropriate way to mark the trend of events covered by this chapter, Fig. 124.

All of the previous chapters describe surprisingly clear-cut periods of advance or decline on the Heath, usually followed by sharp reversals. Since 1980 various factors, frequently relating to its baleful funding mechanism, have given racing a fairly bumpy ride; however, the period has so far been one of marked overall advance for Newmarket which, hopefully, has further to go. The effect of the prodigious investment of foreign capital is very obvious; while the High Street and the little stables in the town clearly have their problems, the relatively depressed centre is surrounded by splendid new or modernised yards and studs of a grandeur that would amaze their previous owners. The whole is enveloped by a Heath which it seems hard to imagine can be very much improved as a place to rear and train horses, even if questions are sometimes raised over the effect of years of irrigation on the racecourse sward.

Most of its old institutions, such as Tattersalls and the principal veterinary practices, have clearly strengthened since 1980, both in absolute terms and relative to the rest

Fig. 120

Peregrine, 12th Duke of Devonshire (b. 1944)

In the period when, as its Senior Steward, the duke persuaded the Club to transfer many of its powers (in 1993) and then chaired the British Horseracing Board during its formative years, he was formally the Marquess of Hartington and almost universally known as Stoker. His achievement in conducting this complex operation so smoothly, so rounding off years of fitful progress in that general direction, will rightly be remembered long after the efforts of his contemporaries are forgotten. Elected in 1980, he became Senior Steward in 1989 and left office in 1993 when moving on to chair the BHB. This he steered through what seemed fairly unruffled waters until 1996, after which inherent problems in its structure became a great deal more apparent under his successors. Unlike his father, who was a conspicuously lucky owner with the great Park Top and several other good horses trained for him at Newmarket among a small string, the new duke has been by no means so fortunate.

of the country. In addition, newcomers like the British Racing School (BRS) and the National Horseracing Museum (NHRM) emphasise Newmarket's claim to be the headquarters of the sport. Meanwhile, its oldest institution, the Jockey Club, is now in a dramatically different position to that of even twenty years ago. At first sight, the revolutionary alterations to its role seem to represent retreat on all fronts; however, things are much more complex than that – with a mixture of gains and losses which, so far as they directly concern Newmarket, represent no discernable downside at all and a marked upside in the concentration of resources both human and financial on the place.

◆◆◆◆

As explained in the preceding chapter, the Club had for some years been looking for the best route to achieve a constructive sharing of the administration of the sport with more people and institutions. With steadily fewer of its younger members able to devote the necessary time to overseeing its many fields, allied to the times themselves being ill-attuned to autocracy, the need for a redefinition of its role was becoming increasingly obvious. As a result the 1980s saw slow but real progress in pursuit of change, represented initially by the 'magnanimity' sought by Lord Howard de Walden when he retired as a Steward in 1979 subsequently to take up his role as first Chairman of the NHRM.

Things did not get off too well under the first chairman of the Horseracing Advisory Council (HAC) designed to introduce democracy, Phil Bull; despite his many talents he was a square peg in a painfully round hole, and he had the commendably good sense to resign within months. Thereafter, the organisation made steady if unremarkable progress first under Major-General Bernard Penfold and by the end of the decade, under Sir Nevil Macready, it was ready to play a full part in the creation of the British Horseracing Board (BHB). This new body was designed to deliver a genuinely democratic form of racing administration with its eleven-member Board having only four Jockey Club nominees. While the Club retained responsibility for discipline and the regulation of licensed people, the other central functions such as the fixture list, race planning, finance and marketing were transferred to the Board, along with Westminster politics in general and relations with the Levy Board in particular.

Even after such a seismic shift in responsibilities things actually changed more slowly for some years than might have been expected. The BHB inherited its principal creator, Lord Hartington (Fig. 120), as its first chairman with your joint author still in charge of fixtures and race planning until 2000, plus almost all the Jockey Club's non-regulatory staff. Accordingly, the transfer of power did not create too many waves in the short or medium term.

The difficult role of running the Jockey Club's activities on a professional basis during the years prior to 1993 fell to Christopher Haynes. It is a tribute to his skills as a manager that the various transfers of 1993 passed off so well and in the end it all resulted in him having worked himself out of a job when the BHB appointed Tristram Ricketts as its first chief executive.

The staff that were transferred to the BHB, as well as those retained by the Club, had historically been employed by Weatherbys to meet its commitments under the arrangements that had existed since the Cooper Brothers' changes of the 1950s. However, a rival firm in Peat Marwick & Co. came to broadly similar conclusions in the 1980s and its report eventually resulted in Weatherbys restricting its direct racing involvement to running the sport's civil service, including everything relating to its ownership of the General Stud Book, just as it does today. Weatherbys' staff, working in London as opposed to Wellingborough, had been transferred to the Club's payroll a few years before the BHB appeared on the scene in the same way that things had happened in Newmarket thirty years earlier. Those acquired by the Club from Weatherbys included Christopher Foster who had succeeded as Keeper of the Match Book on the death of the last Weatherby, Simon, to hold that ancient office, from 1983; he is still handing out sage advice to the Stewards over thirty years later. It was also lucky enough to get Paul Greeves, who eventually became the BHB's Director of Racing and, more briefly, Johnny Weatherby. Both have now returned to their old haunts in Wellingborough, the latter as Chairman and now also as the Queen's Representative at Ascot.

The Weatherbys business has changed a great deal over the years since its close ties with the Jockey Club largely lapsed, after more than two centuries, with the arrival of the BHB. Apart from that major event, the development of a banking arm for the business by Roger Weatherby has radically altered its balance. Unlike his brother he had not been directly involved in racing administration but that changed when he was elected to the Club in 2007, becoming a Steward in 2012 and succeeding as Senior Steward in 2014. Although several members of the family have been elected down the years this has usually been after retirement and such an appointment would have been inconceivable before the advent of BHB altered the balance of its activities.

Over a decade later after the formation of the BHB, the Club decided to relinquish the last of its seats, and so any direct involvement as of right derived from them in the BHB's successor, the British Horseracing Authority (BHA). It also agreed to transfer to this new body its responsibility for regulating the sport. As a result its position in relation to everything at Newmarket and all its other racecourses changed completely. Until then it had been painfully conscious, and accordingly careful, over any emphasis on its ownership of Racecourse Holdings Trust (RHT). After all, the potential conflicts of interest were fairly dramatic over fixtures, the award of Pattern status, and even such things as the arraigning of its own racecourses on apparently minor charges such as mislaying an ambulance or putting out the course markers in the wrong place. Once these became the responsibility of the BHA the Club could happily rename RHT as Jockey Club Racecourses (JCR), a process begun years before in the less contentious case of the Newmarket Estates & Property Company (NEPCO) becoming Jockey Club Estates (JCE). The Jockey Club's whole approach to running the empire could then become much more commercial and indeed, did, initially under Julian Richmond-Watson and then under Nicholas Wrigley as Senior Steward, so that from 2007 instead of the racecourses and other assets being no more than a corner of the Club's overall wood they became the wood itself. The Club and JCR also seem to have found just the man to achieve such ends in Simon Bazalgette, who fortunately combines a proper appreciation of the peculiar demands of a post of this sort in a complex sport with the necessary business skills.

◆◆◆◆

The timeliness of a concentration on assets such as its racecourses, which in the case of Newmarket was almost a reversion to the Club's eighteenth-century role, is emphasised by the increase in their number and importance. Beginning in 1980 with six, of which only Newmarket and Cheltenham could by any standard be called major tracks, the number had risen steadily to fourteen including Aintree, Epsom, Haydock and Sandown, also firmly in the top flight. Indeed, there are fifteen if Newmarket is treated as being two courses. Haydock had been bought for £427,000 in 1980 and Aintree added in 1983 for £3.4 million after a textbook exercise in negotiation by Johnny Henderson.

What is to date the last major acquisition came in April 1994 after the Levy Board under Sir John Sparrow wisely decided that his board was not a suitable vehicle for running racecourses and, as a consequence, put its subsidiary United Racecourses (UR), the owner of Epsom, Sandown and Kempton, on the market. By now Mr Henderson had been succeeded in the racecourse company chair by Captain Miles Gosling, and Colonel Tommy Wallis had retired as Chief Executive in favour of David Hillyard, both the latter being elected members on retirement by a grateful Club. This time the cost came to a rather more significant £30.5 million, and the deal was hedged with assorted restrictions over sales of land and a willingness to guarantee the continuance of racing at the loss-making Epsom, leaving RHT as the obvious candidate for the Levy Board to choose from its various suitors.

Ten years before this purchase, two prescient members had debated the merits of acquiring UR at a Club meeting. Lord Weinstock's opinion that a purchase would be beneficial was agreed by Henderson whose enthusiasm was tempered by the view that RHT's strengths would be best used by waiting for vendors to come to it, as was the usual policy. Both were fully vindicated by events and racing has surely much to gain from the fact that under its Royal Charter the Club is able to take the long view in such matters. Providing it does not get complacent, it is hard to spot the downside. Hopefully this will not happen as it concentrates on running its empire constructively using professional managers rather than relying too heavily on busy amateurs, however competent, as it did for so long. The emphasis the Club now places on helping racing's recurrent funding crises with relatively generous prize money is a good example of what such arrangements can offer the sport. It does not take much of a head for figures to imagine the cost of staging some of the crucial cards on the Rowley Mile in front of only 3,000 or 4,000 payers, but such losses represent a form of dividend paid to the sport which could not be justified on a short-term commercial basis.

Although JCR is much the larger of the two racecourse groups in terms of prize money and attendance, the other, now entitled ARC and formed from the Arena and Northern groups, collected initially by the Muddle family and Sir Stanley Clarke respectively, has more fixtures and 14 active courses (plus Folkestone and Hereford which, at least for the moment, are closed). The extra fixtures largely

Chapter 10 (Since 1980)

arise from the group's ownership of three of the four all-weather tracks (AWTs). JCR has also recently recruited Ian Renton, following his successful reign at Arena, to replace Edward Gillespie in charge at Cheltenham. This is the most significant job that JCR has at racecourse level and it will be hard for him to match the extraordinary achievements of his predecessor in developing the Cheltenham Festival meeting into a genuine rival to Royal Ascot. However, with the course's profitability amply justifying the completion of the overall scheme for the stands, he will have every opportunity under the chairmanship of Lord Vestey's successor Robert Waley-Cohen.

Since 1994 the Jockey Club has added three smaller racecourses in Huntingdon, Carlisle and Exeter as well as the public gallops at Lambourn and, in 2008, the then heavily loss-making National Stud from a disillusioned Levy Board. Collectively such acquisitions have utilised only a small part of its overall cash flow, almost all of which had been devoted to improving the racecourses at Newmarket, Cheltenham, Aintree, Epsom, Sandown and Haydock, as well as reducing debts relating to the UR courses and putting in the AWT at Kempton. Inevitably, not everything has been sweetness and light and this co-author remembers feeling rather inclined to hide under the table at Levy Board meetings when RHT developments were on the agenda. One scheme after another came in delayed and over budget and the other Board members looked as if they thought that they were entitled to an explanation. Fortunately such problems have disappeared in recent times.

◆◆◆◆

The details of the four major phases of redeveloping the courses at Newmarket since the Duke of Norfolk's remarkable efforts in 1968 are set out in Part 2. Among them only the principal one, the construction of the Millennium Stand on the Rowley Mile in 2000, fell into the category that could have made anyone representing the Club want to be somewhere else during Levy Board discussions. In that case the initial problems certainly cost a great deal of money to rectify. However, the result is a stand that now does its job well even if the construction of something so much taller than the buildings erected in the 1980s is aesthetically questionable, surrounded as it is by a sea of grass. The original scheme would have seen the work completed in harmony with the 1987 buildings but this was rejected as being too expensive.

After Pat Firth's reign as Clerk of the Course his successor, Captain Nick Lees, was in charge throughout the first two phases of improving the Rowley Mile Stands. This period saw the racecourse office moved from the Rooms up to Westfield House when JCE, under the chairmanship of Captain John Macdonald-Buchanan, was finally separated from the racing operation, even down to the ground staff on the Heath. When Captain Lees was succeeded for the 2001 season by the present Clerk, Mike Prosser, he had been in charge for some twenty-five years. At that point the Clerk's responsibilities were split from those of the chief executive with the appointment of managing directors Lisa Hancock, Tommy Wallis's son Stephen and the current Director Amy Starkey following in that role in quick succession. The former Senior Steward, Julian Richmond-Watson, is now in the racecourse chair and among his several predecessors Peter Player also contributed a good deal to other institutions in the town, having also been chairman of the National Stud for the Levy Board (before it ran into real trouble one should add) and the BRS.

Robert Fellowes was succeeded in 1992 as Agent, after nearly thirty years in office, by Peter Amos who in turn moved on, in his case to Darley, after another successful reign this time linked to the chairmanship of George Paul. The present incumbent, William Gittus, adds to his other qualifications for this demanding job the fact that in the nineteenth century his ancestors leased the Limekilns and Waterhall from the Chippenham Estate to run their sheep during part of the year. In 1890 the sheep were not removed as expected in March and the then Mr Gittus told the Agent, Mr Gardner, this was in furtherance of a rent dispute with the landowner and not aimed at the Club. His descendant might not see the joke if someone repeated the performance today on his precious sward.

Apart from the decision to set up the BHB in 1993, perhaps the most crucial one taken in the context of the Club since 1980 was made by Christopher Spence as Senior Steward in 2003. This was to relinquish the regulation of the sport gracefully over a number of years rather than to take a stand on the Jockey Club's right under the 1993 arrangements to retain things as they were. A decision was necessary due to the furore following assorted trials of racing's morality by unsympathetic television programmes. These had begun by delving into the behaviour of various trainers, who appeared to have been remarkably imprudent over their choice of confidants, and moved on to question the skill with which regulation in general had been conducted by the Club. It would not have been too difficult to fend off such attacks, but the Stewards were persuaded that to do so would not have been in the sport's best interests.

By ceding regulation as part of the exercise of creating the BHA without any unseemly squabbling, the Club could embark on its new role with a great deal more goodwill all round. As in the first days of the BHB, the fact that so many of the people involved were transferred from the Jockey Club has led to a surprisingly uneventful, and indeed, largely successful, transition for regulation. Apart from something of a hiccup over the use of the whip in 2011 it would be a pretty demanding Club member who thought that the BHA had betrayed the 250-year-old regulatory legacy it had inherited, going right back to the eviction of George Prentice.

◆◆◆◆

Fortunately, it falls outside the scope of a book on Newmarket and its principal landowner to go into too much detail about the broader impact on the sport of the transfer of power from the Jockey Club to the BHB and BHA. That said, such events are of crucial importance to the long-term health of the sport and so in turn to the Heath. While the BHA has undoubtedly made an excellent start in preserving and developing the Club's dominant regulatory position, both it and the BHB in combination, have, however, had rather less success in maintaining the Club's near monopoly of administrative control due to the difficulty of aligning the collective interests of racecourses with those of the other participants in the sport.

If ultimately unsuccessful, Sir Tristram Ricketts' stalwart efforts to bridge the yawning gaps between racecourses and the rest of those directly involved, and between racing and the betting industry were admirable. As Chief Executive of the Levy Board for two decades up to 1993, and then at the BHB until returning to Grosvenor Gardens in 2005, such efforts were unstinting. His premature death while still in office in 2007 was a sad day for the sport he had served for so long under four chairmen from Sir Desmond Plummer (later Lord Plummer) to Rob Hughes at the Levy Board with a dozen years from 1993 under three more masters at the BHB thrown in for good measure.

The key event in which Sir Tristram played a part, and which finally wrecked the BHB's initiative under Peter Savill aimed at replacing the Levy System with a much larger data rights payment, came in the European Court of Justice in Strasbourg in 2004. This scheme would have provided the BHB with a data rights payment of about 80 per cent of an annual sum, expected at the time to be around £130 million, from the betting industry, with only the balance going direct to racecourses for their general picture rights. However, on top of that small slice the racecourses could have expected a further substantial sum when the contract for the sale of their pictures to the betting shops via Satellite Information Services came up for renewal later in the year. Some racecourses were so aggrieved at what they saw as a grossly unfair division of the spoils that they launched an action but subsequently withdrew from the case. Then a more potent threat to the new order emerged in the form of major bookmakers William Hill which challenged the whole data rights concept rather than merely its equitable division. Despite defeat in the courts in this country – both at first instance and also on appeal – they pressed on, with the result that the European Court of Justice overruled the English judgement and effectively scuppered the whole scheme.

The government had previously asked racing to agree a levy replacement with the betting industry, but then showed no enthusiasm for a major quarrel with Europe over the issue of data rights. It is one of the great imponderables of racing's recent history what would have happened had the government shown any enthusiasm for a challenge to the European Court's judgement. However, there was none, and things proved little different over racing's attempt to acquire the Tote but recently the introduction of measures to prevent the avoidance of tax and Levy payments by the betting industry via the simple expedient of removing their non-cash business off-shore seems to indicate a shift in the wind. In the earlier cases the issue that has caused racing so much grief has been the government's fear of European State Aid provisions and the potential infringement of competition legislation. On both issues very real doubt existed as to whether state aid was in fact an insuperable block but the problem has yet to be challenged and at least over the Tote never will be, although it is reasonable to hope that the Levy loophole can be addressed now that the government has blocked the comparable leakage of tax.

While the 2004 reversal of the earlier English judgement was a disaster for racing's funding, it had been preceded four years before, in the early days of the long data rights campaign, by an opportunity which might have been turned to comparable advantage but which was never pursued. In 2000 the betting industry applied to the government to have betting tax set at a higher rate based on gross margins, in place of one calculated on turnover, which would enable it to cancel tax deductions from punters and so greatly expand turnover while checking the drift offshore. In launching its application a very quiet approach was made to racing to elicit support for the switch with assorted nods and winks over the generosity of the Levy schemes that would be agreed in return for such support should the application succeed. The initial view on the racing side was that the government was most unlikely to grant the change with or without racing's support. A debate then ensued in the BHB between those who felt there was little to lose in joining the campaign (and much to gain should it succeed) and those almost ideologically opposed to a Levy based on margins and, in any case, having more faith in a separate data rights route rendering the whole discussion irrelevant. By the slimmest majority, a proper exploration of what might be on offer in return for support was rejected and the betting industry scored a triumph in getting a switch to gross margin tax with no help from, and so no obligation to, racing. Ironically, once the tax was rebased, the Levy could realistically only fall into line so what may have been a great opportunity was missed for fear of a change that happened anyway in pursuit of a scheme which, however well-designed, failed to bring home the bacon. Newmarket and the rest of racing live with the consequences to this day.

The negotiation which eventually ended in the data rights calamity was conducted as skilfully as anything managed on behalf of RHT by Johnny Henderson by Peter Savill but sadly the endeavour met a brick wall in Strasbourg. With the BHB then in need of cooperation all round what appeared on the scene instead was the Office of Fair Trading (OFT), at the bidding of some racecourses, to investigate complaints over centralised control of the fixture list and similar matters such as control of the Pattern and the racing programmes in general. Eventually the OFT sided with racecourses over fixtures and with the racing authorities over almost everything else. Even to this day

Fig. 121

Sheikh Mohammed bin Rashid al Maktoum

Fig. 122

Prince Khalid bin Abdullah

Current Arab owners who have taken the championship

Since 1985, when Sheikh Mohammed from Dubai first topped the list, to 2013 he, his brother Sheikh Hamdan, his wife Princess Haya or their Godolphin operation have only lost the championship on five occasions. On three of these the leading owner was Prince Khalid bin Abdullah from Saudi Arabia. While not all their horses are trained or bred in Newmarket, the majority of their triumphs are scored by horses trained on the Heath, and many have been bred at Dalham Hall or Banstead Manor in Cheveley. The implications for the town of the vast scale of their investment can be seen all around the neighbourhood, and are the basis of its present prosperity.

no alternative funding scheme has been agreed to allow the closure of the Levy Board and until recently the BHA expressed little interest in its broader inheritance from the BHB. No doubt finding the answer to the funding issues would eventually allow a stronger central authority to be resurrected, although it is most unlikely (and probably undesirable) that this authority should apply to the same extent as that which existed before 1993. Fortunately to a degree such political issues pass Newmarket by. It is hard to imagine that even the most trenchant prize money warriors would suggest it would be fair to other claims on Newmarket's resources to devote a much larger slice of its pie to keeping them happy.

The saga of the sale of the Tote, originally the inspiration of Lord Hamilton of Dalzell (Fig. 96) to benefit the sport when Senior Steward in the 1920s, eventually produced a result which nobody could have predicted when it was sold to a major bookmaker. After its near-collapse in the 1970s the Tote had recovered slowly under Lord Wyatt and then rather more speedily with Peter Jones at the helm. As a result of their efforts there was something material to sell and in 2011, after more than twenty years of dithering, sold it was. Sadly, its own bid having been rejected, racing will now get barely half the net proceeds of sale on restricted terms instead of the Tote itself, as it had so long been expecting. The eventual receipts will be channelled to a charitable foundation, which will get the money to support broadly charitable projects within the sport.

◆◆◆◆

Two important initiatives that have had probably more to offer at Newmarket than anywhere else have been the concerts staged after minor evening meetings on the July Course and the introduction of wide screens opposite the stands, originally sponsored by the Tote. The latter have provided a brilliant rebuttal to all the jokes down the years over the folly of standing in Suffolk to watch races in Cambridgeshire and the former have often had a magical effect on attendances even if they fail to delight the Heath's more traditional supporters. As the traditionalists are not usually much in evidence to see the rather moderate racing on offer during such meetings, and can hardly fail to appreciate the result of the proceeds being used to improve the quality of the sport on the Rowley Mile, these initiatives have been an all-round bonus at Newmarket.

Chapter 10 (Since 1980)

Fig. 123

Frankel (2008) by Galileo out of Kind by Charles Church

If Flying Childers (Figs. 10 and 32) was the first great horse to be trained on the Heath, at this juncture Frankel is his latest rival. In fact such supposed rivalry is meaningless. All one can say of such horses is that they were so good they entirely dominated their contemporaries, which seems at least as good a definition of greatness in horses as any other. Between these two paragons very few others– like Eclipse, Highflyer, St Simon and Ormonde – can have claims advanced for them, and it would be impossible to name a British candidate without a win on the Heath. Frankel's career spanned the years 2010 to 2012, during which his fourteen races all resulted in victory, usually by huge margins and, apart from his first race, his dominance was so obvious he was always odds on. If there is any hint of a blot on his escutcheon, it is that he was never tested over the classic distance of 1½ miles, but neither his pedigree nor performance suggests it would have made much difference if he had run in the King George. Owned by Prince Khalid bin Abdullah and ridden by the stable jockey Tom Queally, he represented Sir Henry Cecil's (Fig. 114) swansong and it must be said it was quite a song. The outcome of his days as a stallion at Banstead will be one of the more fascinating aspects of the next few years.

The fact that Newmarket has thrived over the past thirty years has nothing to do with politicking. Mostly it is attributable to the extraordinary impact of the investments made in the area led by the Maktoum family, in particular by Sheikh Mohammed bin Rashid al Maktoum from Dubai (Fig. 121), and by Prince Khalid bin Abdullah of Saudi Arabia (Fig. 122). It is a remarkable thing that, from the first year in which the Maktoum family took the owners' championship, in 1985, they retained it for the rest of the century and have chalked up another eight triumphs since then. Along with Prince Khalid's three years, their twenty-three has left only two seasons in the last twenty-eight when the Gulf has failed to score and in those years the Aga Khan and Christopher Tsui have topped the list with largely Irish-trained stock. Quite what the status of the Heath would now be if the original mission to the Gulf by Colonel Dick Warden and Humphrey Cottrill had not sparked an initial interest is not something the town's supporters would be wise to contemplate when you consider the last native to top the list was Robert Sangster in 1984. Nor need they, as these have developed into family commitments rather than individual ones, as seems also to be the case with the Al Thani family from Qatar.

Naturally, the principal trainers of these mammoth strings will usually take their separate championship. As they have tended to be based in the town it is not surprising that Newmarket has scored more regularly in the thirty-three years from 1981 than since such records began in the late nineteenth century. If you take the ninety-eight years covered by Chapters 8 to 10, the national trainers' championships break down as follows:

	Total	Newmarket	Other UK	Abroad
1915 to 1945	31	12	19	0
1946 to 1980	35	19	10	6
1981 to 2013	33	22	7	4
Total	**97**	**53**	**36**	**10**

If such details were calculable for earlier periods it is most unlikely that the town would have been so consistently triumphant since the days of Richard Vernon and the Prince of Wales in the eighteenth century. The initial monopoly of the local leadership since 1980 by Sir Henry Cecil and Sir Michael Stoute was only broken by Saeed bin Suroor's first triumph in 1996 and, John Gosden in 2012 is the first to score from outside that magic circle since Sir Noel Murless in 1973. Who can tell what is round the corner but a tour of Freemason Lodge, Clarehaven or indeed, Dalham and Banstead Manor hardly suggests that any dramatic change in the town's status is imminent despite the universally lamented death of Sir Henry Cecil soon after Frankel (Fig. 123) retired to Banstead having provided such a fitting finale to a great career.

Unlike owners and trainers, the local jockeys cannot claim the same sort of dominance as they managed in the nineteenth century. For over fifty years the sequences of Nat Flatman, George Fordham and Fred Archer virtually farmed the jockey's championship. However, since the heyday of Lester Piggott the local talent has lost the leadership more often than it has won it, despite the skills of Frankie Dettori (Fig. 124), Ryan Moore (Fig. 126) and Steve Cauthen (Fig. 119).

The Heath has clearly benefited both with respect to trainers and jockeys from the sad decline in Italian racing following the glory days of Frederico Tesio, owner, breeder and trainer of great champions like Nearco and Ribot. Not only Dettori but also the trainers Luca Cumani and Marco Botti come from Italian racing dynasties while Andrea Atzeni looks like becoming the heir to Dettori. Indeed Cumani is not only a successful trainer but breeds quite extensively at Fittocks Stud on the edge of the town in conjunction with his wife Sara and trains some of the produce in the Tesio tradition. Nowadays that is a rare combination in this country on any scale.

Apart from the National Stud the only large breeders in the area in addition to the Middle Eastern interests are

Chapter 10 (Since 1980)

Fig. 124	Fig. 125	Fig. 126
Frankie Dettori	Kieren Fallon	Ryan Moore

The most successful Newmarket-based jockeys of recent years still riding.

It seems that a real racing background is more important in identifying potential champion jockeys than trainers. Of the three jockeys covered by the heading of this piece (Frankie Dettori, Kieren Fallon and Ryan Moore), only Fallon is without an impeccable racing pedigree, while Lester Piggott and Steve Cauthen also qualify. On the other hand, only John Gosden – among five comparable Newmarket trainers – has that background. Apart from these three riders only Seb Saunders, who dead-heated in 2007 and Michael Roberts (who won in 1992) have scored largely when riding for local yards since Steve Cauthen in 1987. Dettori and Moore have so far scored three times and Fallon no less than six, beginning when he came south to ride for Warren Place. The latter also leads in terms of classic winners, with sixteen while Dettori has fifteen on the board from with the much younger Moore on seven.

165

the Thompson family at Cheveley Park and Miss Kirsten Rausing out at Lanwades. Both stand between five and ten stallions and sell many of their colts each year while racing the numerous fillies essential in order to maintain the high-class broodmare bands needed to operate successfully on that scale. Apart from the two large stallion studs mentioned the Hascombe and Valiant studs of Anthony Oppenheimer have produced numerous good animals for him or his father, including the outstanding Derby winner, Golden Horn. Like Patricia Thompson, Kirsten Rausing and all the major Arab owner-breeders, the Oppenheimers were elected to the Jockey Club.

◆◆◆◆

Apart from the individual talents of its trainers and jockeys and the collective ones of its large workforce in stables and studs, Newmarket's claim to be the headquarters of the sport is grounded in its institutions. If the Jockey Club has had a bumpy ride at times it nowadays seems in remarkably good order for what some would see as a relic of the eighteenth century. Meanwhile, almost all the other institutions on which the town's racing future is based appear in rude health. Tattersalls' reputation for probity stands as high or higher than any rival firm around the world in its difficult field. In 1980 it sold 2,931 horses for a grand total of £32.7 million. By 2013 the comparable figures were 4,694 and £261 million, which is a major increase despite the pound losing some two-thirds of its relative value over that period.

As with the major yards and studs, a visit to the bases of Rossdales and the former Greenwood Ellis practice at the new veterinary hospital opposite the National Stud shows what major advances have been made in the veterinary field. Meanwhile, the facilities out at Kentford of the Animal Health Trust put its old home at Balaton Lodge in the shade. The principal national training facility for stable staff at the British Racing School (BRS), until very recently under the tutelage of its long term organiser Rory MacDonald, is a successful if relative newcomer out on the Snailwell Road, while those aiming at careers on studs both in this country and abroad often start on the courses run by the National Stud. The facilities at the stable staff club, known presently as the New Astley, are about to be expanded to offer a gym and other specialist help for those recovering from injuries. Rather sadly it seems old Sir John Astley is to lose his memorial as its founder when it is renamed more prosaically as the Racing Centre.

The BRS began life a few years after Major David Swannell decided in 1979 to develop his original inspiration of a small exhibition in the grandstand at York into the National Horseracing Museum (NHRM). Initially the scheme sought what now seems the pitifully small sum of £80,000 (it didn't seem so derisory at the time) to convert the old Tote building on the Rowley Mile. Fortunately, the Jockey Club Agent, Robert Fellowes, tipped him off in 1981 that the building for long used to house the club known as the Subscription Rooms would soon be available, as that institution was on its last legs. Taking a deep breath, Swannell advanced the target to £300,000 to be raised under the aegis of Lord Howard de Walden, but even as late as December 1981 £130,000 was still needed. In the end the shortfall was made up in time for the Queen to open the place in April 1983, and thirty years later we have been fundraising all over again with £15 million now collected for the Palace House scheme under the leadership of Peter Jensen. Over the years Lord Howard had been succeeded in NHRM chair by Lord Fairhaven, George Paul and now Stuart Richmond-Watson, brother of the racecourse chairman Julian. The funds have been raised with a view to creating what is to be called the National Heritage Centre for Horseracing and Sporting Art, which also encompasses the British Sporting Art Trust and the Retraining of Racehorses charity. Taken in the round, it is rather a neat example of the way things have progressed recently in our corner of East Anglia, but the need to make a success of using such extensive facilities, just as with the other grand developments about the place, leaves little room for complacency.

◆◆◆◆

This final chapter began with reflections on the differences between history and current affairs and ends firmly on the latter. Whatever the future may be for the Heath, at the moment it is enjoying a golden age in terms of the facilities on offer and the size and quality of the horse population which uses them. That said, problems can gather like storm clouds with remarkable speed. Apart from those involved, who could have forecast the outbreak of steroid abuse in Newmarket on a serious scale leading to two important trainers becoming ex-trainers in 2013. When allied to widespread confusion elsewhere in the town over what veterinary products were permissible, it was a real blow to racing's prestige that such things had happened in its headquarters. So far the threat of extensive housing development to the north of the town, more in the interests of Cambridge than Newmarket, remains no more than a threat, but the issue shows every sign of being a recurrent problem in one guise or another over the next few years.

Another serious local problem now in the process of finding a good answer is the autumn racing programme on the Heath following the Club's decision to make the Champions' Day at Ascot possible by releasing the Champion Stakes. While Newmarket has gained several important Ascot races in compensation for its various losses, nobody ever believed the changes were in the Heath's interests – they happened as a response to the view that such a day was in the national interest and its success to date suggests there is little reason to doubt that that opinion was right. However, the Heath's autumn programme has yet to settle into a satisfactory pattern. Most of the necessary races are available, but the right pattern of fixtures and race placement has yet to be in place and in any case it takes time for things to become familiar and accepted even when a suitable local pattern is finally settled.

On the national rather than purely local front, prize money may be miserable when compared with the rewards on offer abroad but, so long as there are enough very rich people attracted to the sport, the place should thrive regardless even if their presence makes it hard for others to compete. Such financial considerations and their various possible consequences, together with the risks they represent to the future of the sport and so to its headquarters on the Heath, are surely so obvious that an answer should be found one day – hopefully before the clock strikes midnight yet again as happened in the 1640s, 1740s, 1840s and 1940s.

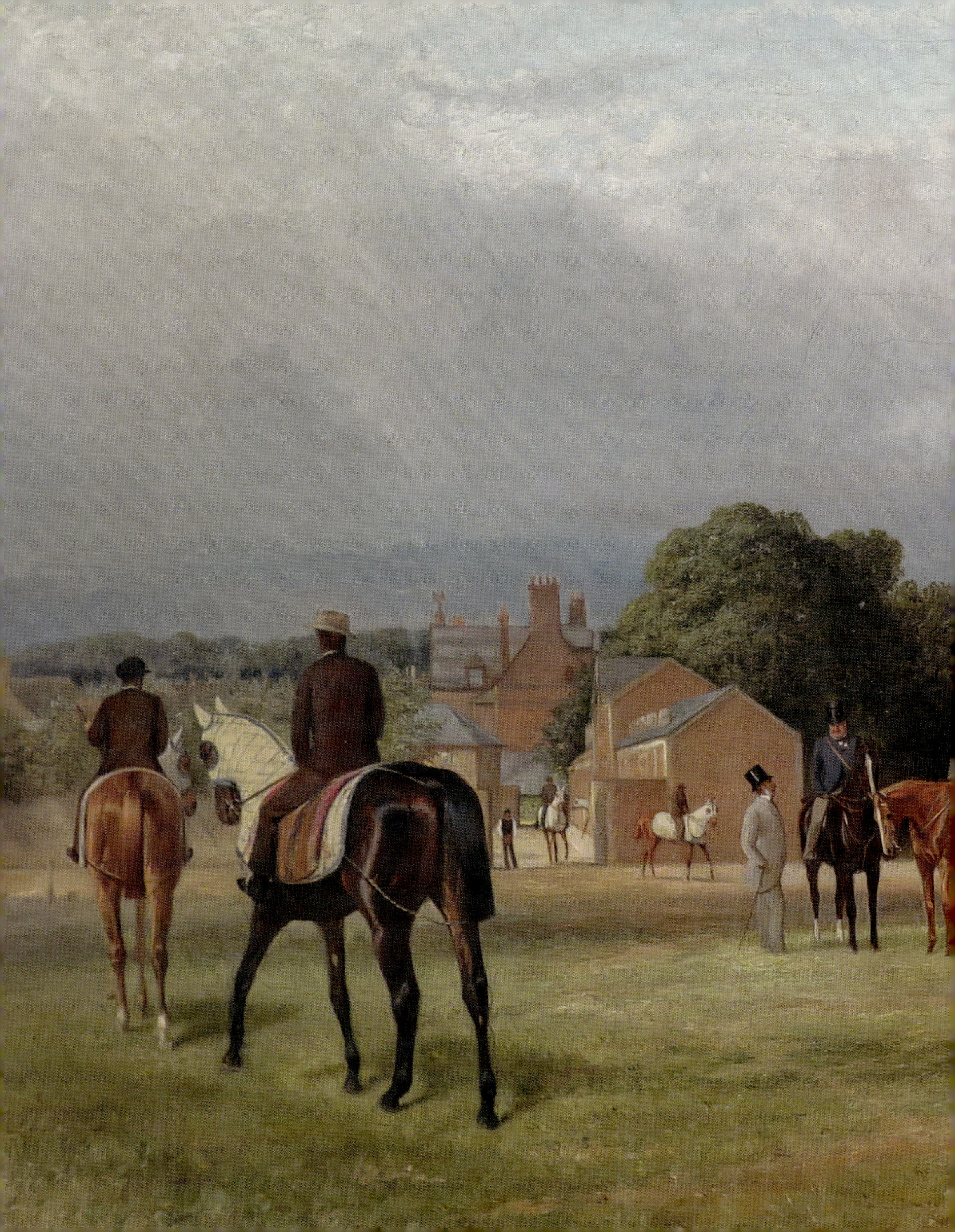

Part Two

Newmarket Heath

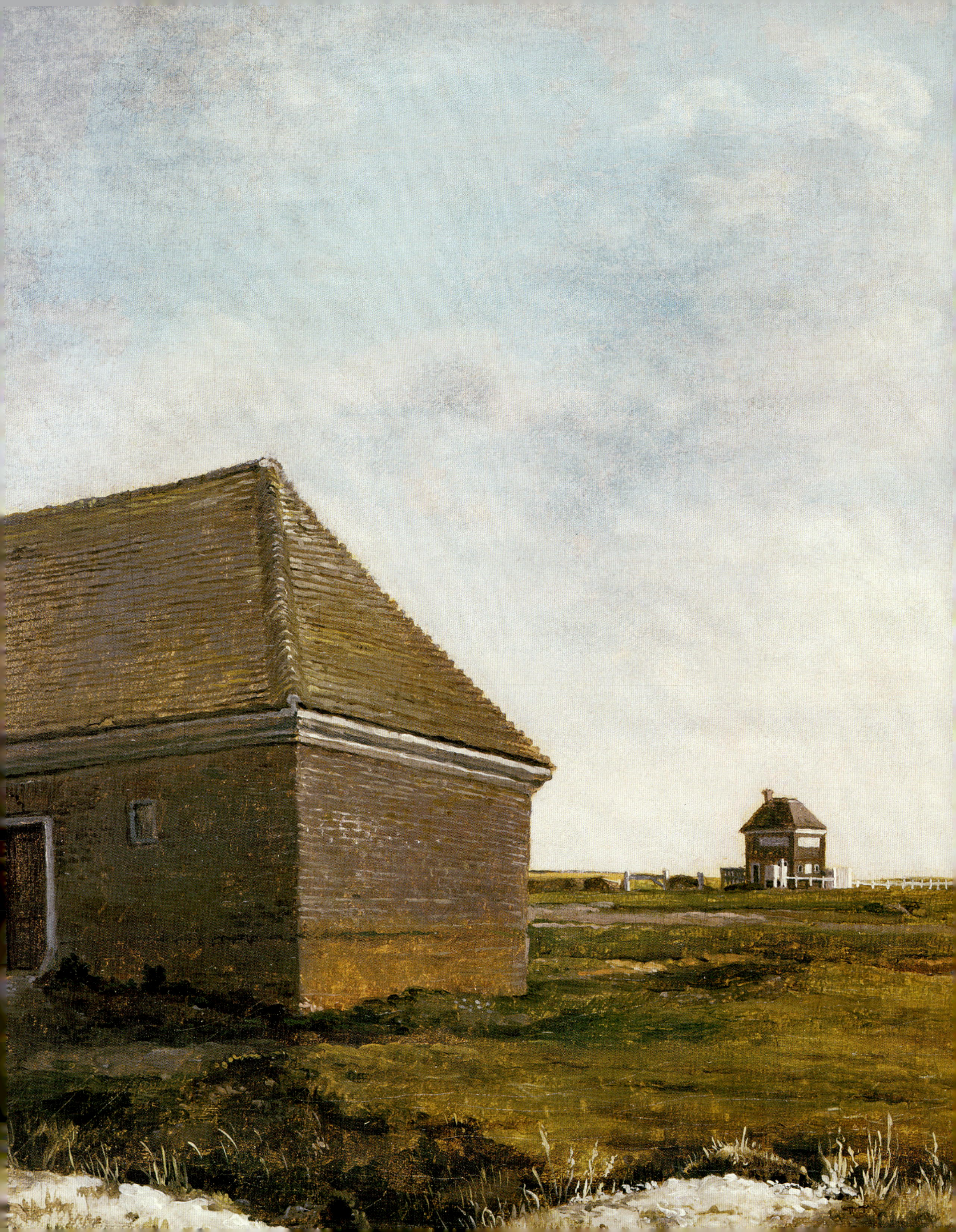

I
Buildings on the Heath

The various structures put up on the Heath over the centuries provoke a level of attention which seems eccentric to those with little interest in racing, its art or its history. As nothing erected before 1850 survived even the next sixty years, our knowledge of what these buildings looked like depends entirely on their images in paintings, prints, plans and, in a few cases, early photographs. However, due to the Jockey Club's resolute opposition until quite recent times to allowing photography during meetings, the latter class is surprisingly rare. Nonetheless, these images of what are, after all, pretty mundane buildings do have a remarkable ability to evoke the essence of the place, set as they were in the same sea of grass you still find today on Racecourse Side.

Perhaps the mystery of the abiding attraction of these ghosts on the Heath was best captured by the late Judy

Study of the King's Stables by George Stubbs (1765), detail of Fig. 157

Previous spread: *Heath House string at exercise* by A.L. Townshend (1884/5), Fig. 73

Egerton in her Stubbs catalogue raisonné of 2007. Writing of his two studies of 1765 (Figs. 157 and 158) depicting the buildings at either end of the Beacon Course, she described them as 'squat, brick-built, utilitarian in design and of no architectural merit'. Yet she saw, as Stubbs before had seen, that 'they testified silently and permanently to victories won and contests endured' more successfully than any scenes of over-excited spectators. She considered that Stubbs's 'focus on these inglorious Newmarket landmarks was a masterstroke in establishing the genius loci'. How right she was, and how lacking in insight was the American critic who railed against the price of £20 million paid for the prime version of the double portrait of Gimcrack in 2011 (Fig. 55) largely because in his view a main element in it was no more than a study of dull little structures.

We are lucky that the buildings on the Heath not only attracted the genius of Stubbs but also the (far less remarkable) talents of John Flatman, son of the fine jockey Nat Flatman (Fig. 60). Trained as an architect, he returned to Newmarket from London in the 1870s and for a while lived in Queen Street, earning his living as an artist. However, his rapidly expanding family (his wife Alice had seven

Fig. 127

July Course buildings by Harry Hall (*c.*1872)

daughters as well as a son, also John) led to a move to Rous Road and a return to architecture and surveying, leaving painting as a hobby. In 1906 he wrote a long article for the *Badminton Magazine* entitled 'Newmarket Heath and Stands', which he embellished with the studies in Figs. 130-1, 134-7, 154 and 155. Both the article and its illustrations form an invaluable source of information, presenting an eyewitness account of the way things happened in the second half of the nineteenth century, before the Heath was swept clean of such antiquated structures by the modernising efforts of Lord Durham and Cecil Marriott.

Among the Victorians not only Flatman but also Harry Hall produced a picture of buildings (Fig. 127), restricted in this case to the two on the July Course about three years before they were removed in 1875. It looks as though he may have had the Stubbs sketches (Figs. 157 and 158) in mind as he soon used his as background for a picture of a horse named Thunder. Inevitably the scrapping of the buildings defeated the purpose of the sketch if that was the use he intended for it.

SUMMARY
There seem to have been ten major stages through which the entirely mysterious arrangements of the days before the Civil War crystallised into the layout of the Heath we know today.

1. The building or reconstruction of stables and stands in the reign of Charles II, which had finished by 1669.

2. The replacement of everything except the old King's Stand during Newmarket's rejuvenation after 1750 as well as the addition of the Duke's Stand.

3. The construction of the Ancaster Mile Course with its Red Weighing House and transfer of saddling to the new Ditch Stables early in the 1770s.

4. The addition of the Duke of Portland's Stand at the north of the Beacon finish in the 1780s, allowing the old King's Stand to become slowly redundant before replacement around 1815 by a second and more adequate Weighing Room.

5. Admiral Rous's reformation of 1858 concentrating activity around the Rowley Mile finish and clearing the Heath to the south and west of the Beacon of all traffic.

6. Abandonment of the old separate Round Course of Charles II after 1872 and concentration of all racing on the July Course into its final mile plus any necessary extensions for longer distances onto the Beacon.

7. Construction of public accommodation for the first time on the Rowley Mile and the consolidation of all betting areas within the enclosures in 1876.

8. Closure over time at both ends of the Beacon of everything beyond the limits of the Cesarewitch Course and removal of related buildings culminating in the 1904 clearances of Lord Durham.

9. Transfer of all activity on the July Course to the west of the realigned track in the 1930s.

10. Removal of the Rowley Mile paddock from the Birdcage area it had occupied since 1858 and the transfer of the Weighing Room in two stages to its present site. Other important events since 1858 have been limited to improving or replacing buildings more or less on their present sites rather than altering the layout of the Heath in principle. This analysis obviously ignores the planning of the gallops dealt with elsewhere.

STANDS AND WEIGHING ROOMS
a) BEACON AND THE OLD CAMBRIDGESHIRE COURSE (the latter originally called the Ancaster Mile Course)
Apart from stables at various starts the only early buildings on the eight miles of the original Long Course were on its final uphill section after the present Rowley Mile finish. These are dealt with first, including those added after that final five furlong stretch was extended to make the Ancaster Mile in 1774, and then by another furlong to form the Old Cambridgeshire Course in 1843. By that time most races actually finished somewhere on the Rowley Mile but the building of stands anywhere on that section of the Beacon was regularly rejected until 1857/58.

King's Stand site
Although it has good claims to being the most historically important of all the Heath's buildings, the much-painted King's Stand (e.g. Figs. 56 and 67) has no known date of either construction or demolition. It appears in many early eighteenth-century pictures and there is no doubt that it was a seventeenth-century structure. The picture recording the scene in a wide-angled panoramic view from Windmill

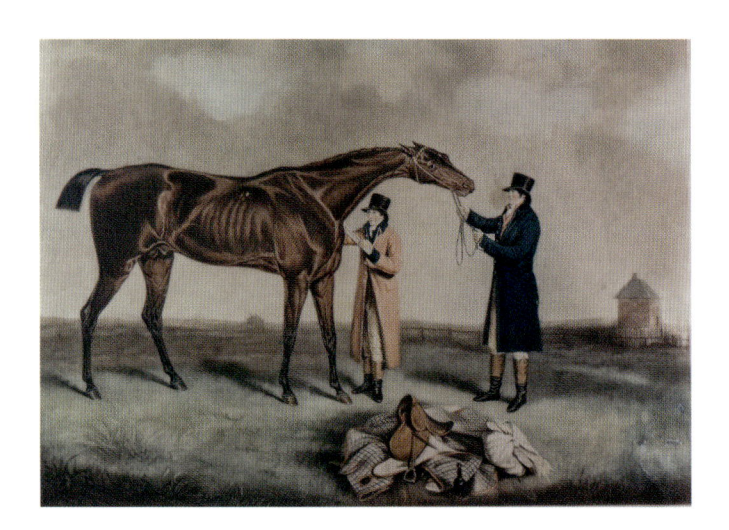

Fig. 128

Engraving of *Orville* after H.B. Chalon (1809)

The horse is being scraped with a strigel behind the King's Stand not long before it was replaced by an earlier version of that shown in Fig. 130.

Fig. 129

Longwaist by Ben Marshall (1825)

A younger Fulwar Craven (Fig. 159) is shown beside the Ditch Stables. In the far distance can be seen the buildings at the Beacon finish, including the King's Stand's replacement demolished in 1858.

Hill which dates from the visit of Cosimo de Medici in 1669 is now in Florence. When reproduced in this country it has usually been cropped at the right to omit the racecourse buildings but, as can be seen in Fig. 21, they already existed. They would either have been built on the orders of Charles II when things were being reconstructed in the 1660s, following the lapse into dereliction of the Interregnum, or may even predate the Commonwealth and have merely been restored after the King returned. There are no earlier pictures and even the detailed records of the Court's transactions do not prove the point either way.

As to the stand's eventual demolition, Flatman states that in 1850 the building on the south side of the Beacon finish was a white brick weighing stand with a flat roof which Admiral Rous allowed residents of the town to use free of charge. In 1840 a map based on a survey by George Tattersall calls the building the Jockey Club Stand and no doubt its roof had originally been used by the Club in succession to the old King's Stand. No references to the old building or its replacement appear in Jockey Club Minutes, available since 1836, but in any case by 1821 the picture of Banker by Ben Marshall already seems to include a corner of the weighing room described by Flatman. On the other hand, the Chalon of Orville published in 1809 (Fig. 128) certainly portrayed the old stand still on that site although already looking on its last legs, so it must have disappeared at some point in that thirteen-year gap.

Its replacement never seems to have appealed much to artists, but it is shown in the far distance of Marshall's 1825 painting of Longwaist (Fig. 129) so we do have some idea of its appearance. Flatman says it was demolished in the 1860s but actually this must have happened as part of the fairly general reorganisation of 1857/58, leading to the building of the first Rowley Mile Stand and Weighing Room. Anyway, the new replacement weighing room at the Beacon finish lasted until 1904 (Fig. 130) and went when the whole set up at the end of the course was removed apart from the vestigial

Buildings on the Heath

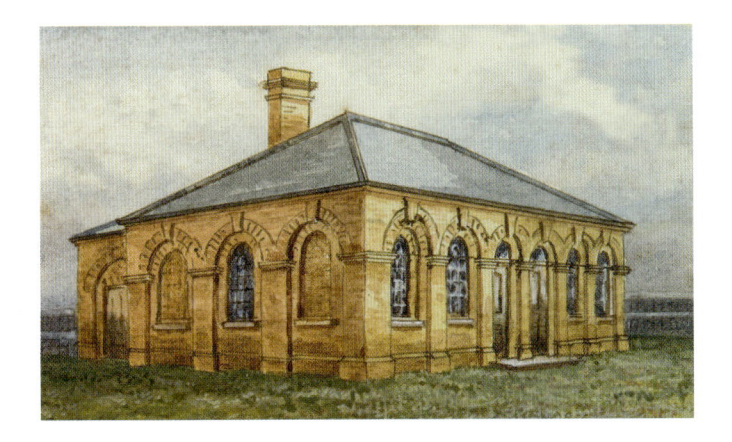

Fig. 130

Weighing Room at Beacon finish (demolished 1904)

remains of the late eighteenth-century Duke of Portland's Stand, which survived the Second World War (as I remember being shown them, such as they were, by my father).

Duke's Stand
Reverting to the mid-eighteenth century, the second stand to make its appearance on this section of the course was the Duke's Stand of around 1760. On contemporary maps it was often called simply the New Stand and the duke in question was that great figure in racing history 'Butcher' Cumberland (Fig. 39), who died in 1765. Fortunately, the plans for the stand have survived in the British Library (Fig. 132) and so we know its ground floor consisted of stabling for twelve hacks with the upper floor for spectators. Overall the building measured 40' x 25' and stood 32' to the pitch of the roof. It also appears in Figs. 4 and 67, and it seems clear from the pictures of the King's Stand that this too had its ground floor arranged as hack stalls. By the time the Duke's Stand was used for the last time in 1858 races finishing beyond the end of the Rowley Mile had greatly declined and in 1859 there were only nineteen divided between long ones over most or

Fig. 131

Duke of Portland's Stand (demolished 1904)

all of the Beacon, five furlong sprints from the Turn of the Lands and races run on the Old Cambridgeshire Course going nine furlongs straight. All had in common that they ended at the Beacon finish and began or ended proceedings for the day so crowds could watch them on their way to or from the main scene of action on the Rowley Mile.

Duke of Portland's Stand
The Beacon acquired its third stand when the Duke of Portland's Stand (Figs.. 65, 131 and 133) was built opposite the King's Stand in the mid 1780s. It appears on the separate maps of the town and the Heath drawn by Chapman in 1787, but there is a considerable difference between the two.

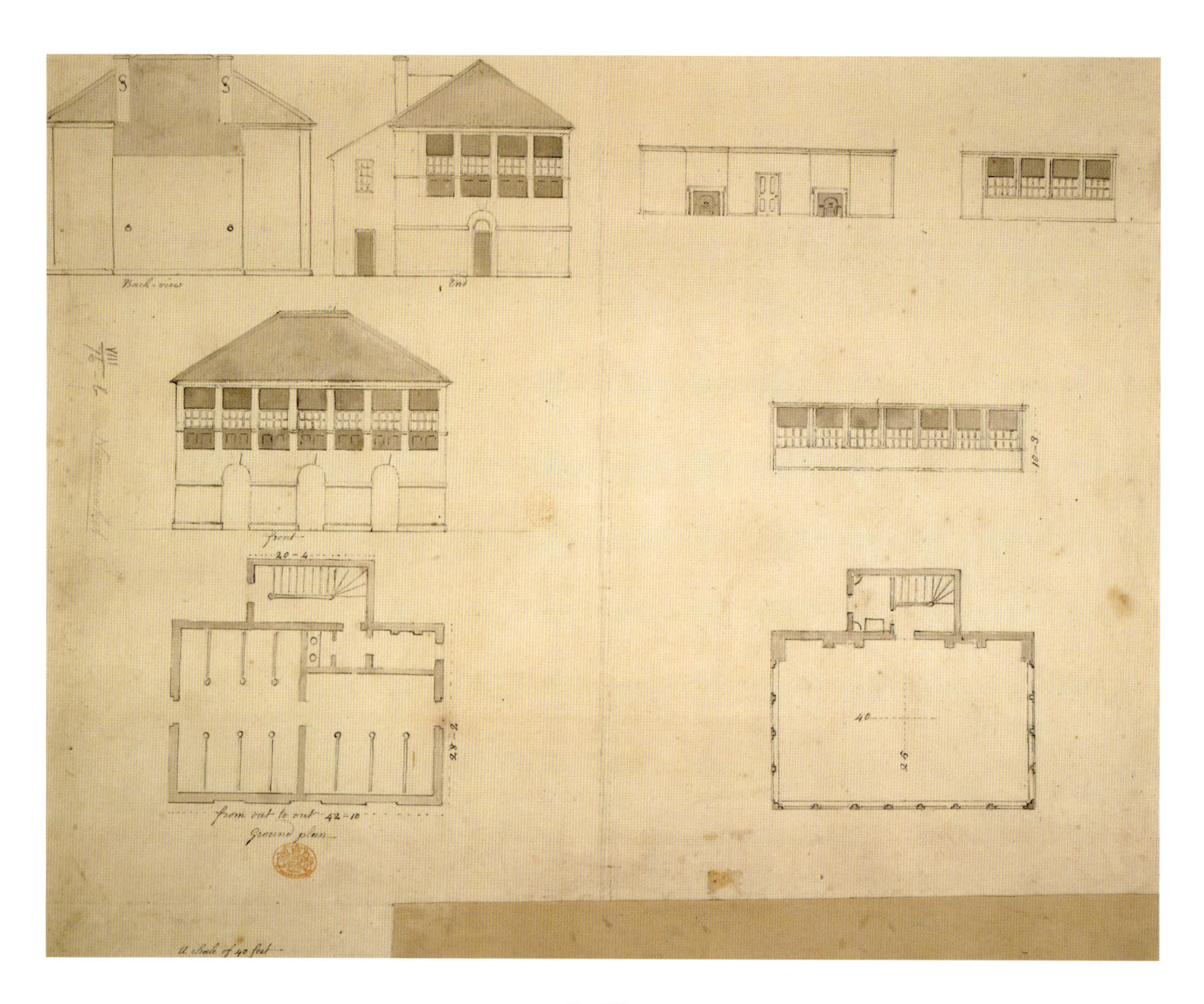

Fig. 132

Architect's plans for the Duke's Stand (*c.*1760)

The layout catered for a dozen hack stalls on the ground floor.
The building was demolished in 1858.

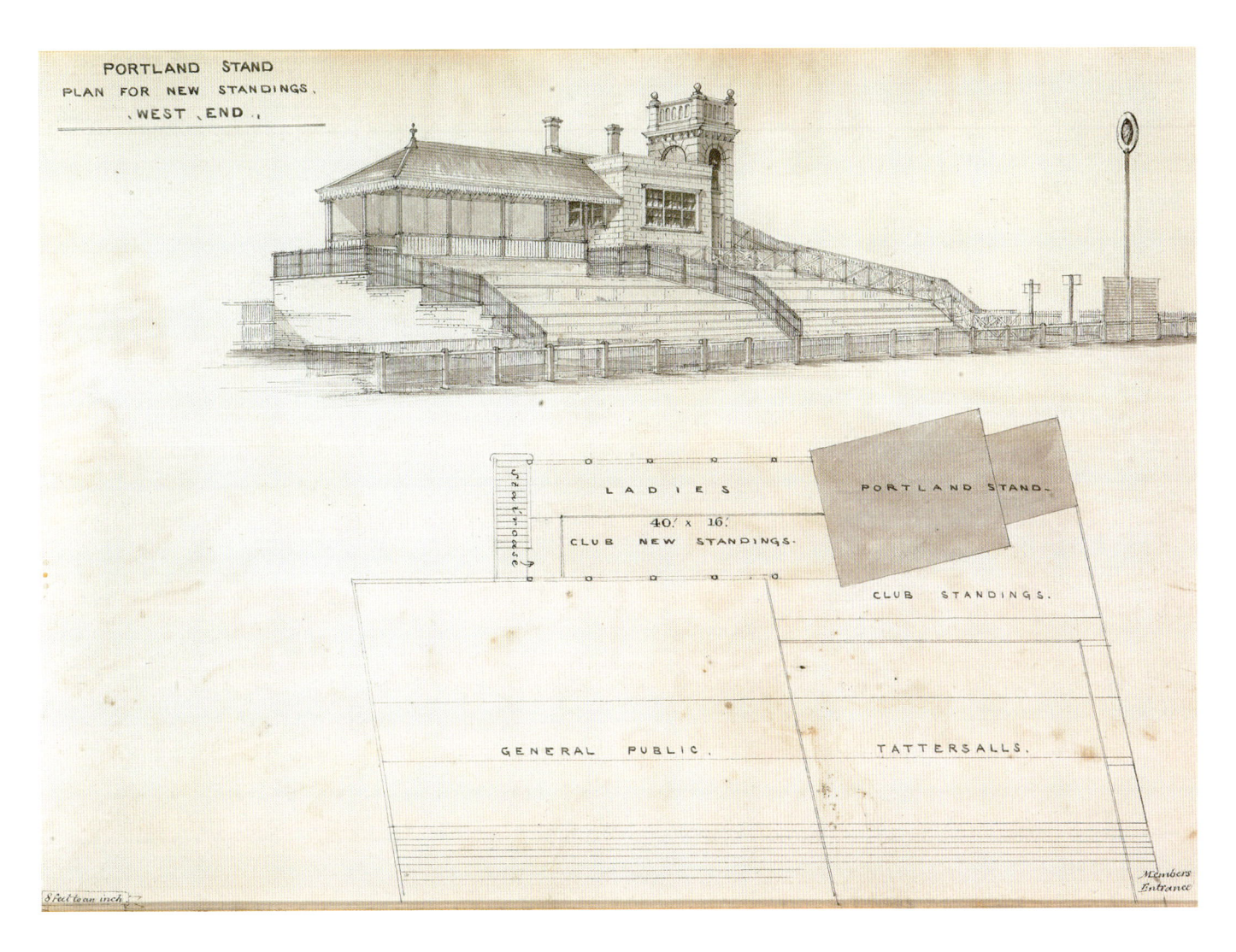

Fig. 133

Sketch of the Duke of Portland's Stand by J. Swain (1889)

The original structure (fig. 65) is shaded above and was almost submerged in later extensions needed for what had become the only stand at the Beacon finish.

Fig. 134

Old Red Weighing House at the Turn of the Lands (demolished 1857)

Fig. 135

Grooms returning jockeys' hacks to the Old Red Weighing House (Fig. 134) from Ditch Stables (Fig. 155)

The first places the track across the Heath to the village of Reach in front of the new stand, whereas the latter, which is clearly correct, sites it behind, more or less on the line of the present road down to the Rowley Mile. Presumably this confusion suggests everything was happening while Chapman was at work so probably the stand came into use for 1786 or 1787 following a Club meeting of December 1785, when various changes were agreed to arrangements at Newmarket. In the Victorian building programme either side of 1880 the Portland Stand was much extended (Fig. 133) to the degree that the old eighteenth-century structure began to look almost irrelevant.

Weighing Rooms

The next building to appear was called the Red Weighing House (Fig. 134) which was put up to the south of the course, about five furlongs out and opposite the Turn of the Lands, so to us where horses pull up after races on the Rowley Mile. Flatman gives an interesting account of the way his father and the other jockeys would ride hacks carrying their saddles after weighing out from this building across to the Ditch Stables (Fig. 155) near the King's Gap to saddle their mounts. The lad who had taken the runner to the Ditch Stables would then ride the hack back to the Red Weighing House and hand him over to the jockey after the race, either to go home or to repeat the performance (Fig. 135). While we do not know when it was built, it was replaced after 1857, in this case by the new structure on the Rowley Mile.

Having two places to weigh out for races on the Old Cambridgeshire Course eventually led to the disaster one could have foretold when in 1863 Catch-'em-Alive won the Cambridgeshire but his jockey, Adams, weighed in some two pounds light. The rider on the second had weighed out as well as in at the scales at the finish and had no apparent problem but Adams had weighed out at the new lower site. Eventually the day was saved by Admiral Rous who ordered all jockeys who had been placed to be weighed again and the rest for the first time. Those unplaced were not usually weighed at the time. This revealed that those who had originally passed the scales down on the Rowley Mile before the race were all a few pounds wrong. Further investigation showed that some bright spark had managed to affix lead to the bottom of the weight side of the balance scales used at the finish; when it was removed Adams could draw the right weight. It was bad luck on the second, who had only been beaten a head, as the removal of the lead naturally showed he had carried overweight. Rous's regular antagonist, Sir Joseph Hawley, launched something of a campaign over the whole thing, but obviously there was nothing which could be done as the villain was never unmasked.

Betting Posts

Apart from assorted Betting Posts at various points near the Old Cambridgeshire Course and the King's Stables at its end, dealt with separately later in the section on Rubbing Houses, no other structures were erected. As the posts were moved about to other sites on occasion it seems pointless to identify any but the Old Red Post painted by Flatman (Fig. 136) which was saved from destruction in 1904 by the trainer Felix Leach. His descendants kindly donated it to the National Horseracing Museum. It stood about a furlong down the course from the Duke's Stand and so was more or less midway between the finishes on the Rowley Mile and on the Beacon. Until 1858, when the main site for betting moved to an area opposite the Bushes, it had been the chief place where fortunes had been won or lost since the early days. When Captain Frank Siltzer wrote his book *Newmarket* in 1923 he, perhaps unwisely, combined a denunciation of vandalism in general, and the 'modernising tendency to iconoclasm' in particular, with asking the 4th Earl of Durham to write his foreword. As a grandson of Radical Jack, the 1st Earl, and as the prime agitator for the removal of the old post, Lord Durham was moved stoutly to defend his position in his foreword. Whatever view you take over the preservation of ancient artefacts, it does seem a bit out of order to quarrel with your author when writing a foreword, particularly as no individual had been named in his general condemnation of vandalism. Fortunately Sir Mark Prescott has been kinder to the present set of authors.

Fig. 136

Old Red Betting Post (removed 1904) and now in the National Horseracing Museum

b) ROWLEY MILE COURSE

Although the course's ancient name (shared with King Charles II and one of his favourite horses) dates from the Restoration, no stand was erected there until 1858. For much of the period it represented little more than a section of the four-mile Beacon Course, but as distances shortened progressively from the mid-eighteenth century the number of races finishing somewhere on it, rather than up at the King's Stand, steadily increased.

By 1845, over three quarters of all races on the Heath finished at some point along the Rowley Mile with only about fifteen per cent ending after the Turn of the Lands and less than ten per cent on the July Course. Efforts to address the absurdity of three stands on the Beacon and a fourth on the July Course with a total of less than a quarter of the races finishing at them had been started by the author, artist and mapmaker George Tattersall in 1840. In 1845 his campaign was taken up by two influential Club members in the Duke of Rutland and Charles Greville but the Club firmly rejected their ideas. However, things did begin to change in 1848 when a committee was set up to consider consolidating the betting areas at the Red Post, the Weighing Stand opposite the Turn of the Lands and the Ditch Stables to the general area of the present enclosures on the Rowley Mile. The aim was primarily to reduce the damage to the Heath caused by traffic of all sorts crossing over to the south and west of the courses and to service them in their new positions with a proper road more or less on the line of the present one from the town.

Betting enclosure and first Private Stand

In 1849 an area for betting was set up opposite the Bushes which was fenced and given a paved surface. As a result, both the old Betting Posts to the west of the course placed little over a furlong apart either side of the Bushes could be scrapped. Although the old Red Betting Post lasted until the twentieth century it will have been much less used and largely abandoned after 1858 apart from any

Fig. 137

First stand on the Rowley Mile (demolished 1875)

use for races on the last few furlongs of the Beacon. This enabled finances to be boosted by charging two Guineas a year for access and the place was progressively improved as the main betting ring until the Rowley Mile got its first proper grandstand in 1876. Long before that the crucial changes had been driven through by Admiral Rous very soon after he became a Steward in 1858. In November he brought forward a 'Proposal for the amelioration of Newmarket Race Course' which is set out later in this section. This built on the 1848 effort and saw the buildings on the Beacon like the lower or Red Weighing House largely replaced by a new private stand at the Rowley Mile finish with facilities for weighing jockeys on the ground floor (Fig. 137). Above was to be accommodation for fifty local worthies, who were allowed to join Club members for a proper view of the races. With saddling now taking place in the area which came to be known as the Birdcage to the south of the new stand, instead of far away at Ditch

Stables, the Admiral had certainly 'ameliorated' the more obvious flaws in the old arrangements. Extensive new hack stables were also built.

The result was that Newmarket at last began to prosper once again after a lapse of more than half a century. The notice submitted to the Club for approval is reproduced here and remarkably it seems the Private Stand was constructed for less than £1,000. In the end, the betting ring seems to have remained near the Bushes rather than moving to the Dip as proposed by Rous. It even acquired a rudimentary stand on its old site called the Ditch mile or later the Old Betting Stand after the ring was moved.

"PROPOSAL FOR THE AMELIORATION OF NEWMARKET RACE COURSE

As the wear of carriages for one mile and a half over the best part of the exercising ground, and the constant crossing backwards and forwards during a wet day, between the Race Course and the Betting Ring, is of very great detriment to the turf, and causes much expense, it is proposed to make a Carriage Road from the Town, passing behind the Portland Stand through Bottom's Land to a point about thirty yards wide of the A. F. Winning Post (meaning Across the Flat or present post on the Rowley Mile), there to erect a small Stand on an improved plan and under the same roof to build a Weighing Room, and attach to it a Saddling Stable for six horses. But to carry this plan into effect, it is imperative to pull down the Duke's Stand, and also the present Weighing House (the Old Red Weighing Stand), which is totally out of keeping with the present requirements: also to take away the old posts and rails between the Duke's Stand and the Weighing House, which would open a fine ground for exercising horses. The said posts and rails are now rotten, and could not be replaced under 100*l*.

If the Duke's Stand, which is now dilapidated, is not pulled down, it will be impossible to prevent carriages going on the wrong side of the Course; therefore this is a *sine qua non*, The Betting Ring it is proposed to place on the left of the Course, between the D. M. and the R. M. Winning Posts, at a reasonable distance from the Course and the New Stand. There are a great many Gentlemen of good standing who would not object to subscribe 2*l* annually to the New Stand, if the expense of building is considered an obstacle by the members of the Jockey Club.

The above Proposal is circulated among the Members of the Jockey Club by direction of the Stewards, in order that they may be better prepared to come to a decision on the question when a General Meeting is called to take it into consideration."

First Public Stand

The next major change came with the decision to build a proper grandstand for public use, which was approved by twelve votes to four in May 1875 after two years of debate (Figs. 9 and 139). With the Club now much stronger financially this would eventually cost over £21,000. It would have been a lot more but for the intervention of Sir John Astley and would be known thereafter as the Astley Stand. Initially, considerably larger figures were quoted by 'the principal building firms in London, Cambridge and Bury'. However, Sir John persuaded the Club to appoint its own Clerk of the Works and let him charge a fee of three per cent on cost. On this basis Mr Jordan worked the oracle using a design by the local firm of Clark and Holland. Clark was one of the semi-hereditary family of Newmarket racecourse judges and Holland was a member of the family that would work for the Club as its main contractor on later buildings for over a century.

Weighing Room and Paddock

At the same period a separate Weighing Room was constructed on the site which is now the Members' Bar between the statues of Eclipse and Persian Punch, as the one which had served since 1858 disappeared along with the old Private Stand.

Fig. 138

The Birdcage by L.C. Dickinson (1887)

The new paddock on the Rowley Mile got its strange name when opened in 1858 because
Admiral Rous objected to the cost of railings to the west, preferring a wire mesh fence.

Part of this new weighing room appears on the left of Fig. 138 set in the corner of the Birdcage which served as the paddock for over a century. It was replaced in the 1920s. The Birdcage itself was an enclosed area without rails in which horses were walked around among those with access to this holy of holies. This came free to Club members, owners and trainers but cost half a guinea for the meeting for anyone else when the Astley Stand was erected. Heaven knows what today's Health and Safety experts would make of the Admiral's arrangements. The paddock got its strange name because the ever-parsimonious Admiral refused to allow a proper fence to be erected dividing it from the racecourse – instead he used wire mesh thereby effectively naming his creation.

Jockey Club Stand

Although we have found no firm evidence, the main betting ring must have been transferred within the enclosures for the new grandstand in 1876 rather than being stranded two furlongs down the course as it had been since 1849. Further change came in 1889 when the Club decided it wanted a separate stand again for its members, who had been lodged in the area under the prominent gable at the southern end of the Astley Stand (Fig. 9). An interesting drawing

Fig. 139

Sketch of the back of the Rowley Mile Stands by J. Swain (1889)

The complexity of the back of the Astley Stand may come as a surprise. As today, the height behind is markedly greater than in front due to the artificial gradient of the betting ring, but it was more noticeable in the past because of the reduced height of the structure and steeper gradient.

Fig. 140

Photograph of work in progress on Rowley Mile (1926)

Colorado wins the 2,000 Guineas, with the roof removed ready for the extra tier to be added.

Fig. 141

Photograph with work nearing completion (1927)

Cresta Run wins the 1,000 Guineas with the Jockey Club Stand still separated.

(Fig. 139) of that year shows the Rowley Mile buildings from behind looking more like a townscape than a grandstand with the Club accommodation showing just over the top of the row of stalls to the east of the Birdcage. Added to its former accommodation, this small independent structure, lasted the Club until it was reincorporated into the main grandstand when this got its new top deck in the mid 1920 (Fig. 142).

Rebuilding of Grandstand

The biggest building scheme since Sir John Astley constructed the first public stand on the Rowley Mile came with the decision to replace it in the 1920s. In fact the old buildings were not destroyed by the scheme – instead the roof was removed and a new top deck created retaining the ground works and steppings of 1876 as the base for a building which lasted until 2000. The various stages of the work appear in Figs. 140, 141 and 142 dating respectively from 1926, 1927 and 1928.

Head On Stand

What we know as the Head On Stand began in the nineteenth century as a small structure in the north-western corner of the Birdcage, which was restricted to trainers and jockeys. In 1889 it was decided that they deserved something grander and the building in the centre of Fig. 143 was constructed for them more or less on the present site. Again it appears just over the top of a range of boxes in the Birdcage in Fig. 139. This lasted until the major works of the 1920s, during which it was replaced by the core of the present structure with some public access and the trainers left with only a section. In the 1987 developments tiers of private boxes

Fig. 142

Photograph of completed work (1928)

Scuttle wins the 1,000 Guineas for King George V with the Club Stand now incorporated.

Fig. 143

Cyllene in the Birdcage by Isaac Cullin (1898)

In the background is the Trainers' Stand, which lasted until 1926. The Admiral's wire mesh fence referred to in Fig. 218 has given way to solid wooden palings.

overlooking the members' car park were added, with ten more very grand ones along the new bridge linking it to the grandstand (Fig. 145).

Silver Ring Stand
At the other end of the enclosures the Silver Ring began as a fenced area tacked onto the northern end of the main stand in 1882. This cost half a crown to enter but punters do not seem to have been provided with a stand of any significance for their money. This was improved in 1894 at a cost of £400, and the stand that appears in an aerial photograph of the 1920s (Fig. 144) looks very similar indeed, to what is still there today, then appearing so pristine it must have just been completed. That photograph should also be a relief to Health and Safety as away on the right it shows the old Birdcage was being modernised out of existence with internal rails.

More recent alterations
After all these works had been completed by 1930 the Club could switch its attention (and by now considerable cash flow) to the July Course, leaving the Rowley Mile buildings little changed until the scheme largely attributable to the Duke of Norfolk of 1968. As explained in Chapter 9, it was the source of major ructions with the Levy Board under its new Chairman Lord Wigg and in the end became a rather inspired adaptation of the old buildings instead of the full-scale replacement originally envisaged. The paddock was transferred to more or less its present site on the far side of the 1920s Weighing Room and the unsaddling enclosure moved to the east – in effect the building was reversed. The old paddock, formerly the Birdcage, disappeared as the members' car park moved to the south giving access to the relevant enclosures from the present direction rather

Fig. 144

Aerial photograph from the 1920s before
the stand got an extra tier

This revealing photograph clearly shows the major works have already begun. The old paddock appears on the right behind the head-on stand, with the still complete court of boxes further east beyond the old weighing room. From its appearance the Silver Ring stand has just been completed, with the work on the main grandstand to follow, dating the photograph to 1925 or 1926.

Fig. 145

Link between the main grandstand
and the head-on stand after 1987

The range of ten boxes at the top of this 1980s development surmount the Jockey Club Rooms lunching facility and bar behind the windows on the first floor. The semi-circle shown linked the Head-on stand to the old grandstand and, since 2000, to the new Millennium Stand.

than over a bridge at the back of the stands, under which Tattersalls patrons got entry to the old paddock.

The penultimate set of changes came in 1987 when the whole footprint of the enclosures was expanded, the present Weighing Room constructed on the far side of an enlarged paddock while the private boxes were added to the new link with the Head On Stand or behind it as explained above. Once again the scheme was considered good value for money and really laid the place out much as it is today save for the main grandstand. One building that disappeared at this juncture was the large one erected by the recently formed Tote about 1930 more or less behind the south end of the Silver Ring with its impressive battery of registers allowing for forty runners showing running totals of win and place bets. It was this by then redundant structure that had been offered to the nascent National Horseracing Museum in 1980 so it might have had a pretty short life there had the Subscription Rooms not fallen vacant in the nick of time.

A seemingly rather odd change made in 1987 was the removal of a third of the excellent courtyard of boxes you can see top left in Fig. 144. Naturally very popular with trainers as a place to saddle, this alteration was essential due to many horses remaining there out of sight for too long, not allowing the public to get a proper view. The result, if you look today, is that the arch leading into the courtyard is still there but with the range of boxes to its north gone it is effectively redundant – it looks rather odd if you consider it without knowing the reason for its existence.

Fig. 146

Photograph of the front of the Rowley Mile buildings today

Millennium Stand

Inflation having run at such an alarming rate since Lord Wigg blocked a replacement for the grandstand in 1967 for £2.5 million, when the Millennium Stand arrived the cost had spiralled to over £20 million by the time it was finished. The structure had to be adapted to save costs from what was originally intended in 1987. The major changes were the cancellation of various planned aerial walkways linking the stand to the paddock, somewhat along the lines of present arrangements at Ascot, and the addition of an extra storey at the expense of chopping more than a quarter off the northern end. Aesthetically it cannot really be questioned that latter change was unfortunate, and the result today is a building which is disproportionately high in comparison with everything else on the site. However, the changes did save a great deal of money as well as generating income from the splendid boxes on the top floor. In the end it was lucky costs had been reduced as most of the savings had to be spent on the rectification of flaws in the design within the building added to problems caused by the failure of one of the main contractors. Even if the result is quite hard on the eye it now works well as a racing plant which, given the problems faced, is a considerably better outcome than at one time seemed likely. Developing old racecourses invariably annoys a great many folk. At least the Newmarket planners of 1968, 1987 and 2000 were largely replacing the concrete monolith unceremoniously dumped on top of Sir John Astley's efforts – so it is hard to think anyone really mourns the old buildings on the Rowley Mile for better reasons than simple nostalgia. Fig. 146 shows what the Club got for its money in 1987 and 2000.

c) JULY COURSE (formerly the Round Course)

Whether there was a separate course to the west of the Ditch before Charles II's 'new Round Course' of 1665/6 is not known. A drawing by Jan Wyck (Fig. 34) cannot predate it as the artist only arrived in this country in 1666. It shows a small circular course making use of the top of the banking between

Fig. 147

Flying Fox in the July Course paddock by Isaac Cullin (1898)

The Weighing Room is on the right, with the small stand used until 1894 by the Jockey Club in the background. As usual with Cullin, many of the people are readily identifiable.

the Cambridge and Well Gaps as a vantage point for carriages. However hare-brained the scheme seems, the combination of this drawing with the increased width and reinforced top of the Ditch between these two points does seem to prove it really happened. Whether Charles's course started like this and was soon extended or alternatively whether the artist has simply compressed the new course for effect cannot be known for sure but there is no later evidence of the top of the banking being used as a carriage stand. Such an elaborate scheme as that must represent would seem quite unrealistic as a way of watching races on the full Round Course of nearly four miles, so it does seem probable the King changed the layout in short order. Fig. 34 shows no buildings at all but only a suitably regal tent and the first to be constructed was the King's Stables or Rubbing House for the new course. There is no way of knowing when it appeared but it is there in all the early eighteenth century pictures by Tillemans and Wootton (Figs. 35 and 37) so probably dates from Charles II's reign and is dealt in page 193.

The first stand (if you exclude the Ditch itself) was erected by 1756 and its roof can be seen in Fig. 3 while all of it is visible in Figs. 127 and 154. This strongly suggests it was contemporary with the Duke's Stand on the Beacon (indeed, it is a smaller version of it) built as Newmarket began to thrive again under the aegis of a more active Jockey Club. It lasted until demolition in 1875, and was replaced by a small stand for the Club's use on the other side of the course (Fig. 147). The Weighing Room attached to the north of the former one also crossed the course to become an independent structure on the present site (Fig. 148). With a stand about halfway down the hill towards the dip on the east the public got a look in for the first time, but with the clear division between those regarded as social sheep and goats. The latter were firmly restricted to the east, and this arrangement, so typical of the period, lasted with one brief interlude until 1930. In 1882 a Silver Ring Enclosure was added north of the public stand with admission fixed at half a crown but with no suggestion of

Fig. 148

Photograph of the new Weighing Room on the July Course (1901)

Whether Mr Marriott adapted or replaced the building with the present structure in the 1930s is uncertain, but the site seems to be unchanged, even if the brickwork is so different that it was probably a complete rebuild.

Fig. 149

Photograph of the Jockey Club Stand on July Course (1901)

Built for the Club in 1894, it was relinquished about a decade later when new accommodation was constructed to the west of the course.

Fig. 150

Photograph of the July Course Stands (1906)

The new Tattersalls and Silver Ring Stands to the east frame that of the Jockey Club and Members across the course, with the Weighing Room partially obscured.

a stand being part of the deal, as happened at the same time on the Rowley Mile.

The next major change came in 1894 when the public stand was enlarged and the Jockey Club temporarily crossed the course again to occupy a new building on the present finishing line to the east (Fig. 149). Their small 1875 structure to the west became known as the Ladies Stand while Club members must have crossed to and fro to see the horses paraded in the July Course equivalent of the Birdcage (Fig. 147).

This proved to be only a brief exile to the east, as the Club's stand of 1894 soon was opened to the public and the members returned to the west to occupy accommodation in the buildings across the course (present in the centre of Fig. 150 with the Weighing Room partly hidden beside them).

This view of 1906 shows them flanked in the foreground by the new public provision to the east, with Tattersalls to the left and the Silver Ring on the right. By this stage the whole area from the Weighing Room down to a point well beyond the dip bounded by the course on one side and a more extensive fringe of trees on the other than remains today was called the Royal Enclosure. It contained several structures including a small Royal Box placed beside the lower winning post but quite who was entitled to use each of the other stands is obscure.

In this period public attendance at the only two meetings held on the Summer Course was small and the limited provision on offer to the east may have been all it justified. To the west things were very different with the large paddock area shown in Fig. 147 including the splendid remains of what had once been called Mr Eaton's Plantation. This enclosure stretched from the boxes beside the present members' entrance to a little beyond the Weighing Room, just as it does today. As crowds steadily grew after the First World War the lack of room for the public, squeezed between the Ditch and the course, became ever more serious and eventually in 1930 a series of rather acrimonious Club meetings resulted in action. Some of the more conservative members objected strongly to what they saw as the likely ruination of the whole picnic atmosphere of the two summer meetings they had enjoyed for so long. This view was not merely selfish but also was backed by the more rational argument that continuing the Club's major building projects of the 1920s into the harsher financial climate of the 1930s was unwise.

The debate between the son of one prime minister and grandson of another is so neat a vignette both of attitudes and individuals it deserves its element of immortality. In 1931 Lord Derby and Mr Reid Walker, who had been a brewer, tried to block change due to the slump following the Wall Street crash. Lord Rosebery accused them of trying to ambush the scheme and acidly observed that the capital expenditure involved 'would not be thought out of order for a brewery'. The public would say the Club was keeping them out in the rain just to preserve its privacy. To this Lord Derby countered that he did not think that was the way to put it only for Rosebery to reply that the public would still see it that way however it was put. The Club's approval of the 1930 scheme was then confirmed.

Part of the project for moving everything to the west of the course involved realigning the track itself to run more or less parallel to the Ditch rather than diverging from it at an angle of about 15 or 20 degrees. When the track was moved before use in 1932 all the starts were also adjusted so that distances were unchanged but naturally times before that year are not strictly comparable with subsequent years. With almost everything now proposed for removal westward, including even the brand new Tote building, it no longer mattered how much space was left to the east and the revised angle would naturally improve viewing from the stands to be erected. Completion of all the changes was celebrated at a party held just before the 1935 July meeting.

In reality the opposition was mainly due to hankering after the freedom of the old days on the Heath – on your hack with no stands at all at most finishes. Lord Hamilton of Dalzell (Fig. 96) was even moved to observe that such things had already disappeared, apart from the example of Lord Lonsdale 'prancing down on the very nice coloured hack he rode'. As Lord Lonsdale was not one of those who opposed the changes Hamilton added that he was confident Lonsdale would not 'ask them to sacrifice the interests of the public seeing the racing' for any such reason.

On the financial wisdom of it all after the Wall Street crash Mr Marriott observed in writing to Weatherbys that the 'pessimists must be convinced'. Once they were he took charge of the construction of the five main buildings we still use today – namely the Weighing Room, Head On Stand and the three very similar structures erected for Members, Tattersalls and Silver Ring patrons. As Figs. 151, 152 and 153 make clear, surprisingly little has changed over the past eighty years apart from some reallocation of space between the enclosures to enlarge the more popular ones, and anyone familiar with the Jockey Club section today would have no problem in recognising it in the 1930s down to most of the finer detail. It was a remarkable feat to have got it all so right that we could spend almost £10 million, during the short recent reign of Lisa Hancock, in making a series of successful improvements without actually needing to alter any of the principles of what was done so long ago. Mr Marriott had been expected to do the whole thing for £65,000, including £8,000 for some extra land. To say that he deserved the formal congratulations he received at a meeting in May 1935 would seem to us a considerable understatement and the success of his efforts is really the foundation of the prosperity of the two racecourses today.

Fig. 151

Photograph of the July Course Stands in 1945 on Derby Day

Even today's pop concerts do not attract such crowds. Nobody knows how many were crammed in, but the whole area between the Ditch and the Plantation was described as 'black with people' down to the dip.

Fig. 152

Photograph of the southern end of the July Course Stands in 1944 on St Leger Day

It seems remarkable how well these stands have withstood the ravages of time and how little has changed over the past seventy years.

STABLES AND RUBBING HOUSES

King's Stable

The first building of this type of which we have firm evidence is the King's Stables, often referred to as the Rubbing House although there were several others. It had been erected by 1669 and is the structure to the right of the print in Fig. 21 with the King's Stand actually bisected by the edge of the plate just beyond it. The appearance of these stables is constant through the earlier work of various artists, as in Fig. 5, but changes quite significantly at some point before Stubbs portrayed the building for the first time in 1765 (Fig. 157). It is reasonable to assume that this happened as part of the general replacement of seventeenth-century structures in around 1760. We know that the Duke's Stand was then added. The stables were more or less on the line of the present Hamilton Road's small extension to join the main London Road. Flatman tells us they were demolished by the former jockey Jack Watts as they 'obstructed the view from Hamilton'. Watts appears in Fig. 80 on Persimmon and regularly invested his money in Newmarket property before his death in 1902 and probably had the stables knocked down when building on the Hamilton Road in 1896.

Unlike the Duke's Stand, no plan has survived to explain what happened in terms of layout inside the King's Stables and the other ancient Rubbing Houses on the Heath like that in Fig. 127. The layout of the hack stalls under the Duke's Stand (Fig. 132) shows that in this case they were accessed along a central corridor with the only entrances at each end of it. On the other hand, the King's Stables for racehorses not hacks had four doors along both the east and west frontages, which appears to show they were favoured with loose boxes rather than stalls on the racecourse even in the eighteenth century when stalls would have been used back in their yards. Presumably the dual use as a rubbing house dictated the need for boxes. It seems likely each door gave access to two boxes with internal doors set at an angle of 90 degrees to each other across the adjacent corners. Probably those on each side of the building backed onto their opposite numbers with no corridor between them. Clearly there must have been fewer than the sixteen inferred by the eight doors to allow for such things as a tack room and feed store of some sort.

Stables on the Long Course

The starts along the first half of the Long Course had smaller stables at the eight, six and five ones and at the four-mile

Fig. 153

Photograph of the July Course Stands today

The retention of the buildings in the recent extensive redevelopment is surely a tribute to the work of the 1930s.

Fig. 154

First stand on the July Course (demolished 1875)

Beacon Post. We have no images of any but the last, which appears in Fig. 158 apart from a distant view on the horizon by Seymour of five-mile stables. The earlier ones would have already been demolished or been taken over by Jenison Shafto in the period after 1750 when he used much of the old course for what Chapman designated his 'Trial Course'. Four Mile Stables at the Beacon Start as painted by Stubbs and Herring (Fig. 159) looks very similar to, if smaller than, the rebuilt King's Stables so no doubt the building was also reconstructed only a few years before it forms the background to fine portraits by Stubbs in the 1760s (Figs. 49 and 50). With the first part of the Beacon largely disused by the mid-nineteenth century, there was a debate in 1857 about moving it to the Cesarewitch start but nothing was done. It was finally demolished in 1869, by which time it was being 'regularly vandalised by gypsies and vagrants' – a sad fate for a building that had begun a century earlier as an important element in Stubbs's establishing the sense of place.

July Course Stables

One of the stables erected around 1760 was that on the July Course, replacing the seventeenth-century version that appears in Figs. 35 and 37. It must have disappeared along with the old stand of Fig. 154 in 1875. After that the July Course never had a separate stable block as such but horses were saddled in boxes or under the trees of the Plantation just as they are today.

Ditch Stables

Slightly later came the important Ditch Stables (Fig. 155) just beyond the King's Gap and quite close to the Ditch on the eastern side. They are absent from the 1768 map but had appeared by that of 1787 and became increasingly important as the use of the Beacon at either end beyond the Cesarewitch Course steadily lessened. As explained above, the Ditch Stables were where the vast majority of horses were saddled throughout the nineteenth century until made redundant for racing purposes by the Admiral's changes of 1858. However, they remained of some use in connection with training on the Heath until finally demolished in 1903.

Other stables

By 1885 another so-called Rubbing House was thought necessary (Fig. 87) although it can never have been used for

Fig. 155

Ditch Stables (demolished 1903)

that purpose in the full pre-Robson sense of scraping a horse after sweating him. It is now the only survivor of all the various stables and was last used for anything more constructive than storage by Sir Alfred Munnings as a studio due to its close proximity to the main starts on the Rowley Mile.

Apart from all the painted or engraved images showing buildings that can be identified, there is one that is much harder to place (Fig. 156). The original Wootton at Badminton, of which this is a copy, depicts the Heath in 1744. From the alignment of the various gaps and other buildings we can deduce that its position must have been quite close to the Cambridge Road, or even just across it in Hare Park. As it is not the Four-Mile Stables and does not appear on the earliest map of 1768 it is impossible to identify, although it looks as though it had been there a long time and might not last much longer. Maybe it was something from the days of Charles II.

On the Bury side of the town there has never been a racecourse and so little call for structures beyond that named the King's Chair constructed for Charles II to watch the gallops on Warren Hill. In fact it stood on the slice of the rising ground known as Long Hill and by the late eighteenth century it had become the rather elegant little gazebo of Fig. 1, which too has long since disappeared. The absence of Rubbing Houses suggests that Warren Hill was thought unsuitable for sweating horses and that this part of training them was restricted to work on Racecourse Side. At least they do not seem to have had to face the rigours of Warren Hill laden with the numerous blankets, headpieces, etc. needed for sweating gallops.

Fig. 156

Trip, after John Wootton (1744)

A mysterious building appears beside the horse. It is not on any map but would seem from the landmarks to have stood near the Cambridge Road perhaps a mile from the Ditch. It seems most likely to be Five-Mile Stables.

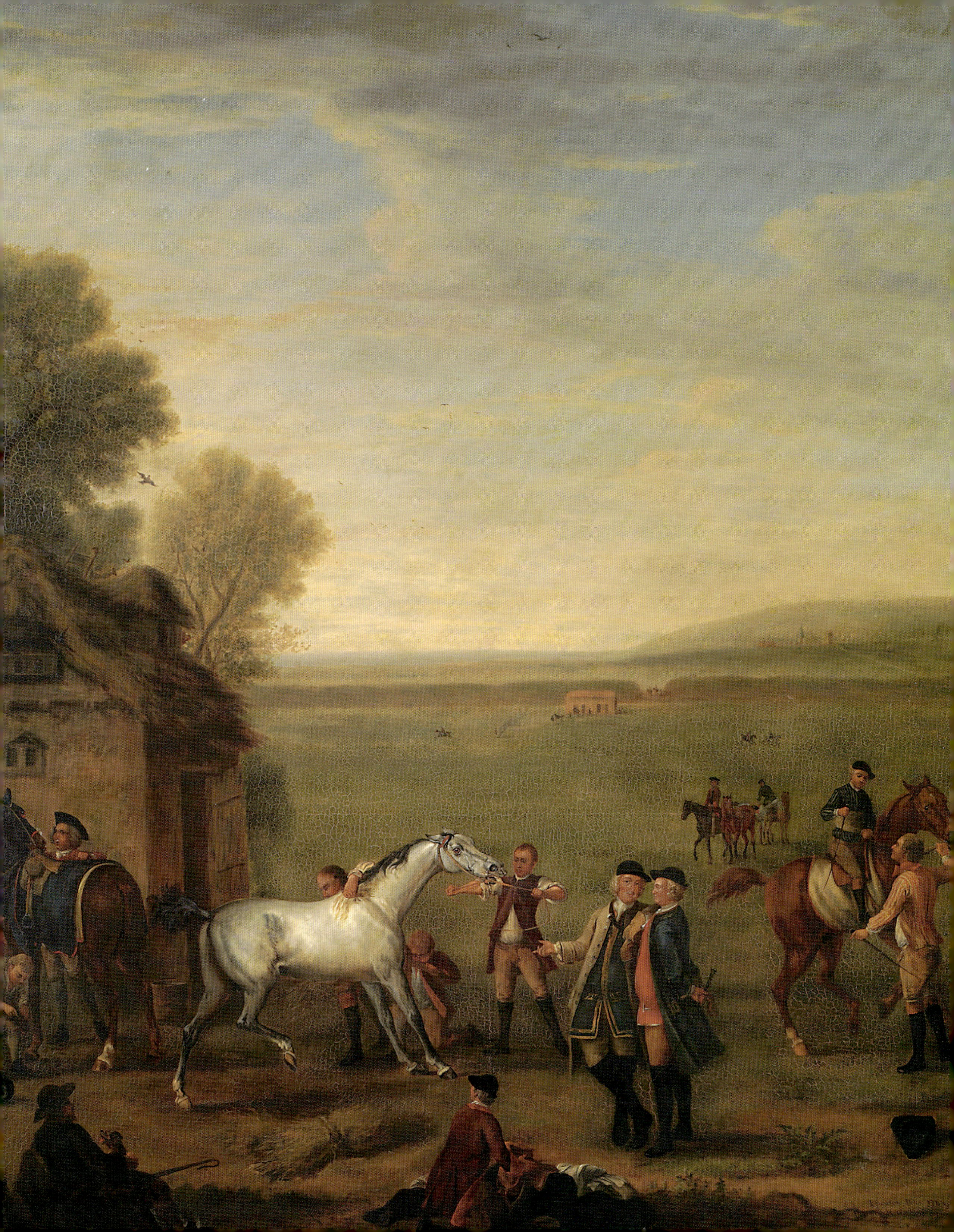

PICTURE PUZZLE 7: IDENTIFICATION OF BUILDINGS

Until recently it was assumed that the two Stubbs sketches of stables on the Heath (Figs. 157 and 158) both depicted different ends of the same building. They were retained by Stubbs for his own use from their creation by 1765 until his death in 1806, as they figured in his studio sale en route to their places today in the Mellon Collection and the Tate. In fact the background of the King's Stand with the Duke's Stand beyond receding into the distance, linked by the rails to the south of the course, shows Fig. 157 to be of the King's Stables as opposed to the eastern end of the Four-Mile Stables which is shown in Fig. 158. In that case the background includes the trees by Four-Mile Farm on the horizon beside the Cambridge Road. Nowadays, as in numerous other places around the town, the wooded area shown here has expanded. The Mellon sketch was later used for such masterpieces as the Gimcrack double portrait (Fig. 55) and the exhausted Hambletonian after his match with Diamond (Fig. 67) of over thirty years later, while the Tate picture was used for another Gimcrack (Fig. 49), Eclipse (Fig. 50) and several other fine portraits of horses before their races.

When the buildings are confused they are usually referred to, rather vaguely, as the Rubbing House or, less accurately, as the Rubbing Down House, although the latter term was never employed when they were in use. In fact there were several other similar structures on the Heath where horses would be scraped after work in heavy clothing, or simply set right after exercise or races or indeed, between heats. Only one later stable of this sort remains. It is situated near the Cambridgeshire start and appears in the background of the picture of La Flèche by Emil Adam (Fig. 87).

There would never have been confusion between these sketches if Stubbs had chosen to make it obvious that the King's Stables at the finish were at least twice the size of their counterpart at the start. This is made clear by Herring when he shows how small the latter seems in the background to his picture of the eccentric owner Fulwar Craven trotting past on his way back to the town along the Cambridge Road (Fig. 159). The extra size of the King's Stables is apparent from a Francis Sartorius (Fig. 53), yet even that shows only three of the four doors which were placed on each side.

The sketch of the King's Stables is of crucial importance to understanding how Stubbs continually used these images even after they became anachronistic – as with this one, that had ceased to be an accurate representation of the Beacon finish after the Duke of Portland's Stand was added in the 1780s. The point is made in detail elsewhere (Figs. 65 to 68) but here it will suffice to say that the large post in the centre of the picture is that on the north side of the Beacon finish. Opposite is the Judge's Box to the south beside the Stand and it appears again in detail behind Trentham (Fig. 164). What is most significant is the bank running north from the winning post before turning west, which marked the limit to the course as horses approached the finish, there being no rails on that side of the Beacon. When exactly the bank was removed is not clear but its disappearance related to the building of the Portland Stand so it had gone some years before Stubbs assumed it was still there when he painted Hambletonian after his triumph in 1799 over Diamond (Fig. 67) in 1800.

Picture Puzzle 7

Fig. 157

Study of the *King's Stables* by George Stubbs (1765)

Fig. 158

Study of the *Four-Mile Stables* by George Stubbs (1765)

Picture Puzzle 7

Fig. 159

*Fulwar Craven on his Norfolk Hackney passing Four-Mile Stables
by J.F. Herring senior (1834)*

II
Layout of Individual Courses on the Heath

The various ways in which different generations have laid out the Heath for racing since the mid-seventeenth century is well recorded. On the other hand, before the Restoration the precise use made of it by the Courts of Charles I and his father remains obscure. At least we know they used what they called the Long Course, and there seems no reason to doubt that it was the same one employed after 1660. This started not far from Babraham and largely followed the ridge overlooking Cambridge for four miles dipping down to the six mile post just to the west of Six Mile Bottom before arriving near the Beacon starting post at its halfway point. From there it ran straight for two miles to the Running Gap and on up the Rowley Mile before a lung-bursting six furlongs uphill to finish at the King's Stand having covered a total of eight miles. Whether there was a stand in the first half of the seventeenth century is not known and the only supposed picture of one (Fig. 4) actually depicts the eighteenth-century Duke's Stand named in honour of the Duke of Cumberland.

In essence, the main racecourse on the Heath has always been based on the old Long Course even if changing fashions have seen six furlongs chopped off at one end and five miles at the other. The two and a quarter miles of the present Cesarewitch course in the middle have thus been raced over for some four centuries and this fact is surely part of the fascination of the place. Quite when Newmarket got its second and largely separate racecourse (originally known as the Round Course and now the July or Summer Course) is a good deal less clear. We know that in 1665 Charles II ordered articles which refer to the race being on the 'new Round-heate'. Whether the word 'new' indicated a revised version of a former Round Course or something entirely novel is uncertain, but the usual assumption has been that he was initiating the first racecourse on the far side of the Ditch. However, in 2002 a fascinating drawing (Fig. 34) was sold at Sotheby's which could well point towards the King much extending an older course. As the note explains, the drawing is not only full of information about the conduct of things on the Heath in the seventeenth century but also seems to be the oldest representation of racing at Newmarket – it is a truly remarkable if somewhat ambiguous relic of the early days.

Whatever form it took in its very early days the Round Course that appears in the first maps was a circuit of about three and three-quarter miles beginning and ending quite close to the present July winning post. In fact it was nearer to being diamond-shaped than round with each side around a mile long. The first leg took the field north-west to a point on the edge of the present National Stud not far from the Cambridge Road before turning due north to cross the Beacon Course and the present bypass before coming back across them and finishing broadly on the line of the present straight but angled more away from the Ditch. Things stayed this way until the early nineteenth century when the start was moved down to the Well Gap and the third eastward leg was realigned to follow the Beacon rather than cross it. By then the Round Course itself was becoming an anachronism and racing beyond the Ditch was largely confined to the straight of about a mile plus as much of the old Beacon as was needed for the longer races.

Until 1846 the concept we have of concentrating summer racing to the west of the Ditch was unknown. There was a July meeting from 1765 but until 1846 its races took place on either course depending as much as anything on which one you decided you wanted to use for your match. Racing commonly took place on both courses on the same day so not merely did you need to get from one finish to another a few furlongs away but sometimes had to cross the Ditch itself to see things properly. With no public stands and the need for a hack all too obvious, it is hardly surprising that before Sir John Astley built the first version of the Millennium Stand on the Rowley Mile the general public was conspicuous by its absence. Indeed, it was not until 1873 that the habit, going right back to Charles II, of running the Royal Plates over the Round Course regardless of what else was happening was finally abandoned. After that the old course itself became redundant apart from its use today for staging the Town Plate with its prize consisting, among other things, of Newmarket sausages.

◆◆◆◆

It is sometimes supposed that having several different finishes on each racecourse served little purpose except to deter too many of the public from putting in an appearance. While it is true that one of the arguments sometimes used at Club meetings for continuing this seemingly odd practice when it came under pressure in the second half of the nineteenth century did have just such a basis, it was certainly not the original reason for such a complex layout. Races could be started from as many as twenty points along the Long Course and end at nearly half that number until distances beyond four miles were abandoned around 1730. One of the last six-mile races came in 1722 when the great Flying Childers beat Chaunter for 1,000 Guineas (Fig. 12).

In fact the reason for the multiplicity of courses within the Beacon, and to a lesser degree the Round Course arrangements, was so that owners could pick the one they thought would best suit their horse when making matches. To take an extreme example, the Ancaster Mile went dead straight up to the King's Stand, having started on a spur which joined the Beacon just after the finish of the Rowley Mile. It was a course of exceptional severity, uphill pretty well the whole way, and the contrast with the Abingdon Mile, beginning at the present Cambridgeshire start and finishing in the dip, is stark. The layout of the Heath thus provided an additional layer to the standard debates over weights and distances when trying to settle the terms of a match or decide which open race to enter. In addition, the younger horses were catered for by the races for two-year-olds usually ending on the Rowley Mile on the down slope before the Bushes while on the July Course their post was in that course's dip, so sparing young horses the stiff uphill final furlong they face today.

Mention of the Abingdon Mile brings us on to the two adjustments added to the latter part of the Beacon and which almost amounted to separate courses in their own right apart from the fact their finishes were shared with the Beacon and the Rowley Mile respectively. Both made extensive use of the area which lies between the Rowley Mile stands and the Ditch with the Ancaster Mile laid out, as explained, as a spur extending the last leg of the Beacon back into what are now just gallops. It was opened in 1774 and named after the 3rd Duke of Ancaster. As made clear in Part 4 the new course became the basis for various shorter races over nearly six furlongs, principally the Criterion Stakes, and in the nineteenth century included some of only just over three furlongs 'from the Old betting Post to the King's Stand'. When the Cambridgeshire was founded in 1839 it began by being

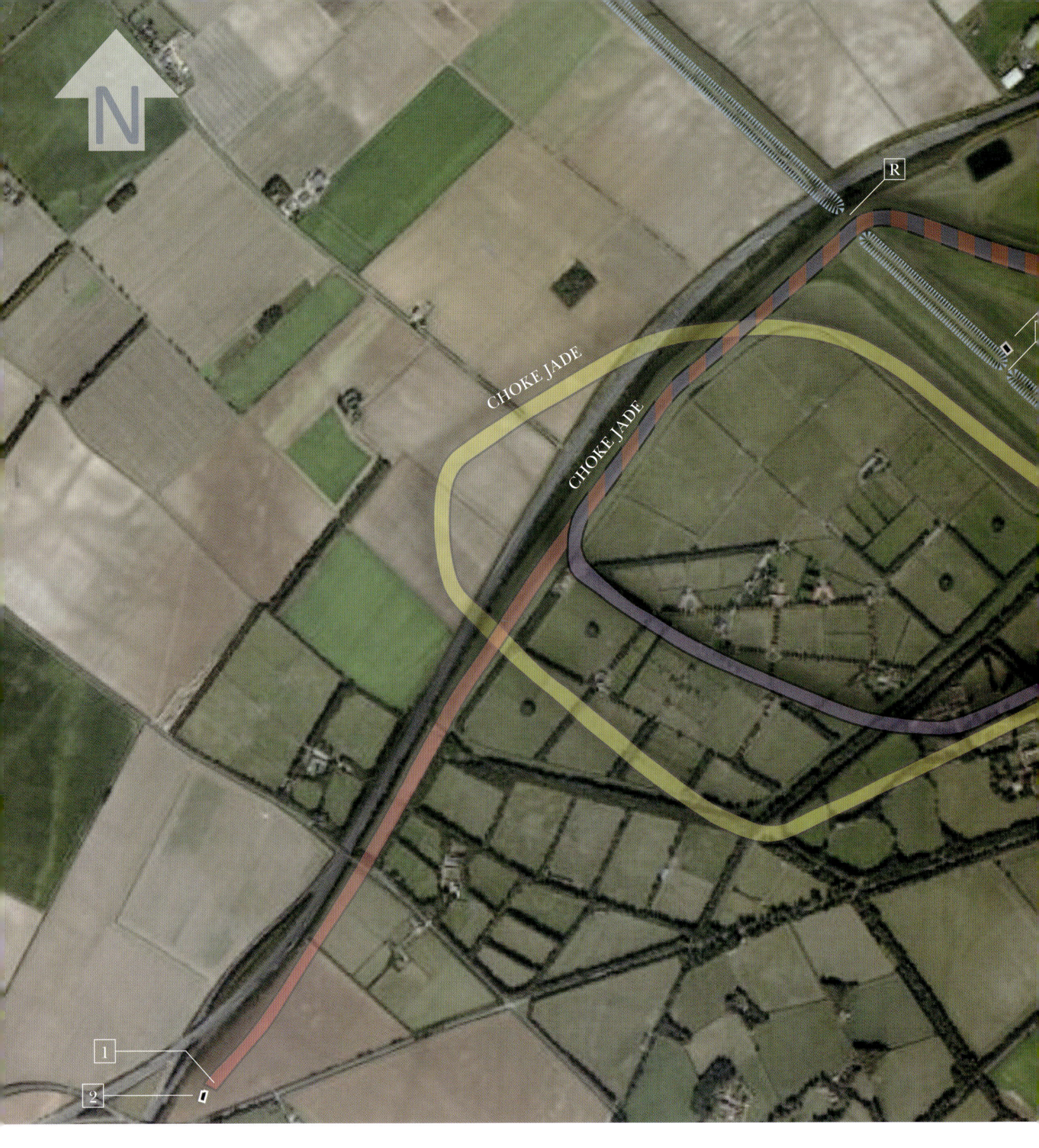

Newmarket Racecourse Historical Course – 1787

The historial details have been added to an aerial map that shows today's buildings, road layout and field boundaries.

Features

	Devil's Ditch	C	Cambridge Gap
R	Running Gap	T	Toll Bar
K	King's Gap	B	The Bushes
W	Well Gap		(The Furzes in 1787)
		Tu	Turn of the Lands

Courses

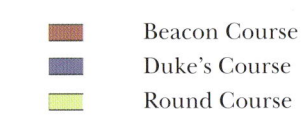

- Beacon Course
- Duke's Course
- Round Course

Buildings

1	Start of the Beacon Course	2	Four-Mile Start Stables	7	King's Stand
6	Beacon & Dukes Course Finish	3	Jockey Club or Ditch Stables	8	Duke's Stand
9	Finish of Rowley Mile	4	Duke of Portland Stand	10	Round Course
11	Starting and Finishing Post for the Round Course	5	King's Stables		Finish Stables
13	Starting Post for Duke's Course			12	Round Course Stand

Newmarket Racecourse Historical Course – 1887

The historial details have been added to an aerial map that shows today's buildings, road layout and field boundaries. Course layout based on Manning Map of 1887.

Features

	Devil's Ditch	T	Old Toll Bar
R	Running Gap	B	The Bushes
K	King's Gap	Tu	Turn of the Lands
W	Well Gap		
C	Cambridge Gap		

Courses

- Beacon Course
- Round Course inc. the July Course
- Ancaster Mile/ Cambridgeshire Course
- Between the Banks Gallops

Buildings

1	Start of the Beacon Course	2	Site of the former Four-Mile Stables	7	Portland Stand
9	Finish of Beacon and Cambridgeshire courses	3	Victorian Rubbing House	8	King's Stables
11	Red Betting Post	4	Ditch Mile Stand	10	Saddling Enclosure
12	Finish of Rowley Mile	5	Rowley Mile Stand	13	July Stand
14	Finish of Round & July Courses	6	The Bird Cage	15	Jockey Club Stand
16	Start of Round Course				

run on a most unsatisfactory course starting in the dip just before the Bushes and racing round the bend at what was known as 'The Turn of the Lands' (more or less the present Members' Car Park) up to the King's Stand. Realising its deficiencies for a big handicap field, in 1843 the Ancaster Mile was extended and the race run on what became the Cambridgeshire Course. After the 1886 running it became the Old Cambridgeshire Course when the race moved again to its present start and from 1912 the Ancaster spur reverted to gallops.

◆◆◆◆

The other addition to the main course came in 1959 when the Club was persuaded that Newmarket needed a circular track in front of the Rowley Mile stands. This could accommodate races of up to two miles, beginning near the Cambridge Road and tracking across the Heath until swinging into the Rowley Mile near the Bushes. The minimum distance on it was ten furlongs and the whole concept, originally named the Cambridge Road Course, was never very popular. However, the fact that the runners seemed suddenly to be swallowed by the earth about a mile out due to a fold in the land caused something of a sensation on the first day. Renamed the Sefton Course in honour of its chief protagonist, the 7th Earl of Sefton, his death in 1972 made it possible to scrap the whole experiment in 1973 without causing too much offence. The Duke of Norfolk then observed that Lord Sefton had once told him that if he refused to remove an adverse comment from a report on the course he would never speak to him again, so the potential for ill-feeling was clear enough. The alternative of naming the Earl of Sefton Stakes in his honour instead has provided a much more satisfactory memorial.

With proper stands due in 1876 at the Rowley Mile finish a second effort was made in 1875 following an earlier failed attempt at a circular course in 1808. It began at the Old Cambridgeshire start and swung in a long arc across the Flat to join the Rowley Mile about six furlongs out. However,

like its predecessor it was used only once, on 28 October, for the two-mile Circular Handicap when Stray Shot beat six others including the prolific winner Lilian. It seems that the Georgians and Victorians were quicker on the uptake than their twentieth-century successors in appreciating the demerits of laying out courses on this ground. Hopefully the large screens now available will deter anyone else from a fourth experiment.

◆◆◆◆

The July Course also had a subsidiary track of sorts in the form of the Duke's Course. This was almost as old as the Round Course itself and must have been named for Charles II's brother and successor James, Duke of York. It began just inside the mid-point of the first leg of the Round Course diamond and curved its way across the middle of the track to join the Beacon just after the Cesarewitch start. Thereafter it followed the normal route to finish at the King's Stand. The fact that the race was named for a different royal duke to the one commemorated by the Duke's Stand explains the seeming oddity of the ducal course failing to finish at the ducal stand. When the Round Course was altered early in the nineteenth century the Duke's Course was abandoned together with its only subsidiary, Dutton's Course, which had a short life from 1793 starting six furlongs along the way just before entry into the Beacon and running three miles up to the King's Stand.

For many years the sport on the Heath was divided colloquially between racing 'Behind the Ditch' as opposed to that which took place 'Across the Flat'. However, this slightly dismissive reference to the July Course seems to have fallen out of favour, which is perhaps just as well as now no less than twenty of the thirty-eight cards programmed for 2014 were located there. Things were very different until 1890 when in July another three-day meeting was added to the four-day July meeting itself. Formerly, only that one was held on it, which had been initiated in 1765 with a win for Gimcrack (Figs. 49

and 55). The necessary preliminary to such a major switch in emphasis between the two courses was the realignment and building works of the 1930s on the July Course, dealt with in the preceding section.

◆◆◆◆

The final and completely separate course which needs mentioning was the one used for Jumping laid out on the Links by Colonel Harry McCalmont in 1893. Although its two-mile circuit proved quite popular, staging a meeting in March and again in November, including the National Hunt Meeting itself in 1897, it did not long survive the departure of the Colonel to the Boer War. A fixture was held in November 1899 and the meeting then lapsed until after McCalmont's death in 1902. Restarted in 1903, it finally packed up in 1905 without the essential support of its founder. It is now laid out as the town's golf course having been bought by the Club when the McCalmont family sold their huge Cheveley Park estate in 1921.

◆◆◆◆

In the tables and maps we have tried to set out all the principal variants available when agreeing terms for a match. Most of the courses regularly used bore the names of important owners or topographical features but a few were entirely idiosyncratic choices and one can sometimes only guess what was meant by such descriptions as 'Start between the two hills and so over the course'. In fact this was probably a four mile race, the two hills being the pair of tumuli which appear in the background of the Stubbs's pictures at the Beacon start but which have long since been levelled.

After the first public grandstand at the present Rowley Mile finish was erected in 1876, pressure mounted within the Jockey Club for the rationalisation of such arrangements – no doubt outside the Club feelings were a good deal stronger. Perhaps the key decisions came when everything beyond the present Rowley Mile finish was abandoned in 1912 under pressure from Lord Durham, apart from very occasional races over the old 'Ditch In' (two miles from the Running Gap to the old Beacon finish) for the Club's private races, the Whip and the Cup. As explained, the old King's Stand and Duke's Stands had been scrapped in the mid-nineteenth century, and after 1912 most of the Duke of Portland's Stand went too, apart from residual bits near ground level from which you could watch the private races. Even that use lapsed in 1963 after Bigamy overturned the three to one laid on Domesday for the Whip. In 1960 the final finishes in the dip on the July Course took place while the comparable post on the Rowley Mile had ceased to be used in 1959. Apart from anything else this decision avoided occasional traumas for all concerned when a jockey got beaten by going easily past the lower winning post in eager anticipation of quickening away up the hill only to find that the race was already over.

◆◆◆◆

In summary, over the years race distances fell steadily from eight miles (there were a few even longer ones but presumably these were achieved by doing three or four laps somewhere as there does not seem to have been a 12- or -16 mile course as such) to consolidate at a standard four miles by 1730. From there on maximum distances have fallen to the 18 furlongs of the Cesarewitch and average ones increased again after initially dropping to very low levels in the late nineteenth century (see Chapter 7). Both racecourses now have single winning posts instead of the proliferation of former days and our forefathers would certainly deprecate the loss of variety even if they would have to concede it makes a day's racing on the Heath a good deal less arduous. That said, the loss is real as the variety added by every distance up to about three miles having an easy or severe version meant that the Heath really represented far more than two racecourses in terms of testing the developing thoroughbred population and the judgement of the main owners and their trainers and jockeys.

Newmarket Racecourse – 2015

The historial details have been added to an aerial map that shows today's buildings, road layout and field boundaries.

Features

	Devil's Ditch	C	Cambridge Gap
R	Running Gap	T	Old Toll Bar
K	King's Gap	B	The Bushes
W	Well Gap		

Courses

- Cesarewitch and Rowley Mile Course
- July Course
- Round Course (used for Newmarket Town Plate)

ROWLEY MILE

THE FLAT

NEWMARKET

Buildings

	National Hunt 1893-1905	6	Finish of July and Round Courses	3	Victorian Rubbing House
	Sefton Course 1959-1973	8	Start of Newmarket Town Plate	4	Rowley Mile Stands
1	Start of the July Course			7	July Stands
2	Start of the Cesarewitch Course				
5	Finish for Cesarewitch and Rowley Mile Courses				

III

Main Races on the Heath

Although we know there was a register kept of forthcoming matches and bets laid in Charles II's reign at the Groom Porter's Office both in Whitehall and at the Newmarket Palace, there is no evidence of any record of results being maintained before the Match Book is opened in 1718. The first volume runs from October of that year to November 1788 and so bridges part of the gap that would otherwise exist at Newmarket before John Cheny started his national record from 1727. Prior to 1718 occasional results are known from various sources, and these were collated in 1892 by J.B. Muir in his 'Ye Olde New-Markitt Calendar'. The earliest one he found was in 1619, so his work covers exactly a century but records only a tiny fraction of the races that would have been run. In any case, there were only a handful of races with names designed to continue for years and almost all the great events would have been matches. As Richard Nash observes, this sudden enthusiasm for record-keeping away from Whitehall mid-season in October 1718 seems to indicate something is really beginning to stir in terms of replacing the Palace at the heart of the sport.

THE SEVENTEENTH CENTURY

The main events now known which happened in the seventeenth century are as follows:

a) The first race unearthed by Muir was run on 19 March 1619 and only appears in Court records because James I attended. No details survive of what happened.

b) On 8 March 1623 came a match for £100 in which Lord Salisbury's horse beat one of the Duke of Buckingham's named Prince, so he becomes the earliest runner with a name.

c) Apart from a reference to a meeting in the spring of 1631 and to Bay Turrall winning a gold cup in March 1634 all is silence until after the Restoration in 1660.

d) After that, in March 1666 Lord Thomond's Thumps won what was referred to as 'a great race' over six miles. If it ended at what was called 'Thomond's Post' it used at least the last part of what became in that year Charles II's new Round Course.

e) It is uncertain whether the Articles for the Town Plate of 1665 (Fig. 18) actually produced a race each year before 1720. However, King Charles rode the winner of Plates in 1671 and 1675 whether or not actually that derived from the Articles. So far as it still can the Town Plate follows the route of the old Round Course using for much of the way a strip of grass left specially across the National Stud (Fig. 160).

f) The final seventeenth-century subject to mention is each monarch's provision of Royal Plates, which only ceased in 1887. Begun by Charles II, the series expanded steadily and eventually formed the nearest thing to a Pattern scheme that the eighteenth century had. Until quite late in the series each race was worth 100 Guineas and until 1720 this came from the monarch in the form of a trophy made of that weight of gold (Fig. 23). By 1800 there were twenty-two such races, almost all over four miles, but Newmarket's allocation of three were run on the Round Course so over some two furlongs less. In 1850 there were thirty-five here and sixteen in Ireland and even in 1887 twelve still survived in this country with Newmarket's three consolidated into a single race of 500 Guineas while the others had 300 Guineas on offer. In Ireland the series only ended after the Second World War and the Royal Whip at the Curragh is a relic of former glories. Given that the ability to win one of these races was the real measure of quality until the Classics arrived in 1776 with the St Leger, the fact that in those days to call a horse a Plater was a compliment is hardly surprising as it was then short for King's Plate horse, rather than a Selling Plater.

PROGRAMMES IN THE EIGHTEENTH CENTURY

While we know so much more of the events on the Heath in the eighteenth century, things only changed fairly slowly until the dramatic expansion following the Jockey Club's real arrival on the scene as the major player in the town after 1750. The great majority of races in the first half of the century continued to be private matches. However, from 1709 there were serious alternatives when proper sweepstakes arrived.

a) On 12 October 1709 Newmarket borrowed or copied a race from Quainton and ran it as the Noblemen and Gentlemen's Contribution money. The race lasted until 1736, by when it was entitled the October Stakes and its disappearance was an early sign of general malaise in the 1740s.

b) The first version of the Great Stakes series came in 1730 followed by the Wallasey Stakes in 1733.

Fig. 160

Photograph of the second leg of the Round Course today

The impact of the tree planting is apparent from a comparison with Fig. 37, showing the same part of the course over two centuries ago.

c) When things got going again after the 1740s it was a resurrected Great Stakes that was the key to the advance. However, by 1786, when it petered out with a whimper rather than a bang, it had ceased to be of great importance.

d) From 1751 expansion was dramatic, but it was very largely constructed on matches and sweeps with no names. They were subject to annual or triennial renewal or were simply one offs. The oldest surviving race, excluding the Town Plate, is the Newmarket Challenge Whip, which really started in

Fig. 161

The Newmarket Challenge Whip

The trophy bears the arms of Barbara Villiers, one of Charles II's mistresses when she was still Lady Castlemaine, so seems to date from around 1670. It was competed for intermittently before becoming a regular event for members of the Jockey Club and Rooms in 1764. Fig. 3 shows one of the earlier contests, that of 1756, won by Matchem. The Whip happened to be held without challenge by the O'Kellys between 1786 and 1792, so when Eclipse died at Cannons, their splendid park in Edgware, it seems entirely plausible that his hair was used to embellish it, as legend alleges forming both the loop at the head and lash.

1764 for members of the Jockey Club Rooms. The Club had run a variety of races for its members since 1752 and continued to do so into the nineteenth century but only the Whip and the now defunct Challenge Cup had traceable identities among these private races. The trophy for the former actually dates from the days of Charles II and is known to have been contested on an occasional basis before 1752 (Fig. 161).

e) A few races began to acquire names such as the Fortescue, Bolton, Grosvenor and Cumberland Stakes and the Clermont Cup but most only lasted a decade or so. One that achieved far greater longevity was the Craven Stakes – founded, like them, as a tribute to an individual – starting in 1771 as a weight-for-age race Across the Flat. However, its conditions eventually changed so dramatically that it would be unrealistic to claim it is actually the forerunner of the present Classic trial of that name. In 1878 it took its present form following a final outing as an optional claimer in 1877, which had produced a walk-over. Such disasters were often the precursor of a race's demise but in this case at least the name survived.

f) Two races which seemed to herald a new approach came in 1786 with the Prince's Stakes followed in 1792 by the Oatlands. The former finally ended early in the next century having been restarted after a pause following the departure of the Prince of Wales from the Heath. Always run Across the Flat for three-year-olds, it was an early sort of Classic trial. Its peculiarity was that it was run in three separate classes with the entries apportioned by ballot and, just as today, provision made to separate each owner's entries if he had two or more. There was then a fourth race or final, called the Main, with that name derived from cockfighting, in which any runner could again compete, paying 200 Guineas entry as opposed to the original 100 Guineas. Winners of earlier classes were penalised 3lbs.

g) Much longer lived and more important was the Oatlands Stakes, with its name derived from the Duke of York's house and effectively purloined from Ascot. The original Oatlands there had been run in 1790 and was the first major handicap ever run. It was a huge success, and in 1791 was won by the Prince of Wales's Baronet (Fig. 56). For 1792 Newmarket prevailed on Ascot to put on identical races with only those which had run at Newmarket eligible to turn out at Ascot. After the Escape Affair one can only assume Ascot cancelled its part of this arrangement in a Royal huff as only the Newmarket race took place. After a gap in 1793, when people were no doubt ruminating on what had happened, Newmarket seems to have rubbed salt into wounds by staging the Oatlands in two classes with a Main in the form of a match between the winners while Ascot continued to sulk. The series was a great success and soon had three classes with the Main now open to their runners along the lines of the Prince's Stakes. Run on the Ditch In for four-year-olds and upwards, arrangements varied as sometimes there was no Main and in other years another series in October and, on occasion, in July. Towards the end only a single race took place. Ascot eventually accepted they had got it wrong and reintroduced their own Oatlands Stakes in 1811 but by 1838 the races at both courses were losing ground due to lack of prize money. Both reacted in the same way on this occasion as Newmarket introduced the Cesarewitch and Cambridgeshire in 1839 and Ascot staged the first Ascot Stakes while the Oatlands became an important footnote to racing history as the origin of the handicap. Indeed, the words Oatlands and handicap were effectively interchangeable as references to running 'our Oatlands' in other places make clear.

h) In 1786 the Heath got the first open race which is still run today under the same title and with similar conditions. Surprisingly this ancient relic is a race for two-year-olds, the July Stakes, run then on the Rowley Mile over slightly under its modern distance of six furlongs. Not all the conditions stand as in 1786 the progeny of the two dominant stallions, Eclipse and Highflyer, were required to carry 3lbs extra and fillies got only a 2lbs allowance. The race moved to the July Course in 1822 and finished in the dip until after the Second World War. It was then shortened to five furlongs, until 1961, and used the modern winning post, so it was over a more severe course if a shorter one than before the war. Now back to six furlongs, the July Stakes is comfortably the oldest two-year-old race in the world and the Heath is a fitting place to run it as the first horse of that age to race anywhere had been Gibsoutski, who beat a six-year-old when receiving three stone over the last six furlongs of the Rowley Mile on 26 October 1769.

i) Apart from serious efforts to programme races to suit the available horses there were some splendidly eccentric efforts to do so for the amusement of the owners. One of the best was the Claret Stakes which was launched in 1780 over the Beacon. Originally it cost 100 Guineas to run plus the contribution of a hogshead barrel of claret. The owner of the second collected two of the hogsheads with which to console himself. This was changed in 1781 to the entry going up to 200 Guineas with the proviso that the winner should find the owner of the second's two barrels, thus depriving Sir Charles Bunbury of a net fifteen hogsheads when his Derby winner Diomed won. However as he collected 1,900 Guineas less two barrels instead of only 1,300 Guineas plus thirteen hogsheads he may not have minded too much. The race continued in fits and starts for a century but shorn of any barrels after 1785. It was even teamed with the Port Stakes from 1810 which had half the entry payment and was only open to horses not entered in the Claret – sadly it never seems to have had any pipes of port attached to its conditions but they did add an Ale Stakes for a while with claiming conditions.

NINETEENTH-CENTURY DEVELOPMENTS

The new century began well enough with the arrival of the 2,000 Guineas in 1809, followed by the 1,000 Guineas in 1814. While the colts' race has always been on the Rowley Mile (Hitler permitting) the fillies faced a considerably easier task over the Ditch Mile and continued to do so until 1872. In some ways more thought seems sometimes to have gone into the programmes at Newmarket with regard to horsemanship in the widest sense than is possible today against the pressures of attracting crowds and satisfying the betting industry.

a) Another chance to show that there was more thought going into such things than might have been expected was missed with the Newmarket Stakes which began in 1804 over the Ditch Mile for three-year-olds. In 1809, when the 2,000 Guineas arrived at the same meeting, perversely it was the Prince's Stakes over ten furlongs that disappeared, leaving the Newmarket Stakes to struggle on rather unsuccessfully over a mile against the Guineas until 1889. Then it was moved to the Second Spring meeting with a huge increase in prize money and run Across the Flat as the main Derby trial and was won by that race's winner Donovan. However, with money again in painfully short supply the race disappeared after the 1961 running, won most appropriately by The Axe. Fortunately, the perceptive bookmaker Michael Simmonds supplied the funds to reinstate it in 1978 and it was run at the Guineas Meeting as the Heathorn Stakes and he was rewarded when the Derby winner Shirley Heights beat Ile de Bourbon by a short head. When Corals took over the sponsorship in 1985 the rules which governed such things under the recently formed Pattern Committee saw the race recover the ancient title that it still retains, now linked to Qatar.

b) Races which survived through the dark years of the mid-nineteenth century without ever being of major importance included the Audley End, Trial, Garden, Bedford, Clearwell, Column, Rutland and Prendergast Stakes. Of more significance if shorter lived were the Riddlesworth Stakes named after Squire Thornhill's estate and the Grand Duke Michael Stakes named for a Russian grandee. The Riddlesworth took various forms beginning in 1815 with a race for three-year-olds over the Abingdon Mile finishing in the dip. Entry cost 100 Guineas plus another 100 Guineas to run and had to be made when the stock in question were foals in 1812. It proved very popular and was often contested by animals that went on to run in one of the Guineas races as it took place at the Craven Meeting. Indeed, the Riddlesworth was so popular that from 1820 it was split between colts and fillies for four years before reverting to being a single race. From 1834 an odder idea for splitting saw two races run on the Mondays and Tuesdays of the Craven with identical conditions. You could enter a foal in either for £100 plus the same again to run. Indeed, you could enter both and decide later which one to pick. The race mirrored Newmarket in general in its steady decline, and by 1858 both races saw walk-overs. With the Admiral's sweeping changes on the Heath coming into force, 1859 saw the end of this race when only one Riddlesworth had been opened and received just two entries. As one was dead before the day, it too was a walk-over and so ended the series after 45 years and 74 races some won by the best horses of the period like Derby winners Priam and Bay Middleton (Figs. 162 and 163).

c) Indeed, Bay Middleton provides a link between this race and the Grand Duke Michael Stakes as he won both in his unbeaten career of six wins and a walk-over in 1836. The first running of the latter came in 1823 Across the Flat for three-year-olds in October. Designed as a final race to decide the champion, its first running appropriately saw the Derby winner Emilius beat the Oaks winner Zinc. It continued to attract some of the best horses on occasion but not so often as its prize money languished. The final running in 1892 saw the great filly La Flèche (Fig. 87) win a match at 40 to 1 on, thereby gaining a very stingy £486 for Baron de Hirsch against the 1,200 Guineas Colonel Udny had collected seventy years before.

d) Both elements of the Autumn Double, the Cesarewitch over 18 furlongs and the Cambridgeshire of half that distance, were introduced in 1839 to replace the Oatlands and have always been by far Newmarket's most important handicaps. The Cesarewitch is in one way like the 2,000 Guineas as they alone of all the early races have always been run over precisely the same courses except in wartime. The Cambridgeshire on the other hand started life with a bend in the middle as it was run over the last part of the Beacon until 1842. After that it had its own course running straight to the Beacon finish until 1887, but then it moved to the

PRIAM AND BAY MIDDLETON

Two fine Derby winners. Both strikingly handsome horses, they represent the end of an era on the Heath as nothing approaching their quality was trained at Newmarket until the 1860s, some thirty years after Bay Middleton retired to stud.

Fig. 162

Fig. 163

Priam (1827) by Emilius out of Cressida
after J. F. Herring, Senior

Bay Middleton (1833) by Sultan out of Cobweb
by W. Willoughby after J.F. Herring, Senior

Perhaps the best horse trained in Newmarket in the first half of the nineteenth century, Priam won fourteen of his sixteen races including the Derby. One of his defeats came in the St Leger when he was caught on the post by the much inferior Birmingham but really beaten by the bottomless going. An outstanding stallion he sired three winners of the Oaks although sold to the USA after only four covering seasons. He was just as successful there being champion four times, before his death in 1847.

Like so many horse portraits of its period this is a copy of the famous Herring in his Derby Winner series. At least the fairly moderate artist was honest enough to sign it with his own name, which is not very usual with Herring copies. A noticeably inferior copy of the same picture has long hung in the Jockey Club Rooms supported by a respectable provenance, and was once thought to be genuine. The horse was never beaten also winning the 2000 Guineas but at stud was not a success apart from siring a champion in the Flying Dutchman. Too many of his stock proved unsound.

present course. In their early days both the handicaps were often contested by Classic horses even including such as the Triple Crown winner Gladiateur, unplaced in the 1866 Cesarewitch. The places in the Calendar of the races have been switched several times and they have been sponsored since the 1970s. In the case of the Cesarewitch the Tote took over in 1978 and added the Cambridgeshire to its sponsorship portfolio in 1997. As a consequence of its acquisition by Betfred both races are now supported by that firm.

e) Newmarket experimented for years with triennial produce races in the autumn and later added biennial ones in the spring. In the first version animals were entered in 1845 for £10 in terms of the matings that year although the entrants only became the foals of 1846. One hundred and twenty-six of the matings produced live foals and the first race went to the useful Tadmor over six furlongs at the First October Meeting in 1848. A year later he was favourite for the three-year-old version open to the same pool of horses with another £10 due to be run Across the Flat but only came third to Vatican. In 1850 the no doubt much diminished pool provided the field for the final race of the series when Tadmor was missing and Vatican was made hot favourite but he was only third in a race over the Ditch In. By then the next pool of horses drawn from the 1847 crop had reached their Across the Flat race as three-year-olds and the lot after that one produced a field of fourteen two-year-olds at the same meeting. Things proceeded on these complex lines until the outbreak of the First World War but ended with the foals of 1915 entered before the war began. Fifty-four were still attracted at the same £10 with a richer Club adding £300 but only two ran for their two-mile race in 1919 and thus the series concluded, having provided 210 races over 74 years (including admittedly a sprinkling of walk-overs in the later stages).

f) A number of races still run today began on the back of the Club's improving finances in the last part of the nineteenth century, usually with good prize money. In sequence the most obvious ones are the Middle Park (1866) and Dewhurst (1875), both named after their original sponsors' studs, July Cup (1876), Princess of Wales and Jockey Club Stakes both in 1894 and the Cheveley Park in 1899. In addition, the Jockey Club Cup started in 1873 and the Champion Stakes in 1877 but both are now transferred to Ascot as part of Qipco Champions Day scheme along with the relatively new Pride Stakes on which to base their fillies and mares championship. In return have come the Group One Shadwell Fillies Mile, the Group 2 Juddmonte Royal Lodge and two Group 3 races.

g) Apart from the Cesarewitch (a slightly eccentric spelling for the heir to the Russian throne) and the Cambridgeshire, other handicaps have tended to arrive and disappear too often to attempt to summarise events. Naturally, in recent times this has been largely a matter of sponsorship. The Newmarket Handicap at the Craven lasted from 1844 to 1877, initially as an important race, and a similar race in the autumn, the Newmarket October Handicap lasted longer from 1861 to 1958, when it too disappeared as a name. Without Pattern race status to keep their names in place the lives of handicaps are usually a good deal shorter nowadays, in any traceable form at least.

h) The longest-surviving name arising from two-year-old races after the July Stakes is the Criterion Stakes, although it does not have a continuous history, disappearing in 1958 having existed since 1829. In this case the grant of Group 3 status to the Van Geest family's race at the Charity Meeting in June meant it needed a handle attached, and the old name was recycled in 1986 for this all-age contest.

i) Almost as old as the Criterion is the still extant name of the Hopeful Stakes, now an all-age Listed race over six furlongs run on the July Course. It began as a race for two-year-olds in October 1832, produced some major winners and lasted until Newmarket's financial problems bit and in 1961 it was converted into a maiden race. As a final indignity the old title was attached for a while to an apprentice handicap before being abandoned altogether. In 1986 the July Course had need of a handle when the present race was introduced with Listed status and somebody thought it would be a good one to resurrect. It has now survived 28 years in this form with ratings more suited to Group 3 status.

j) Almost as old was the Chesterfield Stakes founded in 1834 in honour of the 6th Earl but its demise from 1990 when still a five-furlong race at the July Meeting after 167 years came about for almost the reverse reason. The race had a splendid history, having been won by the great Crucifix as well as several other Classic winners but by 1990 races over only five furlongs for two-year-olds found it hard to justify their places within the Pattern system due to their poor ratings. As a result it was already in decline when a three-horse field of little quality lost it Pattern status and after a few years as a rather nondescript handicap the name was quietly abandoned. Lord Chesterfield has been particularly unfortunate in his races as the Bretby Stakes named after his estate disappeared from 1988 having existed on the Rowley Mile since 1844. It is an odd by-product of changes of this sort that the Bretby Stakes Course is still the final six furlongs of the Rowley Mile, and the defunct Chesterfield Stakes still gives its name to the last five furlongs of the July Course. Accordingly, two of the most used courses on the Heath are named after races linked to one man although neither of the relevant contests actually still exists.

k) As finances improved in the 1860s and 1870s and more money could be added to owners' stakes, matches quickly almost disappeared. For so long the main element in the Newmarket programmes, by the time Admiral Rous (an enthusiastic matchmaker himself) died in 1877 they were already nearly extinct. It is also as well that some of the names which appeared in the early part of the century did not last too long. Quite who thought it a good idea to give races names such as the Weeds or Wretched Stakes or simply The Shorts for a half-mile race one cannot tell, but they do not sound likely to have been too attractive to a winning owner. Even worse was the Rubbish Stakes but at least the stipulation that the winner must be offered for £30 in the first year should have ensured the name was accurate. Other races where the names were linked to the entry qualifications were the Virgin and the Boudoir Stakes. The former was restricted to first foals and the latter to fillies run in the names of lady owners. As this only resulted in owners lending fillies to their wives for a day the race did not survive.

i) Apart from races with eccentric names or conditions a few have terms attached even where in retrospect it seems almost impossible to understand what the programmes were trying to achieve unless it was something rather discreditable. A good example was a race for two-year-olds with 100 Guineas entry and fillies allowed 4lbs. To these standard conditions were added an allowance of 3lbs for stock by stallions yet to have runners and, rather oddly, the same for two-year-olds bred in Ireland. Perhaps the latter was just a generous gesture but none ran and anyway that seems a bit unlikely in view of the final condition of an allowance of three pounds for stock got by three middle-aged stallions in Drumator, Coriander and Whiskey. The plot thickens when it is appreciated that these horses, of very different reputations, all belonged to Club members in Lord Clermont, Francis Dawson and Sir Charles Bunbury. While Drumator's only significance was that he was brother to the major stallion Trumpator both Coriander and Whiskey were important horses. Coriander was the horse who had won the race in 1791 when Escape caused such a sensation by finishing last, and Whiskey's daughter Eleanor won Sir Charles both the Derby and Oaks earlier in 1801. There were eight entries and three ran with victory going, rather unfairly one would feel, to Sir Charles's Julia by Whiskey in receipt of her two allowances. Fate, however, decided to intervene on behalf of the second owned by Mr John Wastell. The following season his defeated filly, by then named Scotia, won the Oaks with Bunbury's Julia in second place. Fig. 57 shows Frank Buckle about to mount Scotia in the Wastell silks so it seems a case of all's well that ends well but still a pretty odd performance all round. At least Sir Charles was quite open in getting his extra allowance.

EVENTS SINCE 1900

Apart from the Rowley Mile and Cesarewitch Courses the names of the rest are rarely used today and other distances are usually identified simply by the number of furlongs. However, names are part of the history of the Heath and it would amaze earlier generations how quickly they have fallen out of use. No doubt those from the eighteenth century would be equally surprised that all races now have names rather than reserving such titles only for the most important. A problem today is the way names are changed so often and there is no point in trying to trace their history below Pattern level since World War II. Apart from the needs of sponsors, the many changes in the Heath's fixture list further complicates the issue, all of which indeed, makes understanding the so-called 'narrative' of the sport much harder than was once the case when titles might last for ordinary maidens and small handicaps for decades.

However, these problems are offset at Pattern level by the rules devised originally by a committee under the Duke of Norfolk within which the major influences were the late Lord Carnarvon and Mr Peter Willett. Since its recommendations were implemented in 1971 their system has spread worldwide and each Pattern race has a continuing 'handle' which can only be changed in the rarest circumstances for races classed as Group One or Two. Those in Group Three or with Listed Status can have their 'handles' omitted from racecards but they are still registered and more often than not stated in full. When a new race is added it too gets its handle, with any sponsor's name attached while support lasts. Accordingly, it seems to us sufficient for present purposes to tabulate the Pattern and Listed races run on the Heath in 2013 plus their present dates in the Calendar, distances and grading together with their dates of foundation and entry into the Pattern scheme.

As will be seen from the latter date, the number of such races at Newmarket has expanded considerably, and if you take the local programme as a whole it constitutes a pretty impressive Pattern in its own right. Indeed, apart from the main racing countries very few of the rest could match its spread in terms of their entire national lists. Its only obvious weakness as a separate Pattern is in races of ten furlongs or more as the transfer of the Champion and Pride Stakes and the Jockey Club Cup has seen them replaced by two-year-old races. No doubt the reason so many black type races can be made to work usually without the injection of enhanced levels of prize money is the huge local horse population, which can run without the additional demands of travel. In our view, racing in general has benefitted enormously from the system and it would be hard to deny that Newmarket has done so as much or more than anywhere else. It inevitably reduces flexibility both nationally and internationally but programmes without the rigidity it introduces would be horribly like a body minus a skeleton.

Experts in marketing are inclined to complain that racing's 'narrative' has become obscure. However, they seem sublimely unaware (my co-author excepted) that the prime reason for this problem is the no doubt excellent commercial advice they hand out to their clients over race titles. Not so long ago one could go to most racecourses and know more or less what races you would see on a given day because they had happened there under the same title for years. Their names were linked in with their class, distance and so forth in the public mind. The best that can be managed today below Pattern level is the Classification system for all races but it is a rather soulless substitute even if considerably more informative – as its inventor I know it was never meant to have anything to do with 'narrative'. The exchange of the old names for those of sponsors' companies is a commercial inevitability, but equally inevitably detracts from the standing of the race itself in the minds of the informed public. Sadly, it is a problem without an answer, but there are a few cases where things might usefully have been done differently. For example, it is strange that, while Sir Charles Bunbury adds rather than detracts from 32red's sponsorship at the July Meeting with his Cup, there is no race on the Heath for Lord George Bentinck or, far worse, Admiral Rous. He did have a five-furlong Listed race until 2010 but it then moved to Ascot. Surely a trick was missed when the new Listed substitute for the Jockey Club Cup acquired a rather pale pastiche version of its predecessor's ancient title when named the Jockey Club Rose Bowl. As a race not aimed at sponsorship, might it not do better as an appropriately forthright Admiral Rous Cup?

During the slump in racing's fortunes after the last war far too many conditions races were being staged on the Heath with poor prize money and hopelessly inadequate fields distinguished by lack of either size or quality. It was a happy coincidence that the strengthening finances of the Club linked so well with the reinforcement of such races' standing due to their new Pattern status. Nowadays the result at all the main meetings is a quality of racing that must be the envy of some courses in locations that enable them to attract larger crowds – on a wet autumn day with the wind from the east all seems rather reminiscent of the eighteenth-century story when the best racing in the world took place before a few hundred folk even if we are no longer on our hacks (Fig. 37). At least they seem to have been lucky with the weather in October 1724.

While not a race of any significance since the seventeenth century it seems unfair to Charles II's inspiration of the Newmarket Town Plate of 1665/6 to omit its history from this section. From foundation as an important race for amateurs like the King himself it became one largely for the local tradesmen in the town from around 1725. After the Match Book ceased in 1788 few details of its presumed annual runnings exist until the 1850s but thereafter its winners are all known from the 1880s. Usually only attracting fields of two or three until after the First World War it then had a startling renaissance once ladies were allowed to take part as the only race in the country where this applied. Fields of fifteen or twenty then arose and the race still continues for nominal prizes over a presently somewhat altered version of the Old Round Course of Charles II. For many years the prize was augmented by the rent of what was apparently known as the 'Plate Land' close by the Jockey Club, but not has long since ceased to yield rent.

Pattern and Listed races on the Heath in 2013

Date	Name of Race (and sponsorship)	Age	Grade	Founded	Gained Black Type status
5 FURLONGS					
4th May	Palace House (Pearl Bloodstock)	3+	3	1961	1971
6 FURLONGS					
18th April	Abernant (Connaught Access Flooring)	3+	Listed	1969	1980
29th June	Empress (bet.365)	2	Listed	1983	1993
11th July	July (Portland Place Properties)	2	2	1786	1971
12th July	Duchess of Cambridge (Betfred)	2	2	1947	1971
13th July	July Cup (Darley)	3+	1	1876	1971
24th Aug	Hopeful	3+	Listed	1986	1986
28th Sept	Cheveley Park (Connolly's Red Mills)	2	1	1899	1971
5th Oct	Boadicea (EBF National Stud)	3+	Listed	1999	2003
12th Oct	Middle Park (Vision.ae)	2	1	1866	1971
1st Nov	Bosra Sham (EBF)	2	Listed	2003	2003
7 FURLONGS					
17th April	European Free Handicap (CSP)	3	Listed	1929	1980
17th April	Nell Gwyn (Lanwades Stud)	3	3	1961	1971
18th May	King Charles II (coral.co.uk)	3	Listed	1988	1993
29th June	Criterion (bet.365)	3+	3	1978	1986
13th July	Superlative (32red.com)	2	2	1972	1987
10th Aug	Sweet Solera (German-Thoroughbred.com)	2	3	1979	1982
26th Sept	Somerville Tattersall (Tattersalls)	2	3	1962	1980
27th Sept	Oh So Sharp (Aqlaam)	2	3	1987	1993
12th Oct	Challenge (Dubai)	3+	2	1878	1971
12th Oct	Dewhurst (Dubai)	2	1	1875	1971
12th Oct	Rockfel (Vision.ae)	2	2	1981	1984
8 FURLONGS					
18th April	Craven (Novae Bloodstock Insurance)	3	3	1878	1971
4th May	2000 Guineas (Qipco)	3	1	1809	1971
5th May	1000 Guineas (Qipco)	3	1	1814	1971
11th July	Stubbs (Hastings Direct - Insure Pink)	3	Listed	2007	2013
12th July	Falmouth (Etihad Airways)	3+	1	1911	1971
27th Sept	Joel (Nayef)	3+	2	1963	1991
27th Sept	Rosemary (Shadwell)	3+	Listed		
27th Sept	Fillies Mile (Shadwell)	2	1		
28th Sept	Royal Lodge (Juddmonte)	2	2		

28th Sept	Sun Chariot (Bahrain)	3+	1	1966	1971
12th Oct	Autumn (Dubai)	2	3		
2nd Nov	Ben Marshall	3+	Listed	1986	1986
2nd Nov	Montrose (EBF Lanwades)	2	Listed	1999	1999
9 FURLONGS					
17th April	Feilden (ebm.papst)	3	Listed	1978	1983
18th April	Earl of Sefton (Weatherbys Hamilton Insurance)	4+	3	1971	1971
5th May	Dahlia (Qatar Bloodstock)	4+	3	1997	1997
13th Oct	Darley (Dubai)	3+	Listed	1987	1987
10 FURLONGS					
4th May	Newmarket (Qatar Racing)	3	Listed	1889	1980
5th May	Pretty Polly (Tweenhills)	3	Listed	1962	1980
18th May	Fairway (coral.co.uk)	3	Listed	1999	1999
6th Oct	Pride (TRM)	3+	Listed	2011	2011
2nd Nov	James Seymour	3+	Listed	1986	1986
12 FURLONGS					
4th May	Jockey Club (Qatar Bloodstock)	4+	2	1894	1971
29th Jun	Fred Archer (bet365)	4+	Listed	1987	1987
11th July	Princess of Wales (boylesports.com)	3+	2	1894	1971
20th July	Aphrodite (Newsells Park Stud)	3+	Listed	1994	1994
26th Sept	Princess Royal (Richard Hambro EBF)	3+	Listed		
27th Sept	Godolphin (Mawatheeq)	3+	Listed	1982	1987
13 FURLONGS					
11th July	Bahrain Trophy (Bahrain)	3	3	1991	1991
16 FURLONGS					
26th Sept	Jockey Club Rose Bowl (Jockey Club Estates)	3+	Listed	2011	2011

	1. Races transferred from Ascot as part of the arrangement for setting up the Qipco Champions Day in 2011 have been omitted from the columns dealing with the dates of foundation and entry into the pattern system. At the same time, the Jockey Club Rose Bowl and the Pride Stakes were created as Listed races to fill gaps caused by the transfer of the Jockey Club Cup (Group 3) and Pride Stakes (Group 2) but have been treated as new races.
	2. The Pattern was created for 1971 but Listed races were not added until 1980 and their number has expanded considerably since. Both dates combined account for the first running with black type status of 22 of the Heath's 52 races of this class showing that number to be as old or older than the system itself.
	3. Determining when races were founded is in some cases a matter of opinion. We have regarded the reuse of a name after any material gap as a new race as well as those with really marked changes in their conditions prior to the grant of black type status. However, in some cases we have accepted continuity despite changes of name or conditions where it is clear that an earlier race aimed to cater for the same pool of horses at the same time of year. In essence we have done the best we can to present an accurate picture and do not feel we would be justified in explaining each of the decisions made in detail in addition to those few more important examples included in the text of this section. Changes in sponsorship have been treated as irrelevant in this context
	4. In summary, Newmarket staged 29 Pattern races in 2013 and another 23 with Listed status. The only comparable British totals are those at Ascot with the same number of Pattern races but only 12 Listed. Naturally, as a proportion of the programme that figure of 41 is much higher as the course only stages 18 cards on the Flat against the Heath's 38. It also has 8 Jumping cards with a separate black type allocation.

PICTURE PUZZLE 8: IDENTIFICATION OF HORSE AND COURSE

These two paintings by Stubbs show contemporaries from the 1770s at different Newmarket finishes. Trentham (Fig. 164) has the King's Stand and its adjacent Judge's Box as a background viewed from the north-west. Thus its distance is occupied by the windmill which stood near the present cemetery. As explained in connection with Gimcrack (Fig. 55), the shutters show that he is not racing but quite what is happening is a little mysterious. Given the angle at which the horse is moving away from the building and the rails, which would have continued without a gap from those you can see starting by the box, he is probably striking off from a standing start to canter over to the King's Stables, as he is aligned to do. Presumably his rider's seat is intended to convey this to the viewer, although the attempt at the position is not wholly successful as the picture has usually been thought to show the horse moving at speed. It is dated 1771 and Trentham's owner at this stage of his career with the harlequin silks was Charles Ogilvy. Mr Ogilvy had no regular jockey so the rider is still anonymous.

At least it has always been known that it is Trentham, and there is a mezzotint of the picture to prove the point – although it is printed in reverse with the horse going from left to right, which is not unusual with prints. In the case of the second picture of a horse by a judge's box, the identity of the animal had become lost, despite the colours being correctly recognised from the painting's provenance as those of Robert, 1st Earl of Farnham. This fact makes it more than likely that it is his Conductor, foaled the year after Trentham in 1767 and of similar ability – indeed, the score was one each from their two clashes. Conductor by Matchem (Fig. 165) was about the only really good horse Lord Farnham raced among a large number of moderate ones, and as he was a chesnut it is probably him, although in the absence of another picture as confirmation one cannot be sure.

The attribution is made the more probable by the site chosen to immortalise the horse: it is the Judge's Box on the much less used Round Course, with the Ditch in the background. On 15 April 1773 Conductor had won the King's Plate, his only victory on this course, so it seems reasonable to assume that this is the occasion Lord Farnham would have chosen to remember. The horse is ridden by his usual jockey John Clark and had something of a history of competing with other Stubbs subjects as he twice beat both Hollyhock and Laura, lost to Mambrino, and compromised matches with Firetail and Pyrrhus apart from his clashes with Trentham. It all goes to show the dominance of Stubbs on the Heath in the early 1770s. In later life Conductor became a better stallion than Trentham and the Matchem sire line, one of the only three still in existence from which all thoroughbreds descend, passed on through his son Trumpator.

That it is John Clark is confirmed by the strange way the brim of his cap seems to dip down on the far side of his face. We know from the Holcroft memoir that the left side and eye had been severely damaged in an accident with a gun some years before so, as usual, an explanation can be found for surprising aspects of the master's work.

These two boxes are among the few permanent ones sited at finishes of the many courses on the Heath. In most cases they were serviced by wheeled contraptions which were dragged about the place by ponies as required. An example appears in Fig. 167. Until the twentieth century the mistake represented by placing the judge as close to the course as possible was pretty universal. With so few runners in the eighteenth century it did not matter too much, but as the years passed errors proliferated when horses finished far apart with one close to the judge and another across the course. Given the breadth of the Rowley Mile the failure to give the judge a proper angle of vision well back from the rails and above the horses was particularly unfortunate. By the middle of the nineteenth century the judge's box on that course was on the far side, firstly in the form of no more than shelter from the weather, and after the 1858 changes as a rather grand sentry box with a cupola on top decorated with a ball finial. Later in the century he was moved to the stand side and relegated to a more mundane structure still placed by the rails at ground level. In the twentieth century the judge migrated back to the far side again and dwelt in a purely utilitarian structure without cupolas, finials and any other embellishment but raised on stilts and set back an appropriate distance from the rails. Nowadays he has returned to the east and is presumably settled there in the Millennium Stand until the grandstand is one day rebuilt.

Picture Puzzle 8

Fig. 164

Trentham by George Stubbs (1771)

Fig. 165

Conductor by George Stubbs (c.1773)

PICTURE PUZZLE 9: IDENTIFICATION OF OCCASION AND RECYCLING OF IMAGES

A series of paintings and prints mainly by or after Stubbs's successor as the leading sporting artist, Ben Marshall, revolves around an outstanding early eighteenth-century sprinter called Eagle. Bred by Sir Frank Standish in 1796, he had started hot favourite for the Derby but was only third to Sir Frank's much inferior Archduke. Due to his wind being defective he was far better at much shorter distances. After various victories, including wins in the Craven Stakes of 1801 and 1803, Eagle was sold for 800 Guineas at the end of that year to Henry Mellish, a friend of the Prince of Wales. Mellish raced on a spectacular scale for a few years and when the money ran out he was given a colonelcy and went off to the Peninsular War to serve under Wellington. Before going soldiering it seems likely that he had commissioned Ben Marshall to produce this pair of pictures (Figs. 166 and 167) showing the start and finish of an extraordinary match which Eagle had won on 31 October 1804 against Sir Charles Bunbury's great mare Eleanor.

The match between the two famous horses was for a restricted 200 Guineas over less than six furlongs of the Rowley Mile, finishing just before the Bushes and so downhill much of the way. Such an undemanding test played to Eagle's strengths but was against Eleanor who had won both the Derby and the Oaks in 1801 and stayed four miles well. To even things up in this very odd encounter Eagle was required to concede the mare no less than 19lbs and, as the picture of the finish shows, just managed to do so, although Eleanor had been 13/8 on to succeed at the weights. As the pictures of both the start and the finish remained in Marshall's studio for many years and the latter is unfinished, it seems reasonable to guess that Mellish failed to come up with the cash.

The resourceful Marshall certainly did not let matters rest as both pictures were quarried to produce other images for smaller paintings or prints. From the Start he recycled the figure of Samuel Betts (Fig. 168), the regular starter on the Heath, and in a separate work, the trainers of the contestants (Fig. 171) seen standing besides each other in a picture which has long been wrongly assumed to show Sir Charles Bunbury (Fig. 47) chatting to his trainer. The rather weaselly-looking chap in the blue coat is indeed, going to be Bunbury's trainer, James Frost, but the much taller figure is in fact Richard Prince, the trainer of Eagle. We know this from a print (Fig. 170) showing Prince, Eagle and the same groom. It has been accepted in recent years by racing historians that Eleanor's original trainer was a Mr Cox and that on his death bed, just before the Derby in 1801, he said to a parson 'Depend on it, that Eleanor is the hell of a mare'. Perhaps it is true, although not traceable as yet to any contemporary sources. However, when Frost did indeed, die in October 1805 an extremely similar story appeared, and the chances that Mr Cox's remarks are apocryphal are increased by other references to James Frost having handled the Bunbury horses 'for many years'.

From the picture of The Finish Marshall has extracted the figure of John Fuller (Fig. 169), whose duties as Clerk of the Course included ensuring the runners did not get interfered with by spectators, on his hack. The picture itself shows the two horses ridden by Frank Buckle on the winner and Saunders for Bunbury, who seems sure to be the portly figure following the runners in the red waistcoat, a form of attire he seems to have favoured at this time (Fig. 47). Beside him presumably rides Mellish as he had black hair, although the picture is not finished to the degree one can be sure of his identity. While it is sad that such a promising painting was never finished, had it been completed it must be admitted that the NHRM could never have afforded to buy it when it came on the market some twenty years ago.

There are at least two versions of The Start but for some unaccountable reason they have regularly been sold as representing Eleanor accompanied by a bad horse of Mellish's named Surprise. As can be seen from Fig. 167, that is nonsense as there are several other paintings of Eagle including in particular a very fine one by James Ward in the Mellon Collection which shows what a striking horse he was. Anyway, The Start shows the horses having just been saddled at the Ditch Stables near the King's Gap while the other connections depart into the distance leaving the trainers behind with their horses as the rest get into position to follow up the runners.

After Eagle's final race in 1805 had resulted in Mellish needing to find the 500 Guineas stake when he failed to give 16lbs to the good class Bobtail over a mile, his owner recouped the sum by selling Eagle to the USA, where he lived to a great age and proved an excellent stallion. His rival was a lot less successful at stud although Eleanor did eventually become the great grandmother of one of the most famous broodmares of them all, Pocahontas.

Picture Puzzle 9

Fig. 166

The Start – Eagle and Eleanor at the post by Ben Marshall (c.1804)

Fig. 167

The Finish – Eagle beating Eleanor by Ben Marshall (c.1804)

Picture Puzzle 9

Fig. 168

Engraving of Samuel Betts after Ben Marshall (c.1804)
(The Starter based on Fig. 166)

Fig. 169

Engraving of John Fuller after Ben Marshall (c.1804)
(The Clerk based on Fig. 167)

The Heath and the Horse

Fig. 170

Engraving of *Richard Prince and Eagle* after John Whessell (1805)

Picture Puzzle 9

Fig. 171

James Frost and Richard Prince, trainers of Eleanor and Eagle with Eagle's lad by Ben Marshall (c.1804), study for part of Fig. 166

IV
Newmarket in Wartime

Over the four centuries that have elapsed since the Heath became a racing centre the country has been involved in all sorts of wars but seven really stand out from the rest in terms of national consequence. They divide fairly equally between the Duke of Marlborough's campaigns, the Seven Years War and the War of Independence in America, which were of limited importance locally, as against the Civil War and the two world wars of the twentieth century, where the reverse is the case. That leaves the Napoleonic Wars, where their impact was distinctly constructive, as the odd one out of the seven. At that time, French prisoners were largely responsible for converting the essentially treeless plain of Wootton (Fig. 37) and Seymour (Fig. 2) into the heath of today by the planting of numerous shelterbelts, even if their handiwork was partially obliterated by the 1987 storm.

The three wars which had altogether bigger implications for Newmarket in the short to medium term were the Civil War, when racing ceased completely for over a decade (Fig. 16), and those of the twentieth century, which saw the racecourses used by more runners than ever. There may have been slightly fewer races but the fields were so large and the proportion of the national programme these races represented so big that the Heath justified its title of 'headquarters' as never before.

Although never the site of any of the battles, Newmarket still took centre stage on two occasions at either end of the conflict between King and Parliament in the 1640s. Having failed in his notorious attempt to arrest five members in the chamber of the House of Commons, King Charles retreated in a hurry from London, arriving at the Palace on 7 March 1642. There he was immediately waylaid by a parliamentary deputation demanding his assent to the Militia Bill, designed to assert joint control over the only readily available military force. After a furious row in the Palace the King flatly refused to comply and also rejected a demand to return to London. Meanwhile, his Queen departed abroad with the crown jewels in an attempt to raise money for armaments. Probably it was already too late to avert the outbreak of the war which would, seven years later, lead to the King's execution but at least in theory this was a final chance; instead he went north to York and the war broke out in August.

With the whole of East Anglia more or less permanently in the hands of Parliament throughout the five years it took to defeat the King, he only returned twice more to his Palace, with a final visit in June 1647. This time his chance to save his crown was far from theoretical. Having paused briefly in Newmarket en route to being held as a prisoner, effectively by the House of Commons, at Holmby House near Northampton for six months, he was sensationally abducted on behalf of the Army by a large troop of cavalry led by Cornet Joyce. They returned him to Newmarket, with his consent to a degree, arriving at the Palace on 9 June. During the next few days he was allowed considerable freedom of movement and treated with something akin to the respect of days gone by as the Army Council led by Sir Thomas

Fairfax and Oliver Cromwell deliberated on what became 'The Declaration of the Army'. The Army had little need to fear his rescue as most of it was encamped on Kentford Heath. Their proposal amounted to a form of constitutional monarchy which clipped the wings of Parliament as well as those of the King. With no support from either side and the Commons demanding the return of their hostage, the Army promulgated its declaration anyway on 15 June and eventually took matters into its own hands by advancing on London with the King in tow. Fairfax and Cromwell having occupied the city without resistance the King finally burnt his boats by escaping from Hampton Court in November 1647 but by then Newmarket's brief place in the political limelight was only a memory. However, the Palace had twice been the scene of great events and at least on the second occasion a shrewder man than King Charles could certainly have saved his crown, and indeed, his head, by accepting a much-reduced role.

◆◆◆◆

Naturally, lesser wars have also had consequences for both the Heath and the sport in general. In the case of the Boer War the departure of the local MP, Colonel Harry McCalmont, in 1899 in command of the Militia Battalion of the Royal Warwickshire Regiment saw the Colonel's brainchild of a National Hunt course on the Links did not long survive its patron, closing in 1905.

As explained in Chapter 8, on 14 May 1917, a Club meeting accepted Lord Rosebery's advice and agreed to allow the Military Aeronautics Directorate to set up a flying school for officers of the Royal Flying Corps based at the Rowley Mile buildings. It was to take over some 250 acres between the stands and Southfields Farm on which fifty pilots were to be trained with seventy mechanics, batmen, etc. also to be accommodated. The pupils and their trainers were to live in the Weighing Room and eat in the Members' Luncheon Room while the rest had the use of the Telegraph Room, Tattersalls Bar and a field kitchen to feed them. These arrangements even allowed for the place to be cleared sufficiently for racing to take place on the Rowley Mile that autumn once Lord Rosebery had prevailed on the government to lift its ban. Throughout the rest of the war the facilities were used for training in night flying by two squadrons, now members of the Royal Air Force rather than the RFC. It was agreed that none of the additional meetings granted to Newmarket should use the Rowley Mile but otherwise events had remarkably little direct effect in marked comparison to the next war. This time the real impact on the Heath was in terms of its enhanced importance as the stage on which the sport could be kept going rather than in terms of local disruption.

◆◆◆◆

From 1939 to 1945 things were very different and even before war was formally declared Mr Marriott must have appreciated his looming problems when on 2 September several Wellington bombers landed on Racecourse Side without any prior notice having been given. He is recorded as marching out of Portland Lodge to remonstrate with the newcomers waving his walking stick. Not only did the RAF stay in occupation of the Heath between the town and the Ditch until February 1945, but he also had to accept the requisitioning of his house for the use of a series of officers in command of the new airfield. The Agent's forceful reputation was further enhanced when a visiting American Air Force general complained to an old heathman that the spreading acres on Racecourse Side would allow most of the Luftwaffe to land. The reply to his complainant is said to have been 'Oh no, I am afraid Captain Marriott would never allow such a thing'. With no Captain Marriott to protect it, the Palace was requisitioned as an officers' mess for the duration of the war.

In the early days aircrews camped in the grandstand in considerable discomfort or were billeted in the town and

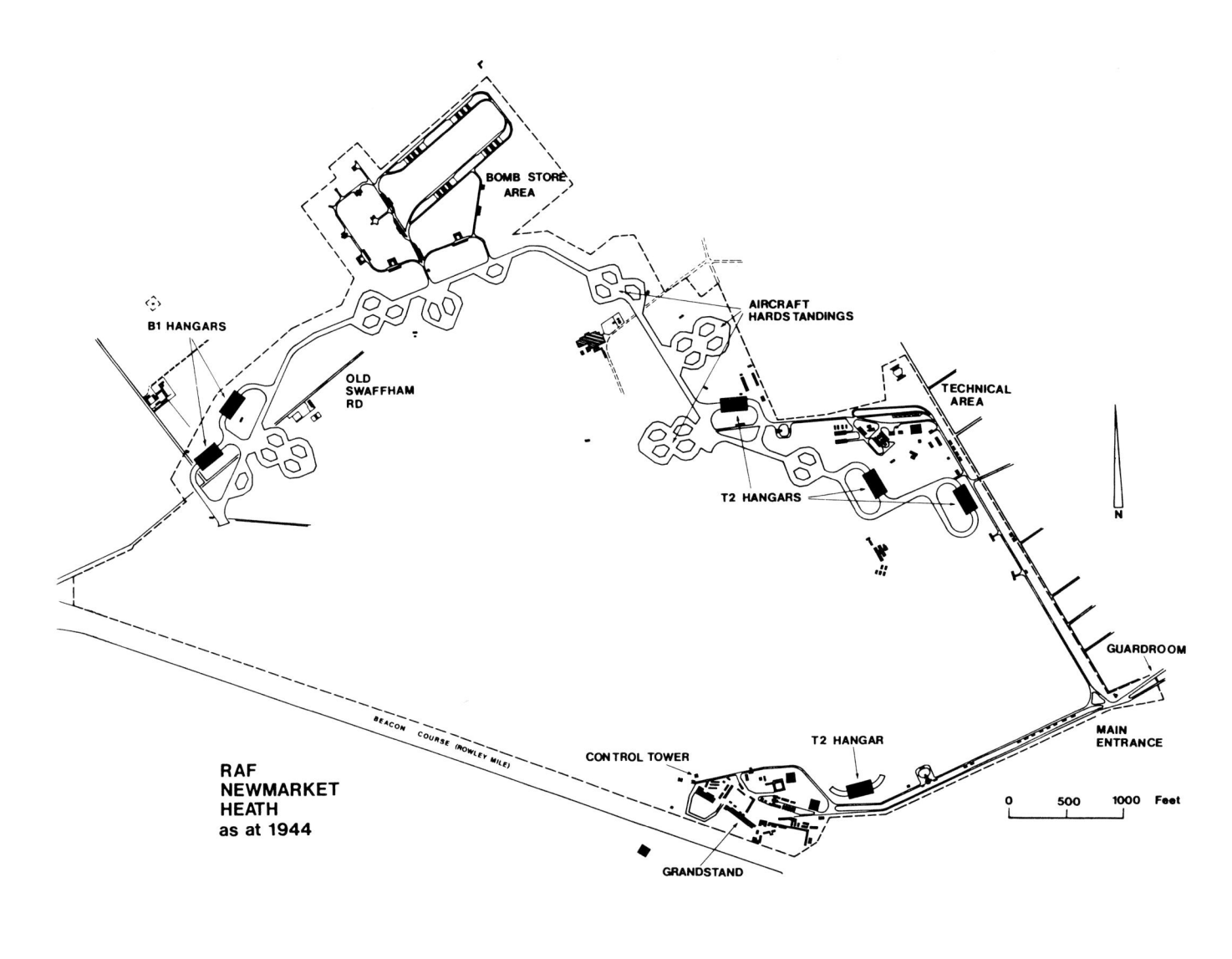

Fig. 172

Map of the Second World War airfield based on the Rowley Mile

so the whole site steadily developed to the degree that racing on the Rowley mile was impossible. Before things had really got under way the RAF actually offered to allow racing there in 1940 but by April it was accepted that this was impracticable and instead the July Course was used for the duration of the war. As early as December the Ditch claimed its first victim since a crash during the earlier war when a Wellington collided with it, killing the crew. However, at this stage the wide expanse of the Heath would have had real advantages for returning pilots, and the fact it had no hardened runways must have made it a relatively unattractive target for German bombers. There were raids on the airfield in October and early in 1941 bombs fell on the July Course and in Exning near a major Group HQ in the village. Yet, in general the Heath escaped quite lightly and later in the war when hangars, taxiways and bomb stores were constructed close to the present bypass near Exning (Fig. 172) offering better targets such raids by the Luftwaffe had largely ceased. In fact by far the most serious disaster actually happened in the High Street quite near the Rooms rather than on the Heath. On 18 February 1941 a Dornier bombed a military column moving through the town and wrecked the Post Office and White Hart on either side of the road leaving twenty-two dead and some one hundred other casualties.

Squadrons came and went on a regular basis, flying different aircraft types, mainly Stirlings or Wellingtons, and the Heath also seems to have been used regularly for the diversion of aircraft that had run into difficulties when heading elsewhere. Later in the war, no less than seventy beds were kept available for such diversions in a period when accommodation was far less spartan than in the early days. However, not all went well as in June 1943 various WAAF drivers became ill as a result of the efforts of the cookhouse. Its replacement was promptly ordered and in July the grandstand was declared unfit for habitation for any of the 550 personnel then based on the Heath. At much the same time the airfield ceased to be used for launching raids on the continent as its grass was less suitable for heavily laden bombers than the hardened runways available elsewhere. Instead it became primarily a training base just as in the First World War and a site for developing aircraft in addition to accepting numerous diversions. In its developmental role the first experimental jet aircraft had its taxiing trials on the Heath and returned there in 1943 for an initial cross-country test flight to a base in Oxfordshire. The aeroplane eventually became the first jet fighter, the Gloster Meteor.

By this time the base occupied over 500 acres and its occupants increased to well over 1,000. The map in Fig. 172 shows the taxiing routes and hangars near Exning to the north, with many of the personnel still based near the stands. By the time the airfield closed in February 1945 numbers had more than halved. Over the course of the war it is thought that 33 Wellingtons and 43 Stirlings were lost flying missions from Newmarket. One of the best-recorded disasters was the fate of a Stirling of 75 (New Zealand) Squadron piloted by Sergeant Franklin on 16 December 1942. Taking off to the west laden with mines to drop in the estuary of the Gironde, the starboard wheel struck the top of the Ditch, ripping it off together with the adjacent oil tanks. As a result that engine seized and the plane crashed one mile away leading to the explosion of two of the mines and the death of the whole crew. Presumably it was this crash which led to the top part of the Ditch being removed for some 200 yards to the south of the King's Gap in the interests of safety. There seems to be no contemporary record of the work being done, merely a vague reference to the disaster leading to 'improvements to the runway'. Given the nature of a grass runway, it seems likely that reduction in the height of the ancient earthwork was the 'improvement' in question.

When the RAF departed in February 1945 normality was restored with remarkable speed. Most of the buildings near the stands except for the control tower (Fig. 173) were quickly

Fig. 173

Photograph of the airfield's control tower in 1985

Fig. 174

Photograph of the finish of Pont L'Eveque's Derby in 1940

Fig. 175

Photograph in running of the 1940 Derby

removed, including the large hangar in the bottom right corner of the map (Fig. 172). The tower itself was still in place in 1985 being used as the centre of operations for the police. Standing just beyond the Silver Ring stand it gave a good view across the airfield stretching out towards Exning. The two hangars near the latter had been constructed in 1942 and remained in place as warehouses until one was destroyed by fire in 1997. The other is still there, looking a good deal less gaunt. Indeed, it is almost the last reminder of the conflict that saw the death of so many of the young men watching Pont l'Eveque win the 1940 Derby on the other side of the Ditch (Figs. 174 and 175). On a lighter note, so precious did his owner Martin Benson rightly consider Nearco that he had a special air raid shelter built for the great stallion at Beech House Stud where he could retreat each night. When he eventually emerged on a permanent basis the war in Europe concluded for Newmarket quite satisfactorily too as Major Gorton, soon to become the Agent, reported in July that the Rowley Mile would be ready for the autumn meetings. This he attributed largely to a group of thirty German Prisoners of War lent for the purpose of straightening things out by a local general. Sir Humphrey de Trafford warned members to keep all that on the quiet in case their benefactor might get into trouble for overstepping the mark.

Once restored to the Rothschilds after being derequisitioned, the Palace took a great deal longer to be made habitable against a background of post-war shortages and a lack of free German labour to do the work.

Actual events on the July Course during the war have been covered in Chapter 8 but it seems worth noting how the programmes were designed in order to fulfil Newmarket's real role – facilitating the continuance of the breed. During 1942 races open to handicappers aged five or more were scrapped and although arrangements were later relaxed the pattern of racing would nowadays be thought extremely elitist. Of the 142 races run in 1943 (there were 334 elsewhere) handicaps accounted for only 55 including nurseries, so less than 40 per cent. They were outnumbered by conditions races at 60 with the balance made up of maidens for two- and three-year-olds only. With only about 1,500 horses in training anywhere and their movement very restricted, sport was inevitably moderate but crowds of up to 35,000 still somehow got to the Heath on Derby days despite all the transport problems most must have faced.

Aureole with owner and trainer by Sir Alfred Munnings, detail of Fig. 105

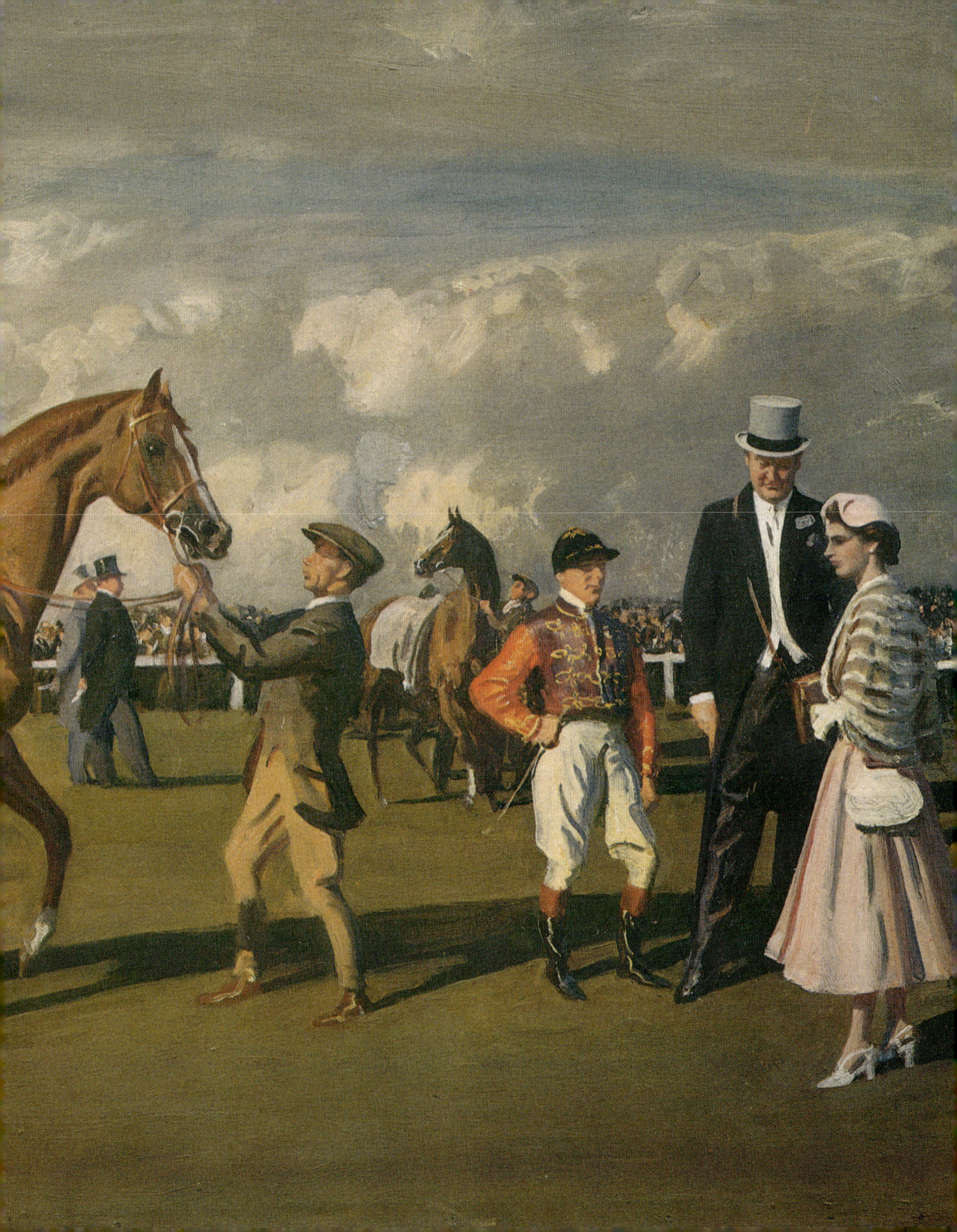

V
The National Stud

Although the thoroughbred originated here our version of a national stud for the breed arrived later than those in almost any other major racing country apart from the USA – where one is still conspicuous by its absence. The main reason for this apparent peculiarity is not too hard to find, stemming as it does from racing here growing slowly and naturally as opposed to being imported after the thoroughbred already dominated proceedings. Developing racing in countries such as France, Germany and Russia meant importing representatives of the breed then generally called the English Thoroughbred. Inevitably this was often some form of governmental exercise, usually royal, and the obvious way to make progress from a standing start was via a heavily- subsidised national stud.

Apart from the dramatically different political background of colonial America and the marked aversion it then shared with this country for central direction of anything, racing took root there well before the thoroughbred really came into existence. Although it was necessary for quite large numbers of horses to be exported from this country the need for a national stud to organise things never arose and in any event would probably have been unacceptable in political terms before or after the Declaration of Independence.

Individual enthusiasm was quite sufficient here to keep things going until the latter part of the nineteenth century but, with agricultural depression a constant factor from the early 1870s, light horse-breeding in general was in severe decline. With cavalry remounts in demand for the Boer War, local deficiencies were ruthlessly exposed and the position began to cause real alarm when contrasted with the situation on the Continent where all the major powers had vastly larger standing armies and better resourced methods of producing adequate numbers of suitable animals. France, for instance, had over twenty heavily subsidised stallion stations spread about the country all linked to their national stud; all we had was a not particularly successful scheme for premium stallions originally adopted in place of the old Royal Plates in 1888. In 1911 the government did make the rather feeble gesture of supporting the scheme with an annual grant of £20,000 but that was only a tiny fraction of what was being poured into light horse-breeding abroad.

◆◆◆◆

Various committees pondered these matters over a period of some forty years, culminating in one chaired by Lord Middleton which reported to the Board of Agriculture in 1915. One of the members was Sir Merryk Burrell, whose son Peter was over twenty years later to become a particularly eminent Director of the future National Stud. In the event, the committee's efforts were rather overtaken by Colonel William Hall Walker's (Fig. 177) offer in October to present his major breeding operation at Tully in Ireland to the state along with his training establishment at Russley near

Fig. 176

Peter Burrell (1905–1999)

Perhaps the most respected stud manager of his generation Peter Burrell took over the National Stud when still in Ireland in 1937. What he inherited was certainly a going concern following the long reign of Sir Harry Greer (Fig. 94) and the short one of Noble Johnson. However, Burrell's 34 years saw their achievements built on with six Classics shared by Sun Chariot, Big Game, Chamossaire and Carrozza while the families they had started (or taken over on foundation) were further developed. He organised the complex move from Tully to Dorset in 1943 in the middle of the war followed by expansion to West Grinstead and eventual consolidation on the Heath. This picture shows him outside the front door at Gillingham in Dorset with the gundogs indicative of his skill as a shot. In retirement he bred some excellent horses for himself trained by Henry Cecil (Fig. 114) including Be My Chief, top two-year-old in 1989 when unbeaten in six races.

Fig. 177

Colonel Hall Walker (later 1st Lord Wavertree) (1856–1933) by Lynwood Palmer

A man of considerable talent in several fields he was also distinctly difficult and by no means universally popular. Tory MP for Widnes for twenty years he also ran the large family brewery Peter Walker & Sons of Warrington, sometimes in conjunction with his several brothers, and was a remarkably successful breeder of racehorses. Beginning with racing ponies, some of which he both trained and rode, he owned the 1896 Grand National winner The Soarer before moving onto the Flat. At Tully he developed an extremely successful stud based on remarkably cheap acquisitions producing several Classic winners and twice making him champion owner with animals he retained before giving the stock to the State to form the National Stud in 1916. Although elected to the Jockey Club in 1919 his racing involvement after the disposal of the Stud was very limited but his influence was credited by the Aga Khan (fig. 94) as inspiring his racing empire's breeding plans. The family was also responsible for Liverpool's Walker Art Gallery and many of Wavertree's pictures ended in the Rooms.

Lambourn. The terms of Colonel Walker's offer were that he would provide all his bloodstock as a gift if the government would buy Tully and its estate of nearly 1,000 acres plus over a hundred more round Russley at valuation.

By refusing the offer the Board of Agriculture initially showed no enthusiasm whatever for its proposed role as owner of a large stud and string of racehorses. However, the support of the influential friends still forming a bridge between the sport and Whitehall saw Henry Chaplin, many years earlier the owner of Derby winner Hermit and a former minister once in charge of the Board of Agriculture, lead the campaign to make it change its mind. It may also have helped that Lord Derby had close links to the War Office, and indeed, became Secretary of State there later in 1916. Anyway, the War Office was instrumental in persuading the Board of Agriculture to change its mind in the nick of time, as following the refusal of his offer all the Colonel's bloodstock had been entered in the sales on 3 December. Not unnaturally it caused a considerable stir and a good deal of criticism when Tattersalls were instructed to withdraw the horses on 2 December. At that stage the idea was that by continuing operations much as before the colts below the highest class would form an ideal base for stallion depots on the French lines.

Eventually, Colonel Walker received £65,625 for his 1,100 acres, and published a lavishly illustrated book recording the details of his stock. The list is set out below, and shows the position early in 1916 before the mares had foaled, treating stock only recently retired from racing as stallions or broodmares whether or not yet productive. The whole lot was valued at £74,000.

Stallions	6
Broodmares	43
Two-year-olds	10
Other horses in training	5
Yearlings	19
Total	83

Born in 1856, a younger son of Sir Barclay Walker and brother to a future Senior Steward in Reid Walker, Colonel Walker raced ponies with great success as a form of apprenticeship before moving on to thoroughbreds in 1895. After winning the Grand National in 1896 with The Soarer he opened Tully in 1900 and very soon produced Cherry Lass, a dual classic winner in 1905, and Polar Star, winner of twelve races in an unbeaten two-year-old career the following season. He was already champion owner in 1905 and 1907, although he was always inclined to sell as well as race stock. Indeed, both his best horses, Minoru, who won the Derby and 2000 Guineas for Edward VII in 1909 and Prince Palatine, whose many victories included the 1912 St Leger, two Ascot Gold Cups, the Eclipse and a Coronation Cup, went on to race for others. If none of the six stallions did great things for the Board of Agriculture, several of the mares like Blanche, dam in 1919 of the great Blandford, produced top class stock and fillies which continued his families far into the future.

Perhaps inevitably the Board rejected the French example of setting up satellite stations and simply sold the colts and many of the fillies to cover costs, initially with the somewhat daunting proviso that official sanction would be needed before export. Much more far-sighted was the decision to appoint the Senior Steward of the Jockey Club, the Irishman Captain Henry Greer (Fig. 94), as an initially unpaid but hands-on manager following his own highly successful career as a breeder at Brownstown. He remained in charge until he died in 1934 and, apart from the final two or three years of his reign during the worldwide crash, he produced excellent results in financial terms and quite adequate ones on any basis. As profound in its long-term effect as the formation of the National Stud itself was the fact that he shared with Colonel Walker the credit for setting the Aga Khan dynasty in motion on the turf.

The old Aga (Fig. 94) said firmly that it was the Colonel who had got him interested in the first place and taught

Fig. 178

Sun Chariot (1939) by Hyperion out of Clarence

This brilliant if wayward filly only lost one of her nine races taking the Fillies Triple Crown in 1942 on the Heath. However she was not trained there being in the hands of the almost equally mercurial Fred Darling at Beckhampton on behalf of King George VI. As an 'invader' the only reason for her inclusion here is that she was bred at the National Stud and returned to it through its various peregrinations from Tully, being a reasonably successful but not outstanding producer. However she proved herself probably the best horse the Stud has ever produced during her two seasons in training. Her portrait by Munnings is worthy of its illustrious subject and her trainer told the artist he was right to try to catch her mulish nature on canvas, which he seems to have done with considerable success.

him the principles on which he afterwards operated, and it was to Greer that he turned to set up his Irish studs as an extramural endeavour in addition to his labours at Tully. The degree to which Colonel Walker's remarkable success as a breeder (he also found time to sit in Parliament as Tory member for Widnes for twenty years until ennobled in 1919 as the first and only Lord Wavertree, as well as running the large family brewery, Peter Walker & Co. of Warrington) can

be attributed to his more outlandish ideas is a moot point. He certainly laid considerable stress on casting horoscopes for horses and people and the evidence that he took it seriously remains at Tully to this day where the stallion boxes have glass roofs to allow for the exposure of their occupants to the heavens. However, he was a pretty arrogant man who seems to have amused himself by obscuring as opposed to elucidating the reasons for his success as a breeder, although he certainly made an exception in the case of the Aga Khan.

Probably the most remarkable feature of the Colonel's efforts as a breeder was how cheaply so rich a man acquired the mares which not only produced such results for him but in some cases started lines which lasted until all the mares were sold in 1964. Part of that success was no doubt due to the quality of his senior staff, headed by William Chisom and Harry Sharpe. However, given his generally rather autocratic approach to things they must have done what they were told to have survived, whereas his numerous trainers were removed with predictable regularity for perceived failures.

◆◆◆◆

After the death of Sir Henry Greer (as he had by then become) the management of Tully briefly passed to Noble Johnson, formerly in charge of Eyrefield for the Loders, but he died in 1937 and was succeeded by the next Eyrefield manager Peter Burrell (Fig. 176). Once again the government had made an unusually good choice and Peter Burrell, who remained in charge until 1971, was probably the most respected stud manager of his generation. After the war broke out he decided in 1940 to dispose of stock privately and keep what he felt to be the best. The three horses which fell into that category in 1940 included the 2000 Guineas winner Big Game and Sun Chariot (Fig. 178), who took the Fillies Triple Crown in 1942. This almost clairvoyant achievement became the basis of the stud's success after the war as both returned having been leased to King George VI and trained for him by Fred Darling at Beckhampton.

In this success Burrell was emulating some of Greer's efforts in the early days, when fillies who later became outstanding mares such as Myrobella had been retained and leased to Lord Lonsdale. Before he found the deal by which he paid the costs of training and only kept half the stakes too onerous for his purse, Lord Lonsdale had some excellent sport, winning for instance the 1922 St Leger with Royal Lancer followed home at a respectful distance by another of his leased horses, the very useful Diligence. Indeed, Diligence was better fancied at Doncaster than the winner and despite being nearly last in a field of twenty-four eventually proved the better stallion.

Relationships with the Ireland of Eamon de Valera in the middle of the war were far from easy and eventually it was decided to leave Tully and migrate to Gillingham in Dorset as Russley had been sold long before when the theory of stallion depots had been abandoned. Naturally, Ireland had no need of a separate national stud until the move and after it Tully became, and still remains, the Irish National Stud. Despite its recent travails Tully can surely be regarded as having been a considerable success overall since the Wavertree inheritance was split between this country and Ireland. The move to Dorset was effected in 1943 and other land in the neighbourhood was added. In 1949 another slightly larger stud was leased near West Grinstead so that total acreage was restored to more than 1,000. Big Game was champion sire in 1948 in tables that excluded Masaka's victory in the Irish Oaks, which pushed Nearco ahead in others. He was succeeded by the Derby and St Leger winner Never Say Die as principal stallion, who was himself champion in 1962. Post-war classic winners bred were Chamossaire (also champion as a result of siring Santa Claus) and Carrozza. Never Say Die came as a present from an exceedingly generous American, Ambrose Clark, whose wife had won the Grand National with Kellsboro' Jack, and prefigured Paul Mellon's later and even more important effective gift of Mill Reef in 1973.

◆◆◆◆

Between these two particularly lucky breaks the government transferred responsibility for the National Stud to the new Levy Board in 1963. In all probability Whitehall sighed with relief, although the Stud's almost unbroken success had provided the Civil Service with fewer reasons for complaint than it had no doubt expected. It was then decided to sell the broodmare band and concentrate on standing stallions at its present base running to 500 acres of the Heath situated to the west of the July Course with New England and Egerton Studs as neighbours. The place was laid out for its new role by Burrell to splendid specifications and over the next twenty years some theoretically very promising prospects like Royal Palace and later Grundy joined Never Say Die and Tudor Melody. However, the newcomers achieved a great deal less than hoped and it must be arguable that the sale of the mares in 1964 was one of Burrell's few mistakes. The nineteen sold averaged a highly respectable figures of nearly 11,000 Guineas with Short Sentence, Aiming High, Carrozza, Persian Wheel and Crepe de Chine figuring among the top seven mares at the December Sales.

After the retirement of Peter Burrell the arrival of Mill Reef to cover a small book in 1973, while still to a degree recovering from breaking his leg the year before, gave the National Stud a new lease of life under Colonel Douglas Gray and Michael Bramwell via the cash mountain built on his success as a stallion. However, the old days during which the stud was as often as not the principal yearling vendor had gone with the broodmares and the new structure of ownership of the best horses meant that the regular appearance of the top classic animals as stallions was also becoming a distant memory.

In 1986 Sir John Sparrow, later to chair the Levy Board himself, wrote a report to it advising the interposition of a separate board for the stud largely made up of racing figures. At that stage the old post of Director of the Stud, in the form of an individual responsible to a ministry or board made up of individuals with little or no breeding experience, became downgraded into a stud manager reporting to reasonably knowledgeable people. Whether one should conclude that breeding horses by committee is unwise, or ascribe the subsequently increasing problems to the times themselves, must be a matter of opinion. Anyway, while valiant efforts were made no corners were turned, and as the money arising from the stud career of Mill Reef progressively melted away the Levy Board became increasingly exercised about the position. At one point most of the stud board resigned when it objected to the appointment of its new chairman. Eventually the Levy Board under Rob Hughes decided to bring things to a head by offering the National Stud for sale with caveats attached over the continuance of its important programme of training courses for stud staff.

In truth the only realistic purchaser was probably the Jockey Club, with over 950 years of its peppercorn lease still outstanding, and a deal was eventually done in 2008. By savagely reducing costs without undermining standards, a new board, initially chaired by former Senior Steward Christopher Spence, followed by the present incumbent Ben Sangster, has restored the stud to profitability, although it will need some luck with its stallions to achieve significant earnings. Its broodmare band was resurrected before the change of ownership and is now beginning to produce reasonable returns in the ring under the management of Brian O'Rourke. The whole place looks as it should in his hands and is an ideal site both for running the stud training scheme and offering an insight into the breeding industry for the many interested visitors that come on organised tours. While its own stallions Dick Turpin, Bahamian Bounty and his best son Pastoral Pursuits may not aspire to achievements on the lines of Mill Reef, they are vital cogs in the wheel of a complete operation offering much needed boarding facilities of the high standard required in a town surrounded by studs standing eminent horses which do not board the mares visiting their stallions. The addition to the stallion ranks for 2015 of the very high class Toronado promises much for the future.

◆◆◆◆

In summary, the National Stud as now conducted on the Heath is certainly not performing the varying roles envisaged for it by Lord Wavertree, Sir Henry Greer or Peter Burrell. However, with such a splendid selection of top class stallions already in the neighbourhood without its intervention what it is achieving as the link between the racing public and the breeding industry, as well as serving the latter in terms of training its staff and boarding its mares, may well be the most constructive use of the stud's slice of the Heath in present circumstances. That such a place exists at no cost to anyone in terms of losses or subsidies must be the cheapest insurance for the future of the breed in an uncertain world as could be imagined. Maybe Lord Wavertree would feel it would have been better if something nearer to his original ideas along the lines of the French arrangements had been the outcome. While the influence of what the French National Studs have achieved in terms of National Hunt horses is clear enough and means we have to import from there to have much chance against the Irish, such schemes cost a great deal of money. As no government here would even contemplate introducing subsidies on the necessary scale or seemingly sanction the Pari Mutuel arrangements that would make them unnecessary his gift may never perform its original purpose but is still something for which racing has good reason to be grateful.

VI
Topography of the Heath and Its Layout

Unlike the great majority of towns of its size and antiquity, Newmarket is unusual in having developed on a site where there is no river or even stream of any consequence. Obviously the main reason is the excellent drainage through the deep layer of chalk underlying the Heath, obviating the need for a watercourse for that purpose. The original settlement also developed here, rather than somewhere else like Kentford on the Kennet, due to the chosen site's closeness to Devil's Dyke, where the roads from London and Cambridge converged to pass through the Cambridge Gap before splitting again below Warren Hill bound for Norwich and Bury St Edmunds. Originally it seems this gap was used, until the routes were moved some six hundred yards south in the seventeenth century to free the area of the Round Course finish.

The drainage, allied to the rise and fall of the topography around the small and already far from new market town, made it ideal for training and racing horses once the Court had fixed on this place as its preferred holiday camp (originally to hunt rather than to race). Thus we should really add King Penda, most probable builder of the Dyke, to later kings like James I and Charles I when thinking of the Heath's founding fathers. Had the Stuarts not found this small town on which to base their amusements and eventually their palaces it is likely that racing's headquarters would have appeared on one of several other downland sites just as convenient for Whitehall; perhaps they would have based themselves at the older settlement at Exning had the Dyke not resulted in the road passing a mile south of it, leading, it is supposed, to the selection of the present site as an off-lying trading post several centuries before the Stuarts arrived on the scene.

Lying on the western edge of the higher part of Suffolk on a chalk ridge, the land falls away just after the old Beacon start to the plain running from Cambridge to the Wash. The core of it used for racing and training tends to fall slightly from Beacon Hill to the hollow in which the town is sited, on the boundary between Suffolk and Cambridgeshire (the Rowley Mile is in the former and the July Course in the latter), before rising quite steeply up Warren Hill. The combination of suitable hills for work each side of the town with the possibility of laying out a course over eight miles avoiding anything unreasonably steep, all on free-draining soil, almost seems like divine providence in action – it would certainly be hard to improve on it.

◆◆◆◆

Over the centuries the acreage devoted to racing and breeding horses has expanded dramatically, but has not kept pace with the burgeoning population of horses. In the early days there were no recorded studs of any significance in the area and the horses raced came largely from Yorkshire. As things have developed, an ever-increasing acreage, largely outside the heart of the Heath devoted to racing and training, has been laid out as stud farms. However, this section of the book is really limited to activities in the central area which, including the town itself, stretches from Water Hall and the Line Gallop halfway to Kentford in the east to the July Course. As explained in Part 3, the whole area apart from the town was acquired by the Jockey Club from local estates in easy stages between the Napoleonic Wars and the Second World War, with much of it rented long before purchase. Meanwhile, before the advent of artificial surfaces the practicable number of horses per acre of gallops was far smaller than today – indeed, it was really a matter of acres per horse.

Inevitably the number in training is hard to calculate before the annual volumes of 'Horses in Training' began appearing in 1894. From the mid-eighteenth century it seems to have varied between around two hundred to four hundred, before the town's fortunes took a turn for the better in the 1860s. A detailed assessment for 1768 suggests a figure of 260. How large the horse population was in Stuart days or how far it had fallen in 1742 when only four races took place is beyond estimation. However, we do know that during the thirty years before full records became available in 1894 it had multiplied almost three times to about 1,100, handled by around forty trainers. With good racing largely restricted to Newmarket during both World Wars, that figure varied very little until the 1960s. Thereafter change has been dramatic, as is shown in the following table:

	Trainers	**Horses**
1958	34	1,004
1968	40	1,388
1978	41	1,640
1988	54	2,787
1998	57	2,468
2008	73	2,755
2014	80	2628

Source: Horses in Training (2008 and 2014 Newmarket Trainers Directory)

We know from debates over the state of the Heath in the 1920s that it was felt that about 1,250 was the limit of the its capacity without serious damage resulting. Yet the area covered today by the gallops (about 2,500 acres) has not greatly expanded in recent times. The main reason that the population could more than double in the intervening period and yet damage the Heath far less is of course the steady expansion in the use of artificial surfaces for the great majority of slower work. Many horses virtually never use the grass unless to do fast work in the run up to a race.

◆◆◆◆

The size of the area laid out as gallops provides a range for trainers which can have no equal. Indeed, it is believed that at over 2,500 acres including the racecourses the Heath is the largest expanse of cultivated heathland in the world. The gallops form two separate blocks divided by the town itself (details appear as an appendix in Part 4). The eastern block falls into three broad sections separated by the Norwich and Bury roads. To the north of the former lie Railway Field and the so-called Private Ground, which used to be what its name implies but is now a sand canter and place to introduce yearlings to their new life. The principal use nowadays of this part of the Heath is the Al Bahathri Polytrack, given to Newmarket by the Maktoum family and named after one of their Classic winners. It stretches over nine gently rising furlongs and is suitable for faster work upsides on its Polytrack surface.

Between the two roads to the east lie the crucially important Limekilns with the best gallops on the Heath for fast work in summer, plus an extension towards Kentford known as Water Hall. Taken together, the whole area between the roads runs to some 750 acres and decades of working peat moss into the sward on the Golden Mile and Long Straight have produced a surface perfectly adapted for use in dry weather. The process began about a century ago, and the subsoil now contains a considerable element of peat in its top six inches. The Golden Mile is only available for serious work on request, usually by useful horses, and the Limekilns in general are always withdrawn from use if the ground gets soft, to avoid damage. The name is derived from the original use of the area for pits in which to burn chalk to produce lime. Although the land was only rented in 1840, Mr Pettit, foreman of the day on Bury Side, was allowed £55 to pay for the cost of filling the pits – for which every trainer of a Derby winner from the town since then should be grateful as all must have used this splendid gallop in the days before their charges triumphed.

South of the Bury Road lie four linked areas on the slopes of Warren Hill. These are the northern section known as Bury Hill beside that road, the adjacent Long Hill even closer to town, Warren Hill proper and Side Hill on its southern flank facing towards Cheveley. Apart from the summer gallop up Long Hill very close to the town, the rest are devoted largely to slower work, most of it nowadays on the three Polytrack canters and two other artificial surfaces, one parallel to the Bury Road and the other further across up the face of Warren Hill itself.

It was in this section of the Heath that the first efforts at surfaces other than grass came in the mid-nineteenth century. In 1838 the trainers of the day demanded a ploughed gallop to try to combat Newmarket's fall from grace due to a reputation for the ground becoming too firm in dry weather. Debate rambled on for years about who should pay for it and eventually one was created but was never at all popular. However, in 1860 the Duke of Rutland granted permission for a ten-yard-wide tan gallop of one-and-a-half-miles using tannery residue to be laid out round the bottom of the hill. This was as popular as the plough had been unpopular, and was replaced in 1882 with what was said to be the finest tan gallop in existence. What is still known as 'The Tan' today by those with long memories runs straight from the neighbourhood of Heath House for just over half a mile to end near the Bury Hills depot. However, it ceased to have a tan surface many years ago and the elm trees you can see near its start in Fig. 73 were lost to Dutch Elm Disease.

Work on grass is conducted up narrow strips of land which are moved almost daily across the face of the hill to allow each strip a year to recover from the pounding it gets from several hundred hooves. Parts of the Heath are operated on a two-year cycle. The process involved in organising all this was originally known as 'Bushing the Gallops', as the ground to be used was marked by a line of sprigs of gorse plucked from the abundant bushes around when the Heath was a great deal wilder than it is today. As improvement choked off the supply, gallops were marked with perhaps slightly twee little sprigs of imitation bracken made from black plastic, nowadays in turn superseded by more prosaic white discs. Each day a board outside the Rooms announces which gallops are open on a first-come, first-served basis and subsidiary ones show those available on the respective sides of town at the Bury Hills depot to the east and Southfields depot on the west.

The extensive gear needed to maintain the Heath is based at these depots and the stabling at Southfields still provides ample evidence of the large number of carthorses needed for

Fig. 179

Heavy Horses working on the Heath

Two of the large number of heavy horses needed to keep the Heath in trim before the arrival of the tractor. Here two horses are rolling Long Hill in 1896.

such work before the advent of the tractor (Fig. 179). Mowing, rolling, spiking the sward and moving strips, together with tending the artificial surfaces and the myriad other tasks involved in maintaining such an acreage to high standards is now achieved by Nick Patton and his team of about two dozen which is split fairly evenly between the two sides. At one stage they had available what is thought to have been the gang mower with the broadest cut in the world, but problems with moving it about eventually led to the use of less ambitious alternatives. In much earlier days the job was done by flocks of sheep, as is suggested in Fig. 36, a process only brought to an end in the twentieth century. Part of the responsibilities of the gallops teams are the miles of horse walks across the Heath, which used to be plagued with flints working up through the soil. Indeed, until about 40 years ago gangs of women were employed to pick any up, but nowadays a layer of carstone, known locally as gingerbread, has done the ladies out of a job. There is also a main horse walk stretching right across the town to enable strings to move safely from yards on one side to use the gallops on the other, or indeed, for those placed centrally to get access either to Racecourse or Bury Sides. Before a separate staff, complete with its own equipment based in a depot at the Rowley Mile, was set up in the 1980s to deal with the racecourses, the entire Heath was treated as a unit under the eye of the Jockey Club Agent. A separate foreman ran things on either side of the town and a picture of Mr Jackson, foreman of the eastern section in late Victorian days perched on his donkey, hangs in the Rooms (Fig. 180). It was recently joined by one of John Taylor (Fig. 181) who has only just retired as overall foreman of both teams after a lifetime of service to the Heath. Indeed, we would know

Fig. 180

Heath Foreman on Donkey (*c.*1870) by A. L. Townshend

Down the years heathmen have frequently had extremely long careers in their specialised job and developed a good deal of individual character. Mr. Jackson, foreman at times of the Limekilns only and later Warren Hill too would seem to have been a case in point. In 1878 there was no doubt some upset when a large part of his garden was taken away to build houses for heathmen and there was even some debate over the cost of the keep of the donkey. This charming picture was acquired by another great Newmarket character in Mathew Dawson (Fig. 69) of Heath House and came to the Rooms at the sale following his death in 1898.

a good deal less than we do without a guided tour he was kind enough to give us.

Nowadays the ground on the racecourses is the responsibility of Jockey Club Racecourses (JCR) and William Gittus at Jockey Club Estates (JCE) runs an entirely separate show with Andrew Merriam in the chair. JCE handles not only the rest of the Heath including the Rooms and their collection but also the Club's many properties in and around the town as well as the vexed politics of what does (or does not) constitute a desirable development in such an unusual place. The job of Agent was split from that of Clerk of the Course some while after the racecourse company had been transferred to Racecourse Holdings Trust (now JCR). The racecourse team now consists of eleven permanent staff under Alan Hathaway bolstered by six casuals for the race meetings.

◆◆◆◆

On the other side of town the gallops form a more compact square of much the same overall size as those to the east, with a spur running off it alongside the Cesarewitch Course. The spur is known as Choke Jade, a name that can be traced back to the seventeenth century when it appears in a play by Colley Cibber. Why it should be so named has often puzzled people as that section of the Beacon and Round Courses runs downhill. The answer to the conundrum is that the original Round Course crossed the present by-pass and went up quite a steep bank before swinging back to join the Beacon before the Running Gap. When they met it a field would have been galloping slightly downhill for the best part of a mile so the reason for the ancient name seems clear enough. While the name is unchanged, the place it describes shifted two or three furlongs when the Round Course re-opened, after considerable changes, in 1819, having been closed since 1810. Reverting from the Choke Jade spur to the east of the Devil's Ditch, nearly half the square block lies in a triangle, two sides of which are the bypass and the Hamilton Road. This area is largely devoted to bringing on yearlings and canters for winter work conveniently close to the town. The two artificial canters there are known as the Southfields Woodchip and the Rubbing House Polytrack, near the last remaining Rubbing House on the Heath. Apart from them the area is effectively restricted to use in the months October to March.

Either side of the Rowley Mile and occupying the rest of the square lie the main gallops on Racecourse Side. The area between the winter ground on Southfields and the racecourse is known as 'Back of the Flat' and is only used for fast work before the turf season really gets under way after which such work is conducted across the Rowley Mile over what is known simply as 'The Flat', with its gallops running up the hill towards the Cambridge Road. This is the crucial section for gallops on Racecourse Side right through to the end of the season, and it is bounded by the important Cambridge Road Polytrack of nearly a mile and a half, and the even longer Summer Gallop on grass stretching to a full two miles – both of which are suitable for fast work. The 'Watered Gallop' runs parallel to the Rowley Mile itself and is irrigated with bowsers rather than pop-up sprinklers, which proved unreliable in their spread of water.

Across the other side of the Flat against Devil's Dyke is the unique seven furlongs known now as 'Between the Banks' and formerly as the 'Trial Ground'. This provides particularly good ground being, like the Golden Mile, dressed with peat moss – but its unique characteristic is not its ground but the second bank on the town side, which was constructed with a view to preventing touts from spying on trials. In 1852 it was even proposed that a bank should be added across the southern end to obscure the vision of anyone persistent enough to watch head-on from the Cambridge Road. Eventually a structure called 'Astley's Bank' was effected to block the view but no doubt the touts usually found a way round such efforts and it has since been removed. Finally, on Racecourse Side there is provision across the Cambridge Road for jumpers to work and be schooled on gallops, inevitably known as 'The Links' being adjacent to the golf course.

Naturally, all this activity on so many sites costs a great deal of money. By 1819 the Club was finding the expense more than it could manage against the background of the cost of its steady accumulation of land, so the decision was made to impose a Heath Tax on horses trained in the town for use of the gallops. The varying charges adopted to levy a Heath Tax to pay for the cost of maintaining the gallops provide a graphic illustration of the way the Club

Fig. 181

John Taylor, recently retired foreman in overall charge of the Heath by Marcus Hodge (2010)

has thought it right to fulfil its role over the centuries. The overall switch in policy shows it is an entirely different role today and the way the charges have increased down the years gives a pretty accurate guide to the degree to which the place was prospering at any particular time.

Prior to 1819 horses trained in the town, mostly belonging to members, paid nothing at all towards the upkeep of the gallops. In that year an annual charge of one guinea was introduced and, with Newmarket in an increasingly depressed state, it remained fixed at that figure until 1862. Clearly the £300 or £400 being raised annually would have covered only a small fraction of the cost of rent and upkeep, even if not much was on offer beyond the efforts of the flocks of sheep in keeping the grass down.

With things steadily improving locally from the 1860s the charge went up to two Guineas in 1863 and then climbed steadily to seven by 1887, during a period with no inflation at all. There it stuck until 1927 and then stayed at only £10 annually until after the Second World War. None of these figures can ever have recovered more than quite a small part of the costs and by 1945 the percentage retrieved after the inflation of the two wars can have been little if any higher than in 1819. Since 1945 what is on offer has escalated and the Club's whole approach to cost recovery has changed so that nowadays a monthly charge of £112.50 represents what is needed to make a moderate profit to plough back into facilities.

The necessary change came quite slowly and did not really begin to take effect until the town was beginning to thrive again in the 1980s. For instance, until 1967, when the payment was raised to £30 annually, it had only crept up to £25 from £10 over 40 years of inflation since 1927 and in the 1970s the increases really only represented the savage rate at which the latter was running. It is all a demonstration of the way the Club has steadily switched to adopting a properly commercial approach to its role – even at a rate over a thousand times the original charge of 1819 not too many owners seem to feel they do not get good value for money at £1,350 a year in 2014.

Visitors from elsewhere to The Links now pay £29.17 daily and special charges are levied on every horse using the Watered Gallop or the peat moss ones on the Limekilns (£20.83 and £40 respectively). Inevitably not everyone has always been happy and in 1863 Sir Joseph Hawley, a key Club member and owner of four Derby winners, protested bitterly at the unfairness of being made to pay a full guinea when any of his horses came up from Berkshire for the big meetings. Compared to the two Guineas annual charge then current for locals maybe he had a point, but nobody seems to have felt particularly sorry for him. Not only Sir Joseph had problems as an attempt to set up a Trainers' Committee to help in liaison with the Agent, Mr Gardner, was an abject failure. One of the three illustrious members, Tom Jennings, was dismissed after a quarrel and within a year of its foundation it was dissolved in 1890 on the grounds it was an unworkable division of responsibility. Fortunately, things work a great deal better today and the trainers in the town are represented by a committee under Mark Tompkins dealing with everything except the gallops which are covered by a branch called the Trainers' Heath Committee chaired by Sir Mark Prescott since 1974.

◆◆◆◆

Not a lot in terms of exercise now happens on the Heath beyond the Ditch, although Egerton is these days the site of training operations as well as breeding ones. However, there is a seven-furlong canter between the July Course and the Ditch, while Choke Jade is used a little during the later stages of the winter. Given that the gallops are in essence a preserved eighteenth-century landscape, parts of which have never been cultivated, it has been designated a Site of Special Scientific Interest. While the scale of irrigation necessary on the racecourses has tended to change the nature of the sward, with the hardier natural grasses capable of withstanding drought giving way to lusher meadow ones without the same depth of root, that on the gallops is unaltered. One effect is certainly that the surface tends to be looser even on good ground as is clearly visible after a big field throws up divots. There are also complaints that the Rowley Mile in particular has developed slight undulations due to irrigation, but the degree to which there is really a problem in races because of this is debateable. In any case, as with the naming of races for advertising purposes undermining the so-called narrative of the sport, any problem that does exist is without an effective answer. The provision of good ground is nowadays considered essential if you really want to attract adequate fields. Days like that on which Come to Daddy won the 1959 Cesarewitch in mid-October after months of drought on ground officially returned as hard amid clouds of dust are gone forever.

With a landscape so well preserved for centuries, essentially unchanged apart from the introduction of numerous shelter belts, the place does have an appeal which is both timeless and slightly mysterious. All sorts of legends and mysteries have proliferated as a result, from the regularly reported sightings of a spectral Fred Archer on his horse, to wondering who may have been buried in 'The Boy's Grave'. The latter is at least finite, lying as it does at the far end of Water Hall and flowers have quite regularly been laid on it, supposedly reflecting a gypsy origin. Who, one wonders, was the medieval Clark of 'Clark's Path', an ancient trackway running from the town towards Swaffham Prior through the Well Gap?

Of considerably greater significance for the future of the Heath was the decision to put on what was variously described in the Press as a 'great' or 'grand' cricket match in 1751. The game, to be decided on a best of three basis, was spread over five days from the 2nd to the 6th of July with numerous other attractions such as cockfighting, wrestling, football, cudgelling and, most alluring of all, a race for women with a smock or smocks as a prize. Given that all this was put on in the wake of the Prentice scandal and never repeated it seems hard to avoid the conclusion it was part of the special efforts to relaunch Newmarket, and with it the Jockey Club, after the fallow years of the 1740s.

It is reported that all this entertainment attracted crowds of 6,000, with the cricket matches as the central feature. The teams were chosen by the Earl of Sandwich, whose choice was made first but was limited to anyone who had been to Eton, and the Earl of March whose eleven could be picked from among any 'noblemen or gentlemen in England' not already selected by Sandwich. Professional cricketers were excluded and their lordships each put up a 1,000 Guineas and captained their own sides. With £20,000 in side bets it is one of the first cricket matches where accurate details of what happened have survived, which only seems to have happened because Lord March's ally John Pond printed the scores in the annual Kalendar he produced that year in succession to John Cheny. Sadly he did not print individual contributions, but we know each match had two innings per side, with All England scoring a total of 194 to beat Eton by 37 runs on 2 July, Eton making 235 and winning by 70 runs on Thursday and All England clinching things on Saturday with a splendid 242 to land Lord March his Guineas by 95 runs.

One cannot be certain but the chances surely are that the scene of these epic encounters was the flat area at the end of the Beacon between the King's Stand near the Cambridge Road and the Rubbing House on Hamilton Road. Still called 'the Cricket Pitch' today, we know from Thomas Holcroft that it was in regular use for games later in the 1750s. The King's Stand would have made an ideal pavilion. With Lord March's new 'villa' only a stone's throw away it is tempting to imagine him along with his merry men trooping off down the hill to celebrate their triumph in style, no doubt cheered by the huge crowd which, playing as All England, they effectively represented. Coming less than three months after the Prentice scandal, and with no racing scheduled between spring and autumn, the success of 'the great match' does seem to have represented the turning of the tide for Newmarket and its Heath.

VII
Training at Newmarket – Changing Methods for Preparing the Racehorse

While there are numerous early commentaries on the layout of stables, stable management and on diseases and other veterinary subjects relating to horses in general, information on the changing approaches to the basic business of getting the horse fit enough to race is not extensive. This is no doubt because, even among the best training grooms, many (probably the great majority) would have been illiterate. In addition, in the days before veterinary science really existed (from around 1800) they would have been highly protective of the mysteries to which they attributed their success. However, the same considerations would not have applied to the riding and management of horses in general in an age when anyone likely to be interested in racing would have been involved with horses all their lives. Accordingly, there were always plenty of enthusiasts happy to instruct the rest of the world in print how such things should be done.

The best very early work on training came long before the racehorse in our terms arrived well over a century later. Gervase Markham was no training groom, being a younger son of Sir Robert Markham, and was among other things a soldier of fortune, probable owner of the eponymous early Arabian and author of books on all sorts of subjects in the early seventeenth century. His various works on equitation included one thought to date from 1599 called *The Compleat Jockey* which sets out to instruct an amateur how to get his horse ready to ride in a match. His connection with the Courts of James I and Charles I would have ensured that he was familiar with Newmarket. However, the details of his life are very vague apart from the fact that he was once fined the sum of £500 in a case about duelling in 1616 and the same year he or his father sold the Markham Arabian to James I for £154. He died in 1637.

From the eighteenth century much the most interesting source of information came in the unlikely form of a memoir of his early life by the playwright Thomas Holcroft, written just before he died. His remarkable life had seen him progress from trailing around the country as a child to help his peddler-father, to being thought worthy of a three-volume biography based on his diaries, largely produced by the famous essayist William Hazlitt after Holcroft died in 1809. Fortunately, the first few chapters of the biography were written by Holcroft himself, covering his life to the age of fifteen when he left Newmarket after two-and-a-half years as a lad in three of the best stables in the town in the late 1750s. As these were the yards of the Duke of Grafton and

Captains Richard Vernon and Jenison Shafto they provide such a unique perspective on Newmarket's second golden age that the wider aspects of the memoir are dealt with separately. Meanwhile, Holcroft's reflections on the way the Vernon yard was run for him by John Watson and how his horses were prepared are covered here.

The third work taken to show how far things had progressed towards today's methods is that of Richard Darvill, published in 1828. Darvill spent his youth in stables before eventually becoming a vet and joining the 7th Hussars in 1815. His two volumes (he had intended three so some subjects are missing altogether) are much the most detailed of the books used here to illustrate the trends. In some areas one gets the suspicion that the fact his adult life had largely been spent as a soldier-vet rather than in a trainer's yard may have led to some of his views being a little behind the times, as training had recently been much changed by the influence of Robert Robson (Fig. 57).

Accordingly, what happened on the Heath in terms of readying a horse for a race as opposed to general practice in other parts of the country is not covered until Holcroft's memoir, based on working in the town from 1758 to 1760. The next key date locally is the production of John Chapman's maps of the district in 1768 and 1787 (see endpapers). Fortunately the gap between these events is short and Chapman is in effect mapping Holcroft's Newmarket and so in fact lends the latter's account a firmer base.

◆◆◆◆

Chapman's first map identifies the sites of twenty-six yards, of which twenty-two were in the town. Naturally Chapman's details are a snapshot at the date of production and can mislead as a result. For instance, Lord March's yard is shown occupied by Lord Eglinton, which is no doubt explained by the fact that March took a two-year break from racing from 1767. Lord Eglinton presumably leased the yard until murdered by an aggrieved trespasser in 1769. As he is the same man who was a leading figure in the riot of 1751 it seems he must have been a rather belligerent figure. A few owners like Bunbury out at Great Barton were also Newmarket orientated but too far out to figure in 1768 although he did also keep a yard near the bottom of Warren Hill for most of his long career. Both the Duke of Bridgewater and Richard Vernon had subsidiary yards in the town and a total of just over forty owners were clearly Newmarket-based as most or all of their runners were on the Heath. Those not named by Chapman must either have used one of the six training grooms who he states ran yards or shared facilities with one of those grandees where only the main owner's name appears on the map.

In all it seems that 260 horses entered in races somewhere in the country that year were trained on the Heath although there were no doubt a few more now not traceable as they never got as far as an entry. This suggests an average of about ten horses a yard, which seems surprisingly low. However, even more surprising is that they only ran in 403 races – so turning out on average only 1.55 times each season. When this is contrasted with a national average today of approximately three times that figure on the Flat, which is itself reduced by the number of two-year-olds having one or perhaps two races only, an explanation is clearly needed.

In fact the reason for this extraordinary disparity must largely be traceable to what owners sought from their strings in the mid-eighteenth century. Obviously there are other reasons, like the difficulty of travel, the length of the courses and the limited number of races on the Heath, but surely the main factor was that the real prize being sought was the making of an advantageous match or victory in the few early-closing sweepstakes. Engineering oneself into the position to achieve such a result in the small world of Newmarket would have been no easy matter and doing so more than once or twice a year with any horse at this period seemingly virtually impossible.

The programme on the Heath in 1768 can be broken down as follows:

Race Type	Note	No. of races	Value
Matches	(1)	49	£15,850
Plates	(2)	20	£1,719
Sweepstakes with £500 or more on offer	(3)	17	£13,020
Other races	(4)	13	£3,161
		99	£33,750
Forfeited matches		18	£2,861
		117	£36,611

Notes:

1) Matches ranged from as little as the nine worth only 100 Guineas to one for 1,500 Guineas in which Captain Vernon's Marquis beat Captain Shafto's Caliban.

2) Most of these races were worth only the statutory minimum of £50 but good horses occasionally ran, presumably when it had proved too difficult to fix suitable matches for them.

3) The most valuable of these races in 1768 was the 1,200 Guineas or Great Stakes run in the spring and one worth 1,400 Guineas in October. The latter was won by Shafto's best horse, the unbeaten Goldfinder by his famous stallion Snap.

4) Precise values are not always calculable as some Jockey Club races were expressed as being worth '100 Guineas or upwards'. In all sweepstakes the winner's own stake has been included in the value of the race.

It should be appreciated that most of the matches and entries for the major sweepstakes had been published in 1767, or even earlier in a few cases, and, as events developed, opportunities would appear based on trials or problems to back or lay horses. Owners of the day would be dumbfounded by our rules forbidding laying your own animal. Trying to get into a position to win whatever happened (or at least not to lose money in defeat) was the real target and men like Vernon and Shafto, professional racing men living in the area and with the largest strings of the day, must have had major advantages over the bigwigs like Cumberland, Rockingham and Grosvenor. Holcroft quotes one example towards the end of his time in Newmarket when on 2 May 1760 Richard Vernon got into the position of winning a fortune despite his own runner finishing last of six. Unfortunately for the gallant captain his choice could only make it a dead heat and as it was not run off all bets were void. Holcroft says Vernon would also have won on his own entrant and broken even anyway had the other dead-heater prevailed so he amply justified his reputation for shrewdness.

Against such a background it is surely understandable that horses ran so infrequently and that the lengthy preparations for these epic encounters bore some resemblance to the way boxers' lives are organised today before occasional appearances in championship bouts. The whole performance of match racing really did bear quite a close relationship to eighteenth-century prize-fighting as a concept. Set out below are some of the more interesting aspects of getting your horse as fit as conceivably possible to race over four miles just once or twice a year.

◆◆◆◆

TRAINING DOWN THE AGES

As this is no treatise on modern training methods but instead aims at showing the main trends over the past four centuries, it seems sensible to recognise that many seeming oddities will not be evidence of ancient mistakes but instead practical responses to the changed circumstances of the different periods. In particular are reflected:

1) The different demands placed on the horse by both race distances and the ages of the runners sharply reducing.

2) The arrival of alternative surfaces to grass such as first ploughed gallops then tan, watered gallops and finally the various all-weather surfaces now available on the Heath.

3) The spectacular increase in the cost of labour relative to anything else in an activity which is as labour-intensive.

4) The equally spectacular effect of the development of veterinary science from little more than folklore and nostrums to what it is today.

5) And probably most important of all, the changing nature of the horses themselves as selective breeding added at least two hands to average height and almost as certainly markedly reduced the hardiness of the original racing Galloways.

Clearly, points 4 and 5, representing as they do suitable subjects for tomes on veterinary history and the whole development of the thoroughbred, cannot be covered in any detail here. Equally, the other points touch on all sorts of things that have changed radically over the centuries, so perhaps the best approach is to outline shifting views and trainers' policies on specific subjects. Collectively, they seem to cover enough of the field to give a picture of the speed and direction of travel at Newmarket as racing's headquarters has grappled with the implications of points 1 to 5.

◆◆◆◆

Perhaps the right place to start is with something that in principle has never really changed at all. However long the distance covered and in whatever clothing to induce sweating, work as conducted by good trainers seems to have assumed that horses should not be pushed to their limits at home. They have always wanted fit horses to be able to quicken up towards the end of their gallops and still not quite to be at full stretch. No doubt relatively moderate animals that are worked with better will be pushed very near their limits in fast work, but even they will not be pressed to the extent that would happen in the finishes of their races. Although old fashioned private trials did approximate to races, even then experienced operators found out what they needed to know by juggling with the weights carried rather than by driving horses to their limits with whip and spur.

Another common factor down the years has been the understanding that horses must progress relatively slowly from an unfit state to a race only being able to stand the essential faster work and more of it as the weeks passed. Markham may seem a bit optimistic in advising his amateur that a horse could be got ready for races over four miles (or frequently more) in only about eight weeks from grass. However, he was handing out his opinions based – in our terms – on tough little racing ponies and the amount of work he thought they would take in that period would certainly be too much for the modern thoroughbred.

◆◆◆◆

ABANDONED PRACTICES
Most of the major changes in the regime in training stables have moved pretty steadily in one direction all the way through. Yet, some of the once universal schemes for readying horses have simply been phased out altogether and the more important of these are seen as being:

1) Horsebread
In Markham's era to eat horsebread was virtually synonymous with a horse being in training and really defined the exercise of getting one ready to race. He went into great detail of how loaves should be made and varied over the eight weeks as the race approached. The main constituents were shelled beans and fine wheat with the proportions changing towards the latter as things progressed in order to produce a finer flour. This was turned to dough with varying quantities of brewing residue, water, milk or egg white and then baked into large loaves. Left at least three days to become a little

stale, several slices without their crusts were crumbled into the horse's normal feed of oats.

The idea was that as a high-energy food it would help the horse to stand his necessary work and the race itself. One wonders whether the practice was the origin of the expression 'full of beans'. Quite when it was phased out is unclear but Holcroft made no mention of it a century and a half later.

2) Sweating

This practice had a much longer history, lasting to the mid-nineteenth century, although it was becoming steadily less fashionable at Newmarket by the end of the eighteenth. Indeed, the most detailed account of the procedure is in Darvill but it was already history at Newmarket soon after he wrote. As a result the various rubbing houses where horses were scraped after sweating, which were dotted about the Heath, became redundant unless near one of the starts or finishes, justifying their retention as simple stables. Sweating a horse was thought essential to get flesh off early in the season and to clean him of grease through the pores in the skin. First he would be completely covered with one or two serge-lined hoods over head and neck plus a body sweater from neck to tail. Over this was fastened a blanket and one or two quarter pieces, and sometimes a special long breast sweater before the horse was saddled. The length of work would vary from two and a half to five miles dependent on age and was conducted at about half speed or even less, ending near one of the Rubbing Houses. Inside he would be loaded with further clothing (Fig.182) and the stable closed against draughts while he stood for up to a quarter of an hour pouring sweat. Then he would ideally be attacked by four lads, one to each quarter, while a fifth held his head (Fig. 182). With the hoods and quarter pieces removed and the other clothing he had worked in folded over the saddle they stripped away the sweat with strigels. An example can be seen in Fig. 53, beside the bottle, and another in Fig. 128, where it is in use, as

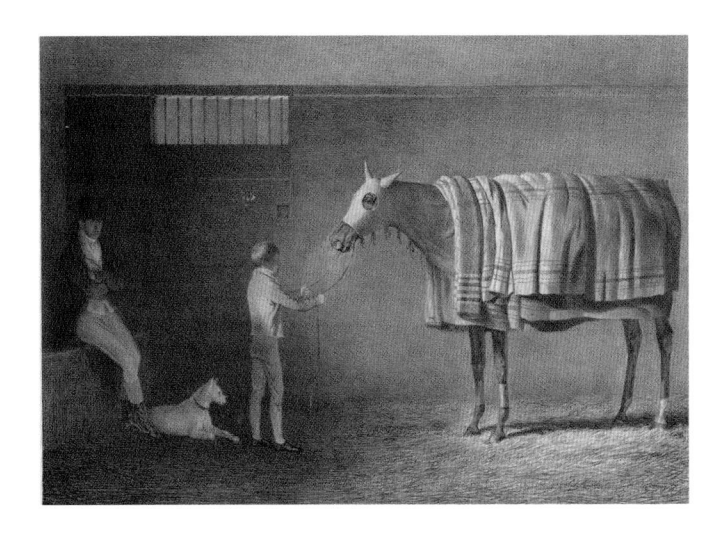

Fig. 182

Etching showing rubbing after sweating (1823) by John Doyle
(Series: Life of the Racehorse)

Once the long sweating work in plenty of clothing was over the horse entered a rubbing house. Here he was loaded with yet more rugs and left to stew for about a quarter of an hour, the procedure in the first etching. This was followed by the point of the exercise in the second when, with the horse awash with lather, a lad would be allocated to each quarter and a fifth used to restrain the no doubt often infuriated animal.

it was quite normal to scrape a horse after a race. Once the quarters and shoulders were dealt with the saddle was removed along with the remaining clothing and the job completed. After that the horse was resaddled with only light clothing and did a short canter before returning to his own stable. Given a horse might be sweated like this anything up to ten times a year it is hardly surprising that far more became savage than happens today.

3) Stables

In the days of Markham and Holcroft stalls for most horses including those in racing stables were almost universal. However, by the time Darvill was writing early in the nineteenth century the majority of racehorses would have stood in looseboxes, although stalls were still the norm for most other horses. This posed about the only real problem Darvill noted in switching to boxes – horses being walked from inn to inn to race at distant meetings would be lucky to find boxes available and being unused to standing in stalls could potentially be unsettled by having to do so. The other argument that a building could take more stalled horses he dismissed with somewhat cavalier disregard for his readers' pockets, while the objection that early boxes usually resulted in horses suffering from isolation was naturally remedied in the end by the removal of bars from the half-doors or placing grills between adjacent boxes.

4) Trials

While trials no doubt still occur occasionally they would be pale shadows of those recorded in such detail in the reminiscences of nineteenth-century trainers. By the days of Holcroft they were certainly already an important part of activities at Newmarket and Jenison Shafto had a special private trial course of his own beside the original eight-mile track beyond Six Mile Bottom. However, Holcroft makes no detailed reference to them in the memoir. Perhaps this is hardly surprising in view of the fact he was only fifteen and the training groom John Watson and his chief assistant John Clark (Fig. 165), were both first-class jockeys who would have monopolised such specialised and secret work. Gimcrack's trial (Fig. 55) came only five years after Holcroft had retreated to London and sixty years on from there Darvill goes into considerable detail about just how these exercises should be conducted, often concealing from the riders the weights they had carried for fear of leaked information. At Newmarket the trying of horses belonging to different owners was prohibited unless the ground to be used was formally reserved and the animals involved named. Once these preliminaries had been completed no unauthorised people were permitted to watch the trial, which explains the absence of any spectators in Fig. 55. Darvill dilates on various other types of trial which fell well short of private races of this type. For instance a trainer would normally try each generation in his care as soon as they were ready, with a view to categorising them for the longer term. References to such events were to yearling trials, which naturally looks odd to our eyes but arises from the fact horses did not formally become two-year-olds until the standard date for aging them of 1 May, which only changed to January in the 1830s at Newmarket. Naturally, the need for formal trials arose from the fact that during the eighteenth and much of the nineteenth centuries the majority of the major yards' and owners' activities were based on gambling. Given that there was very little prize money being added to owners' forfeits and match stakes, and that even good horses were worth relatively little compared with the bets that could be won, this emphasis on trials and gambling is not surprising. As steadily fewer major owners have had much involvement with serious gambling from the later nineteenth century onwards so the need for private advance information has dwindled and formal trials along with it.

◆◆◆◆

CONTINUED PRACTICES VARIED BY TIME

Turning from the practices once thought of crucial importance to training racehorses but now largely abandoned to those elements which are just as important today as in the past, we have again selected four to cover the field adequately. There are clearly others like feeding (quite apart from the central one of simply riding the horses) but we have felt them too extensive or specialised for it to be practicable to include them as separate subjects.

1) Temperature in stables and ventilation

Changes adopted in this area are probably the most complete of any of those considered. Markham, in recognising the eastern roots of the warm-blooded horse, was strident in his advice to keep stables as warm and dark as possible. The thought of ventilation being necessary does not seem to have occurred to him and that would have been the general view in his day. By the eighteenth century things have not changed a lot and Holcroft refers to entering stables in the early morning and opening 'the few places for fresh air' so that 'the great heat of the stables gradually cooled'. Darvill as usual goes into a lot more detail and actually includes a short chapter on ventilation. However, too much should not be read into the way he stresses its importance although he does say firmly that stables should be much cooler and that the old practice of hot ones was most improper. He castigates the practice which had even extended to laying 'long dung' at the bottom of the doors to close off draughts as well as shutting every other opening to fresh air on cold nights. These practices had largely been abandoned (to his considerable satisfaction) but he then rather spoils things by advising that a temperature of 62 degrees is the ideal in winter and spring. Nonetheless, vents for admitting fresh air and allowing foul out are accepted as being important even if by no means as extensive as you would find today in any modern yard, mostly with the airy spaces of boxes laid out as pens in large barns.

2) Physicking horses

This is another area which has seen dramatic changes much to the advantage of the modern horse. Dosing horses with aloes used to occur with monotonous regularity for all manner of reasons quite apart from dealing with worms. For instance, if a horse knocked a leg which filled at all as a result the use of physic was automatic both to reduce the swelling and to keep the horse from putting on weight and thereby holding up his preparation once the inevitable box rest was over. Recovery after a race was to be another cause of recourse to the medicine cupboard as was general staleness in the middle of a hard campaign. Darvill records that it was not uncommon for horses to be killed by illiterate grooms who became confused over the correct dosage or impatiently decided to repeat it just before their first administration was effective. Indeed, he was so horrified by the practices of earlier days that physicking merited two long chapters but even then what he did advocate for horses in training goes far beyond modern practice.

3) Staff arrangements

Many of the key changes in working practices in Newmarket and elsewhere have arisen not with a view to the advantage of the horses but that of the staff and in the interests of cutting costs, which reflects the inflation in the cost of labour relative to anything else. Markham is not relevant as he was writing for an owner preparing his own horse and has nothing to say on such matters, but Holcroft thought himself very lucky to be paid four pounds a year when on trial plus his keep and livery. In his day an ordinary lad dealt with only one horse in a stable like Richard Vernon's so the total number of people employed would have much exceeded that of the horses in the yard. Considering that the lad would be out with his horse on the Heath for around four hours in the morning and only slightly less each evening it could not be otherwise, although no doubt riders were switched as needed to reflect their skill. Rising at 2.30 each morning in spring and summer the whole string would be out on the Heath from about 3.30 until around 7.30. From then until about 9 o'clock, when the stables could be shut and the lads depart for a well-earned breakfast, the time would be occupied with grooming, feeding and setting things right in the yard and stable. From then until 4 o'clock the staff's time was their own but woe betide anyone late back, an offence which Holcroft never repeated after enraging John Watson as he happened to pick a day for his misdemeanour when Captain Vernon was in the yard. Back in the stables from the neighbouring Heath around 7 o'clock the staff groomed their horses, fed them twice and had a meal themselves in between before going off to bed around 9 o'clock to start again at 2.30 am the next day. One would imagine nightlife in Newmarket was a good deal less exciting than it is today.

By the nineteenth century life was a little more like today, although horses would still go out for a shorter period during summer evenings. Mornings began much later with breakfast splitting two quite separate lots now normal and the timing of sweats as between first and second lot dependent on the weather. Obviously the demands on staff time of sweating several horses must have made for a much less regular pattern as between first and second lot and the whole exercise could continue until nearly 1 pm. Evenings seem to have begun at 5 o'clock and proceedings concluded by 9 o'clock when the stables were shut for the night, the lads having had their dinner before 8 o'clock. Probably the ancient ritual of the trainer's formal inspection of all boxes, sweeping around with an entourage of any visiting owners and his head lad while boxes were opened in a prearranged sequence with almost military precision for their inspection together with that of their inhabitants (known as Evening Stables), was already being enacted in the larger yards.

As strings are now so much larger than even fifty years ago, and the cost of labour so much increased, the whole system of staffing yards has had to change out of all recognition. The eighteenth-century arrangements of each horse having the full attention of a lad changed to 'doing his two' then three and now most yards have entirely different arrangements based more on function rather than a precise linkage between individual lads and horses. Putting a string out in the evening on a regular basis is unheard of today. While no doubt inevitable due to the pressure of costs, it is hard to think all these changes are an unmixed blessing for the horses.

4) Work

It is impractical to try to make detailed comparison between periods, as apart from anything else practice varies greatly between different yards. We have already dealt with sweating, an exercise which would have occupied a lot of time prior to the early nineteenth century, but a few general conclusions can be drawn over the activities on the Heath. Whenever possible, work has always finished uphill, or indeed, been entirely conducted on the rise now it tends to be shorter. The view that horses' stamina could be stretched by working over further than it was intended to race may or may not be true, but would find no favour today where the emphasis is on developing speed. However, the original extension of good two-year-old races to seven furlongs in the late nineteenth century and to a mile after the last war, which seems innocuous today, caused some outrage among traditionalists on the grounds it would blunt the speed of future classic horses. One may fairly reflect that what constitutes a traditionalist is by no means a fixed standard.

Thomas Holcroft's four hours of a morning on Cambridge Hill consisted of a good deal of walking and two 'brushing' gallops (the old term of 'brushing' meant no more than good, fast work finishing uphill at something well short of top speed without overdoing the horse) interspersed with canters and a visit to the stable's private horse troughs this side of the Well Gap. A major trainer had his own locked water trough and one of the lads' duties was to draw water from the well daily to refill it. It would be used between the two gallops and the number of gulps each horse was allowed was a figure preordained by John Watson. It was into one of these troughs that Daniel Dawson introduced poison, killed some horses,- and was hanged at Cambridge in 1812. Markham's pupil would have done a real gallop three times a fortnight over considerably longer distances and also spent much longer out of the stable each day than is now practicable. The concept fashionable today derived from athletics known colloquially as interval training was unheard of until recent years and is clearly much facilitated by the all-weather surfaces.

◆◆◆◆

We have explained elsewhere how stables developed originally in the town and as things expanded tended to gravitate outwards. Of the three yards where Holcroft was employed Vernon's was on the High Street just across the Avenue from the Rooms, Grafton's at the foot of Warren Hill on the edge of town and Shafto's some five miles out between Hare Park and Balsham.

No doubt the trend away from the centre to the outskirts in part related to the increasing population both human and equine. Later in the eighteenth century, following Shafto's suicide in 1771 and Vernon cutting right back, the influence of the old order increased steadily with the likes of the Prince of Wales, Duke of Bedford and Lord Grosvenor replacing them as the largest owners. By this stage what was wanted was generally a younger horse capable of running far more often (well over three times a season soon became the average) in the new races like the Derby, Oaks or St Leger, together with the early major handicaps like the Oatlands. There were far more horses and prize money began to matter, along with match stakes and gambling, so that racing, and the way to prepare horses for such different tasks, began to take a more recognisable form. Such expansion resulted in a Heath and infrastructure generally that in our terms had been grossly underused developing on more rational lines towards the point where it could cater for today's local horse population of 2,700 or so in training, roughly ten times the eighteenth-century population.

A dispassionate review of the content of this section could lead to two seemingly very different conclusions. One would be that over the past four centuries the many changes have altered the way horses are prepared for races out of all knowledge. On the other hand, it can be argued that in essence the exercise is still what it has always been: namely, getting the horse as fit as possible for the task it faces based on as much work as it will stand (within the constraints of what the owner will pay for) on a high energy diet. In the final analysis we suggest that both views are true.

Training at Newmarket by John Ferneley, detail of Fig. 183

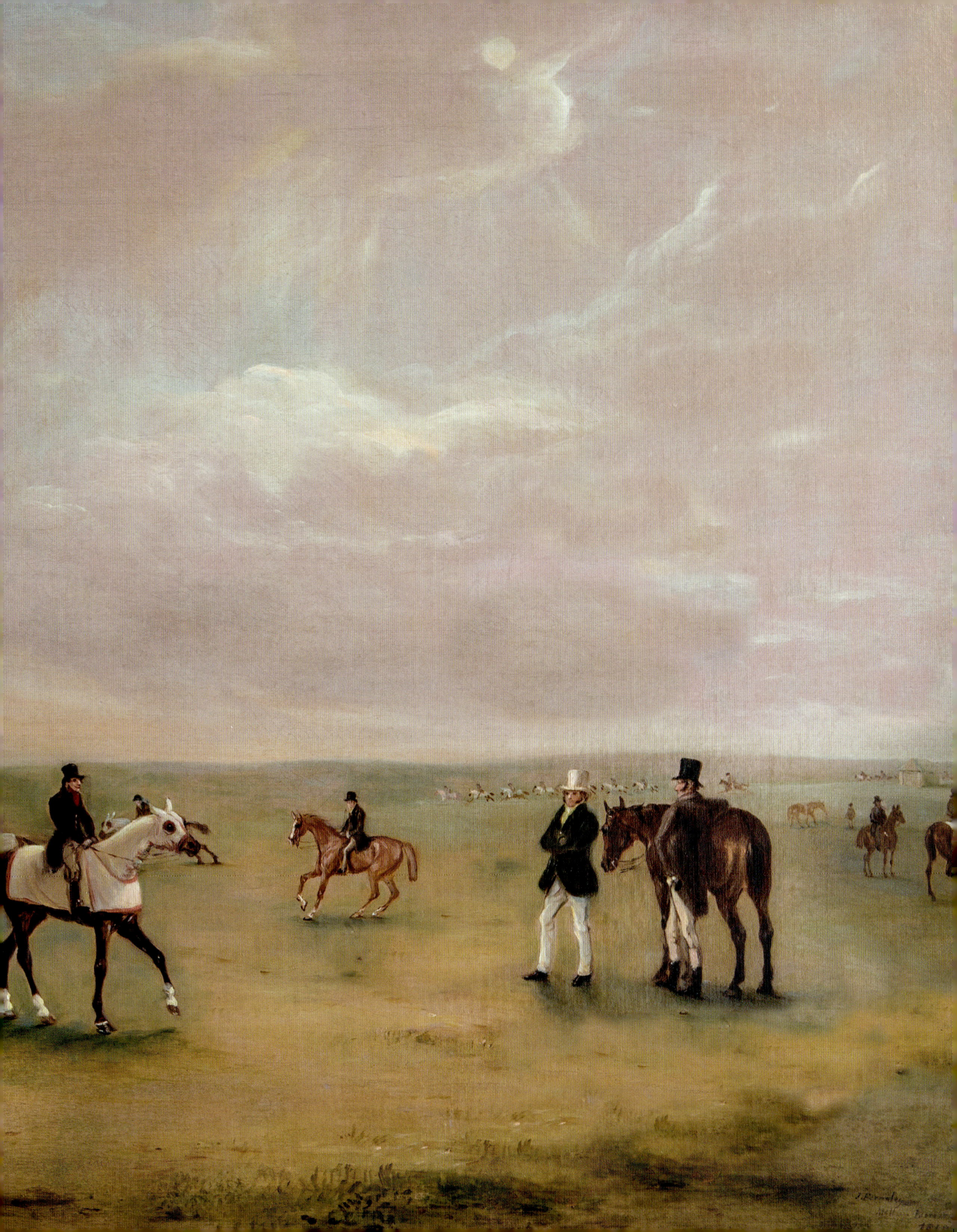

PICTURE PUZZLE 10: IDENTIFICATION OF PEOPLE AND OCCASION

The practical significance of getting things right rather than leaving pictures as anonymous scenes is well made by this fine Ferneley (Fig. 183). It appears as entry 597 in his splendidly detailed account book under the dull title of 'Training at Newmarket'. It had been commissioned by Mr C. Townsend of Aldersgate in the City for the seemingly very reasonable sum of 10 Guineas. When it recently came on the market at a somewhat more exalted price, the scene was recognised as being of exceptional interest in the context of the history of the Jockey Club. As a consequence, a member, Prince Khalid bin Abdullah, was kind enough to add it to the collection in the Rooms. What his generosity actually delivered is a picture painted to mark the tragically early death of Lord George Bentinck at only forty-six in 1848, the year before the work is dated. Lord George is the tall figure in his favourite mulberry coat negligently leaning on the hack. He is inspecting the string of his great friend James, the eccentric 5th Earl of Glasgow, who was a retired sea captain and habitually dressed like one in naval ducks instead of normal trousers or breeches, a reefer jacket, and with a white top hat reflective more of his eccentricity than the sea.

The relationship between Bentinck and the immensely rich Glasgow, provided the former with a large and steady income from the matches they arranged between their horses on the Heath. In some years these could number well over twenty and Bentinck always won the overwhelming majority, as might be expected given the strength of his huge string over the invariably inferior horses owned by Glasgow. After the sale of all his horses in 1846 for £10,000 – a fraction of their real value, Bentinck concentrated on politics and even sold his stud at Doncaster to Glasgow. It subsequently became Glasgow Paddocks, for many years the site of Tattersalls' principal yearling sales.

Even after he and Benjamin Disraeli lost the battle over the Corn Laws (they were abolished in 1846) and Sir Robert Peel lost power, Bentinck continued to combine the roles of Leader of the Opposition with serving as a Steward of the Club until June 1848, and visited Newmarket for the last time during the Guineas meeting that April. If the occasion of this picture has a specific origin presumably it was that visit which Townsend commissioned John Ferneley to commemorate in this memento mori. It obviously depicts a morning scene on the Heath with the two friends standing more or less on the July Course to the west of the Ditch, their shadows pointing westwards. Behind Glasgow's string, their white rugs trimmed with pink as you would expect, can be seen the small Well Gap with its rails running up the face of the bank.

Contrary to the normal course of events, Glasgow did win some races that week including the Queen's Plate with Miss Whip run over the Round Course and so finishing somewhere near the little building in the distance. Perhaps she is the bay leading his string. Who the chap with the greyhounds might be has yet to be discovered – if he is Glasgow's trainer he is unlikely to have lasted more than a few months as he sacked them frequently. In any case, the temporary occupant of that very hot seat is more likely to be the figure on the chesnut hack, centre stage.

Picture Puzzle 10

Fig. 183

Training at Newmarket by John Ferneley (1849)

VIII

Holcroft's Memoir of Life in a Newmarket Yard (1758–1760)

Thomas Holcroft (Fig. 184) was a most unusual stable lad. Born in 1745, his early life was mostly spent helping his father peddle a variety of different goods around the country, walking vast distances between towns and villages in the north and midlands even as far south as Ascot. However, by the time he died in 1809 he had become a successful playwright and novelist. He also became notorious for his political views in alliance with Tom Paine and others which, following the French Revolution, led to his trial for high treason in 1794. Although acquitted he fled abroad for several years before returning to England in 1801. The memoir forms only a fraction of his biography, the rest of which was written by William Hazlitt after his death, based on his diaries. Fortunately, the slice of his life Holcroft wrote himself covers his first fifteen years and ends when he left the turf in 1760. As it provides a unique insight into Newmarket life at a crucial point in the sport's development, and shows the status of stable jobs with some clarity, it is covered here in some detail. It also forms the basis of the section on training with respect to technical detail in the mid-eighteenth century.

Holcroft's father was always poor, and became steadily more so, but before he took to peddling he had lived a more settled life in London and his son had at least learnt how to read. After several years on the road, in June 1758 they were in Nottingham at the time of the assizes and poor Thomas, aged thirteen, was horrified when his father insisted it would further his moral education to take him to see one of those convicted being hanged. Despite his hard existence, Holcroft senior had strong views on morality and sought to teach them to his son. However, things took an altogether happier turn when the race week began on 4 July with the King's Plate. On the 7th the famous horse Careless (Fig. 185), which Holcroft had been watching all week, made a deep impression on the boy by stretching his so far unbeaten career to fourteen races going back to its start in 1755.

At this point Holcroft becomes fairly confused over the details of which race happened where but writing over fifty years later with no racing calendars to prompt his memory that is hardly surprising. But it is easy enough to piece together the correct sequence of events with a calendar to help, and it is no wonder that the whole thing greatly impressed the thirteen-year-old. In particular he was struck by the smartness of the lads in their owners' liveries and found them 'healthy, clean, well-fed, well clothed and remarkable for their impudence'. He immediately decided the sport was the life for him and fortunately Captain Richard Vernon had sent a horse from Newmarket to contest the King's Plate. Holcroft struck up an acquaintance with John Clark (Fig. 165), some three or four years his senior, who had brought the horse to Nottingham. Clark agreed to take him back along with his horse and Thomas was delighted to find they could eat 'excellent cold beef, bread and cheese, with the best table beer and as much as one pleased'. This gave him 'a foretaste of the fortunate change I had made'.

So the journey proceeded pleasantly enough at ten or fifteen miles a day until they reached Huntingdon for the races which began on 1 August. Then disaster struck as the now revered Careless was beaten for the first time in his life by the Duke of Devonshire's Atlas after three heats. This difficult lesson did not deter youthful enthusiasm and Holcroft eventually reached Newmarket, where Clark found him a job with Captain Jenison Shafto's trainer John Woodcock just beyond Six Mile Bottom. Like most trainers of the period, Woodcock was also a noted horseman and in 1761 won Shafto a famous bet of no less than 2,000 Guineas by riding one hundred miles each day between 4 May and 1 June. He could use as many horses as he liked overall (he actually used fourteen) but only one each day and as one animal broke down after covering sixty miles Woodcock had only just long enough left before midnight to complete his daily stint on a fresh one.

The job did not last more than a few weeks as Holcroft's inexperience led to a bad fall, but he was enjoying his new life and when he recovered Woodcock took pity on him and found him a place in the Duke of Grafton's yard at the foot of Warren Hill. That arrangement proved even shorter term as Grafton's trainer, thought to be Mr Johnstone, decided he did not have the necessary experience. However, his riding was improving and Clark then got him a job with John Watson, Captain Vernon's trainer, at the same place where he worked himself on the corner of the High Street and the Avenue. Watson took the sporting view that everyone has to learn somewhere and in his hands it seems Holcroft progressed quickly to become one of the more proficient horsemen in a yard where Watson, Clark and indeed, Vernon himself were all good jockeys.

Contrary to what one might expect, life seems to have been a good deal easier for the staff than it became a century later in the notoriously harsh regimes of Victorian racing stables. Food remained good and plentiful and while the discipline may seem strict to us it did not approach the severity of post-industrial times. Relationships within the yard were extraordinarily democratic, a good example of which was the fact that the trainer was simply known as 'John' to his face, not even 'Mr. Watson', much less 'Sir'. Holcroft states that he was 'John Watson' to the lads from other yards and, writing in 1828, Richard Darvill quotes all this rather disapprovingly as already seeming far too lax an attitude. That view steadily strengthened and held sway until very recently in any large yard. Even allowing for the fact that Watson was quite a young man whose status acting for Vernon was probably somewhere between that of a trainer and a head lad, it does seem surprising and Holcroft makes it clear that other yards were much the same.

As with farm labourers of the period, the younger staff were almost part of the family and in general good stablemen seem to have been regarded as something approaching a working class aristocracy. It is hard to think too many factory workers in the next century would have been able to expect 'milk porridge, cold meat from the preceding day, most exquisite Gloucester cheese, fine white bread and plentiful draughts of beer' for breakfast each day. While 2.30 am in summer is indeed, an early start, to have your freedom from 9am to 4pm and only one horse to worry about certainly has its attractions. Meanwhile £4 or so annually at the age of thirteen must have been far in advance of anything a farm boy could expect. While Holcroft does not mention

Fig. 184

Thomas Holcroft (1745–1809) by John Opie (*c*.1804)

After spending most of his early years helping his father peddle goods round the northern half of the country he made a break to work in three major Newmarket yards from thirteen to fifteen. His life in stables forms most of the first volume of his three-decker biography by Hazlitt and fortunately he contributed that part himself in old age. After Newmarket his varied career encompassed success as a playwright and prosecution for treason, and consequent exile during the early years of the French Revolution for his support of radical causes. Given the quality of his vivid account of life in an eighteenth century yard, it is sad he was not spared long enough to have made it an autobiography.

Fig. 185

Careless (1754) by Regulus out of Silvertail, Francis Sartorius (*c*.1758)

Owned and bred by Mr Borlace Warren, Careless was eventually beaten after fourteen wins at Huntingdon on 3rd August 1758 as witnessed by the horrified Thomas Holcroft. He was trying to concede the only other runner, the Duke of Devonshire's Atlas, 11lbs and won the first heat but lost the next two. Atlas won again on 10th May 1759, at level weights at Newmarket, with high class Sweepstakes third. However on 21st August 1760 honour was restored at York when Careless inflicted the first and only defeat of Atlas's career at levels in the Great Subscription. Retired to stud for the 1762 season he was only moderately successful.

his wages increasing as his skill in the saddle progressed it seems likely they would have risen over his two years from thirteen to fifteen in the Vernon yard.

Unlike his contemporaries Thomas spent some of his free time in educating himself, learning to sing and read music and in other distinctly atypical activities. Indeed, he seems cordially to have despised his fellow workers for their complete lack of ambition, and his efforts to persuade them to learn to read and write were contemptuously rejected. He says at one point the only two he respected were Watson and Clark, either or both of them may well have been literate. There is also a detailed account of Clark having the left side of his face shot away when larking around in their lodgings across the street with lads from Lord March's yard when a gun was pointed in fun without realising it had been charged. In general the accounts of horseplay and initiation rites were much as you might expect in an all-male environment of this type. At the same time, Holcroft's tales of the degree to which life among the lads was governed by assorted strange superstitions, all of which he scornfully rejected, seems almost medieval in its intensity.

In October 1759 Holcroft realised that even Vernon made mistakes when he matched his Forester, by then rather unsound and aged ten, against Jenison Shafto's six years old Elephant at level weights for 500 Guineas over the Beacon. Shafto was to ride his own horse with Watson up on Forester and on the great day Forester certainly tried hard to save Vernon's Guineas. In fact, on finding near the finish that he could not get by Elephant he seized hold of his opponent and they reached the King's Stand locked together in the most literal sense. Whether encouraged by the fact he had spotted this rare example of the Captain's fallibility in advance or by that master gambler's usually high rate of success, Holcroft decided he was fully equipped to take the ring by storm at the April meeting in 1760. To his horror, he discovered that it was by no means as easy as he thought and his 'crowns and half crowns were dwindling away'. By the end of the meeting he had lost over half a year's income and was so disconsolate that he spent many hours in an unavailing search for any coins that might have been dropped on the Heath rather than admit to his father what had happened.

The whole experience so soured Holcroft that he decided to abandon Newmarket and seek his fortune in London where, after a much longer apprenticeship, he eventually achieved the success already described. He gave several months, notice to John Watson with real regret, admitting to the trainer he could not expect a better place than the one he had. On being asked what he proposed to do Holcroft said he thought he would become a shoemaker to which Watson replied that he was a blockhead but a good boy who would do far better if he stayed where he was.

Although he went through with his scheme and severed his links with the turf he seems to have retained a fondness for his life in stables in general, and the thoroughbred horse in particular, even if he lamented his contemporaries' refusal to embrace self-improvement. If that makes him seem something of a prig, the memoir as a whole suggests that would be an unfair judgement of a remarkable life. Certainly the lively style in which he wrote is a good deal easier for modern eyes than the rather pompous offering of Hazlitt in the final two-and-a-half volumes of the biography.

IX

History of the Palace and its Development as Part of the National Heritage Centre for Horseracing and Sporting Art

Perhaps the most striking thing about the story of the buildings on the Palace House site is how closely they have reflected the fortunes of Newmarket itself. That stayed largely true from the start of things in the early seventeenth century, when James I's initial move was to rent and then buy the Griffin Inn, until the Rothschilds finally sold his grandson's Palace to Forest Heath District Council around 1980. Thereafter, their house and the yard across Palace Street have at times fallen out of favour almost as dramatically as during Newmarket's total eclipse during the Commonwealth, whereas the town has largely prospered. Hopefully the development of all that remains on a reduced site as a cultural centre will see their fortunes go forward in step again.

Developments before the Civil War

The Griffin stood on the High Street to the east of Sun Lane, and by 1610 James's fairly modest construction was complete, representing the first attempt at a palace. Unfortunately subsidence led to serious cracks appearing and when the king's lodgings started to sink a major rebuild began in 1614. By then the site had been expanded on the west of Sun Lane to include what later maps call 'Old King's Yard' stretching back to All Saints Church to the south.

In 1615 the famous architect Inigo Jones was appointed to the office of King's Surveyor and began adding separate buildings called the 'Brew House' and the 'Dog House' plus a later 'Office of Works'. More ambitious was his construction of the 'Prince's Lodgings' for Charles I (then Prince of Wales) which were finished in 1619. The architect's drawing of its façade shows an imposing structure which figured on a postage stamp of 1973 (Fig. 186) issued to mark the four hundredth anniversary of its designer's birth. It appears to have stood east of Sun Lane in Old King's Yard if indeed the elaborate design was ever completed before the Civil War.

Throughout the period before the civil war pieces of property were bought as they became available, such as the 'King's Close', some six acres lying south of All Saints, and an acre behind the Greyhound Inn on the High Street rather to the east of the original Griffin purchase. Thus when Charles I was finally removed from Newmarket by the Parliamentary forces in 1647 the quite extensive site would have contained a rather odd assortment of buildings with various special uses, rather than just a conventional palace. Over the next two decades, apart from those sold off for building materials, the rest were largely left to decay as Newmarket became a backwater with no obvious future.

Fig. 186

The Prince's Lodging designed by Inigo Jones

This impressive building was constructed before 1620 for the occupation of the Prince of Wales, later Charles I. The image was used for a commemorative stamp issue of 1973 marking the four hundredth anniversary of the great architect's birth. The structure did not survive the Interregnum.

Reconstruction and Royal occupation

Charles II would have known Newmarket well as a boy but did not return to his old haunts until six years after his restoration to the throne in 1660. Prior to that work had begun on restoring the buildings but does not seem to have progressed very fast as the place was not habitable in 1666. However, after that things speeded up under William Samwell's guidance and Charles bought both the Earl of Thomond's house and the adjacent Greyhound Inn, thereby increasing the High Street frontage of the site. Stables appeared across Palace Street, the foundations of which were recently exposed as part of a Time Team investigation for Channel 4. One cannot be sure but it seems unlikely these were the King's racing stables and much more probably they were the mews for the Palace riding and carriage horses.

Despite the scale of these works, their position in the middle of town and their lack of architectural distinction when compared to the old 'Prince's Lodgings' caused the diarist John Evelyn to condemn them in 1670. That severe critic objected to their being placed 'in a dirty street without any court, or avenue, like a common one'. Instead he considered the Palace should have been built 'at either end of the town upon the very carpet where the sports are celebrated' and, much as modern planners would object to such a procedure, it is hard to deny that in his day he had a point. Further buildings were added and in 1672 it seems there was a total of 124 rooms on the site with the King's eldest illegitimate son, the Duke of Monmouth (Fig. 188), ensconced in lodgings on the old Greyhound site as Master of the Horse. Across the other side of the site the King's last mistress, Nell Gwyn, eventually had lodgings next to the mews (it is said connected to the Palace by a tunnel under the street but no one has proved the point by finding it), while the grander ones like the Duchesses of Cleveland and Portsmouth resided in the Palace itself. Presumably it was here that Nellie dangled her son from an upstairs window (if indeed, she ever did) threatening in jest to drop him if he was not made a duke – as indeed, he was in 1684. At least this legend seems to reflect the easygoing personalities of both the principals.

The only pictures of the main buildings are those which appear in the distant backgrounds of the many panoramas taken from various vantage points on Warren Hill and Fig. 29 is an early example.

The great fire of March 1683 which destroyed most of the town to the north of the High Street caused no serious damage to the south. However, due to all the disruption the King and his brother left early for Whitehall which may well have saved their lives from the Rye House plotters. Although as a response to the crisis Charles threatened to take his pleasures in future near Winchester, building a new Palace there took time and he did in fact return for three weeks in October and twice more in the spring and autumn of 1684 but died in the following January. As a result Newmarket saw no more royalty until after James II's deposition and the appearance of William III regularly during his fourteen year reign. He does not seem to have made many changes and when Queen Anne succeeded him in 1702 she did little more than make some alterations including the removal of buildings that obscured the view from her apartments.

By the time the Queen died in 1714 the site had a High Street frontage in the west from a little short of Sun Lane to about halfway to the Rutland Arms (then known as The Ram). Across Sun Lane the Crown still owned the buildings in Old King's Yard extending as far west as the present Museum and running back to All Saints Church. Beyond All Saints the pasture called 'King's Close' was also retained but the field between the Palace mews and what is now Rous Road, which will be part of the Heritage Centre, does not seem to have been acquired by that stage. After the death of her husband Prince George of Denmark in 1708 the Heath saw no more of the increasingly overweight and immobile Queen and her Hanoverian successors were drawn to the town only once or twice respectively. Their Palace in the background of so many pictures by Wootton, Seymour and Tillemans looks much the same as it had fifty years before in Fig. 12.

The Palace between the death of Queen Anne and the arrival of the Rothschilds in 1857

Over the ensuing period of almost one-and-a-half centuries the site was usually let in sections to various people, often to several at the same time. The only two significant Royal occupants were the Duke of Cumberland either side of 1760 (he was content with a redesigned building on the Greyhound site) and the Prince of Wales for most of the decade before the Escape catastrophe of 1791. Before their day, the Duke of Somerset (Fig. 37) took a thirty-one-year lease in 1721 and on his death in 1748 it passed to his heiress, who was married to the notable general after whom so many pubs are named: the Marquis of Granby. As she was the mother of the 4th Duke of Rutland the principal lease remained with that family until Queen Victoria finally severed the Crown's connection by selling what was left on the site in 1855 after Charles's tapestries had been divided between Holyrood and Hampton Court. Baron Meyer de Rothschild bought both the main house and the stables which had been separated briefly by the 1855 sale.

Before either the Palace or the new Coffee Room became available, the Red Lion had traditionally been the haunt of the important figures, but in 1752 soon after the Marquis of Granby took over he made part of the site available for the entertainment of the grander racegoers, even importing Mr Maskell, mine host from the Jockey Club's London haunt at the Star and Garter, to run things. Quite how much of the still very extensive Palace buildings were thus employed as an early version of the present Jockey Club Rooms is uncertain. We know the Long Room was included and from its shape on the plans it seems likely this was the room more formally called King William's Picture Gallery, which was on the first floor just to the north of the present Palace House. There are records of those frequenting the site quarrelling over games of hazard and the present entrance hall of Palace House, then known as the Old Hazard Room, was presumably included in the deal. The room would have allowed access from Palace Street and on to the Long Room up the stairs. There is a contemporary note stating that John Pond of Calendar fame was in charge of the Hazard Club in the town at this period so he may have run it in the old room among his various other activities.

These included winning a race on the Thames with a fellow oarsman 'from Westminster Bridge to the Temple' in 1754 'for a considerable sum', as well as acting as the Tattersalls of the day. In that guise he or his son sold both Herod and Eclipse in 1765 after the death of the Duke of Cumberland, the latter by auction.

The facilities were only available on an occasional basis and the grandees would no doubt have been among the 364 subscribers to Mr Deards's Coffee Room, which had been run by the family for much of the century and in 1752 attracted nearly 400 subscribers, more people than ever before. In the Chapman map of 1768 the buildings next to the Rutland Arms (then called the Ram) running through from the High Street to Palace Street are marked as the 'Old Coffee House' and this was presumably the one run by Deards. John Deards had been succeeded by his son William in 1731 and the latter died in 1761. His son seems to have severed the family's business links with the town. As the Deards family worked for the Club in various roles it seems likely that either they ran both establishments or the earlier version was closed soon after the Rooms opened, leaving its name attached to the premises.

What pictures the Long Room contained is unknown apart from the Chatsworth portrait of Flying Childers (Fig. 10) and we only have that information due to an 1844 memorandum by the 6th Duke of Devonshire that has survived. In it he stated that the picture had 'long adorned the long room at Newmarket, and, when that room yielded up its treasures, was received here' (i.e. Chatsworth). Records there show that it was already in Derbyshire by 1792 and so, as explained in Chapter 5, it seems probable that the transfer had come in the early 1770s when the Marquis of Granby's death was immediately followed by the major extension of the Rooms, presumably as a replacement for the Palace.

Before its long decline and eventual sale the Palace had a final fling in Royal occupation when the Prince of Wales made it the centre of Newmarket life in the 1780s. Indeed, it must have reverted to something approaching its palmy days under Charles II. An inventory of the contents was made in 1783 which must have been done in preparation for the arrival of the Prince of Wales as he had his first runners in 1784. One yarn from the period which does seem to be true is that the Prince pushed the Duc d'Orleans into the fountain when he caught him unawares in contemplation of the goldfish. The Duc, known as Philippe Égalité, even took his opinions so far as to vote for his cousin Louis XVI's execution but ironically soon followed the French King to the guillotine. It seems he did not share the Prince's sense of humour, and returned to his rooms in the Palace in high dudgeon to dry out after too close an inspection of the goldfish.

The Palace site bought by Baron Meyer was a very much reduced version of what had stood there in the Prince of Wales's day seventy years before. The main changes had come between 1815 and 1819. These represented a retreat from the High Street as first what was called the 'Lord Chamberlain's Office' was demolished for its materials and two years later the 'Queen's Apartments' went the same way in a sale for £500 to the notorious William Crockford. In 1819 that exercise was almost completed when the building on the site of the Greyhound Inn went to the local Holland family for £1,010. What remained on the main site was reported by the *Sporting Magazine* as about to be restored in a way that would make it 'very much resemble a lunatic asylum at Hoxton' rather than a palace, but in 1825 the Duke of Rutland's lease on 'Queen Anne's Pavilion', the last building on the High Street, was confirmed. It eventually became a Congregational Chapel in 1863.

At some point which cannot now be precisely identified King Charles's mews had become a racing establishment and in the first half of the nineteenth century was principally the base of the Edwards family, who trained at various times for the Duke of Rutland and Earls of Jersey and Chesterfield. Beginning with James, who, as well as siring a series of trainers and jockeys from his three marriages, handled fourteen Classic winners between 1811 and 1837, it passed to his sons – by which time Newmarket was in severe decline. William and John trained there but the yard had left the family before the Rothschilds took over. The final severance of Royal ownership seems to have been precipitated when the aged Duke of Rutland retired from the turf (he died in 1857); the 6th Duke was not interested in racing and anyway still owned the whole Cheveley Park estate until it was sold on his death to Harry McCalmont in 1890. In all probability their long interest in the Palace site was always due as much to its stables as its house.

Occupation by the Rothschild family

Baron Meyer de Rothschild had horses in training elsewhere in the town for some years before the chance came to acquire the remains of the Palace as a residence and stables over the road for his string. The trainer there at the time was James Godding and, after he retired on the back of his final triumph in the 1863 Derby with Macaroni, the Baron appointed Joseph Hayhoe to succeed, building for him the present 'Trainer's House' which is to accommodate the National Horseracing Museum when it switches from the High Street to open its doors in 2016. The stables were reconstructed outside Hayhoe's front door and Palace House across the street greatly improved by the architect George Devey.

After the remarkable series of triumphs, which resulted in 1871 being known as 'The Baron's Year', the owner died in 1874. As his only child, Hannah, had yet to take much interest in racing the Palace and yard passed to his brother Lionel's third son, Leopold.. The process by which it passed from Meyer's executors to Leopold has been obscure, but Rothschild family tradition says that it was first sold to the Graftons and almost immediately bought from them by Leopold. Why the Grafton family would have wanted the Palace and yard is not obvious, as they had little connection with racing at the period; perhaps they saw it as an investment, and simply sold because they were offered a profit. Anyway, in Leopold it passed to someone with a deep interest in the sport and the whole site for forty years. Leopold had great success as an owner and after Joseph Hayhoe was succeeded in 1881 by his son Alfred the latter added a third Palace House Derby in 1904 to Joseph's wins with Kisber and Sir Bevys. In the 1890s Leopold owned the outstanding St Frusquin, principal rival of his friend the Prince of Wales's Persimmon and the Palace, stables and Trainer's House were all much improved. With no palace of his own the Prince both stayed at and visited Leopold's and crowds used to gather to watch his comings and goings up the flight of stairs leading from Palace Street to the main front door, set in the wall at the level of the first floor windows of today. Indeed, you can still see where it was bricked up when the stairs were removed and the entry reverted to former arrangements at ground level via the stone-paved Hazard Room. The steps had been one of Leopold's changes.

Work continued on the house, much of it designed by the architect John Flatman, son of the famous jockey Nat, who produced the watercolours used to illustrate the chapter on Buildings on the Heath. In 1903 he built what is called the Rothschild Yard to the south of the King's Yard more or less as it stands today, including very original arrangements for ventilation with a tower. He also added a three-storey wing to the north of the Palace in 1906, and in 1908 the splendid circular manure pit which will pass to the Retraining of Racehorses (ROR) charity complete with its listed status when they take over the old Rothschild Yard. Flatman's final addition to the Palace before Leopold de Rothschild died in 1917 was the oriel window overlooking the garden added to the King's Bedroom.

After Alfred Hayhoe retired in 1905 John Watson took over as the trainer with still considerable if somewhat less conspicuous success than his predecessor. He remained in charge until he died in 1934 working for Leopold's son Anthony. However, the latter never raced on the same scale as his father and the yard's major successes were mainly for other people. After 1934, Anthony de Rothschild actually had his string in other yards while the stables at Palace House were used as an overflow for Jack Jarvis, based nearby in Park Lodge. With the outbreak of the Second World War Anthony and his family, including his children the future long-term chairman of Epsom and Club member Sir Evelyn de Rothschild and National Hunt trainer the late Mrs Renée Robeson, left the Palace for the duration of the war as it was requisitioned to serve as an officers' mess. As a partnership they were still actively involved in Leopold's old Southcourt Stud near Leighton Buzzard and the horses they bred are still trained by Sir Michael Stoute. After peace came Anthony presented the Palace to the Jockey Club with the intention of again providing a base for Royal visits to the Heath. However, the only visitor was the aged Princess Royal, Countess of Harewood, and eventually it was returned to the donor as being prohibitively expensive to keep going for such limited usage. Before the gift in 1948, following it being derequisitioned, there had been a gap before the place was fit for occupation and from 1950 until the sale of the house to FHDC over thirty years later it was occupied by the Rothschild family on an occasional basis, plus continuing usage by the Princess Royal as their guest until her death.

Uneven progress since the sale by the Rothschilds

Following the Palace's purchase by FHDC a great deal of money was spent on its restoration with support from English Heritage and the Heritage Lottery Fund (HLF). As a result it eventually reopened with a tourist information centre in the ground floor Hazard Room, plus function and meeting rooms above, but in truth has remained considerably under-utilised resulting, at least in part, in FHDC's crucial support of the Heritage Centre project.

Across the street the Trainer's House and the two yards initially had a much happier time, as after Sir Jack Jarvis gave up the lease the place was taken over by Bruce Hobbs in 1966. He had twenty distinctly successful years both before and after the sale of the Palace itself but by the time he retired in 1985 such a big yard in the town centre was by no means a popular choice for a large string. Without a tenant in the offing the yard was sold by the Rothschilds, who thereby severed their long connection with the site and it suffered serious neglect in the hands of property interests seeking development. Following refusal and eventual compulsory purchase by FHDC, the whole Palace site was again reunited but the buildings south of Palace Street stood empty and boarded up as they slowly decayed, until the decision was made to support the Heritage Centre scheme over a decade later. After that, further deterioration was prevented during a long process while the Home of Horseracing Trust (HOHT) gathered the necessary £15 million that enabled it to start the works. These will see the Palace converted to a national home for sporting art under the aegis of the British Sporting Art Trust, with the Trainer's House and King's Yard housing a much enhanced NHRM and the Rothschild Yard occupied by the ROR plus a few equine celebrities of earlier years in a more extensive arrangement with ROR.

Having been a Trustee of NHRM from its foundation, as well as one of HOHT since it appeared on the scene, I can bear witness to how lucky both have been in their godparents, the Jockey Club, Suffolk County Council and FHDC. The former let us paddle our own canoe without interference at any stage but with a good deal of help when needed, including a substantial donation towards the new scheme. It has provided all four chairmen for the NHRM plus the only one of HOHT, while a majority of the larger private donations have come from its members. Indeed, in giving a long lease on the Subscription Rooms without rent one could say it provided the original canoe. When that home was outgrown along came the equally generous local Council with the offer of a much grander location on an even longer free lease, as well as a grant only exceeded by the HLF – if nothing else, all the organisations now involved in the site have been formidably lucky in their godparents and it is now up to them to show that the generosity of their many supporters was not misplaced.

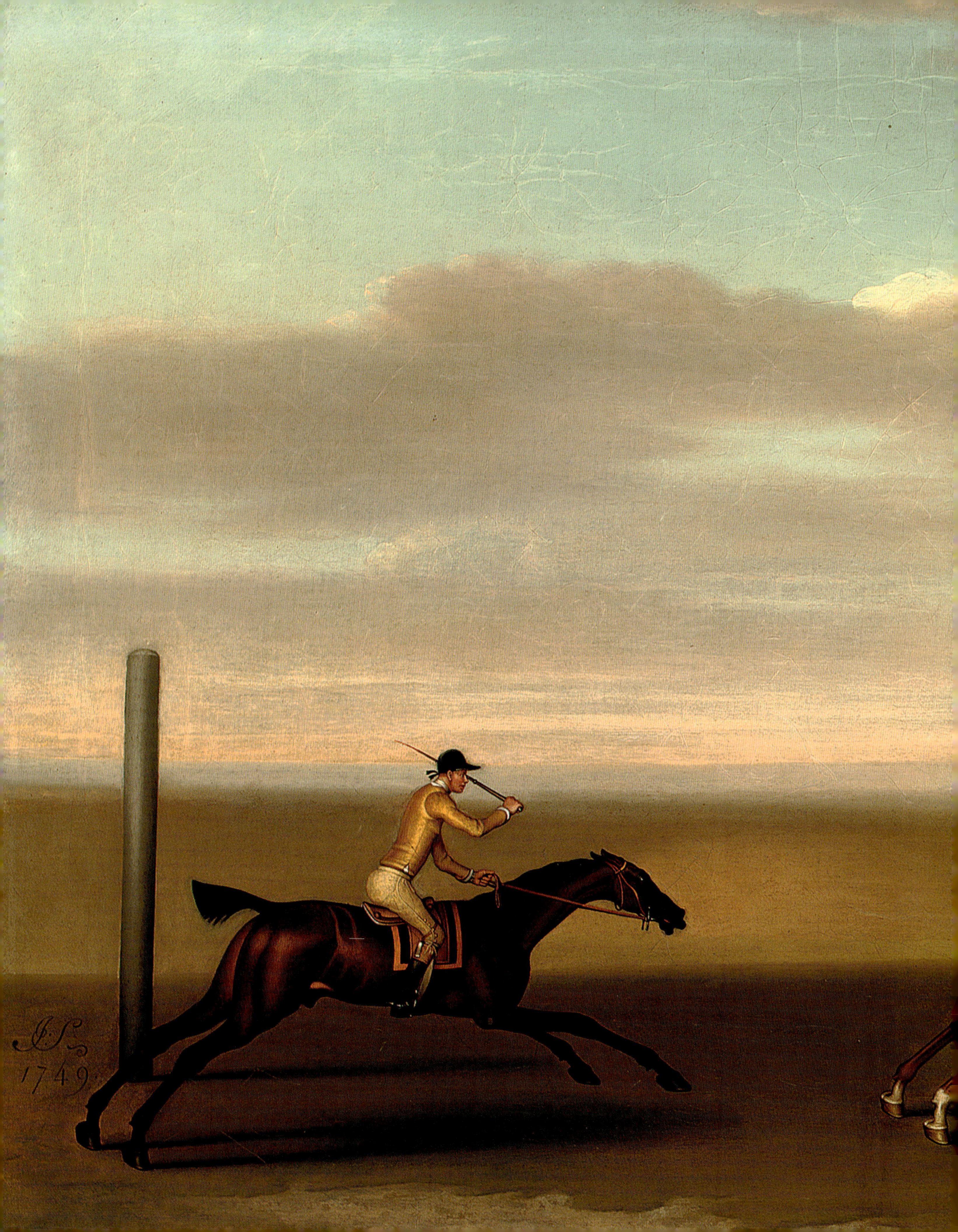
1749

Part Three

Early History of the Jockey Club and Its Links to the Collapse and Sudden Recovery of Racing in the Mid-Eighteenth Century

I

The Jockey Club Before 1750: Politics, Art and Sport in the Early Formation of the Jockey Club

Richard Nash

Historians have long identified the earliest record of the Jockey Club as being this 1751 advertisement of a meeting: ' 'This is to acquaint the Noblemen and Gentlemen of the Society call'd the Jockey Club that the first Weekly Meeting will be held on Thursday, as usual, at the Star and Garter in Pall Mall.' (*General Advertiser*, 19 November 1751)

Throughout the twentieth century, racing historians accepted without serious question two inferences Robert Black writing in 1891 had drawn from this advertisement: 1) that the Club had been formed at some point prior to that autumn, but presumably not long before; and 2) that the Club in this earliest form was primarily a social club of noblemen and gentlemen drawn together by sporting interest, and only became a regulatory body a generation later. When the British Library digitized the many seventeenth- and eighteenth-century newspapers that constitute the Burney Collection, however, scholars were able to uncover several references to the Jockey Club earlier than the 1751 notice.[1] As a consequence, historians now face the challenge of constructing an account of the Club's earliest years. This chapter will provide a foundation for that reconstruction, on which future research can build.

The references in newspapers reveal public notice of the club of 'Noblemen and Gentlemen... call'd the Jockey Club' sporadically for a generation prior to 1750, with the greatest frequency of mentions occurring in the 1730s and the earliest explicit reference in a notice of August, 1729: 'The Jockey Club, consisting of several Noblemen and Gentlemen, are to meet one Day next Week at Hackwood, the Duke of Bolton's seat in Hampshire, to consider of Methods for the better keeping of their respective strings of horses at Newmarket.' (*Daily Post*, 2 August 1729)

While 1729 is the earliest date that we can yet assign to the Club's public announcements, there is good evidence to believe that the Club was active before that. Though traces may date back to the end of the reign of Charles II, currently available evidence allows us to develop a sustained, consistent history of the Club and its activities from 1717

Previous spread: Thomas Panton's Conqueror beating the Duke of Bolton's Looby in 1735 over the Beacon for 300 Guineas by James Seymour. The horses have just passed the Turn of the Lands with the King's Stand at the end of the Beacon in sight, Fig. 187

forward. In that year, Newmarket hosted for the first time a Hanoverian monarch at a meeting rich in social and political significance (Fig. 29); and a variety of activities and events in the years immediately following suggest that whatever social or sporting organization existed before the royal visit took on a more permanent and lasting form in its immediate aftermath.

Earlier possible antecedents, 1681–1717

When Charles II made Newmarket his preferred sporting resort, disputes (if any arose) would be adjudicated by the monarch himself. J. B. Muir records that two such disputes occurred in the Spring Meeting of 1682, and 'the King with the Jockeys at nine o' clock at night decided' the result. While one could think of this as, in Muir's terms, 'an embryo Jockey Club', it might make more sense to say that at this time, for all practical purposes, the Club was the Court. From Muir's 'embryo Jockey Club', the most important name may very well be that of the Duke of Monmouth, Master of the Horse to Charles II (Fig. 188), whose political cause during the exclusion crisis of 1679–81 was supported by many who came to play an important role in forming the Jockey Club, some time after Monmouth's ill-fated rebellion. After Charles II's death, his brother, James II, did not patronise Newmarket, and there is no record of racing there during his reign until 1688, when 'Nobility and Gentry' were invited to contribute to a £100 plate to be run for in Easter Week, gentlemen only to ride. The group of 'nobility and gentry' who contribute to the 1688 race appear to be the direct precursors of the Jockey Club itself, and they and their descendants further a connection between racing at Newmarket and a construction of a distinctly Protestant Royalist national identity.

Contribution purses or plates were not, in themselves, new, but a few features of the plate advertised in 1688 deserve attention. Most contribution races were funded by contributions of two to five pounds; this race required a £20 annual contribution for five years from prospective competitors, effectively restricting participation to a small elite. At the same time, it created a

Fig. 188

James Scott, Duke of Monmouth (1649–1685)

The eldest illegitimate son of Charles II (Fig. 19) born over a decade before his father's restoration and the subsequent appearance of numerous half-brothers. Monmouth's career brought disaster on an epic scale both to himself and his supporters. Personable and popular, he was actually an unintelligent libertine who attempted to usurp his uncle James II's crown having failed to persuade his father to alter the succession in his favour as the only potential Protestant heir. A fine athlete and noted horseman, he built a faction favouring his succession partly on his triumphant progress round assorted race meetings in the early 1680s prior to his exile following the 1683 Rye House Plot (Fig. 22). His later attempt to seize the crown by force from his uncle in 1685 was badly bungled and ended after the battle of Sedgemoor with his execution, along with that of many of his supporters. As explained, the first stirrings of what would eventually become the Jockey Club can be traced to his faction.

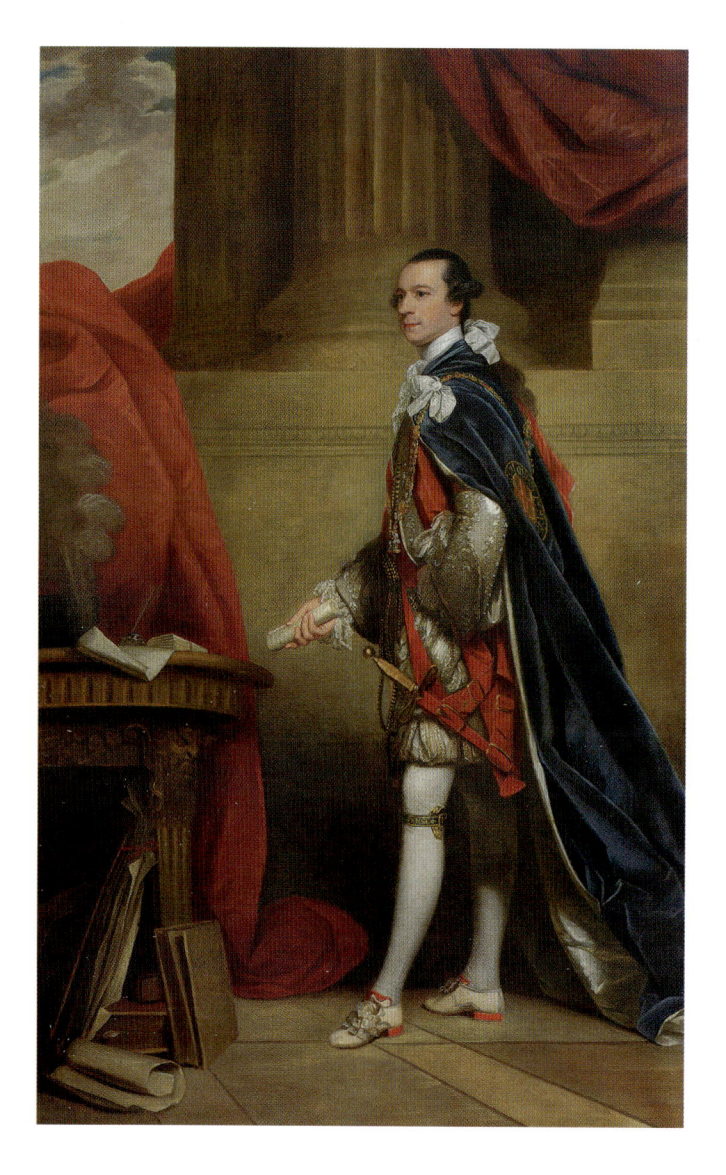

Fig. 189

Charles, 2nd Marquis of Rockingham (1730–1782)
by Catherine Reid after Sir Joshua Reynolds

One of the most influential early members of the re-formed Jockey Club of the 1750s, Lord Rockingham was a major owner until his death while Prime Minister in 1782. He owned some fine horses, including Bay Malton (Figs. 52 and 53). Good-natured and popular, his two brief periods as Prime Minister were separated by seventeen years and his leadership of the Whigs during the period of Tory dominance savoured more of duty than conviction. He would have been happier at Newmarket.

£100 prize equivalent to the Royal Plates initiated by Charles II. The only precedent for such a large prize outside royal sponsorship seems to have been when, during the last years of Charles's reign, Thomas Wharton had offered 'the Great Prize at Quainton Meadow,' as a focal event for assembling supporters of the Duke of Monmouth, who won the prize, riding one of Wharton's horses. At the very least, there is a high likelihood of a significant overlap between those 'nobility and gentry' who subscribed to this series and those who had participated at Quainton Meadow, a few years earlier; and also those who, soon after, would invite William of Orange to invade England. Indeed, the first running of this contribution plate coincides with receipt of a message from William indicating his willingness to 'rescue' the nation, 'if he was invited by some men of the best interest.' At least one of the signatories of the letter inviting William – William Cavendish, Earl (and subsequently, Duke) of Devonshire was almost certainly one of the 'noblemen and gentlemen' to subscribe to this plate, as was in all likelihood his close friend Thomas Wharton, who was among the first to greet William on his arrival in England. Moreover, advertisements indicate that the £100 plate first run for in 1688 was designed to initiate a five-year series, establishing a pattern that would become a signature of the Jockey Club when it emerged in the decades that followed: a series of races restricted to 'noblemen and gentlemen' subscribers, subscribed to for several consecutive years, at high stakes, to be contested at Newmarket.

However volatile and troubled may have been the political issues of royal succession in St James's during the reigns of the late Stuart monarchs, at Newmarket continuity reigned in the person of Tregonwell Frampton (Fig. 28). While his activity on the turf can be traced back to the reigns of both James II and Charles II, his official service as Keeper of the King's Running Horses at Newmarket began in the reign of William and Mary, continued through Anne's reign, survived the Hanoverian succession in 1714, and just outlasted George I, retaining his post under George II until his death in the spring of 1728. For a long time, Frampton's status as 'Father of the Turf' has encouraged a notion that (if not, perhaps, on the throne of England) he at least effectively replaced Charles on the turf at Newmarket. That view is neither entirely accurate nor entirely misguided. It may be hard to exaggerate Frampton's importance, but much of his authority derived from the support of those people of influence who participated in the sport there every spring and autumn.

By 1713 Frampton was 72 years old, and while there may have been little enthusiasm for dismissing him from his post, many must have thought that the (anticipated) death of Anne would be a likely time for a change. In addition to being Keeper of the King's Running Horses, Frampton had also long been associated with Lord Godolphin in a racing partnership; Frampton never matched a horse against the first Lord, and only once (on express orders from the Queen) did he match against Lord Ryalton, Godolphin's son (Fig. 31). Godolphin, however, was removed from his position as Lord Treasurer in 1710, and died in the autumn of 1712. In a letter to the 2nd Duke of Devonshire the following spring Frampton wrote that the new Lord Godolphin had recommended that Frampton retire from his post. Perhaps Devonshire intervened, for Frampton remained, but shifted tactics. Giving up on a recent experiment of 'feathering' opponents (in which he had been matching the Queen's horses against superior opponents in return for large weight concessions) he issued a public challenge, offering to match the Queen's horses against horses owned by the Dukes of Devonshire, Rutland, and Somerset, acting as a consortium, with a separate offer extended to the Duke of Bolton. It is tempting to see in this alliance of dukes something of an inner circle of what would become the Jockey Club, descending directly from those who had established the Noblemen's and Gentlemen's Contribution Purse at the time of the Glorious Revolution. We can see an early Jockey Club at work from 1717 onwards, and I think we can discern three phases from 1717–1750, each lasting roughly eleven years: emergence (1718–1728), flourishing (1729–1739), decline (1740–1750).

The First Phase: 1717–1728

After Anne's death in 1714 and the ensuing Hanoverian succession, royal visits to Newmarket, planned for 1715 and 1716, were disrupted by the Jacobite rebellion. In 1717, George I made his first and only Royal Progress anywhere, in the form of a visit to Newmarket in October. This visit was an important, well-choreographed moment of political theatre, and (not insignificantly) it was recorded for posterity in paintings undertaken by John Wootton (Fig. 29) and Peter Tillemans (Fig. 35). In April, the Duke of Devonshire had stepped down as President of the Privy Council as part of what is sometimes known as 'the Whig schism of 1717.' Originally more ambitious in scale, the royal progress was put off to the autumn and reduced in scope to a visit to Newmarket and Cambridge. Explicitly named as dining with the King on his arrival in Newmarket were the Dukes of Devonshire, Kent, Montague, Rutland, Roxburghe, and Portland; the Earls of Sunderland and Halifax, the Lord Viscount Lonsdale, and the Lord Harvey; these may be thought of as being among those at the core of the early Jockey Club. On Thursday morning, the King hunted hare, and witnessed the King's Plate in the afternoon, won by Mr Pelham's mare. On Friday, it rained all day, but he attended the races throughout. On Sunday, he visited the university at Cambridge, returning at night, with the intention of watching the Noblemen's and Gentlemen's Contribution Purse on Monday. He cut the trip short, however, returning to Hampton Court on Monday and proroguing parliament the next day.

Over the winter, there were several expressions of how much the King had enjoyed the visit to Newmarket, and he was expected to return in the spring. But it was a cold spring, many matches were settled by forfeit, and the King changed his plans, choosing 'to keep his court at Kensington until the weather grows warm'. He was expected to attend the King's Plate in the autumn, but again changed his plans. If, as seems likely, the royal visit to Newmarket in 1717 (by a king who avoided such travel at every opportunity) was intended to exploit that year's sport as an occasion for political theatre, promoting a spectacle of national unity to offset the appearance of political division triggered by the changes in the King's ministry, then the cancellation of the projected royal return may well have galvanized the Jockey Club to more sustained efforts. One of the most valuable early documents that we have could very well be the Newmarket Match Book, on loan from Weatherbys to the National Horse Racing Museum. This is a leather-bound volume of nearly a thousand manuscript pages recording the results of all races at Newmarket from October 1718 to 1788. Although it is bound as a single volume, it appears to have been compiled from several volumes over time. And although it is known as the Newmarket Match Book, it is actually a record of results rather than of prospective matches. Scattered references make it seem likely that true match books were recorded prior to this time, most likely under the supervision of the Groom Porter's Office but the consolidation and preservation of results recorded in the Newmarket Match Book, beginning with the autumn meeting of 1718, points to an active recording of events for the Jockey Club in the era before what has generally been considered its foundation date. The initial import of the evidence of the Match Book would suggest that the commitment to regular record-keeping enshrined in the volume dates the early activity of the Jockey Club to 1718; but I am inclined to push that originating moment back one year to the royal visit of 1717, identifying the Match Book as an artifact that emerged from the first year of the Club's activities, rather than seeing the book itself as an initial action of the Club, although it must be admitted that the Spring meeting of 1718 is omitted.

For the royal visit to Newmarket in 1717, a new race was created and a different model was chosen for it: like the 1688 Contribution Plate, it required a five-year commitment to an annual series of races, funded by subscriber contribution, but in the form of a single heat of four miles. Originally termed the Noblemen and Gentlemen's Contribution Purse, this race became known as the October Stakes and introduced the notion of restricting weight to 9st. and eligibility to horses under six years of age, thereby making this event at the end of the racing season a prelude to what would be the following year's royal plate season. Though Newmarket had hosted contests under this or a similar name in earlier years, those races had been renewals of the Great Prize at Quainton Meadow, originally sponsored by Thomas Wharton to promote the Duke of Monmouth. Like that race and the Royal plates that it deliberately set out to imitate (and rival), the October Stakes was for aged horses under high weight, contested in multiple heats. The original subscription undertaken in 1717 was renewed in 1721, 1726 and 1731, each time losing some subscribers and recruiting new ones. Because the original terms of subscription allowed a subscriber to race a horse that was not his own property, the subscription list is not the same thing as a membership roster of the Jockey Club, but it points strongly to certain names at, or near, the centre of the Club in these early days.

We can see in the early phase of the Jockey Club the development of stakes racing, and it is possible to discern in that development a deliberate association with the centrist values of a protestant monarchy championed by moderate Whigs and Tories in support of the Hanoverian succession. The primary focus of the early Jockey Club was certainly on Newmarket, but one event held elsewhere seems particularly significant in terms of the organization's early history. The culmination of the Duke of Monmouth's Western Progress in the autumn of 1682 had come at Wallasey in Cheshire. Tories, having learned that Monmouth was to compete in the 12-stone plate there, had sponsored a rival race in nearby Delamere Forest. A horse bred by Thomas Wharton carried off that prize for the Whigs, while Monmouth raced and won at Wallasey on another horse bred by Wharton. The ensuing celebration by Monmouth's supporters touched off a small riot that included, among other offences, drinking Monmouth's health before that of the Duke of York. When word of this reached court, Charles issued a warrant and Monmouth was taken into custody.

Forty years after this event, in 1722, those at the centre of the early Jockey Club commemorated it in a significant way by subscribing to articles modelled on the October Stakes. Like that race, the purse was generated by 20 Guineas contributions from subscribers for a race of a single four-mile heat; it was scheduled for the first Tuesday in May so that it would follow the Newmarket Spring meeting and would mark the first time horses were asked to carry 10st. While the subscription to the Wallasey Stakes was the same value as to the October Stakes, and owners were permitted to join the subscription with the approval of those already subscribing, the original term of subscription was for a 10-year commitment, from 1723 to 1732, and in the last five years of the subscription, owners could only race horses bred by themselves, indicating that from the outset that one intention of the Wallasey race was to create an incentive for breeding as well as racing.

The Great Stakes, initiated in 1729, builds on the precedent of the October Stakes and the Wallasey Stakes, while also introducing new features that mark significant change. The October Stakes may have followed a pattern of subscription initiated by the Noblemen's and Gentlemen's Plate of the time of the Glorious Revolution, and the Whig-sponsored Great Prize at Quainton Meadow that preceded that race and continued afterwards, but it also shifted from the heat racing format of plate races for older horses to a single race for younger horses. In doing so, it effectively introduced stakes racing. Collectively, these three stakes races (October Stakes, Wallasey Stakes and Great Stakes) usher in a new model of racing in contrast to plate racing, each requiring multi-year subscriptions. They worked to define the racing calendar, bookending it with spring and autumn meetings, and they focused on owner/breeder development. This is the model resurrected a generation later in the 1200 Guineas in the 1750s. The Great Stakes quite literally raised the stakes on its two precursors, with the October Stakes falling away, and the Wallasey Stakes upgrading to comparable value (£100 subscriptions) when it relocated to Newmarket. Originally, the Great Stakes, like the Wallasey Stakes, was envisaged as a ten-year event, but for whatever reason it reverted in practice to the five-year subscription of the October Stakes.

Second Phase: 1729–39

Just how important the new style of racing for much larger sums being developed at Newmarket by the Jockey Club was can be seen by comparison with what was happening in the rest of the country. In 1732, the last year before the Wallasey moved to the Heath and had its value multiplied, only one race elsewhere was worth as much as the 100 Guineas Royal Plates. This was a one-off sweepstake match at Hambleton in Yorkshire where four subscribers each hazarded 50 Guineas for a race in a single heat. Indeed, it was the only sweepstake of any sort apart from the Wallasey not run at Newmarket in 1732. Apart from that race Lincoln's Ladies Plate offered a Gold Cup valued at £90 and races at Stamford and Oxford were best of the rest with 80 Guineas Plates. Otherwise most prizes fell in the range £10 to £25. Compared with these sums Newmakrket's three major sweepstakes totaling 1,475 Guineas and seventeen major matches worth 200 Guineas to 500 Guineas represented an entirely different world. The matches dwindled in importance over the centuries but the Jockey Club's early development of sweepstakes foreshadowed their successors' approach after 1751 and has become the formulation, shorn of five year guarantees, of racing all around the world.

Tregonwell Frampton had survived the Hanoverian succession, retaining his position as Keeper of the King's Running Horses during the reign of George I, but dying in March 1728, shortly before the Newmarket Spring Meeting in the first year of the reign of George II. The post of Keeper of King's Running Horses was in the gift of the Master of the Horse, a preferment George II had granted to Richard Lumley, Earl of Scarbrough. He in turn, now appointed his kinsman, Thomas Panton (Fig. 33) (who had for some time been a racing partner of the Duke of Devonshire) to

Frampton's old post. Plans for a royal trip to Newmarket made shortly after the coronation, postponed from the previous autumn, were fulfilled in April, 1728. When Frampton's will was proved, he left to the Earl of Godolphin, his longtime patron, among other things, the stables at Wandlebury, not far from Newmarket. This property had not been the primary training facility for Frampton and was in significant disrepair. A few years before Frampton's death, Defoe had described the place in his *Tour of the Whole of Great Britain*:

'As I said, I first had a view of Cambridge from Gog Magog Hills; I am to add, that there appears on the Mountain that goes by this Name, an antient Camp, or Fortification, that lies on the Top of the Hill, with a double or treble Rampart and Ditch, which most of our writers say was neither Roman or Saxon, but British: I am to add, that King James II caused a spacious Stable to be built in the Area of this Camp, for his Running-Horses, and made old Mr Frampton Master or Inspector of them: The Stables remain still there, tho' they are not often made use of.'

Here, the Earl set about building stables that became a prototype for the next generation, while racing at Newmarket now entered a new phase with Panton as Keeper of the King's Running Horses.

The first public notice of the Jockey Club in the *Daily Post* of 2 August 1729, is very close to, but not quite identical to, an announcement in the *Universal Spectator* on the same day: 'The Earl of Godolphin, and a great many other Noblemen and Gentlemen who keep running horses, are to meet next week at Hackwood, the Duke of Bolton's seat in Hampshire, to consider of methods for removing their strings of horses at Newmarket.' While this notice does not explicitly name the Jockey Club, it clearly describes the same meeting as in the *Daily Post* notice. Two other differences in this version of the announcement may also be worth attention: 1) that the Earl of Godolphin is specified alongside the Duke of Bolton, and 2) 'the Methods for the better keeping' being considered in the *Daily Post* announcement here are revealed to consist of 'removing' their strings of horses at Newmarket.

Just one week before the announcement of the Jockey Club meeting at Hackwood, the *British Journal* reported that Godolphin was visiting the site at Wandlebury with the intention of building a 'Hunting Seat': 'The Earl of Godolphin, Groom of the Stole to his Majesty, is gone down to Cambridgeshire, to give directions for building a Hunting-Seat near Gog-Magog hills, within three miles of Cambridge and ten miles of Newmarket, where the late Tregonnel Frampton, esq. kept the King's Running-Horses.' This became the stud made famous as the home of the Godolphin Arabian, but at the time Frampton's one-time associate may very well have been contemplating the idea of 'removing [the] strings of horses of several Noblemen and Gentlemen from Newmarket' to a new centre to be established at Gog Magog.

Alternatively, another option before the Club might have been removing from Newmarket to Winchester, where Charles II had contemplated relocating royal sport at the end of his reign. The Duke of Bolton's seat at Hackwood was only 20 miles away, and the month before the August meeting, he had offered a Gold Cup to be run for there. Alas, if Bolton had thought he might make a bid to put himself at the centre of racing, he overplayed his hand. Arguably, at the time, the foremost horse in England was the daughter of Bay Bolton, the excellent Camilla, who had won most of her races in the previous four years. But after retiring her, Bolton tried to win his own cup in a fashion not unlike the notorious practice of a Smithfield distiller whose case had only recently been concluded (see page 285). Assigning ownership to the Dowager Duchess, Bolton had entered Camilla under the name 'Fair Rosamond'. He had, however, not thought this plan through because, even though Camilla was plain enough to look at, she was immediately detected by the grooms of the other horses:

'the Grooms knowing the mare, none started against her: Camilla was her name, she started by herself and ran about 3m, which so exasperated the people that his Grace gave orders to ride her off the course without coming in, and that it should be run for the next day, which was won by the Earl of Essex's Smiling Ball.'

Whether or not Bolton was seeking to make Winchester a new centre of national sport, there is more than a little irony in the first known meeting of the Jockey Club being hosted by one who was himself detected running a ringer only the month before.

Another item that conceivably could have been factored into the August 1729 meeting of the Club might have been the death just two months earlier of William Cavendish, 2nd Duke of Devonshire, racing associate of Thomas Panton. If Bolton and Godolphin were two of the leaders of the early Club, Devonshire would certainly have been a third. Most significantly, he had been the owner of Childers, arguably the first racehorse in England to achieve widespread popular fame in his own lifetime. Childers, a son of the Darley Arabian, had raced exclusively at Newmarket, thoroughly dominating all opposition, before retiring to Devonshire's stud, where he was bred almost exclusively to the Duke's own mares. For decades after his death, 'Flying Childers' was held up as the acme of racehorse speed, having supposedly been travelling as fast as a mile a minute at top speed, and having been clocked completing the round course (just under four miles) in six minutes and forty-eight seconds.

The royal procession from London to Newmarket in the spring of 1728 was an elaborate affair, with no fewer than five well-armed escorts handing the monarch on from one militia to the next on the way to Palace House; the details of this procession were painstakingly described in the papers of the day. The attendance at Newmarket that spring, in pointed contrast to the previous years, where interest seemed to have been waning, was extraordinary. Panton provided scarlet livery for all servants in the King's stable, and arranged for the combined strings of all horses owned by Noblemen and Gentlemen to be paraded, stripped, before the monarch. Attendance was so great, one paper noted after the visit, that one gamekeeper was killed in the crush of the throng and many were injured.

While Charles may have looked longingly to Winchester at the end of his reign because Newmarket was a Whig stronghold, the royal progress to Newmarket at the outset of George II's reign attempted to consolidate a spirit of national unity around the Whig virtue of Protestant Succession. Eustace Budgell, a kinsman of Joseph Addison whose public falling-out with the Duke of Bolton had been a small scandal a decade earlier, now sought to capitalize on the promise of the moment. His estate lay on the way of the royal progress, and he prepared several tents, well supplied with 'a cold collation' and wine and ale for toasts to refresh the royal party. No doubt at Budgell's instigation, the papers covered this entertainment as thoroughly as they did the dinner at Trinity College Cambridge, and Budgell sought to capitalize on the moment by publishing a poem in praise of the new king on this occasion. Throughout this event, the echoes of the first George's progress a decade earlier are clear; and behind both of these, one could hear (perhaps more faintly) echoes of the Duke of Monmouth's progresses a little more than a generation earlier. Where the public support for protestant succession had failed in Monmouth's case, it could now be safely celebrated as triumphant in the seamless succession whereby '[George] II reigns like [George] I'.

Whatever enthusiasm may have been generated in the spring, the autumn meetings had to have been disappointing. In August, newspapers reported that only five matches had been arranged for the autumn, and with such limited sport scheduled, the palace was changing their plans to attend and would hunt at Windsor instead. The major participants at

Newmarket that autumn were the Dukes of Devonshire and Bolton and Lord Godolphin. When the races ended, those who had been in attendance returned to London … with one notable exception. The Duke of Devonshire would die the following June, and he was clearly in poor health with what the newspapers reported to be gout. Over the months of November and December, he seems to have been quite ill and staying with Godolphin: 'The Earl of Godolphin is at Newmarket, accompanying the Duke of Devonshire, who is so ill of the Gout, that he is unable to stand.' It would be welcome, indeed, if one could have a record of whatever conversations were carried on between Godolphin and Devonshire during the latter's illness, as it seems likely that the impulse for the Great Stakes may have begun here.

By January, Devonshire was back in London, able to attend the marriage of his son, Charles. As winter drew to a close the following March, the newspapers were alive with the prospect of another royal presence at Newmarket in the spring: while Devonshire struggled with illness, Prince Frederick arrived that winter from Hanover, and was created Prince of Wales on 8 January 1729. The grooms of George I, who had lost their employment at the succession of George II, were now brought back into the Royal Household to serve the Prince of Wales, and it was soon announced that Frederick would attend the races at Newmarket. Throughout March, the papers were again full of updates about the approaching race meeting, and when it arrived, Newmarket was again unusually vibrant, even though Frederick failed to appear.

The race meeting began on 5 April, and we begin to see notices of the Dukes of Bolton and Bridgewater and other Noblemen and Gentlemen travelling to Newmarket by 29 March. But the most important development in racing in the spring of 1729 was the signing of articles for what became the Great Stakes. I believe it makes most sense to imagine those articles agreed to and signed in London, at the final meeting of the Jockey Club preceding the Spring Meeting at Newmarket, but allowing an opportunity for additional Noblemen and Gentlemen to join at the meeting. The first public notice of this innovation is in the *Daily Post* of 15 April, and it is soon repeated in the *British Journal or the Censor*, *Fog's Weekly Journal*, and *The Country Journal or The Craftsman*:

'There's a Subscription carrying on for a plate of a thousand Guineas to be run for annually at Newmarket in the following method, i.e., Ten Noblemen and Gentlemen to engage for ten years to pay 100 Guineas each year, and to run a five year old horse, &c that has been in their possession for two years before the time of starting, and to carry ten stone.'

The subscription announced in the newspapers during the spring 1729 meeting, following the winter in which an ill Duke of Devonshire was attended by Lord Godolphin follows the Wallasey Stakes plan of a 'ten-year subscription,' and dramatically increases the ante from the 20 Guineas subscription of the October and Wallasey Stakes. In practice, although the newspaper accounts all follow the Wallasey model of a ten-year subscription, the terms set forth in Cheny's *Historical List* at the end of the year (and these are the terms that are followed) establish a five-year subscription. The articles were signed on 25 March, calling for the first running of the race to be on 23 April 1730 and for annual renewals for the next five years (1730–34). The appearance of the announcement in the newspapers of 15 April corresponds to a term in the agreement that allows interested parties one month (until 15 May) to enter the subscription, after which time 'no person can be concern'd as a Principal therein, but by the Approbation of the Majority of those Noblemen &c as before that day had subscribed to the said Engagement'.[2] The race to be run in late April by 4yos (rising five), carrying 8st 7lbs, for one four-mile heat, 'but none can start for the same but Contributors and for which Contributors themselves can only start such four year olds, as have been their property full two years before running.' The contribution required for this single heat was 100 Guineas each year, immediately making this race far and away the most lucrative race in the country. This was, for all practical purposes, the first Breeders Cup.

The original subscribers to this event were the Duke of Devonshire, the Duke of Somerset, the Duke of Bolton, the Earl of Godolphin, the Earl of Lonsdale, Sir Michael Newton, KB, Anthony Henly, Esq., and Thomas Brodrick, Esq. Accordingly, the prize was set originally at 800 Guineas, then, following the death of Devonshire, the announced prize was reduced to 700 Guineas, but when all subscribers agreed to let the 3rd Duke of Devonshire into the engagement made by his father, the purse returned to 800 Guineas in time for the first running. To put the prize money in perspective, the entire prize money combined for all the other races conducted at this spring meeting totalled only 1,200 Guineas. It is understandable that the race quickly became known as 'the Great Stakes.' In 1732, anticipating that the original five-year subscription would come to a conclusion in 1734, a second edition of the subscription, on similar terms but this time specifying horses to be 'of their own breed,' was entered into. The subscribers for this second iteration of the 'Great Stakes' were: the Dukes of Devonshire, Somerset, Bolton, and Bridgewater, the Earls Godolphin, Hallifax and Portmore, Viscount Lonsdale, Lord Weymouth and Sir Michael Newton. Thomas Brodrick had died, Anthony Henly had dropped out, but the original noblemen re-subscribed and were joined by Bridgewater, Halifax, Portmore and Weymouth, raising the prize to 1,000 Guineas. At the same time that the Great Stakes was renewed, the Wallasey stakes was relocated to Newmarket officially, and the value raised accordingly; the new terms for this race called, like the Great Stakes, for a subscription for five years at a 100 Guineas contribution, 'for horses &c of their own breed not rising more than six years of age to carry 9st. one four mile heat.' These subscribers included a considerable overlap with those subscribing to the Great Stakes: the Dukes of Devonshire, Ancaster and Bridgewater, the Earl of Portmore, Viscount Lonsdale and Lord Gower. In addition to these core events with multi-year, large money commitments to races for homebreds during this period of the thirties there was a noticeable spike in smaller versions of such stakes racing, matching more than two parties for large amounts, winner take all, sometimes on a multi-year commitment, sometimes on an individual basis. For the most part, the participants are the individuals who had subscribed to the second round of the Great Stakes; especially active in these events seemed to be Bridgewater, Portmore, Gower and Sir Michael Newton.

We can see the activity of the early Jockey Club at work when we focus on the innovation of stakes racing during this period. With the period from 1718 to 1750 divided into three eleven year periods: from 171 to 1728 there is one stakes race every year, the Noblemen's and Gentlemen's Contribution Purse or the October Stakes; from 1729 to 1739 that increases to 48 races. That's an average of more than four a year, with a high of eight in 1736, and nine of the eleven years having at least four; then, from 1740 to 1750, we drop back down to twelve with one or none in eight of the eleven years. Essentially, racing from the year of the first public mention of the Jockey Club (1729) to the Horse-Racing Bill (1739) is marked by a significantly altered model of racing. When the remodelled Jockey Club reasserts itself after the events of 1751, it returns to that model as its way forward.

Thus far, by reviewing changes in the conduct of racing, particularly at Newmarket, in the years immediately connected to the public notice of a Jockey Club in 1729, and attending to the most directly relevant political events associated with those changes, we can establish with a fair degree of confidence some of the most important activities engaged in by the Club, a possible mechanism that would explain either its rise or its more explicit self-conscious denomination in the early days of the reign of George II, and a strong sense of which participants would have been most centrally involved in its organization circa 1729. The short list of those Noblemen and Gentlemen would include: the

Dukes of Devonshire, Somerset, Bolton, Bridgewater, and Rutland; the Earls of Halifax, Godolphin, Derby, Bristol and Essex; Lords Lonsdale, Gower, and Weymouth; Sir Michael Newton, Sir Richard Grosvenor, Sir William Morgan of Tredegar, Thomas Panton and Edward Coke, Esq. To these names a handful of others might be added as very likely to have been significantly involved (the Dukes of Ancaster, Bedford, Dorset and Grafton, for instance) at one point or another, to varying degrees. Certain family lines, kinship ties and political allegiances are strongly marked in this group, with a strong commitment to the Whig principle that the Hanoverian succession had preserved protestant monarchy as the defining feature of English national identity. We might think of this collection of roughly two dozen generally Whig political leaders as the Noblemen and Gentlemen at the heart of the early Jockey Club.

Roger Williams and the Middle Class Infrastructure of the Club

We should, however, also consider those tradesmen and merchants who played a critical role in the early development of the Jockey Club; by doing so, we can develop a significantly more detailed picture of the various activities that comprised, and gain greater knowledge of the ties of commerce and art that wove the Club into the social fabric of the era, while simultaneously gaining a richer appreciation of how topographical networks and print technologies worked together to reinforce one another. Three enterprising merchant families in particular play a critical role here; the principals of these families are John Deards, toyman and silversmith, and Roger Williams, coffeeman and vintner, and John Cheny, coffeeman.

Our picture of the early Jockey Club begins to come more clearly into focus when we attend to the other active roles played by those in the merchant class who in their own ways played parts every bit as important as Frampton's. Of these, the most important was certainly Roger Williams. His name figures most prominently in early histories of the turf as it appears in 1730 in the will of Edward Coke, who left all his racing horses to the Earl of Godolphin, and all his breeding stock to Roger Williams, who ran a coffeehouse in St James's. Relatively little attention has been paid to the social imbalance of those paired bequests, even though the importance of the bequest is that Coke's breeding stock passed to Williams and then silently on to Godolphin, where one stallion in particular achieved fame as the Godolphin Arabian, one of the breed's three foundation sires. It may well be that a racing partnership existed between Coke and Godolphin, like that which had united the racing interests of Godolphin and Frampton; Williams may or may not have been involved in some way in any such confederation. Secondly, and perhaps more importantly, Williams was clearly a central figure in many of the practical activities of the Jockey Club, and particularly was involved in the commercial transactions of bloodstock, and quite possibly with the importation of foreign horses. Certainly, Williams had been active and instrumental in the activities of the early Jockey Club for some time prior to Coke's death; and his coffeehouse in St James's should be properly considered to be the Jockey Club's first home.

We cannot be sure exactly when Williams opened his coffee shop in St. James' Street, almost directly across from the palace; it was sometime after 1707, and the earliest advertisement I have found alluding to it dates from 1713. Pursuant to a crown lease, dated 29 January 1717, the site itself was leased by the Nelthorpe family, of which one member (Richard) had been among the original Rye House plotters, going into exile with the Duke of Monmouth, returning in arms during that rebellion, and being among the first executed during the bloody Assizes that followed. It had been sublet from the Nelthorpes by a Richard Frith, who erected the building in which Williams established his coffeehouse. By 1719, Williams covenanted with the crown lessee, Henry Nelthorpe, to rebuild the building, incorporating space for the Jockey Club rooms into the plan; sometime later, in 1736, Williams sought and received permission to make additional changes to the premises. It may be worth remarking that the very first entry in the Newmarket Match Book from the autumn 1718 meeting records that 'Mr Howard's Burgundy paid forfeit to Mr William's Sampson.' While the entry does not specify that 'Mr Williams' was 'Roger Williams,' it is certainly a likely possibility, as 'Roger Williams' is specified in subsequent years. Indeed, in 1730, the *Grub Street Journal* had some fun with a rival paper, inadvertently conferring a knighthood on Williams: 'In the list of the horse matches to be run at Newmarket in March, April, and May, printed in the Morning Post, the most remarkable is the Earl of Portmore's Gudgeon against Sir Roger Williams's Whipper Snapper; which Sir Roger Williams, we hear, keeps a coffee house in St James.' Among the more well-known Newmarket racing scenes from this era is John Wootton's portrait of Sir William Morgan of Tredegar's Lamprey. Lamprey's jockey stands with his back to the viewer, dressed in the straw colour that comes to be associated with the Duke of Devonshire, speaking to Sir William. Sir William, in red coat, with the sash of the Order of the Bath, was one of the founding knights when that order was restored in 1725, and married (in 1724) Devonshire's daughter. In the background can be seen Morgan's African servant holding a horse. Less often commented on is the fourth man in the painting, who wears clerical garb. This would almost certainly be Morgan's chaplain, Rev. Walter Williams, who may have been a relation of Roger Williams who kept the coffeehouse where the Jockey Club met.

If the subscription stakes races at Newmarket and Wallasey point to an active club of politically well-connected Noblemen and Gentlemen that we can safely identify as the early Jockey Club operating during the reign of George I, it may be helpful to contrast that group formation with a cause célèbre of the period that originated in Smithfield and Banstead Downs, but attracted the active attention of the Noblemen and Gentlemen of St James's and Newmarket. In 1724 a distiller matched a mare against a gunsmith's mare to be run at Banstead Downs, and then substituted a ringer:

'We hear a remarkable Jockey Cause, which has been depending 3 years in the Court of Exchequer, (so much noticed in Westminster hall by many heats run there Whip & Spur) . . . is at last finally ended . . . . N.B. The Defendant in this piece of Jockeyship, wherein (for the honour of Smithfield) is said to have refined on all the Gentlemen of the Whip, as well Newmarket as Yorkshire and others.[3']

This and similar accounts in the contemporary press indicate that the Club at Williams's Coffeehouse was not only following the trial with interest but wagering among themselves as to the outcome. Subsequent notices linked to Williams's Coffeehouse reveal that sporting wagers constituted no small part of the activities of the Club.

Among the most interesting advertisements of the 1720s, suggesting an active Jockey Club based at Williams's Coffeehouse, is the following notice from the *Daily Courant* of 18 February 1724:

'On Friday the 21st of this Instant February, at Eleven of the clock, will be raffled for at Williams's Coffee-House in St James's Street 12 Arabian Horses: Any Gentleman may come into this raffle who will subscribe his name in a book for that purpose at Williams's where the conditions of that raffle are to be seen.'

One hardly knows where to begin with this audaciously abrupt public announcement that Williams's coffeehouse had become the central location for racing interests in London, but certainly our understanding of the activities of the early Jockey Club would improve enormously if we could locate the abovementioned book, kept by Williams, in which subscribers entered their names. While historians have attempted to trace as thoroughly as possible the importation of as many of the early oriental influences on the breed as they can, such importations have been notoriously difficult to track; and have generally been considered to be relatively rare events, undertaken at significant cost. Here we have a dozen such horses, given away as prizes in a lottery. While this is the first and largest of these raffles, it is not the only one. It may be worth considering that this was an early attempt on the part of the Jockey Club both to stimulate interest and generate speculation. Another advertisement from the spring of 1727 (this time for an auction, rather than a raffle) offers 'Ten Arabian and Turkish Horses, and Two Mares, at the White-Bear at Hyde-Park-Corner. To be seen there any Time before the Day of Sale, which is to begin at Eleven of the Clock precisely'.[4]

By 1735, a similar significant auction of Arabians is being delayed by request of several Noblemen and Gentlemen of the Jockey-Club, the sale of those exceeding beautiful ARABIAN HORSES, which were to have been sold on Thursday the 17th Instant, at Williams's Chocolate-House [sic], St James, will be by Auction on Tuesday the 29th Instant, at Mr Cock's in the great Piazza, Covent Garden, to be the two last lots in Mr Hubert's second day's sale. The horses may be viewed from the hour of 9 to 5, every day at Mr Cock's.

In addition to the 1735 auction which was delayed at the request of several Noblemen and Gentlemen of the Jockey Club, one can find several other such auctions of Arabian Horses in London during the twenties and thirties, most of them in one way or another associated with Williams. Not infrequently, the method of sale was not auction, but raffle. The horse would be advertised at a set valuation and available for inspection at a convenient location; tickets could then be purchased at Williams's Coffee House. If a sufficient number of tickets were sold by the advertised date, each ticket-holder would be entitled to three rolls of the dice, with the largest total rolled winning the horse. In this fashion in 1730, 'Mr. Bromley, a sadler in St James Street' won an Arabian valued at 300 Guineas; and another Arabian, valued at 100 Guineas 'was won by Mr Abbott, a merchant of this city, by a waiter of the said coffee house, who in his absence threw for him 44 in three throws'. An advertisement a year earlier suggests that when an Arabian was won in this fashion, as one paper put it 'against the Quality', the payoff came by selling the horse in a more usual fashion: 'The Hautboise Arabian lately thrown for at Williams's Coffee-House in St James's-Street being a beautiful, strong horse, is now to be sold by John Cornforth at the Golden Lyon, Hyde Park Corner.'

John Cheny

For some time historians have recognized that the earliest systematic recording of racing results at a national level in a reliable, ongoing record begins when John Cheny begins to publish his calendars, entitled *Historical List of Horse Matches*. The first volume, reporting the results of 1727, appeared in 1728; and immediately became a standard authority. This has always been viewed as the happy production of a single enterprising individual, which may be the case, but has always seemed most unlikely. Cheny's obscurity remains profound, even among those who are extremely familiar with the *Historical List*. Virtually nothing is known of him except that he published the *Historical List* every year from 1727 to his death in 1750, relying on both extensive travel and a wide network of correspondents to do so. An advertisement of 1723 shows that at that time he maintained a coffeehouse in Arundel and served as Clerk of the Course there, though he had relocated to London by the time he began publishing the *Historical List*. It seems unlikely that someone remote from London with no known connection to the print trade could have initiated and then maintained such an enterprise without visible support beyond the volume's subscription list. Indeed, it seems at first glance somewhat implausible that a coffeeman from Arundel would be able to generate such a subscription list without advertising. From the outset of the venture, however, subscribers were informed that they could receive their copies at Williams's Coffeehouse in St James's; and it seems likeliest that the very idea of the *Historical List* was one of the first enterprises of the early Jockey Club, with Cheny serving much in the role of recording secretary.

Promotion of Sporting Art

In addition to the notice of the 1729 meeting at Hackwood,

the Burney collection identifies three other references to the 'Jockey Club' prior to the oft-noted meeting at the Star and Garter Tavern in 1751; a fourth can be found in the number of Eustace Budgell's *The Bee* for 26 June 1733: 'This day the Right Hon. The Earl of Hallifax gives a grand entertainment, at his house in Bushy Park, to several Noblemen and Gentlemen belonging to the Jockey Club.' The 'grand entertainment' on that occasion may have been at least largely a social meeting, as the principal event seems to have been announcing the engagement of his daughter, Frances, to Sir Roger Burgoyne. Similarly, an announcement in 1743 that 'several Noblemen belonging to the Gentlemen's Jockey Club' had been to see the 'wonderful Gigantick Prussian horse' who had been the principal attraction in London since his arrival at Christmas indicates that the early Club was at least as interested in clubbable sociability as it was in legislating or directing the business of racing, or even supporting and promoting equine sport. But the other two notices in the daily papers point to ways in which the social dimension of the Club was fully woven into the entrepreneurial aspect of its activities, and how tightly woven together one can see are the networks of politics, sport, commerce, and art in the institution's formative years. In 1731, the *Daily Advertiser* announced that 'The Picture of Lord James Cavendish's Horse which his Lordship rode on some time since for a very considerable Wager to Windsor, being near finish'd, we hear the same will be plac'd in the Jockey Club-Rooms at William's Coffee-House, St James.'

However early Williams's Coffee House became the London headquarters for the Jockey Club, the notice about the painting of Lord James Cavendish's horse makes it clear that by 1731 it was well-established. This Lord James Cavendish was brother to the 3rd Duke of Devonshire (not to be confused with his uncle of the same name); the wager had been with Sir Robert Fagg (Fig. 7), reportedly for 200 Guineas, and called for him to ride from Hyde Park Turnpike to Windsor Lodge, a distance measured at 21 miles and one furlong, in one hour and five minutes.[5] The most detailed account can be found in the *London Journal*:

'On Sunday Morning about eleven o clock started Lord James Cavendish from Hide Park Corner, on a horse a little above a Galloway (not Mr Humberton's) and rode to the Lodge in Windsor-Forest for a very considerable wager: Upon his Lordship's arrival the three stop watches were unsealed and it appeared by the first he had won by 16 seconds, by another by one minute, and the third by one minute and four seconds. It is reckoned 5000L was depending on this match. The Earl of Portmore won 800 Guineas and General Harvey lost 200 Guineas. And Yesterday between three and four he returned to St James in good health: his Lordship hath ordered a handsome sum be distributed among the receivers at the various turnpikes through which he passed, the gates being all left open on that occasion for many hours and all passengers rode through toll free.'

His Royal Highness the Prince of Wales, and a great Number of Nobility and Gentry went to Hyde-Park Turnpike to see his Lordship start.[6]

the *Daily Courant* reported that on Monday, 'the Lord James Cavendish came to town from Windsor in good health, and gave a fine entertainment to several persons of quality and distinction at Williams's Coffee-House, St James.'[7]

Within a few months, Cavendish accompanied the Earl of Portmore to France where they presented the King of France with a gift of a set of horses. So, we can see a network of sport and high-stakes gaming integrated into games of political diplomacy, but we should also keep one eye on the role of art in this developmental process. As far as I know, the painting of Lord Cavendish on his Galloway that was hung in the Jockey Club-Rooms at Williams's Coffee House has been lost, but there is good reason to believe that it did not hang there alone. The style of the day would suggest that then (as still today) the Jockey Club-Rooms would be decorated with such sporting art. In his will Roger Williams left his paintings to Lord Godolphin, continuing the pattern of bequests of Frampton and Coke. William Sandiver, an early surgeon of Newmarket, familiar with the Jockey Club in the later eighteenth century, related that many pictures were collected with some definite aim in mind, but they were left in a damp cellar and ruined by neglect; it is possible that these were the remnants of the early Jockey Club collection.

Throughout the 1720s one can begin to map a pattern of related activities that coordinate well with the activities of the club after 1729, and indicate that the Club was active during this period immediately prior to its first explicit identification in news accounts. Not surprisingly, one sort of activity that can be associated with the Club is wagering, particularly sporting wagers. But equally important would seem to be the support and patronage of British Sporting Art at this time. By the time Wootton painted his large canvas of George I at Newmarket (Fig. 29), he had already become noted for his paintings of racing subjects: his portrait of Tregonwell Frampton is dated 1715 (Fig. 28), and his painting for Edward Harley of horses exercising on Warren Hill is variously dated 1714 and 1715. Wootton is soon joined in depicting Newmarket scenes by other artists, Tillemans and Seymour being of particular note. In the same week that George journeyed to Newmarket, the *Original Weekly Journal* reported: 'the Famous Painter, Mr Halton, is Drawing a curious fine Piece, representing the Horse-Races at New-Market, for the Duke of Rutland, which is near finished, and is to be sent into Lincolnshire, to be hung up in the Gallery of his Lordship's seat, called Belvoir-Castle' (28 September 1717 – 5 October 1717).[8] To varying degrees, these artists and the 'British sporting art' that they jointly introduce can be seen as being sponsored by the collective patronage of the early Jockey Club.

Closely associated with the early Jockey Club would be a significant commercial enterprise by Peter Tillemans, who offered engravings of 'four prints of Newmarket races and the Fox chace'; his engravings were undertaken at roughly the same time that John Wootton advertised a set of four engravings of hunting scenes by subscription at Williams's Coffee House. Tillemans' engravings (announced after Wootton's, but delivered before those are completed) have no direct link to Williams's Coffee House, but are closely tied to Newmarket racing. But there is good reason to associate Tillemans with the Jockey Club in what seems to be a conscious effort to aestheticize sporting culture. Indeed, it is precisely this apparent urge to create such links which later led to the lampooning by Philip Parsons in his 'Essay on the Turf' of 1771 of what he saw as the pretentiousness involved. His work is outlined later in Part 3. The four engravings of Tillemans' paintings are unusually large and detailed productions, depicting 'The view of a horse match over the Long Course at Newmarket,' dedicated to 'George, Prince of Wales'; 'A View of the Noblemen's and Gentlemen's Strings or Trains of Running Horses Taking their Exercise up the Watering Course at Warren Hill, Newmarket', dedicated to the Duke of Devonshire; and 'View of the Round Course or Plate Course . . . with horses going Down to the Start for the King's Plate', dedicated to the Earl of Derby. These engravings sought to combine elements of high art and the commercial marketplace; they were mass-produced but designed to be status objects, of significantly higher quality than many slighter productions, yet marketed to a mass audience.

More clearly in keeping with traditional high art landscape paintings, but sympathetic with the sensibilities of the Jockey Club would be his paintings of Chatsworth, undertaken for the Duke of Devonshire. The Derbyshire estate of the Duke is familiar to twenty-first-century audiences as one of England's great houses. But when Tillemans painted Chatsworth, it may have been as well-known for its racing stud, where the great Childers stood. Tillemans's paintings do not magnify the house, however, almost concealing it among the trees in the middle distance. Nor is the stallion whose portrait was so frequently painted anywhere in evidence. Instead it is that landscape that is featured, and dominating that landscape in the foreground are the broodmares and foals of the Duke's stud. Four versions of this painting are known to have been executed, each differing slightly, and apparently each foregrounding the broodmare band.

Tillemans was asthmatic and had left London for a rural climate in Suffolk, where he died in 1734. By that time, the London activities of the Jockey Club seem to be on the wane, and Roger Williams seems to have altered, at least to some degree, his arrangements at his Coffee House. Building on his success as a coffeeman, Williams had steadily advanced his position socially and economically, and in the thirties, became a vintner and a 'purveyor to his Majesty's household.' He sought and received in 1736 a Crown Lease to significantly renovate the building he had leased from the Nelthorpe family; and the alterations made suggest that he may have been increasing his storeroom capacity, perhaps at the expense of what had previously been 'the Jockey Club rooms.' In the fall of 1736 – indeed, on the last day of the October meet, when the Town Plate brought the racing season to a close – his daughter, Anne, married Thomas Salter, a member of the Board of Green Cloth. During the last dozen years of Williams's life, there is very little evidence of activity on the part of the Jockey Club, either at Williams's Coffee House or anywhere else.

When Williams died in 1747, notices identified him as a vintner, rather than a coffeeman, but they also identified him as Clerk of the Course at Newmarket, so he is likely to have retained his connection to what remained of the Jockey Club. In his will, he left to the Earl of Godolphin all his racing paintings, just as the Godolphin Arabian had passed from Coke to Godolphin by way of Williams in 1733. If, however, the Jockey Club was at or near the peak of its activity in the early thirties, it was almost completely moribund by the time Williams died in the late forties.

Final Phase: the forties, the Deards Family

When Roger Williams died in 1747, he seems to have been succeeded in the role of Clerk of the Course at Newmarket by William Deards. The Deards family had been closely associated with racing at Newmarket from at least the beginning of the eighteenth century. The earliest advertisement I have found for John Deards (1700) is as a 'cutler,' but almost immediately he is operating a toyshop at the Dial at St Dunstan's. In the eighteenth century, toyshops served many functions, making items of jewellry, and many small adult accessories, such as snuffboxes, candlesticks, ornamental canes, spurs, whips, etc. They were, as was the case with the Deards family, silversmiths who often served as pawnbrokers and small private bankers. In this trade, the Deards family quickly became quite prominent.

John Deards who died in 1731 and maintained toyshops at St Dunstan's in Fleet Street and elsewhere had two sons: John, who predeceased him; and William, who succeeded to the family trade; as did two daughters, Mary, who maintained the toyshop at Bath which became Bertrand's after she married Paul Bertrand; and Elizabeth, who ran a shop at Charing Cross that became Chenevix's, after she married Daniel Paul Chenevix. Even before opening his toyshop in Fleet Street, Deards was advertising at the Newmarket meeting:

'Any Gentleman during the Meeting at New-Market, may be furnished with all sorts of the finest Whips and Spurrs, Silver or others, that are made, and all sorts of the finest Toys to be Sold (by John Deards's from the Dial in Wesminter-Hall) at Kate's Coffee House in New-Market.'[9]

While I have found no direct evidence linking the first John Deards to the early Jockey Club, it certainly seems worth noting that tradition has long maintained that (in spite of the doubt registered by nineteenth-century historians) the early meetings of the noblemen and gentlemen of the club were conducted 'booted and spurred'. Silver spurs, such as those noted in Deards's advertisement, were fashionable accessories of the era, and may well have been (officially or otherwise) an identifying sign of membership in the club.

After the death of John Deards in 1731, William seems to have taken on a greater role; and seems to be the member of the family most responsible for taking on a more active role with respect to racing at Newmarket. We see in the 1730s more advertisements for subscriptions being taken at both Williams's Coffee House and Deards's Toyshop. It is not clear when exactly William Deards opened his toyshop at the corner of Dover Street and Piccadilly, but this seems also to have been the location where Williams maintained his Coffee House while the main premises in St James' Street were being rebuilt. Whatever the nature of the connection between Deards and Williams, we find that Williams was identified at his death in 1747 as 'Clerk of the Course at Newmarket', and in 1761, we learn that John Deards takes on the role 'in the room of his father'. By 1742, there are regular advertisements for Newmarket Races, in which the public is informed that 'subscriptions may be paid at Mr Deards Toyshop'. By 1747, when more than 330 were counted, we see the practice begin of recording and publicizing the number of those 'listed in the subscription book kept by Mr Deards' at Newmarket. Given the year, it may be that William Deards succeeded Roger Williams in maintaining the Coffee House at Newmarket Meetings that is identified as the early locus of Jockey Club activity; and it is certainly not impossible that this coffeehouse was the same venue identified in that early advertisement as 'Kate's Coffeehouse'. Deards is noted as one of the three official timekeepers for Lord March's famous carriage match against time in 1750 (Fig. 192). In his history of the Jockey Club, Black noted:

We do (in 1754) read of 'Mr Deard, the judge' at Newmarket, as if he were a regular official, whether appointed by the new Jockey Club or by the stewards of Newmarket races, but it is just as likely that he was the keeper of 'Deard's Coffee-house' at Newmarket, enlisted for the occasion. Anyhow, the first recorded regular judge at Newmarket (though he may have been really the second, successor of Mr. Deard) was Mr. John Hilton (appointed about 1772, died 1806) whose office was in time extended to Epsom, Brocket Hall, Bibury, and probably to other meetings; and he was succeeded by the dynasty of John Clark (grandfather, father, and son) lasting down to the recent accession of Mr Robinson.[10]

In light of our better understanding of the activities of the Jockey Club before 1751, and particularly of our awareness of the roles played by Roger Williams and William and John Deards, we should revise Black's judgment accordingly, including these three Clerks of the Course as regular officials of the Jockey Club, with Williams serving until he was succeeded by William Deards (presumably at the death of Williams in 1747, though possibly at some point prior to that date), who was in turn succeeded by his son, John, when William Deards died in 1761. John Deards seems to have retired from the position by 1777, which may fit with Black's starting point of 'about 1772' for John Hilton's appointment.

◆◆◆◆

The nadir for Newmarket racing came in 1742 when there were no matches, one stakes race, and only three plates totalling a combined value of only £400. During the latter half of the 1730s, as gambling became more popular and widespread in various forms, so, too, did opposition to its spread. Something of a tipping point seems to have occurred in early 1739, almost certainly triggered by an event recorded in several papers in February that 'a person of distinction' lost £3,000 in one night at a noted gambling house in Covent Garden. There are, of course, many people who might be so designated, but I will note in passing that William, Duke of Cumberland would have been 18 at the time, and he shipped off to begin military service the following year. Within a month of the first notice of this extreme loss, several notices appeared to the effect that a vigorous prosecution was under way against a noted gaming house in Covent Garden. By midsummer (of 1739), a bill to suppress excessive and deceitful gaming had been passed by Parliament and signed by the King. While early drafts seem to have targeted primarily the proliferating games of skill and chance that were growing in popularity, the final drafts also regulated horse racing, significantly curtailing racing for smaller prizes.

One view seems to be that the attempt (one that has recurred from time to time in racing) was intended to squeeze out low-value racing (which was presumed to be the corrupting influence), thereby permitting high-class recreation to continue. The effect, however – as is generally the case – was more universally destructive to racing. While there was a small, brief resurgence in the mid-forties, it may have been only a celebratory spike in the aftermath of the defeat of the Jacobite rising of 1745. The major players who had been active in the early Jockey Club were now either dead or discouraged; many gave up the sport entirely, and even those who remained, like Godolphin, who stood the stallion commonly agreed to be the best in the country, were going through the motions, but with little of the energy that had characterized the activity of the early Jockey Club in its prime.

The three-phase organization of the activities of the early Jockey Club can be seen clearly by looking at purse values and the forms of racing in each of the three phases. Simply in terms of total purse value, the most money was on the line in the earliest phase, but mostly located in direct match racing: the second phase saw a small drop off in total value, but reoriented value toward stakes racing, where average race value reached its peak. By every standard – value of races, number of races, average value of races – racing experienced a steep decline throughout the decade of the forties. Against the backdrop of that steep decline the Jockey Club reasserted itself to relaunch racing. When it did so, it turned back – notably the creation of the 1200 Guineas—to the innovations that had been introduced by the early Jockey Club, at least a generation earlier.

Endnotes

[1] Mike Huggins, 'University Professor Casts Doubt Over Jockey Club Foundation', *Thoroughbred Owner and Breeder* (June 2013–14): 12. Donald W. Nichol, 'Lost Trousers,' *The Times Literary Supplement*, 26 July 2013, pp. 14–15. Richard Nash, 'Sporting with Kings,' *The Cambridge Companion to Horseracing*, ed. Rebecca Cassidy, Cambridge University Press, 2013: 21. Information and original research in this chapter is extracted from a larger monograph on the origins and early history of thoroughbred racing currently nearing completion.

[2] 161.

[3] *The London Journal*, December 26, 1726.

[4] The *Daily Courant*, 4 May 1727.

[5] Immediately after Cavendish's wager, there were reports that Fagg had repeated the same wager for 500G against Coke and his mare, Statira, but nothing seems to have materialized, and it may have been a rumour generated from the fact that Coke had matched his Statira for that amount against a horse of Fagg's at the next Newmarket meeting; that match was called off by consent.

[6] *London Evening Post* (London, England), 6 February 1731 9 February 1731.

[7] *The Daily Courant* (London, England), Tuesday, 9 February 1731.

[8] No painter, famous or otherwise, named 'Halton' can be found in England at this time. Most likely, 'Halton' is a mistake of the typesetter for 'Wootton', who was famous, and was executing several paintings at this time of the scene of the Tillemans painting that hangs at Belvoir Castle. Wootton and Tillemans may have been painting scenes to commemorate the royal visit for the leading members of the Jockey Club.

[9] *The Post Boy*, 4 April 1700 – 6 April 1700.

[10] 166–67.

II
The Newmarket Bank and the Beginnings of Bookmaking

Richard Nash

Of particular interest in the second phase of the early Jockey Club is the brief appearance (and abrupt disappearance) of the 'Newmarket Bank' very soon after the Hackwood meeting of the Jockey Club in the summer of 1729. The first public notice of the existence of this bank seems to be in 1731, by which time it was already functioning with a Governor and board of directors; and several scattered references indicate that it flourished over the next five years, was intended to be of long duration, but terminated abruptly and without notice. Private banks were not uncommon at the time, and this one may have functioned, at least in part, on behalf of and in support of initiatives undertaken by the Noblemen and Gentlemen of the Jockey Club. The precise nature of its activities remains unclear, but it was certainly an early gambling enterprise, a precursor of later bookmakers. It may be noteworthy that its known years of operation coincide with that phase of the early Jockey Club that saw not only a dramatic increase in Contribution or Stakes races, but an even more dramatic increase in the magnitude of the purse structure of those races.

In the spring of 1729, as in all previous spring meetings, there were no stakes races; that autumn, following the August meeting of the Jockey Club, the traditional October Stakes with a purse value of 180 Guineas was joined by a second stakes with a purse value of 300 Guineas. The following spring meet saw two stakes races (of 200 Guineas and 800 Guineas, respectively); and in the autumn, two more (of 700 Guineas and 180 Guineas, respectively). From here, in concert with the operation of the Newmarket Bank, the number and magnitude of stakes races increased until the sudden disappearance of the bank, after which time no new subscriptions were made, and the existing subscriptions ran their course over the remainder of the decade. The apex of stakes racing activity occurred in 1736, the year immediately following the last known activity of the Newmarket Bank; in that year eight of the twenty events carded at Newmarket (40 per cent) were stakes races, and the combined value of their purses (£3,308) was the highest amount to that point in history, and remained the high value amount until after the Jockey Club reorganized after 1751, constituting 70 per cent of the purse money on offer that year.

One possible purpose of the Newmarket Bank may have been to collect, hold, and disburse contributions and subscriptions for these lucrative events; the Great Stakes advertised in the spring of 1729 had explicitly restricted participation to those who had subscribed by 15 May 1729, permitting late subscribers to be included only by a majority vote of the original subscribers. If we look all the way back to the original Noblemen and Gentlemen's Subscription Purse of 1688, the advertisements for that event specified that subscriptions would be collected by 'Richard Hoare, at the sign of the Golden Bottle'. Hoare's was one of the earliest banks, and is still the longest continuously operating private bank in London. While that may have been one purpose it must be said that we know that in the 1750s the system worked on the basis of signed agreements promising to pay after the event, rather than cash deposits. With so few people involved in the 1730s, all of whom would have known each other well, such arrangements probably predate the later agreements, some of which survive. What we know for sure comes from the few scattered notices in the newspapers, which indicate clearly that the bank took an active part in conducting wagers on these events, functioning like a faro bank, rather than a private savings and loan bank. These notices indicate that the bank was closely affiliated with Roger Williams's coffee house and with the Protestant Hanoverian allegiances of the Jockey Club. The most detailed notice of the bank appears in the *Daily Advertiser* (Monday, 31 May 1731):

'On Friday last, being the 28th of May, the Governor and Directors of the Newmarket Bank met at Williams's Coffee House in St James Street and divided fifty-eight pounds per cent for last April meeting.

At the same time, they chose two new directors, viz. Mr Bennett of the Admiralty Office in the room of Mr Thomas Smith, lately deceas'd; and Mr Blackmore, gentleman of his Majesty's Ewry, in the room of Mr Trunckett, lately deceas'd.

N.B. The Governor and directors have fixed the 28th of May, being the Birth-Day of his late glorious Majesty, King George the First, to divide the profits of the April meeting; and the 4th of November, being the Birth-Day of his late

Fig. 190

Plate Six from *The Rake's Progress* by William Hogarth (1734)

The scene is a gaming house and has long been supposed to relate to the major fire in St. James's in 1733. Considerable additional losses were caused by the amount of cash which happened to be there at the time. Whether the scale of the losses related to the profits from the Newmarket Bank is questionable but, given the identity of the principal loser, quite possible. Anyway the assembled gamblers seem too concerned with the game to notice the disaster unfolding in the background.

glorious Majesty, King William the Third, to divide the profits of the October meeting, for ever.'

This notice makes clear that the bank has been in operation previously (with former directors being replaced), but also suggests that it may not have been in operation for long, with the date of its twice-annual meetings now being regularized. At first glance, one might think that the death of two directors suggests that their appointments were *not* recent, but they could have been. One of the two recently deceased directors, Mr Trunckett, was a suicide, while both of the replacements chosen appear to have been elderly. In fact, without more information about the bank's organization, it appears as though the position of 'Director' may have been something of a sinecure for a trusted pensioner.

We can be certain that a primary (perhaps the sole) purpose of the Newmarket Bank was wagering from an account of a match in the *Derby Mercury* of 1732: 'The same Day Mr Cook's *Bauble* beat the Earl of Portmore's *Miss Essex* for 200 Guineas. The Bets at the Ditch were Twelve Pounds to Ten on both Sides. The Newmarket Bank took the Odds on both Sides, by which Means they got 2 per Cent on their Capital without any Hazard'.[1] In 1733 several notices indicate that that year's spring meeting was again profitable for the bank, although apparently the intention of honouring Protestant succession by dividing profits on the birthdays of William and George had already by then been discarded. While news of the bank's success was announced as soon as the Newmarket meet ended in May, it is not until late in July that a notice appears of the biannual distribution of profits: 'Last Wednesday, the Newmarket Bank din'd at Williams's Coffee-House, and divided above Forty per Cent. out of the last Half Year's Dividend.' The various references to dividing the profits seem to infer splitting them between individual shareholders in the bank (some no doubt club members) rather than paying them to the Jockey Club as the investor.

The distribution of profits in July seems to have been celebrated prematurely and almost catastrophically in an event depicted in a famous scene in the sixth plate of Hogarth's series, *The Rake's Progress* (Fig. 190). It has often been noted that in the background of this plate the gamblers fail to notice that their quarters are catching fire; this has generally been identified with the famous fire at White's in 1733. White's burned completely in the spring of that year, and in the autumn Hogarth began taking subscriptions for *The Rake's Progress* (Fig. 190), completing the series of engravings in 1734 and publishing them in 1735. The last day of the Spring Meeting at Newmarket was Friday 27 April, when the Newmarket Bank closed its accounts, declaring a profit of more than 40 per cent for the meeting. The newspapers report that the fire that consumed White's and two neighbouring buildings broke out sometime after 4 o'clock the next morning, and the losses were considerable: 'It is said there was a large Sum of Money, and a great many Bank Notes in the House, which had been disposed in Mr Arthur's hands by several Gentlemen for their Conveniency, and particularly a large Chest of Plate and other Curiosities, belonging to a Gentleman of Distinction, all which were consumed by the Flames'.[2] The *London Evening Post* subsequently identified this 'Gentleman of Distinction' as Sir Andrew Fountain, the Warden of the Mint: 'Sir Andrew Fountain has lost by the said Fire, in Notes and other Things of Value, which were locked up in a room of the said House, to the Value of near £10,000'.[3] It may be worthy of note here that before being made Warden of the Mint in 1727,

Sir Andrew had been Vice-Chamberlain of Her Majesty's Household; on his being advanced to Warden of the Mint, he was succeeded in his previous post by Thomas Smith, who could be the Mr Thomas Smith who served as one of the directors of the Newmarket Bank. The last notice we have of the Newmarket Bank is during the Spring Meeting of 1735, and while it seems to indicate that for once the gambling activities of the bank were losing, the losses do not seem to be devastating:

'On Monday the Sweep Stakes appointed in the list for yesterday were run at Newmarket... but only Sir Michael Newton and Lord Essex's colts started; the bets at starting were 35 to 10 on Sir Michael's colt and he won the Stakes.

The Newmarket Bank took the odds on Monday and have lost £40 since the meeting.'

If taken literally, such a loss hardly seems devastating, but given that results were previously declared in percentage terms, with the 1731 dividend being announced as 'fifty-eight pounds per cent.', the sentence presumably means that the Newmarket Bank had lost '£40 per cent since the meeting began' as the meeting did not finish until the end of the month. The *Daily Courant* reported then that the Noblemen's and Gentlemen's Contribution Money 'was won by the Duke of Bolton's Merry Andrew, and was taken before starting against the field.' However the Newmarket Bank fared at the spring meeting in 1735, there is no final declaration, nor any subsequent mention of any kind. Instead, even before the spring meeting concludes, new matches (rather than stakes races) are being announced, with one in particular, in which the Duke of Bolton's horse, Looby, is matched against Mr Panton's gelding, Conqueror (Fig. 187), recently purchased from Capt. Appleyard. Throughout the summer, there are numerous allusions to this match as the most eagerly anticipated in years, and in the end over £30,000 is said to have been pending in wagers. The change in 1735 brings to an end what seems to have been a brief but important era in racing's early history, introducing both a model of stakes racing and a model of wagering that provided the prototype that modern racing would build on.

Why did the Newmarket Bank suddenly cease activity? At the moment, that question cannot be answered definitively, but the wagering model associated with it of one horse 'taken against the field', and odds changing between heats and in the running, continued until the appearance of bookies offering odds on each runner near the end of the century. Whether or not there is a more significant connection, the abrupt disappearance of the bank coincided with a period in which the stakes racing introduced by the early Jockey Club went into abeyance and in which Roger Williams made changes in his life that seem to suggest that this early Jockey Club's activity was beginning to wane.

Endnotes

[1] *Derby Mercury*, 4 May 1732.
[2] *The Daily Courant*, 30 April 1733.
[3] *London Evening Post*, 28 April – 1 May 1733.

III

Comparison between the Effects at Newmarket and Elsewhere of the Catastrophic Decline of the 1730s and 1740s

Chapter 4 of Part 1 outlines how disastrously racing collapsed in this period and tries to provide reasons. The statistics used there to show what was happening give only a very sketchy picture of events; this section provides supporting detail. While the decline was on a national basis, the scale of these trends at Newmarket was much more dramatic and the explanation of them materially different. As mentioned, things became so bad on the Heath that in 1742 only four races were run and it must surely have seemed to contemporaries that the end of the sport was nigh. In such circumstances Newmarket can hardly have seemed a viable proposition even to a congenital optimist.

It appears all the more surprising that this collapse took place at more or less the time that the thoroughbred really emerged as a separate breed following the tremendous impact of the last of the great Eastern sires, the Godolphin Arabian (Fig. 30). Perhaps recovery when it came in the 1750s was driven to some degree by an appreciation of the quality of the horse population that had been developed by nearly a century of testing it on the racecourse following the Restoration. Anyway, this section is devoted to drawing various comparisons between the racing programmes which could be put on in five seasons selected to show the trends with a decade between each one. The years in question are:

1731 Before the crash.
1741 After the 1740 Act of Parliament requiring £50 for any race came into effect and racing plumbed the depths.
1751 Before the real recovery, showing some progress elsewhere but very little on the Heath.
1761 Dramatic recovery, especially at Newmarket.
1771 Newmarket in the ascendant and its racing at a peak of prosperity not exceeded until the late nineteenth century.

◆◆◆◆

In considering the figures involved allowance should be made for a degree of exaggeration due to change in the value of the currency. However this was a relatively marginal factor in the eighteenth century and from 1731 to 1751 no discernable change occurred. By 1761 approximately 12 per cent of value had been lost and by 1771 this figure had risen to about 27 per cent due to the implications of the Seven Years War. Since then this figure has risen into the high nineties – certainly over 98 per cent. Although such calculations become steadily less reliable spread out over protracted periods, it is reasonable to multiply mid-eighteenth century numbers by a factor of a hundred to give a very rough guide to monetary values.

| | Table 1: Number and value of race runs ||||||
| | Newmarket || Elsewhere || GB Total ||
	Races	Prize Money (£)	Races	Prize Money (£)	Races	Prize Money (£)
1731	35	£7,938	373	£9,482	408	£17,420
1741	10	£973	112	£6,174	122	£7,147
1751	23	£2,123	192	£11,004	215	£13,127
1761	76	£26,530	216	£16,483	292	£43,013
1771	174	£58,949	311	£24,886	485	£83,835

a) The fact that the number of races run in the rest of the country had not recovered to the 1731 figure even forty years later shows the impact of the 1740 Act that required the value of each race to be at least £50.

b) The effect on the number of racecourses was even more marked. In 1731 there were 143 on the mainland, excluding Ireland, staging 391 cards. On a few occasions only the month rather than the precise date on which a race was held is recorded and one cannot be certain whether consecutive entries refer to races which took place on the same day or on one which followed. However, until racing really recovered in the 1760s even small meetings would sometimes run for four or five days with only a single race on each. Two on the same day hardly ever occurred away from Newmarket. A decade later, in 1741, the figures had declined to 56 putting on 121 days with only Newmarket on one occasion staging two races on one day. By 1771 neither total had recovered fully as the 99 courses staged 305 cards. Yet the impact of setting a minimum value had the effect of raising the average away from the Heath from only £25 to £80 by 1771. Indeed, in that year the Newmarket figure of £339 for each winner would equate to a modern figure in the order of £30,000 roughly twice what is on offer today, albeit with the vast majority then put up by the owners themselves.

c) The nineteen matches run in heats during these years have been classed as matches and excluded from the heats total. Only two of these were run at Newmarket and none was of particularly significant value so the treatment has little overall effect.

d) By comparison with the rest of the country the scale of Newmarket's progress seems remarkable and the pace of its recovery from the depths of the slump almost beyond belief. Expressed as the Heath's share of the mainland totals the percentages for the period derived from Table 1 are as follows:

	Races (%)	Prize Money (%)
1731	9	46
1741	8	14
1751	11	16
1761	26	62
1771	36	70

◆◆◆◆

Such a degree of dominance as had arisen in the first twenty years of the re-formed Jockey Club's operation at Newmarket was of quite brief duration. By the end of the century the rest of the country had caught up and for much of the nineteenth century the positions were really reversed. As explained in Chapters 4 and 5 of Part One, the abyss into which sport fell on the Heath in the 1740s arose from entirely different considerations to the national problem with the 1740 Act and related to a combination of the loss of Royal support added to the absence of any central authority to check the gravest malpractice.

Table 2: Constrasting the nature of the sport on the Heath and elsewhere

	1731		1741		1751		1761		1771	
	Races	£	Races	£	Races	£	Races	£	Races	£
Newmarket										
Matches	26	£5,439	5	£588	13	£1,513	49	£17,310	109	£33,359
Heats	2	£210	3	£260	5	£255	5	£331	3	£260
Other races	7	£2,289	2	£125	5	£355	22	£8,889	62	£25,330
	35	£7,938	10	£973	23	£2,123	76	£26,530	174	£58,949
Elsewhere										
Matches	32	£956	2	£105	19	£1,587	18	£1,955	18	£4,729
Heats	285	£6,741	97	£5,433	150	£8,107	169	£9,188	248	£13,288
Other races	56	£1,785	13	£636	23	£1,310	29	£5,340	45	£6,869
	373	£9,482	112	£6,174	192	£11,004	216	£16,483	311	£24,886
Mainland totals										
Matches	58	£6,395	7	£693	32	£3,100	67	£19,265	127	£38,088
Heats	287	£6,951	100	£5,693	155	£8,362	174	£9,519	251	£13,548
Other races	63	£4,074	15	£761	28	£1,665	51	£14,229	107	£32,199
	408	£17,420	122	£7,147	215	£13,127	292	£43,013	485	£83,835

a) Newmarket's historic dependence on matches is a significant guide to the ethos of the sport on the Heath. Something of the flavour of the medieval tournament still lingered on from racing's days as a courtly amusement and reflected the attitude of its main aristocratic supporters. Although their number was still limited, the major sweepstakes developing during this period were having a material impact on total prize money. For instance, the forty-six sweepstakes run in 1771 on the Heath averaged £518 while the more numerous 109 matches produced a figure of only £306. However, matches remained an important if declining element in the sport until disappearing almost completely by the last quarter of the nineteenth century.

b) Away from the Heath, programmes were always shaped by different and more practical considerations. Firstly, match racing, for all its attractions to the grandees, was almost invariably a matter between only the two owners without any outside contribution to the prize on offer. A few matches involved three or more people and so took on something of the form of a private sweepstake but they were never common. On the contrary, the great majority of racing around the country consisted of £50 plates with that sum guaranteed by the racecourse or sponsor and with owners contributing nothing or only £1 or so as an entry payment. Secondly, there were so few horses in the early days of the thoroughbred that cards often consisted of a single race. Thus, programming in heats usually led to several contests for spectators to watch instead of only one at many of the small country courses. It did not always work, and even York's six days in August 1750 saw only one race programmed on five of them and two on the other so

Eclipse in 1769 (detail of Fig. 40). The great horse did not directly contribute to Tables 1 and 2 as he retired to stud at the end of the 1770 season after his eighteen victories had yielded only £2,078. Of that figure 750 Guineas came from his two victories and two walk-overs on the Heath in 1770.

the need for the 'Great Subscription' of 1751 seems clear enough. However, our ancestors were clearly less demanding, as William Pick records, 'the greatest appearance of company this day upon the course known for many years' to see only two contests, a 200 Guineas match and a Royal Plate of 100 Guineas, which produced only a single race when the loser was scratched after the first heat.

c) As Table 2 makes clear, racing everywhere in the mid-eighteenth century was based, and always had been, on either matches or races run in heats. Even by 1771 they combined to constitute 78 per cent of the sport on offer, and around 90 per cent if the extra contests inherent in heat racing are included. Yet heats were prohibited in the nineteenth century and matches had become virtually extinct by its end, so the changes wrought everywhere by the development of the breed and the arrival of gate money meetings were on an immense scale.

◆◆◆

In summary, racing at Newmarket still bore very little relationship in 1771 to the sport on offer elsewhere. This gulf closed only very slowly as the Heath went into decline in the nineteenth century. By the time it recovered locally in the 1860s the national control of the Jockey Club was clearly an important factor in largely bridging the gap by 1900, based – it must be said – much more on changes to practice at Newmarket than elsewhere.

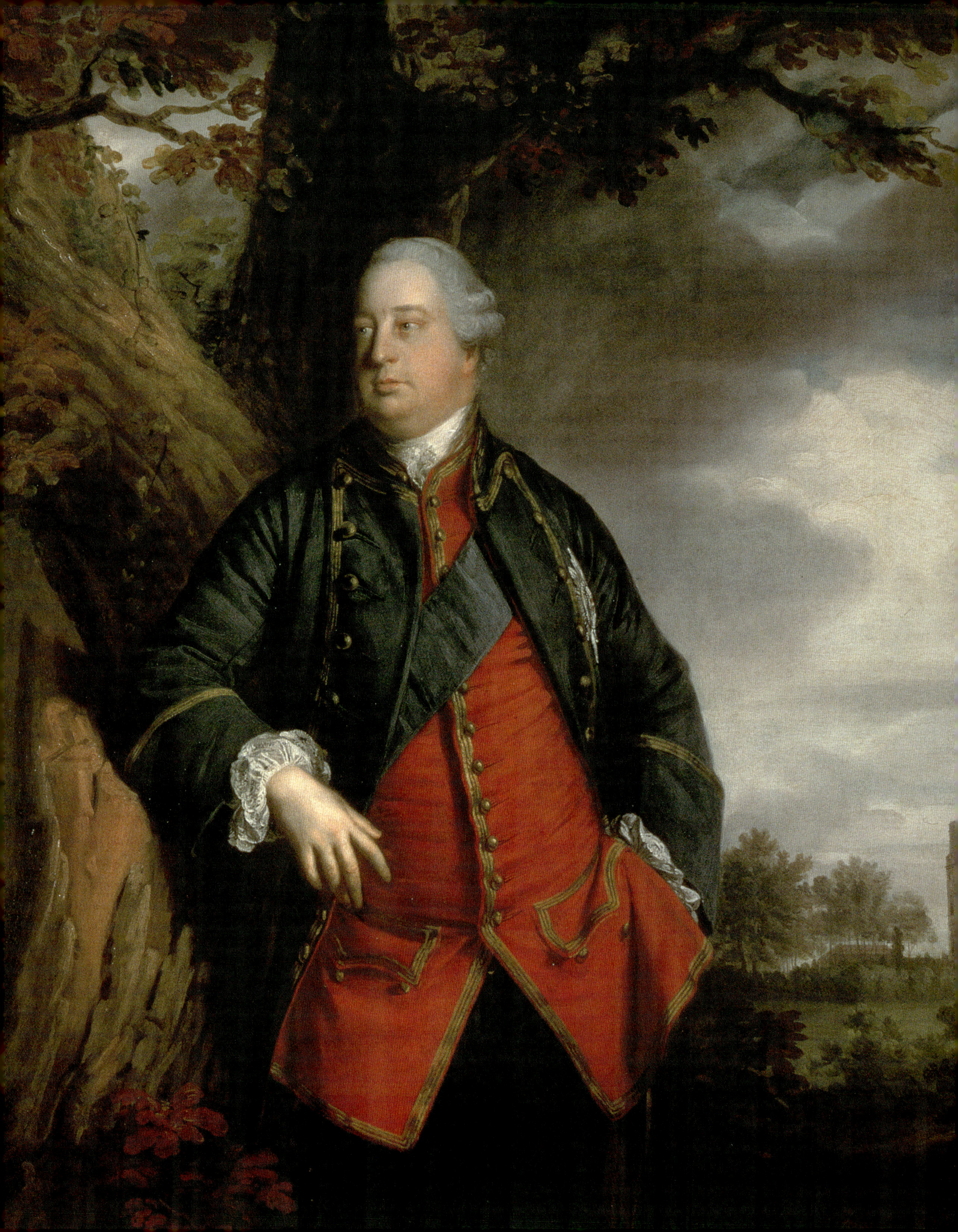

IV
Commentary on the Letter Published in the London Evening Post *in March 1752 and signed 'Philo-Hippos'*

Because it casts so much light on the crucial events of 1751/52 following the Prentice scandal, the letter is reproduced below together with a commentary. This section is based on the letter recently unearthed by Professor Richard Nash and should be read in conjunction with his reconstruction of the formation of the Jockey Club and its activities in the first half of the eighteenth century. The paragraph reference numbers have been added to the text in order to link it to the notes below.

London Evening Post (London, England), 3 March, 1752 – 5 March, 1752; issue 3803.

'To my Brethren of the Bridle, Breeders, &c. Gentlemen,

1) Having lately received more Letters from you than at any other Time, except the Spring that produced the Horse-

Fig. 191

William Augustus, Duke of Cumberland, c.1758 by Sir Joshua Reynolds (1723–92)

Race Bill, I must on Account of ill health &c, humbly entreat you to accept this publick and imperfect Acknowledgement of your Favours, and my own Respect, in the *Evening Post*.

2) I therefore can answer you Affirmatively, as to the New Grand Subscription, the Parchment having been lately shewn me, by the very Amiable and Great Person who has now perfected this Plan; whereby, 1200 Guineas, at the least, will be annually run for by the Subscribers, for five successive Years, and the Things bred by themselves, excepting those started in 1757; when the Sport commences.

3) And thirteen or fourteen Noblemen and Gentlemen have agreed to stake twenty Guineas each, in much the same Sweepstakes Way with the former; But in this they are not confined to their own Breeds.

4) On these, and a great Number of Matches to be run next Month at Newmarket, I send you my Joy, and hope, that as but one Prentice ever appear'd there, that no Age will produce another; and congratulate with you all, on Account of the many Engagements enter'd into at Burford, Stockbridge, and all those Courses in the South and West, as well as the North.

5) And it is observable, that the Royal Diversion of Horse-Racing, ever encourag'd by the Crown, has not only, at this Time, double the Number of Royal Plates for its Support, than it ever had in the Sportly Reign of King Charles the Second, its first Parent; and that his present Majesty has sent a Barb or two into the North for the Benefit of the Breeders there; but that his R. H. the D. has now deign'd to enter the Newmarket Lists, and is at the Head of this Grand New Subscription, and will, 'tis said, grace the Turf with his Appearance. Nor can I conclude without acquainting you, that there is a Report in Town of Mr. H–s's having sold several of his Mares for more than 300 Guineas each, and of Mr. L–s's having asked a much larger Sum for several in his Stud; and I have seen a foreign Stallion of one Mr. Salway's, a Turky merchant, who will take no less than 500 Guineas for him: and though I wish that these Gentlemen may get their own sums, yet I have my fears, that they may overstand their present high Market; and if they'll forgive the Presumption, I know a Western Breeder, when, if that Air has not corrupted the Blood, will sell two young Mares, as large, handsome, and strong, as any in the North, for 100 Guineas each; and they shall be allow'd, by Mr. Panton, or any Judge of Pedigree to be as well bred; and they will soon be cover'd by an Arab of nine years old, bought three years ago, by the Advice of Lord William Manners, Mr. Pelham, and Mr. Bilton; who thought him the finest Arabian, as well as the largest and strongest, they had ever seen; and the Gentlemen having many hopeful Things of his getting, will sell him for much less than Half the Price of Mr. Salway's.
I rest,
Gentlemen,

Your obedient Servant,
Philo-Hippos

6) P. S. I have heard, from good Authority that if illegal Plates are advertis'd, or short Payments made to the Winners, that a Club of Gentlemen, of Quality and Figure, will prosecute any Clerk of a Course for so doing, as well as for withholding the Purses after they are won, as those were at Houn- [here a line is clearly dropped by the typesetter] which were paid but a few Days ago, after Prosecutions commenced against Mr. C–x.'

Commentary on text of letter
(Paragraph references have been added to the text)
1a) The rather pompous author of this highly informative letter seems to have been very well connected and in a position to indulge in a wide correspondence on racing matters since at least 1740, when the Act was passed. The reference to that correspondence suggests he must have represented some form of central point for the gathering and exchange of information. This in turn suggests he was either John Pond or Reginald Heber, who continued to produce Calendars in competition after John Cheny's death or, perhaps most likely, the son of Cheny, also John. The latter had been involved with his father's work and seems to have meant to carry it on separately or in conjunction with Heber but does not seem to have done so at all. As Richard Nash points out, his style was more in line with the rather florid one adopted by Philo-Hippos than either of the others. In addition, neither Pond nor Heber would really have been as old as the tone of the letter suggests and there is no evidence of the younger Cheny after this period.

1b) Of the former pair the evidence points to Pond rather than Heber as he seems to have been much better connected. When his book was published in 1751 all those among the twelve Great Stakes subscribers who had bought Cheny's book (six of them) switched to Pond not Heber and by 1752 he had all twelve, with Heber still to attract any of them. Pond's first volume also contained two features underlining his position, as he included numerous details of races back to 1718 and the first proper set of rules ever published which survived to the end of the century as the prime source of guidance. He or his son conducted the sale of the Duke of Cumberland's stock at Windsor in 1765 which included the yearling Eclipse. His calendar ceased after

Fig. 192

Engraving of the Carriage Match won by Lord March,
after James Seymour (1750)

1757 leaving the field clear to Heber until the latter's death in 1768. The cessation of Pond's work saw Heber become the accepted figure operating on behalf of the Club and it seems very probable that the change after that date was entirely amicable. How long Pond survived after 1765 is uncertain and his death or retirement probably opened the way for Richard Tattersall to develop operations at Hyde Park Corner from 1766 so in effect replacing him. Sadly Pond's son chose to lead the high life beyond his means and by 1775 was bankrupt. Things only got worse, as it is known that for a time he was committed to Bedlam and he died in debtor's prison in 1782 while his mother Sarah died in the workhouse in 1785.

2a) The stress laid on the 'New Grand Subscription' is interesting and shows how important the new races seemed to an informed observer.

2b) The reference to the organiser of the new race being both 'very Amiable and Great' strongly infers in Georgian England that he was a peer. It seems likely that this grandee, who had dreamed the scheme up and showed Philo-Hippos the parchment on which he was collecting signatures, would have been a signatory himself.

2c) We know from other sources that Lord Hartington, soon to become the 4th Duke of Devonshire, was the 'steward' for the great Subscription at its outset. This seems to suggest either that he was the 'perfector' of the scheme or that he provided a suitable front for someone else whose name would not have been as acceptable to the very grand list of subscribers. Being steward entailed being responsible for the cash and acting as judge – it was an appointment for a single year with the right to nominate a successor.

2d) Much the most closely involved in the affairs of Newmarket at the time among the signatories was the Earl of March and Ruglen. Fresh from his assorted triumphs on the cricket field and in the famous Carriage Match (Fig. 192), he was only 26 at the time, and must already have been notorious. In later life he became the 4th Duke of Queensberry and even more notorious as the lecherous 'Old Q' (Fig. 38). It would seem quite possible that his inventive mind devised the Great Stakes at much the same time that he landed large bets on sending a message fifty miles in an hour (by inserting it in a cricket ball and using professional cricketers to throw it round a circle) and covering nineteen miles in a four-wheeled vehicle in that time (Fig. 192). He is also credited with putting on the 1751 cricket match at Newmarket which is one of the first ever recorded in any detail, between an Eton team and an All-England eleven. On balance it does seem most likely that 'the Amiable and Great' founder of the Great Stakes was March and in that case both racing and the Club owe him a considerably larger debt of gratitude than has ever been appreciated. At about this time March became resident in the town in a large house near the Heath with stables across the London road and a stud farm out at Saxham. Few other notables became so involved at that stage.

2e) If the 'perfector' was Lord March then the fact that John Pond was allowed to publish the print after the picture by James Seymour (Fig. 192) that came out immediately after the Carriage Match in turn seems to confirm that Pond probably was a close connection and so the more likely of the two Calendar publishers to have been Philo-Hippos.

Pond's closer connection with March is also suggested by the fact that his 1751 book recorded the three cricket matches in reasonable detail but Heber completely ignored the events, although in March's case his involvement was much reduced after these early years.

2f) The crucial point in the conditions for the Great Stakes is that it was limited to homebreds and so conducive to promoting breeding by subscribers. The importance of persuading people like Cumberland and Rockingham to set up stud farms is stressed in the letter.

3) This race was the one worth £273 referred to in Part 3 (thirteen people paying 20 Guineas each) as being the most valuable run in 1752. Lord March was one of the four people who subscribed to both stakes.

4) The importance of the Prentice scandal is firmly underlined as is Philo-Hippos's delight at the progress in terms of regulating racing that all these events represent.

5a) This is about the best reference to confirm the view that Charles II originated the first King's Plate although no details are known until later reigns.

5b) Philo-Hippos stresses the importance of having got the Duke of Cumberland as the ideal representative of the Royal family involved in racing and breeding. Its lack of interest since the death of Queen Anne in 1714 had proved a serious weakness. Another pointer towards the author being Pond is that he always described Cumberland as H.R.H. the Duke as in the letter and indexed him under the 'Ds'. On the other hand Heber put him in the Cs for 1751 and only changed tack in 1752. In fact whether Philo-Hippos was Pond or the younger John Cheny may be interesting but of much less significance than the light his letter shines on events at this crucial period.

5c) The missing names in the middle of the paragraph will probably be those of the great Yorkshire breeders Mr Hutton of Marske and Mr Leedes of Milford near Thirsk. The presence of the second 's' in Hutton's case is likely to be a printer's error and he and Mr Leedes are the obvious candidates to fill these gaps. No name beginning with an 'H' and ending in 's' would make sense. What is being recorded is the effective end of Yorkshire's dominance as the cradle of the thoroughbred. The later speculation over the next important Arabian after the Godolphin is less prescient – none ever appeared.

6a) Here again the writer holds out his hopes of the Club taking effective control of the sport. If it took rather longer (some eighty years) than he might have hoped, he got what he wanted in the end. The evidence provided by this paragraph that the reformed Club was designed for much broader than merely social ends seems clear. If the Jockey Club had really sprung into existence in the autumn of 1751, as so long supposed, would it be credible that Philo-Hippos would have written in the terms of his PS only three months later?

6b) Past problems in getting some stakeholders to pay out rather than embezzle the prize money had been one of the reasons for racing's collapse in the 1740s. The missing line will refer to the Hounslow meeting and the defaulting clerk was probably Mr Chevenix. You could hardly ask for firmer evidence than this that the Club of 1751/52 had far more than social activities in mind. It is also interesting that the Chenevix family not only kept one of the principal rival toyshops to the Deards family but William Deard's sister was married to its proprietor. Those who provided services to the Newmarket grandees like the Ponds, Deards, Chenys and Roger Williams seem to have been a close-knit society before being entirely replaced by the Weatherby family in the affairs of the Club.

In summary, the rather pompous ponderings of Philo-Hippos illuminate with startling clarity the scene in 1752, just before the Club ran its first private race that April. The links between this seemingly very active body, set on rejuvenating the turf, and the former institution of Bolton and Godolphin dealt with by Richard Nash are much less clear and his work on the subject is of corresponding importance.

V
Reaction around 1770 against Activities in Newmarket

When Newmarket prospered in the seventeenth and eighteenth centuries an almost automatic response seems to have arisen in condemnation of its perceived excesses. That is hardly surprising given the nature of the Restoration Court during the Heath's first golden age under Charles II. The reaction as things flowered again in the early days of the Jockey Club was perhaps less obviously justified. However, the view that people who should have known better were wasting their time and resources on the Heath seems to have been fairly general in polite society. There are quite frequent sour references from Horace Walpole, younger son of Sir Robert, along the lines of his description of Tregonwell Frampton's successor on the Heath as the royal representative as 'a disreputable horse-jockey' although Mr Panton's daughter became a duchess.

More informative is Philip Parsons's extended exercise in heavy sarcasm of 1771, entitled 'Newmarket, or an Essay on the Turf'. It pokes fun at what the author saw as gross excess, made worse by pompous pretentiousness over improving the breed, from those with too much money and/or too little sense. The two sections quoted below to give a flavour of things have the virtue of describing the Coffee Room and the racecourse just before the former was rebuilt but with the new little buildings described in Part 2 having recently sprouted on the Heath.

Extract from 'Newmarket: or, An Essay on the Turf' by Philip Parsons (1771)

The Coffee Room
Come, Sir, I have interest enough with Mr Davies, master of the coffee-room, to procure the key – here it is – we shall soon be there – we are now arrived – walk in, Sir, if you please.

'And this is the coffee-room, which so modestly turns its back upon the street, as if to shun the public view in silent retirement'.

Yes, Sir, this is the coffee-room – how do you like it? – 'Mighty well; large, plain, and elegantly neat, but not grand enough, methinks, for the noble company that frequents it'.

Oh, Sir, that is the modest humility of the noble company – but I see you are particularly engaged in examination; favour me with your opinion of what you see.

'Why, I must confess, I think the place admirably adapted

Fig. 193

Frontispiece to Volume One of Parson's essay

The author of the book in which this illustration appeared was mocking
the classical pretentions of the early members of the Jockey Club.

to the intention of stillness, social amusement, and wise discourse, for which it was doubtless designed. Those boxes are, I dare say, purposely divided, to avoid the confusion and hurry of a general mixture of company, and to receive a select party, of half a dozen gentlemen, who, leaving the bustle and hurry of the Turf, and the tide of anxious passions that attend it, meet here to unbend the mind with calm and amusing conversation'.

Good! – But pray, Sir, go on. –

'But what pleases me particularly is the great number of books that lie yonder together; they are, I suppose, books of morality, of wise sayings and instructive maxims, kept here for the use and improvement of the noble company that frequent the place. They are, I see, all bound alike to the simplicity of every thing else in the room, and to make the outside agreeable, in honest plainness, to the solid wisdom and depth of science, which, I presume, are contained in the inside; – but you smile; have I said anything?'

Indeed, Sir, you entertain me highly; I beg of you to continue your remarks.

'Upon the table I observe, what gives me the highest satisfaction to see – a large FOLIO BIBLE.'
(A Bible! I shall certainly burst – *Aside*)
'This is, doubtless, a very wise sign, to keep that book here for many reasons, as –'

Ha! Ha! Ha! – I can contain no longer, nor suffer you to continue in your mistake; that, Sir, which you suppose to be a Bible, is no other than a *book of matches*, fairly entered, and kept here for annual use.

[Note: The Match Book into which future engagements were entered has survived for the 1750s and will be one of the series to which Parsons alludes. So too do 'the boxes ... to receive a select party, of half a dozen gentlemen', although nowadays such parties are usually leavened by a sprinkling of ladies.]

'You astonish me' –

Fact, I assure you; you need only look into it to be convinced – Now, Sir, what do you think?

'Think! Why, I think I was never more mistaken in all my life.'

Before we leave the room, Sir, I will just desire you to take notice of that map; it represents Newmarket, and the country round it, for a few miles; methinks there is great propriety in hanging it there, as every hero of the Turf may, occasionally, feast his eyes with the spot, in which he so much delights; and as the course is most exactly delineated, may run over again at night, in fancy, the races, which he so happily enjoyed, in reality, by day. – You have heard what delight the great Tully rode, in fancying while he walked along the academic groves, that he conversed with the wisest philosophers, and trod in the very footsteps of the immortal Plato. – Such a rational delight may the frequenters of the Turf take, in contemplating this map; they may dwell with pleasure on the delightful scene, and fancy they can lay a finger in the footsteps of their dear horse, and point out the very spot, where he first appeared to gain a head of his rival coursers.

[Note: The Chapman map of the Heath of 1768 still hangs in the Coffee Room today. It may well be the copy Parsons saw if he actually entered the Coffee Room before writing his book in 1771.]

Stay a moment; – we must not forget those books, which you supposed, Sir, to contain wise maxims and moral sentences – please to open one of them – well, what do you find? –

'This is a calendar of the races of the year – but let me another –'

Nay, Sir, *ex uno disce omnes* – if you see one, you see all – for they are every one the same – but I would only ask – would you desire to see wiser maxims, and more moral sentences, than are contained in these instructive pages?

I think we have now taken a full view of the coffee room – and I hope, reader, we have spent no disagreeable half hour in it; we will now take our leave of it, and return the key to the master of the room.

Mr Davies, here is your key – and we are much obliged to you for the use of it.

A ha! Mr Author, cries an hero of the Turf, have I caught

you at last! You are a stranger, I am sure, and know nothing of the place – the master of the coffee-room's name is not Davies; you have betrayed your ignorance; you have got the wrong name, I assure you –

Have I, my hero? Then you may put in the right name, if you like it. –

[Note: Sadly we cannot be sure of the correct name to insert instead of 'Davies' but we can be quite certain that Philip Parsons would think it silly to be interested in what it was. In fact the chances are quite high that it was 'Deards'. The family had kept a coffee house in the town for years and would seem natural candidates to take charge of the new one erected by the Club. Indeed, John Deards himself figures in the Match Book as the collector, distributor and recorder of matches for the Club. The fact that both names start and finish with the same letters is probably not coincidence.]

The Race Course
Enter we now upon the scene of action; the course itself demands our attention, to compare it with the Olympic stadium.

If much of pomp, ostentation, pageantry and pride, demand regard; if narrow and straitned [sic] boundaries, encircling the allotted space with marble, perhaps (for here, our accounts are wretchedly imperfect) be objects worthy of attention and respect, then we may allow the Grecian Raceground its share of honour.

But it must be after (and with a long interval between) the plains of Newmarket have justly claimed and received their tribute of respect. Here nature, undebauch'd by art, spreads her ample bosom to receive her sons, ambitious of renown; here no pillars of marble, no narrow and contracted limits, cramp the spirit of an Englishman: a wide and extensive carpet is spread indeed, but it is spread by the hand of nature, as if on purpose to form a stage, every way fit for the scenes that are acted upon it.

Long and laboured are the descriptions given us by Pausanias, and Wheeler, and West of the Olympic Race-ground, but from what we can gather, with any certainty, it appears to have been the scene of the amusements of children rather than of men, when viewed, in comparison, with the course at Newmarket. It would be making a vain parade of learning, to enter into the particulars of the Grecian scene of diversion, and it would besides fatigue too much the attention of my Newmarket readers, whose heads are not to be set aching with intricate differentiations, when I mean rather to enliven and animate them, with the great superiority of their own scenes of amusement, over those of the most celebrated among the ancients; – Suffice it, that I assure the reader, that the *Beacon Course*, the *Duke's Course*, nay, *Rowley's Mile*, are, by infinite degrees, beyond the celebrated spots where Greece used to assemble, and which poets and historians have strove to render immortal as their writings – an attempt, the vanity of which time is shewn, for it has overthrown the *immobile saxum*,[*] and scarcely left the traces of former grandeur – This, by the way, is a fate that the Newmarket course need never dread, for as it is formed by the hand of nature, and so it will remain and flourish in immortal green, till nature's self shall fail, and only perish with a falling world.

[Note: Volume One contains a splendidly sarcastic vignette (Fig. 193) of the winners being paraded down the High Street preceded by a choir of beautiful maidens strewing flowers in their path and singing in their honour in harmony with a band of violins and trumpets. Mr Parsons clearly had no time for the Turf and its grand supporters or their supposed pretensions.]

immobile saxum = immovable stone

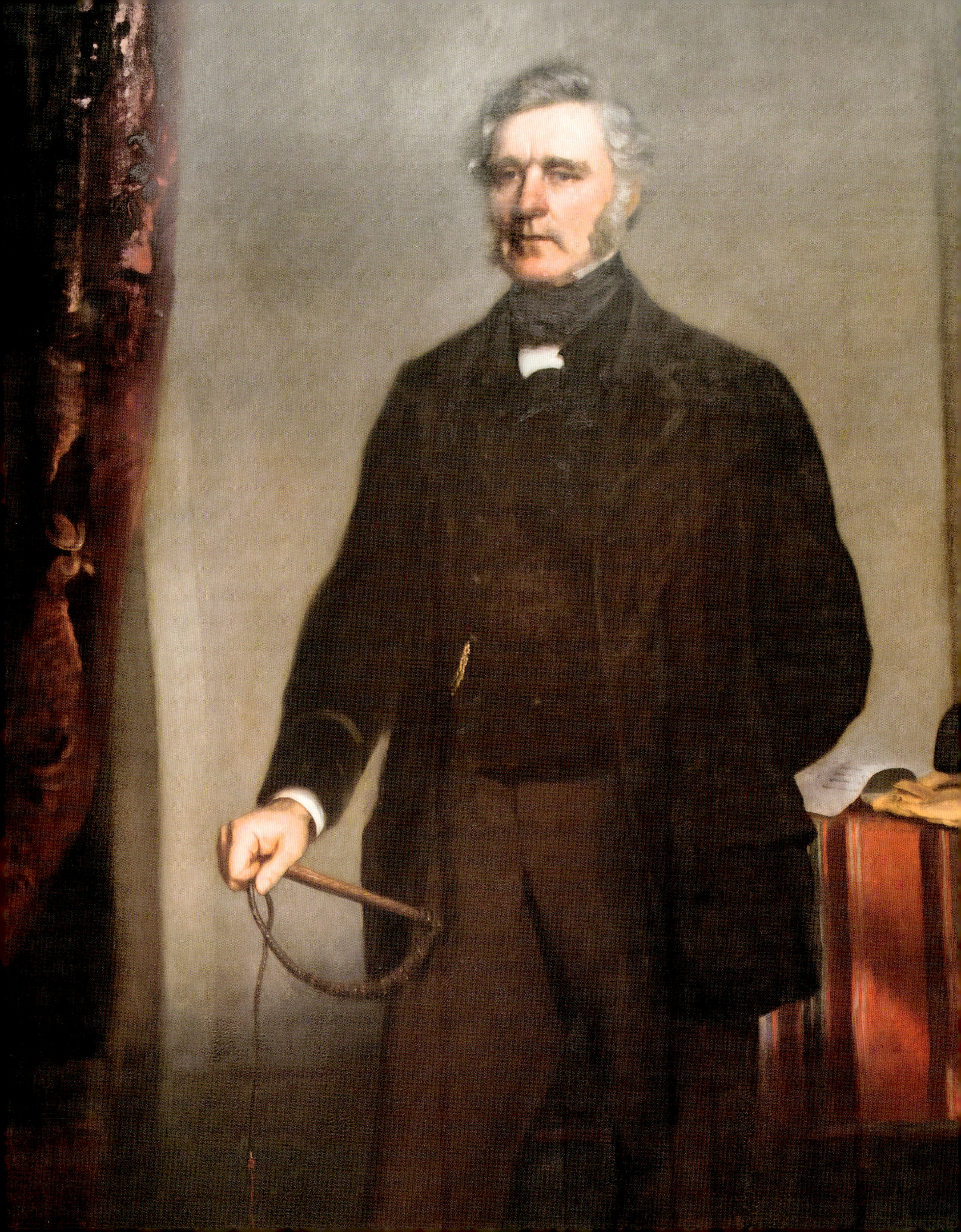

VI

Acquisition of the Heath by the Jockey Club

Before the Club took its first lease in Newmarket on the site of the present Coffee Room in 1752 from the Erratt family of horsedealers, trainers and jockeys, a good deal is known about the ownership of the Heath itself. (Incidentally, the man riding ahead of Lord March's strange carriage in Fig. 192 was one of the Erratt family). However, one needs to understand and so be able to assess and explain medieval land tenure before launching out on that subject. Perhaps fortunately, neither of us is remotely qualified to pontificate on the precise influence derived by the Argentine family from their Lordship of the Manor of Newmarket before they died out in 1423. Then came the Alingtons until they too ran out of puff in the male line in 1722 after which things get rather more comprehensible. Indeed, their name was

Fig. 194

Admiral the Hon. Henry Rous by Henry Weigall (1866).

This painting was presented to Admiral Rous at a dinner in 1866 to celebrate twenty-five years of his work for the turf.

resuscitated in 1876 when Gerard Sturt, whose wife was the Alington heiress, took the name for his title when created a peer. He was a Club member who later won Derbys with St Blaise and the Triple Crown winner Common and in the circumstances it seems almost disloyal that he had them trained by John Porter at Kingsclere.

The original Long Course stretched for its eight miles through various other manors with a mixture of rights to own or occupy sections of the course. Certainly before the Beacon start the Heath would very largely have been uncultivated common land and the existence of the racecourses in the early days seems to have relied more on sporting rights than any modern concept of property law. The Stuart Kings regularly issued edicts and appointed overseers of the game to be found within a huge area around the town aimed at the control of poaching of what was regarded as their property although not based on land they owned or leased.

Eventually, after the Stuarts were replaced by the Hanoverians, the largest freeholder in the area was the Proud Duke of Somerset (Fig. 37) based on Cheveley Park,

Fig. 195

Fig. 196

William, 4th Duke of Portland (1768–1854)

Son of a Prime Minister, the duke inherited land on Racecourse Side and proved a most benevolent landlord to the Jockey Club. He devoted large sums of money and a good deal of his time to improving the Heath, on top of which he funded the purchase of the freehold and the subsequent rebuilding of the Rooms in the 1830s. His most important legacy to the turf in general was to sire Lord George Bentinck (Fig. 62). As an owner he never raced on anything approaching the scale of his son but did at least manage to win a Derby, with Tiresias, in 1819.

John, 5th Duke of Rutland (1778–1857)

A close contemporary of the 4th Duke of Portland, Rutland's estate in the area was much larger and mainly lay on the other side of town. Based on Cheveley Park it encompassed Warren Hill as well as the finish of the Beacon. While the duke lived all was well, but his successor was a much less complacent landlord, having none of the family's traditional interest in racing. Also, like Portland, his main claim to fame as an owner was to win the Derby; this he did with the excellent Cadland in 1828 after a dead-heat, having earlier won the 2000 Guineas. In all, his owner won five classics with only quite a limited string.

an estate extending from the southern part of Warren Hill round to the end of the Beacon Course and the land along the London Road out of the town. The Jockey Club does not seem to have managed to do more than enter into leases until the series of Enclosure Acts for Swaffham Bulbeck (1798), Swaffham Prior (1805) and Exning (1807) made it possible for the various occupiers to sell formerly common land freehold. As a result, by 1819 most of the gallops on Racecourse Side belonged either to the Club or its close allies such as the 4th Duke of Portland, Lord George Bentinck's father. The Enclosure Acts had in any case included provisions which ensured that racing was safe in perpetuity over both courses. Regardless of ownership, the tracks plus a fifty-yard strip either side were always to be available under these provisions so the various vendors would not have been in a position to demand ransom prices. How much was paid for the freeholds that were acquired is not known and the purchases excluded various crucial areas like the finishes on both courses and the early part of the Beacon. The outlay was reduced by the transfer of the area called Bunbury Farm lying in the ring formed by the Round Course. While presumably this was necessary, it eventually had to be bought for £12,000 over a century later from the Allix family of Swaffham House having had its use restricted to sheep in the interim under the sale contract.

The Allix family seems to have been long-term allies of the Club but an even more crucial one was the Duke of Portland (Fig. 195). After the Enclosure Acts he helped by buying property, much of it between the Hamilton Road and the Rowley Mile which is still known as Portland Farm. Unlike the Rutlands at Cheveley he had no big local estate and his interest, which extended to overseeing progress himself, seems to have been the altruistic one of protecting and improving the Heath when to do so was beyond the Club's limited means. In 1842 he offered some 250 acres for £10,000 which the Club could not afford and at some stage the 5th Duke of Rutland (Fig. 196) began expanding on Racecourse Side. However, the main change was the acquisition around this time of the Portland acres by the Exning Estate.

With Newmarket in decline there had been little chance of buying anything for some time, but just before that decline set in the Erratts' sixty-year lease of the Rooms came to an end in 1831. The Club then bought the freehold from them, at a cost of £4,500, but could only do so on the basis of a 4 per cent loan from Portland. Paying the interest was made easier by the fact that the annual sum due to the family of Richard Vernon, also at 4 per cent for the recovery of the original building costs of 1771, had at last expired. Over the years the Vernons had thus collected nearly two and a half times their shrewd forefather's outlay.

When the first stand went up on the Rowley Mile after the 1858 alterations to arrangements by Admiral Rous (see page 181), the local landowners, like the current heads of the Allixes of Swaffham, the Dobedes of Exning and the Tharps of Chippenham, were made honorary members. It must have been a wise move and between 1881 and 1932 all their relevant land came to the Club although it does not look as though it came at a discount.

By 1873 the stronger finances saw Stetchworth Heath acquired from Mr Eaton for £7,000, which was a vital addition as it included the area around the finish of the July Course and the remains of his Plantation are still enjoyed today in the paddock area and behind the stands. On Bury Side the Club remained content with leasing Warren Hill, the Limekilns and Water Hall well into the twentieth century. Probably it had no choice but anyway looks to have treated Racecourse Side as its first priority. Indeed, it was as well it had been husbanding its increasing resources as a potential purchase of major consequence came up which turned out to be the key to the town's future success. In 1881 Mr Dobede decided to sell the entire Exning Estate of 2,867 acres in nine lots. Attempts to buy before auction failed and on 21 July 1881 the Club bought the two principal lots, covering 2,538 acres including the main house. There is a detailed and quite amusing account of the interchanges at the sale between the auctioneer, Mr Stanley, and Mr Fenn, acting for the Club, over promises said to have been given in connection with the linkage between lots. The former seems to have made his point over the promises but the latter got what he wanted from the sale.

In the end some £190,000 had to be found for completion in October and in December the Club convened a meeting to reflect on what it had done. It was then agreed that the whole Newmarket estate must be pledged. The unfunded balance cost the usual 4 per cent interest on a loan from an insurance company. Quite how long it took to repay is uncertain but part was still outstanding until at least 1895. The purchase led to considerable internal reorganisation, beginning with the formation of an Exning Estates Committee. Over time this became transformed in various stages to the Jockey Club Estates company of today.

Odd little additions here and there sometimes came at an extortionate price (for instance in 1884 Pembroke College extracted £120 for each of twenty acres on the Flat) but taken in the round there seems little ground for complaint over the bigger deals. At much the same time rather fraught debates took place with the 6th Duke of Rutland's agents – unlike his ancestors, the Duke had no involvement in racing. His father had never demanded any rent for the crucially important 59 acres he owned around the Beacon finish including the Cricket Pitch but his agent now argued in 1884 that nearly £4,000 was due in back rent since the 5th Duke's death in 1857. Eventually it was accepted that £160 a year would be paid in future with the past forgotten and it took until 1921 for the freehold to be acquired. Occasional purchases were made before the First World War of which the most important was from the estate of a member, Sir Blundell Maple of furniture fame, when his extensive private training grounds linked to Falmouth House were added for £9,500 in 1904. Of that sum £5,000 had to be borrowed from Lord Rothschild.

The early years of ownership at Exning coincided with serious agricultural depression and large annual losses became a real problem. With the value of land tumbling major sales were an unappealing answer but in 1891 it was decided to bite the bullet. An auction was held in June and a total of 1,224 acres was sold in various blocks to realise £69,000. As the sales included Exning House the Club had certainly lost quite badly on its land deal but some of the purchasers were members like Lord Durham acting on their own behalf, and so they were leaving their acquisitions in friendly hands. The house and over 300 acres went to Captain (later Brigadier) E.W. Baird, who was promptly elected a member and remained one for over sixty years. Ned Baird had already won a Grand National as a young man and later took the St Leger with Wool Winder, trained for him by Harry Enoch, who he had set up as a trainer when buying Exning. Despite these sales the Club kept what really mattered in Portland and Southfields Farms and all the land along the Hamilton Road which has since provided space for so many new yards.

Soon after the 1919 purchases of Bunbury Farm for £12,000

from the Allix family, together with an additional bit from the Council for £1,800, came the biggest catch of all. In 1920 Major Dermot McCalmont, owner of The Tetrarch, decided to sell the huge Cheveley Park Estate. He had inherited it from the owner of Isinglass (Fig. 77) who had bought it from the Rutlands in 1892 having rented it for several years but he then died in 1902. Although still a fairly young man, Colonel Harry McCalmont MP's vast expenditure on living at Cheveley on the grand scale appropriate to the place, added to the cost of his racing and political activities, had made quite a large hole in even his immense fortune. Facing agricultural depression for the foreseeable future, his heirs must have been wise to put the whole estate of over 8,000 acres on the market. After protracted negotiations and considerable ill feeling the sale was completed for £300,000 plus another £22,700 for extra land near the present golf course.

The Club could neither afford nor indeed, did it want the whole of the vast tract of land stretching from Warren Hill around the south of the town to the Ditch. After its chastening experience at Exning it clearly did not fancy taking on a farming estate beyond activities incidental to running the Heath itself. However, it most certainly did want over 700 acres on Bury Side and another 400 on either side of the London Road. The whole of the rest was sold on in various deals leaving the Club to find only about £57,000 for land it thought worth over £80,000. Thus, at a cost of under £50 an acre for much of Warren Hill, the Links and some of the Cambridge Hill gallops it is easy to see why Mr Marriott was again congratulated for his efforts at a meeting in April 1922. Even the ill will those efforts seem to have engendered disappeared when the Club eventually elected the vendor as a member after the next war. By that time Marriott had retired after half a century of labour which had transformed the prospects of what he could have been forgiven for regarding as his Heath.

Small purchases and various sales have happened since the Cheveley deal but, with one exception, the important events have been the development of different bits of what was already owned. That exception was the conclusion of the saga which ran for some forty years over the future of the Limekilns and Water Hall Farm, plus Railway Land, part of the Tharp family of Chippenham's estate to the north of Warren Hill. Mr Montagu Tharp who, as mentioned in Chapter 10, seems to have been on poor terms with his tenants died in 1890. Thereafter, intermittent negotiations with Mrs Tharp and her agents over leases and efforts to buy culminated in the purchase of these important gallops for £75,000 in 1932 from Colonel Gerald Tharp. Despite the dire financial climate, finance was not as much of a problem as in the past.

All the acquisitions since the Enclosure Act for Swaffham Bulbeck in 1798 now see the Club owning 4,500 acres in or around the town including 11 yards and other residential properties as well as the Rooms, the two racecourses and the National Stud. Relations between the Club and the local trainers may have been rather fraught at times but now seem to run pretty smoothly and racing in general surely has a good deal to be thankful for in the foresight of those who built the estate at Newmarket which ensures the future of the sport's headquarters.

Racecourse Side

1. Reverend Thomas Mills   Pre-1819
2. The Crown   1819
3. Stetchworth Farm   1873
4. Exning Estate with land acquired separately   1881
5. Beacon Farm   1911
6. Bunbury Farm   1920
7. Cheveley Park Estate   1921
8. Heath Stud Farm   1930
9. Sir William Buchanan-Jardine   1931

BACK OF THE FLAT

THE FLAT

NATIONAL STUD

NATIONAL HUNT TRAINING GROUND

WATER HALL

RAILWAY FIELD

[11]

PRIVATE GROUND

LIMEKILNS

[12]

BURY HILL

LONG HILL

[10]

WARREN HILL

NEW GROUND

SIDE HILL

NEWMARKET

Bury Side

10	Cheveley Park Estate including The Severals	1921
11	Chippenham Estate	1932
12	Earl of Derby	1976

The Jockey Club has acquired land in and around Newmarket since the 18th Century. This simplified map shows when the main parcels of land were added to the Estate and the vendor.

N

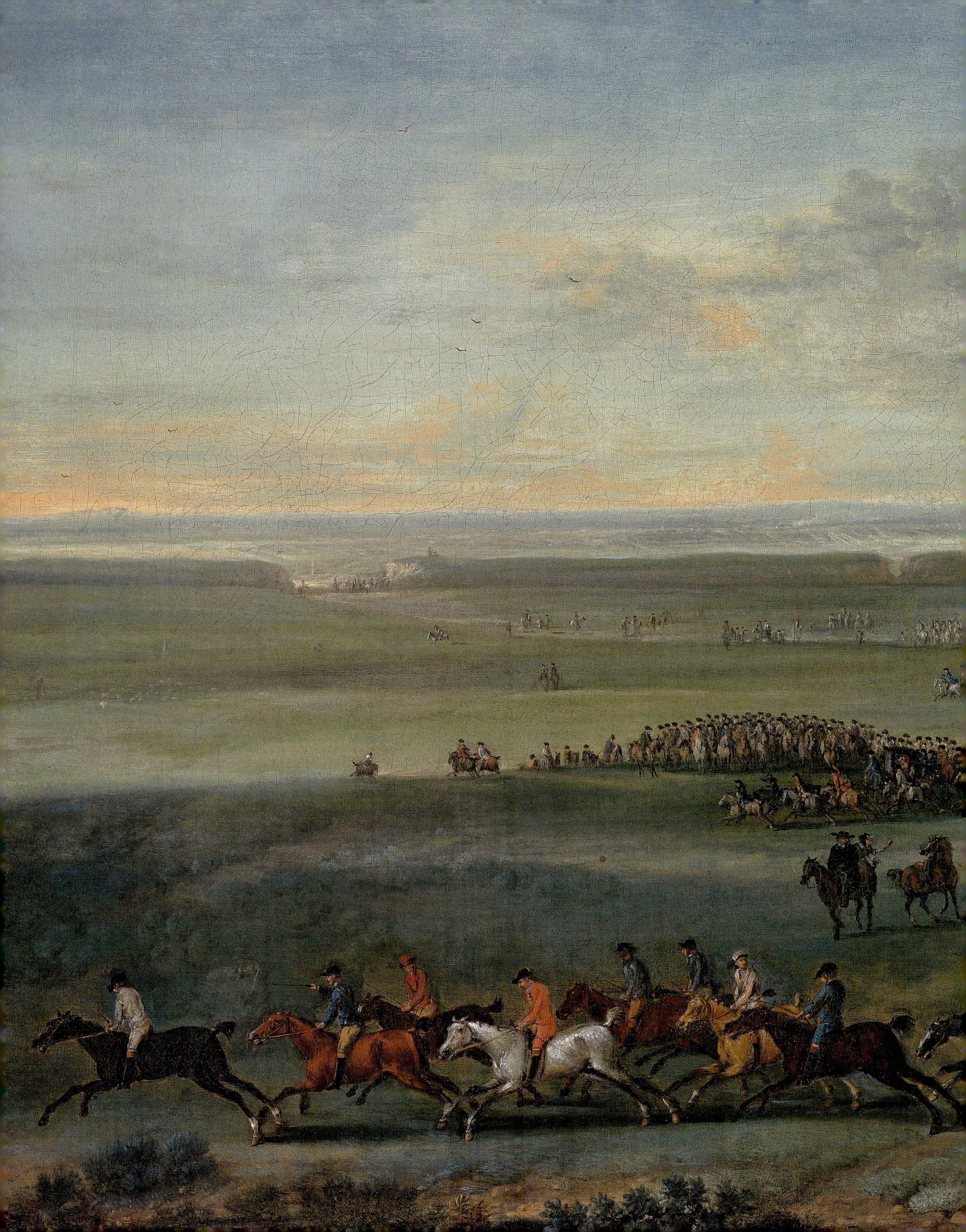

Part Four

Appendices

Appendix One deals with the names of all the courses on the Heath and gives the period when they were in use as well as a background to their titles. It is divided between those on the original Long Course starting near Balsham followed by the Old Cambridgeshire Course across the middle of the present gallops. Finally come the list of courses on the original Round Course of Charles II, and the little used Sefton and Duke's Courses.

APPENDIX ONE
DATES OF USE AND DISTANCES OF THOSE COURSES WHICH HAD NAMES

	Name	Initials	Dates	Distance	Background
1	**LONG COURSE**		Early 17th to mid 18th century	8 miles	Earliest known course ending at King's Stand with 7, 6 and 5 mile starts.
a	Beacon	BC	Early 17th century to 1912	4 miles	Named for Beacon site near to start
b	Last 3 miles of Beacon		1750 to 1912	About 3 miles	Same start as (c) but continuing to King's Stand
c	Cesarewitch	Ces	1839 to date	2m2f	Named for Alexander II before becoming Tsar and race sponsored by him until 1849
d	Two Middle Miles	TMM	1793 to 1959	Almost 2 miles	Ces start to Bushes so central part of BC
e	Ditch In	DI	1760 to 1912	About 2 miles	Running Gap to King's Stand so name is descriptive
f	Audley End Course (ver 1)	AEC	1809	Over 14 furlongs	Running Gap to Green Post (after Duke's Stand), named for house near Saffron Walden
g	Clermont Course		1793 to 1858	About 14 furlongs	Running Gap to Duke's Stand; named for 1st Earl Clermont
h	Across the Flat	AF	1793 to date	10 furlongs	Running Gap to present finish; name topographical
i	Ditch Mile	DM	1786 to 1912	About 1 mile	Running Gap to Bushes; name topographical
j	Audley End Course (ver 2)	AEC	1811 to 1912	Over 15 furlongs	Cambs start to King's Stand; named after house near Saffron Walden
k	Cambridgeshire Course	Cambs	1888 to date	9 furlongs	Cambs start to present finish; race moved from former course in 1888
l	Abingdon Mile	AbM	1776 to 1959	About 1 mile	Cambs start to dip; named for 4th Earl of Abingdon
m	Two-year-Old Course	TYC	1790 to 1930	Over 5.5 furlongs	Cambs start to dip before Bushes, descriptive of main use
n	Peel Course		1883 to 1959	6 furlongs	Slightly extended version of TYC; named for General Peel
o	Yearling Course		1790 to 1881	Over 2 furlongs	Cambs start to starting post of Bretby Stakes Course; descriptive of use
p	Fox's Course		1786 to 1809	About 14 furlongs	RM start to King's Stand; named for Charles James Fox
q	Old Champion Stakes Course		1850 to 1858	About 12 furlongs	RM start to Duke's Stand; short-lived early version of later race
r	Rowley Mile	RM	Late 17th century to date	8 furlongs	RM start to present finish; Charles II's nickname thought to be derived from that of a favourite horse
s	Dewhurst Stakes Course	Dew	1882 to date	7 furlongs	Last 7 furlongs of Rowley Mile; named for Thomas Gee's Stud (original sponsor)
t	Bretby Stakes Course		1853 to date	6 furlongs	Last 6 furlongs of RM; named after house of 6th Earl of Chesterfield
u	Rous Course		1871 to date	5 furlongs	Last 5 furlongs of RM; named for Admiral Rous

	Notes
1	The opening dates refer to the naming of each course but in some cases there was an earlier unnamed course
2	Closing dates mark the formal abandonment of courses but actual usage will often have ceased considerably earlier
3	Some of the distances changed slightly over the years, often due to remeasurement rather than alterations

Appendix One

4		Some courses used occasionally were identified only by the starts and finishes of other courses. Those never given a name have been excluded from Table A as have unnamed courses used today such as that over 12 furlongs on the Rowley Mile Course			
5		Originally some of the older courses named in honour of individuals were spelt by contemporaries with apostrophes as in Rowley's Mile but this usage is now archaic.			
	Name	**Initials**	**Dates**	**Distance**	**Background**
2	**OLD CAMBRIDGESHIRE COURSE**		1843 to 1912	Over 9 furlongs	Extension of Ancaster Mile finishing at King's Stand
a	Ancaster Mile		1774 to 1912	Over 1 mile	Straight mile to King's Stand; named for 4th Duke of Ancaster
b	Bedford Stakes Course		1885 to 1858	Nearly 6 furlongs	From the start of (a) to Duke's Stand; named for 7th Duke of Bedford
c	Criterion Stakes Course		1853 to 1912	Nearly 6 furlongs	Originally known as 'From Turn of the Lands In' which was descriptive of the place where village lands met at an angle
	Notes				
1	The Bedford Stakes was transferred to the Rowley Mile in 1860 after the Duke's Stand was pulled down and run over 5 furlongs. The course was then known as the Bedford Stakes Course but renamed for the Duke's racing confederate Admiral Rous in 1871 by which time the Bedford Stakes had moved to the Bretby Stakes Course.				
2	Although not formally shut until 1912 in fact the last races were run over this course in October 1903 when the final running of the Criterion Stakes saw things brought to a fitting conclusion with a win for the great Pretty Polly				
	Name	**Initials**	**Dates**	**Distance**	**Background**
3	**ROUND COURSE**	RC	1666 to 1810	Over 3 miles 6 furlongs	Charles II's course closed in 1810 for alterations
a	New Round Course	RC	1819 to 1959	Over 3 miles 4 furlongs	Reopened with start at Well Gap and no loop beyond BC but not used after 1873 for races under rules
b	Summer Course		1853 to date	2 miles	Start on old BC just before Ces to July Course finish
c	Sufffolk Stakes Course		1853 to date	12 furlongs	As for (b) less half a mile
d	Ellesmere Course		1889 to 1959	11 furlongs	As for (c) but ending in dip; named for 1st Earl of Ellesmere
e	Bunbury Mile	BM	1772 to date	1 mile	As for (c) but another half mile less; named for Sir Charles Bunbury
f	Beaufort Stakes Course		1884 to 1961	7 furlongs	As for (e) but ending in dip; named for 8th Duke of Beaufort
g	Exeter Stakes Course		1883 to 1961	6 furlongs	Start at 7 furlong post but ending in dip; named for 2nd Marquess of Exeter
h	New Two-Year-Old Course	New TYC	1882 to 1961	About 5.5 furlongs	As for (g) but about 80 yards shorter ending in dip
i	Chesterfield Stakes Course		1882 to date	5 furlongs	Last part of BM; named for 6th Earl of Chesterfield
j	Old Chesterfield Stakes Course		1853 to 1881	4 furlongs	Shorter version of (i)
4	**SEFTON COURSE**	Sef	1959 to 1973	Various	As no distances had separate names detail is unnecessary; named for 7th Earl of Sefton
5	**DUKE'S COURSE**	DC	Late 17th century to 1806	4 miles +	Running across the RC and following the RM to the King's Stand. It effectively linked the two main courses; named for Duke of York, later James II
a	Dutton's Course		1793 to 1807	3 miles	Last part of Duke's Course; named for Ralph Dutton, brother of 1st Lord Sherborne

321

APPENDIX TWO

Tables of the starts and finishes on the Heath and the distances between them. Table 1 deals with the Beacon and so includes the whole of the present racecourse used for the Cesarewitch. It is based on the position in 1853, when the Beacon was still in occasional use. Table 2 sets out the use made of the present Cesarewitch Course while Table 3 bases the details on 1939 for the July Course, since when the only significant change has been the abandonment of the first winning post set in the dip a furlong out. Tables 4, 5 and 6 cover the defunct courses known as the Old Cambridgeshire Course, the Sefton Course and the Duke's Course, dropped respectively in 1912, 1973 and 1806.

DISTANCES BETWEEN THE STARTS AND FINISHES ON THE VARIOUS COURSES

1. STARTS AND FINISHES ON THE BEACON (NOW THE ROWLEY MILE COURSE)

(Based primarily on 1853 measurements - the initials indicating some courses are shown in full

		Distance from start			Distance from King's Stand		
		Miles	Furlongs	Yards	Miles	Furlongs	Yards
	Length of Beacon Course in 1853	-	-	-	4	1	173
1	BC start to start Cesarewitch, TMM and last 3 miles of the BC	1	1	99	1	1	99
		1	1	99	3	0	74
2	From (1) to the Running Gap being the start of AF, DM, DI and Clermont Courses		7	175		7	175
		2	1	54	1	7	56
3	From (2) to the start of AbM, TYC and New Audley End (later moved slightly for Cambridgeshire)		1	63		1	63
		2	2	117	1	7	56
4	From (3) to start of RM and the Old Champion Stakes Course			213			213
		2	3	110	1	6	63
5	From (4) to start for Bretby Stakes Course		2	17		2	17
		2	5	127	1	4	46
6	From (5) to mid-point in AbM (now the 5 furlong or Rous start)			215			215
		2	6	122	1	3	51
7	From (6) to finish of TYC		1	135		1	135
		3	0	37	1	1	136
8	From (7) to finish of DM and TMM at the Bushes			218			218
		3	1	35	1	0	138
9	From (8) to finish of BM in dip		1	74		1	74
		3	2	109		7	64
10	From (9) to finish of AF, RM, Cesarewitch and Bretby Stakes Courses at the present finish		1	18		1	18

322

Appendix Two

		3	3	127		6	46
11	From (10) to Turn of the Lands being start of Criterion Stakes Course			84			84
		3	3	127		6	46
12	From (11) to Duke's Stand being the finish of the Clermont and Old Champion Courses		3	118		3	118
		3	7	109		2	64
13	From (12) to Green Post being the finish of the Old Audley End Course			159			159
		4	0	48		1	125
14	From (13) to the King's Stand being the finish for the BC, DI, last 3 miles of BC, Criterion and New Audley End Stakes (plus various races on the Old Cambridgeshire Course		1	125		1	125
	Overall length of the Beacon in 1853	4	1	173	-	-	-

Note: Distances beyond the start of the Beacon had been abandoned soon after 1730 but there were starting posts set at eight, seven, six and five miles from the King's Stand. There are no records of finishes on this part of the course.

2. STARTS AND FINISHES ON THE CESAREWITCH COURSE TODAY

		Distance from start			Distance from finish		
		Miles	Furlongs	Yards	Miles	Furlongs	Yards
	Length of Cesarewitch Course today	-	-	-	2	2	0
1	Cesarewitch start to 2 miles start		2	0	2	2	0
		2	0	0	2	0	0
2	From (1) to 14 furlong start		2	0		2	0
			4	0	1	6	0
3	From (2) to 12 furlong start		2	0		2	0
			6	0	1	4	0
4	From (3) to start of Across the Flat		2	0		2	0
		1	0	0	1	2	0
5	From (4) to start of Cambridgeshire Course		1	0		1	0
		1	1	0	1	1	0
6	From (5) to start of Rowley Mile		1	0		1	0
		1	2	0	1	0	0
7	From (6) to start of Dewhurst Stakes Course		1	0		1	0
		1	3	0		7	0
8	From (7) to start of Bretby Stakes Course		1	0	1	1	0
		1	4	0		6	0
9	From (8) to start of Rous Course		1	0		1	0
		1	5	0		5	0
10	From (9) to finish of Rowley Mile		5	0		5	0
	Overall length of Cesarewitch Course	2	2	0	-	-	-

3. STARTS AND FINISHES ON THE JULY COURSE (FORMERLY THE ROUND COURSE)

(Based primarily on 1939 measurements)

		Distance from start			Distance from Thomond's Post		
		Miles	Furlongs	Yards	Miles	Furlongs	Yards
	Length of the course in 1939	-	-	-	3	4	138
1	Thomond's Post to start of Summer Course	1	4	114	1	4	114
		1	4	139	2	0	0
2	From (1) to the start of the Suffolk and Ellesmere Stakes Courses		4	24		4	24
		2	0	138	1	4	0
3	From (2) to the start of the Bunbury Mile and Beaufort Stakes Course		4	0		4	0
		2	4	138	1	0	0
4	From (3) to the start of Exeter Stakes Course		1	0		1	0
		2	5	138	1	0	0
5	From (4) to the start of the New TYC			80			80
		2	5	218		6	140
6	From (5) to the start of the Chesterfield Stakes Course		1	140		1	140
		2	7	138		5	0
7	From (6) to the end of the New TYC, Ellesmere, Beaufort and Exeter Stakes Courses		4	0		4	0
		3	3	138		1	0
8	From (7) to Thomond's Post at the present finish of the Bunbury Mile and Chesterfield Stakes Courses		1	0		1	0
	Overall length of the Round Course in 1939	3	4	138	-	-	-

Note: In fact the Round Course has not been used since the nineteenth century and the precise position of Thomond's Post, which marked the start and finish in the seventeenth century, is to a degree uncertain.

4. STARTS AND FINISHES ON THE OLD CAMBRIDGESHIRE COURSE

(Based primarily on 1853 measurements)

		Distance from start			Distance from King's Stand		
		Miles	Furlongs	Yards	Miles	Furlongs	Yards
	Length of Old Cambridgeshire Course in 1853	-	-	-	1	1	020
1	From start to beginning of the Ancaster Mile		1	002		1	002
			1	002	1	0	018
2	From (1) Turn of the Lands and start for Criterion, Rutland and Granby Stakes		2	056		2	056
			3	058		5	182

3	From (2) to the Old Betting Post (a 19th Century start)		2	129		2	129
			5	187		3	053
4	From (3) to the King's Stand being the finish for the Old Cambridgeshire, the Ancaster Mile and Criterion Stakes Courses as well as others on the Beacon Course (Table A)		3	053		3	053
	Overall length of Old Cambridgeshire Course	1	1	020	-	-	-

5. STARTS AND FINISHES ON THE SEFTON COURSE (ABANDONED 1973)
(1959 to 1973)

		Distance from start			Distance from finish		
		Miles	Furlongs	Yards	Miles	Furlongs	Yards
	Length of Sefton Course	-	-	-	2	0	0
1	From beginning to 14 furlongs start		2	0		2	0
			2	0	1	6	0
2	Turn of the Lands to 12 furlongs		1	120		1	120
			3	120	1	4	100
3	From (2) to 10 furlongs		2	100		2	100
			6	0	1	2	0
4	From (3) to finish at the present winning post on the Rowley Mile	1	2	0	1	2	0
	Overall length of Sefton Course	2	0	0	-	-	-

6. STARTS AND FINISHES ON THE DUKE'S COURSE
(Based on 1806 measurements after which the course was abandoned)

		Distance from start			Distance from finish		
		Miles	Furlongs	Yards	Miles	Furlongs	Yards
	Length of Duke's Course	-	-	-	4	0	184
1	From beginning to start of Dutton's Course	1	0	184	1	0	184
		1	0	184	3	0	0
2	From (1) to the finish at the King's Stand	3	0	0	3	0	0
	Overall length of the Duke's Course	4	0	184	-	-	-

APPENDIX THREE

List of the leading Newmarket trainers each year since 1899 by earnings and by number of races won (where the leader by earning was national champion a (c) appears).

	BY VALUE		Races	£		BY NUMBER OF WINS	Wins	
1899	J. Huggins		72	£42,799	Heath House	J. Huggins	72	Heath House
1900	Richard Marsh	c	31	£43,321	Egerton House	E. Wishard	54	Red House Stables
1901	J. Huggins	c	42	£29,142	Heath House	W. Waugh	58	Falmouth House
1902	Richard Marsh		22	£21,998	Egerton House	W. Waugh	67	Falmouth House
1903	George Blackwell	c	24	£34,136	Lagrange	W. Waugh	58	Falmouth House
1904	P P Gilpin	c	44	£35,695	Clarehaven	A. Sadler, junior	45	Freemason Lodge
1905	P P Gilpin		38	£27,132	Clarehaven	Hon G Lambton	25	Stanley House
1906	Hon G Lambton	c	46	£34,069	Stanley House	Hon G Lambton	46	Stanley House
1907	Hon G Lambton		34	£13,401	Stanley House	R. Sherwood	46	St Gatien House
1908	P P Gilpin		25	£19,494	Clarehaven	R. Sherwood	37	St Gatien House
1909	Richard Marsh		16	£20,757	Egerton House	R. Sherwood	40	St Gatien House
1910	Hon G Lambton		54	£24,765	Stanley House	Hon G Lambton	54	Stanley House
1911	Hon G Lambton	c	47	£49,548	Stanley House	Hon G Lambton / J Butters	47	Stanley House / Kremlin House
1912	Hon G Lambton	c	55	£22,887	Stanley House	Hon G Lambton	55	Stanley House
1913	Hon G Lambton		53	£24,673	Stanley House	Hon G Lambton	53	Stanley House
1914	Hon G Lambton		35	£14,666	Stanley House	Hon G Lambton	35	Stanley House

1915	P P Gilpin	c	12	£15,324	Clarehaven	R C Dawson	29	Note 1
1916	R C Dawson	c	32	£16,477	Note 1	R C Dawson	32	Note 1
1917	Hon G Lambton		26	£10,958	Stanley House	Hon G Lambton	26	Stanley House
1918	Hon G Lambton		23	£12,045	Stanley House	Hon G Lambton	23	Stanley House
1919	F B Barling		44	£30,242	Falmouth House	Hon G Lambton	66	Stanley House
1920	Hon G Lambton		57	£27,915	Stanley House	Hon G Lambton	57	Stanley House
1921	Hon G Lambton		37	£23,533	Stanley House	Jack Jarvis	39	Park Lodge
1922	Hon G Lambton		56	£38,440	Stanley House	Hon G Lambton	56	Stanley House
1923	Hon G Lambton		43	£37,920	Stanley House	Hon G Lambton	43	Stanley House
1924	Hon G Lambton		61	£48,256	Stanley House	Hon G Lambton	61	Stanley House
1925	Walter Earl		48	£35,894	Moulton Paddocks	Walter Earl	48	Moulton Paddocks
1926	Hon G Lambton		55	£46,208	Stanley House	Hon G Lambton	55	Stanley House
1927	Frank Butters	c	54	£57,468	Stanley House	Frank Butters	54	Stanley House
1928	Frank Butters	c	50	£67,539	Stanley House	Frank Butters	50	Stanley House
1929	Frank Butters		60	£35,861	Stanley House	Frank Butters	60	Stanley House
1930	Frank Butters		60	£41,418	Stanley House	Frank Butters	60	Stanley House
1931	Jack Jarvis		43	£32,849	Park Lodge	R J Colling	58	Ellesmere House
1932	Frank Butters	c	62	£72,436	Fitzroy House	Frank Butters	62	Fitzroy House
1933	Frank Butters		65	£42,573	Fitzroy House	Frank Butters	65	Fitzroy House
1934	Frank Butters	c	79	£88,844	Fitzroy House	Frank Butters	79	Fitzroy House
1935	Frank Butters	c	48	£59,687	Fitzroy House	Frank Butters	48	Fitzroy House

	BY VALUE		Races	£		**BY NUMBER OF WINS**	Wins	
1936	Cecil Boyd Rochfort		42	£54,265	Freemason Lodge	R J Colling	57	Ellesmere House
1937	Cecil Boyd Rochfort	c	43	£61,212	Freemason Lodge	Frank Butters	57	Fitzroy House
1938	Cecil Boyd Rochfort	c	44	£52,350	Freemason Lodge	R J Colling	58	Ellesmere House
1939	Jack Jarvis	c	34	£56,219	Park Lodge	R J Colling	40	Ellesmere House
1940	Frank Butters		13	£4,757	Fitzroy House	Jack Jarvis	14	Park Lodge
1941	Cecil Boyd Rochfort		9	£6,669	Freemason Lodge	Jack Jarvis	19	Park Lodge
1942	Walter Earl		19	£8,892	Stanley House	Jack Jarvis	23	Park Lodge
						Frank Butters		Fitzroy House
1943	Frank Butters		23	£8,360	Fitzroy House	Frank Butters	23	Fitzroy House
1944	Frank Butters	c	34	£17,585	Fitzroy House	Frank Butters	34	Fitzroy House
1945	Walter Earl	c	41	£29,557	Stanley House	Walter Earl	41	Stanley House
1946	Frank Butters	c	61	£56,478	Fitzroy House	Frank Butters	60	Fitzroy House
1947	Frank Butters		43	£57,867	Fitzroy House	R J Colling	60	Ellesmere Lodge
1948	Frank Butters		39	£50,883	Fitzroy House	R J Colling	46	Ellesmere Lodge
1949	Frank Butters	c	42	£71,422	Fitzroy House	Jack Jarvis	48	Park Lodge
1950	Marcus Marsh		36	£56,180	Fitzroy House	Jack Jarvis	48	Park Lodge
1951	Jack Jarvis	c	62	£56,464	Park Lodge	Jack Jarvis	62	Park Lodge
1952	Marcus Marsh	c	30	£92,093	Fitzroy House	Jack Jarvis	60	Park Lodge
1953	Jack Jarvis	c	60	£71,545	Park Lodge	Jack Jarvis	60	Park Lodge
1954	Cecil Boyd Rochfort	c	39	£65,326	Freemason Lodge	Jack Jarvis	61	Park Lodge

1955	Cecil Boyd Rochfort	c	38	£74,524	Freemason Lodge	Geoffrey Brooke	59	Clarehaven Lodge
1956	Cecil Boyd Rochfort		32	£46,290	Freemason Lodge	Geoffrey Brooke	49	Clarehaven Lodge
1957	Noel Murless	c	48	£116,898	Warren Place	Noel Murless	48	Warren Place
1958	Cecil Boyd Rochfort	c	37	£84,186	Freemason Lodge	Jack Jarvis	69	Park lodge
1959	Noel Murless	c	63	£145,727	Warren Place	Noel Murless	63	Warren Place
1960	Noel Murless	c	42	£118,327	Warren Place	Geoffrey Brooke	57	Clarehaven Lodge
1961	Noel Murless	c	36	£95,977	Warren Place	Geoffrey Brooke	61	Clarehaven Lodge
1962	Dick Hern	c	39	£70,206	Lagrange	Fred Armstrong	65	St. Gatien
1963	Noel Murless		42	£55,467	Warren Place	Fred Armstrong	59	St. Gatien
1964	Jack Watts		19	£67,236	Fairway House	Jack Jarvis	54	Park Lodge
1965	Noel Murless		35	£54,974	Warren Place	Fred Armstrong	76	St. Gatien
1966	Noel Murless		49	£92,285	Warren Place	Fred Armstrong	70	St. Gatien
1967	Noel Murless	c	60	£256,899	Warren Place	Fred Armstrong	68	St. Gatien
1968	Noel Murless	c	47	£141,508	Warren Place	Ryan Jarvis	51	Phantom House
1969	Doug Smith		63	£94,792	Park Lodge	Doug Smith	63	Park lodge
1970	Noel Murless	c	53	£199,524	Warren Place	Doug Smith	65	Park lodge
1971	Noel Murless		63	£154,259	Warren Place	Doug Smith	74	Park lodge
1972	Bernard van Cutsem		49	£105,751	Stanley House Stables	Bruce Hobbs	55	Palace House
1973	Noel Murless	c	34	£132,984	Warren Place	Paul Davey	67	Clarehaven Lodge
1974	Bruce Hobbs		45	£86,721	Palace House	Robert Armstrong	51	St. Gatien
1975	Henry Cecil		82	£205,345	Marriott Stables	Henry Cecil	82	Marriott Stables

	BY VALUE		Races	£		BY NUMBER OF WINS	Wins	
1976	Henry Cecil	c	52	£261,301	Marriott Stables	Michael Stoute	62	Beech Hurst
1977	Henry Cecil		74	£168,888	Warren Place	Henry Cecil	74	Warren Place
1978	Henry Cecil	c	109	£382,301	Warren Place	Henry Cecil	109	Warren Place
1979	Henry Cecil	c	128	£683,971	Warren Place	Henry Cecil	128	Warren Place
1980	Henry Cecil		84	£461,036	Warren Place	Michael Stoute	101	Beech Hurst
1981	Michael Stoute	c	95	£723,783	Beech Hurst	Henry Cecil	107	Warren Place
1982	Henry Cecil	c	111	£872,614	Warren Place	Henry Cecil	111	Warren Place
1983	Henry Cecil		92	£440,022	Warren Place	Henry Cecil	92	Warren Place
1984	Henry Cecil	c	108	£551,939	Warren Place	Henry Cecil	108	Warren Place
1985	Henry Cecil	c	132	£1,148,189	Warren Place	Henry Cecil	132	Warren Place
1986	Michael Stoute	c	76	£1,269,933	Beech Hurst	Henry Cecil	115	Warren Place
1987	Henry Cecil	c	180	£1,882,314	Warren Place	Henry Cecil	180	Warren Place
1988	Henry Cecil	c	112	£1,186,083	Warren Place	Henry Cecil	112	Warren Place
1989	Michael Stoute	c	117	£1,469,171	Freemason Lodge	Michael Stoute	117	Freemason Lodge
1990	Henry Cecil	c	111	£1,519,864	Warren Place	Henry Cecil	111	Warren Place
1991	Michael Stoute		83	£825,838	Freemason Lodge	Henry Cecil	118	Warren Place
1992	Clive Brittain		63	£972,327	Carlburg	Henry Cecil	109	Warren Place
1993	Henry Cecil	c	94	£1,248,318	Warren Place	John Gosden	109	Stanley House Stables
1994	Michael Stoute (note 2)	c	109	£1,913,026	Freemason Lodge	Michael Stoute	108	Freemason Lodge
1995	Saeed bin Suroor		14	£1,877,486	Godolphin Office	John Gosden	86	Stanley House Stables

Year	Trainer		Wins	Stakes	Yard	Trainer	Wins	Yard
1996	Saeed bin Suroor	c	48	£1,932,235	Godolphin Office	Henry Cecil	113	Warren Place
1997	Michael Stoute	c	84	£2,009,436	Freemason Lodge	John Gosden	91	Stanley House Stables
1998	Saeed bin Suroor	c	38	£2,214,651	Godolphin Office	Henry Cecil	100	Warren Place
1999	Saeed bin Suroor	c	40	£2,643,088	Godolphin Office	Sir Michael Stoute	81	Freemason Lodge
2000	Sir Michael Stoute	c	91	£2,807,216	Freemason Lodge	Sir Michael Stoute	91	Freemason Lodge
2001	Sir Michael Stoute		75	£1,967,583	Freemason Lodge	Sir Michael Stoute	75	Freemason Lodge
2002	Sir Michael Stoute		105	£2,263,315	Freemason Lodge	Sir Michael Stoute	105	Freemason Lodge
2003	Sir Michael Stoute	c	115	£3,608,776	Freemason Lodge	Sir Michael Stoute	115	Freemason Lodge
2004	Saeed bin Suroor	c	115	£4,146,844	Godolphin Office	Saeed Bin Suroor	115	Godolphin Office
2005	Sir Michael Stoute	c	95	£2,110,528	Freemason Lodge	Sir Michael Stoute	95	Freemason Lodge
2006	Sir Michael Stoute	c	107	£2,837,612	Freemason Lodge	Sir Michael Stoute	107	Freemason Lodge
2007	Sir Michael Stoute		113	£2,400,234	Freemason Lodge	Sir Michael Stoute	113	Freemason Lodge
2008	Sir Michael Stoute		88	£2,521,539	Freemason Lodge	Michael Jarvis	100	Kremlin House
2009	Sir Michael Stoute	c	99	£3,296,912	Freemason Lodge	Saeed Bin Suroor	148	Godolphin Office
2010	Sir Michael Stoute		73	£2,797,412	Freemason Lodge	John Gosden	105	Stanley House Stables
2011	Sir Henry Cecil		55	£2,623,303	Warren Place	John Gosden	99	Stanley House Stables
2012	John Gosden	c	119	£3,505,346	Stanley House Stables	John Gosden	119	Stanley House Stables
2013	Saeed bin Suroor		106	£2,458,615	Godolphin Office	John Gosden	108	Stanley House Stables
2014	John Gosden		132	£3,927,739	Stanley House Stables	John Gosden	132	Stanley House Stables

Note 1 – Richard Dawson was champion due to training Fifinella in Newmarket to win both the Derby and the Oaks for Edward Hulton. However he also retained his own yard at Whatcombe. The leading wholly local trainer in 1916 was George Lambton at Stanley House with 21 wins worth £13,778.
Note 2 – Since 1994 place money (1-2-3) has been included as that is the basis on which the national championship is decided.
Note 3 – In terms of money the leading trainer on most occasions in this period was Sir Henry Cecil in 17 years and the yard most successful has been Warren Place 25 times. The most successful trainer by stakes won is Sir Michael Stoute (16 times) and Stanley House's stables have the most years by wins with 28 including one dead heat.

Index

All horses are listed under heading 'horses'. Races and courses are treated the same way. Page numbers in italics are figures.

acquisition of the Heath 311–15
Acts of Parliament,
    1740 Act 43, 45, 55, 296, 302
    1879 Act 109
    Betting and Gaming Act (1960) 144, 147
    Horse-Racing Bill (1739) 283, 290–1
Adam, Emil *112–13*, 113
    La Flèche at the Cambridgeshire start 114, 196
    Ormonde with Fred Archer and John Porter 110
Aga Khan III 125, *125*, 128, 130, 164, 237, 238–9
Al Thani family 164
all-weather tracks 159
America 39, 65, 116, 119–20, 129, 236
American seat *113*, 115, 116
Amos, Peter 159
Ancaster, Peregrine, 2nd Duke of 57, *57*–8

Anderson, George 109
Anne, Queen 25, 35, 37, 268
Anscomb, R., *Meld 140 Pinza 140*
Arabians 8, 14, 26, 33, 35, 286
Archer, Fred *9*, 92, 107, 110–11, *110–11*, 116, 249
Armstrong, Robert 150
Armstrong, Sam 137
Articles of the City Bowl at Salisbury *21*
Articles related to the Newmarket Town Plate *27*
Astley Club (later New Astley, and now the Racing Centre) 121, 166
Astley, Sir John 121, 166, 181
Astor, Sir Jakie 144
Astor, Waldorf, 3rd Viscount 144
Atzeni, Andrea 164
auctioneers 65, 69, 164, 166

Baird, Captain E.W. 314
Barbs 14, 20, 33
Barlow, Francis *29*
Barrett, George 110, *114*
Beacon Course *1*, *4*, 6, 43, 56, 193, *202*–5, 213
    buildings 98–9, *100–1*, 171,

173–9, *174–7*
Bedford, Francis, 5th Duke of 70, *72*, 73, 258
Bell, Michael 139
Benson, Martin 234
Benson, Sir Henry (later Lord Benson) 142, 153
Bentinck, Lord George 89, 93–5, *94*, 97, 260, 312
Beresford, Lord Marcus 114
Bertie, Norman 141
betting 66, 133, 153, 288
    and data rights payment 160–1
    Gimcrack and Ascham race 62
    and the Newmarket Bank 292–5
    see also Acts of Parliament; Levy Board; Tote
betting enclosures, Rowley Mile course 173, 180–1
Betting and Gaming Act (1960) 144, 147
betting posts 179–80, *179*, 205
Betting Ring 181
Betts, Samuel 224, *227*
Bin Suroor, Saeed *151*, 155, 164
Birdcage 173, 180, *182*, 182, 185, *205*

Black, Robert 274
Blackwell, Tom 150
bleeding of horses 78
Bloss, George 108
Boadicea, Queen 14–15
Bolingbroke, Frederick, 2nd Viscount 65, *68*, 74, 82
Bolton, Charles, 3rd Duke of 45, 52, 280–1, 283
bookmakers 66, 97, 292–5
    see also betting; Tote
Botti, Marco 164
Boyce, Dixon 90
Boyd-Rochfort, Captain Sir Cecil 137, *138*, 140–1
Bramwell, Michael 240
British Horseracing Authority (BHA) 149, 157–8, 160, 162
British Horseracing Board (BHB) 8, 143, 148, 156–7, 160, 161
British Racing School (BRS) 156, 166
Buckingham, George, 1st Duke of 19, *19*, 20
Buckingham, George, 2nd Duke of 27
Buckle, Frank 47, *90*, 91, 217–18
Buckle, Samuel 47, 90

Budgell, Eustace 281, 287
buildings *30*, 171–3
   stables/rubbing houses *170, 174, 178*, 192–4, *194*
   stands/weighing rooms 173–9, *174–80*, 180–7, *182–90*, 187–91, *192–3*, 209
Bull, Phil 156
Bunbury, Sir Charles 65, 71, *71*, 89–90, 97, 213, 217–18
Burney, E. F., *Warren Hill 2*
Burrell, Peter 236, 237, 239–40
Burrell, Sir Merryk 236
'Bushing the Gallops' 244
Butler, R.A. (later Lord Butler) 144
Butters, Frank 118, 125, *130*
Byerley, Captain Robert 35

Cannon, Joe 115
Cannon, Kempton 113, *113*
Cannon, Mornington 111, *112*, 113
Cannon, Tom 110
Cauthen, Steve *152*, 164
Cavendish, Lord James 287
Cecil, Sir Henry 137, 138, 147, 150, *150*, 163, 237
Chaplin, Henry (later Lord Chaplin) 238
Chapman, John 98, 175
Charles I 19, 20, *20*, 22, 23, 230–1
   as Prince of Wales 267
Charles II 24, 25, 27–8, *28–9*, 30–1, 210–11, 275, 280, 306
   King's Plate 304
   and the Palace *18*, 267–8
   scandalous activities 32
Cheny, John 41, 42, 210, 249, 284, 302, 305
   Historical List 282, 286
Chesterfield, George, 6th Earl of 217
Chetwynd, Sir George 119
Cheveley Park 59, 115, 127, 207, 270, 311, 313, 315, *317*
Chifney, Sam, senior *6*, 70, 71, 86, *87*
Chifney, Sam, junior 90, 91, *91*
Chifney, Will 91, *91*
Chisom, William 239
Choke Jade 246
Churchill, Sir Winston 134
City Bowl at Salisbury 21–2, *21*
Civil War 20, 22, 23, 230–1, 266
Clark, John 222, *223*, 263, 265, 290
Clarke, Sir Stanley 158
Clayton, Jack 143
Clermont, William, 1st Earl of 217
Coffee House 46, 47, 285, 287, 293
Coffee Room 46, 59, 269, 306–8, 311
Coke, Edward 42
colours 74, 78, 82, 97
Cooper, Abraham, *Elis and The Drummer at Lichfield* 97
Cooper Brothers 96, 157
Corals 214
Cotton, Sir John *24*, 26, 27
Cottrill, Humphrey 164
courses,
   Aintree 115, 126
   Ascot 37, 134, 167, 212–13, 216, 219, 221
   Canterbury 56
   Cheltenham 115, 148, 159
   Datchet 29
   Doncaster 37, 123
   Epsom 37, 45
   Gatwick 123, 126
   Goodwood 37, 93, 94, 95
   Haydock 115, 158, 159
   York 37, 45, 55
courses at Newmarket,
   Ancaster Mile Course 173, 204–5
   Cambridgeshire *204–5*, 206
   Cesarewitch 200, 207, *208–9*
   Duke's 206
   Long Course *192–3*, 200–1, 311
   National Hunt (or The Links) 115, 207, *209*, 231, 247, 248, 315
   Round Course 27, 44, *48–9*, 52, *53*, 74, 127, 200–1, *202–3*, *208*, 210–11, *211*, 246
   Sefton Course 206, *209*
   Summer Course 190
   see also Appendix 1 and 2 321–5
   see also Beacon; buildings; July Course; Rowley Mile

Craven, Fulwar 196, *199*
Crockford, William 269
Cromwell, Oliver *8*, 22, 25, 27, 231
'Cross and Jostle' 82
Cullin, Isaac,
   Cyllene in the Birdcage 185
   Flying Fox in the July Course paddock 188
Cumberland, William Augustus, Duke of 43, *54*, 56, 57, 59, *61*, 62, 78, 268, *300*
   and the Duke's Stand 175, *176*
Cumani, Luca 164

Darcy, James 25
Darling, Fred 140, 239, 240
Darvill, Richard 251, 254, 255, 256, 263
Dawson, Daniel 91
Dawson, Dick 125
Dawson, Francis 217
Dawson, Mathew 95, 106–7, *106*, 107, 109, 110, *110*, 111, *112*, 246
Day, John 93, *97*, 106, 129
Day, William 93
de Trafford, Sir Humphrey 234
Deards family 46, 47, 289–90, 305
Deards, John 2, 47, 269, 284
decline of racing in the 1730s/40s 39, 41–3, 45–7, 51, 297–9
Defoe, Daniel 31, 280
Derby, Edward, 14th Earl of 106
Derby, Edward, 17th Earl of *118*, 127, 128, 130, 191
Dettori, Frankie *154*, 164, *165*
Devil's Ditch *4*, 27, *48–9*, 52, 202–4, *208*
Devonshire, Peregrine, 12th Duke of 148, *156*, 157
Devonshire, William, 2nd Duke of 10, 43, 277, 281–3
Devonshire, William, 3rd Duke of 283, 290
Devonshire, William, 4th Duke of 303
Devonshire, William, 6th Duke of 269, 276
Dighton, R., *4th Duke of Queensberry 60*
Dilly, W. *117*
Ditch Mile 181, *207*, 213, 214
Ditch Stables 173, 193, *194*
Doe, John 97

Donoghue, Steve 128
doping horses *117*, 119–20
Drogheda, Henry, 4th Earl of 10, 43
Duncombe, Thomas 59
Durham, John, 3rd Earl of 119, *119*, 179, 207, 314
Dutton, Ralph 71

Eclipse 20, 42, 62, *63*, 64–5, *76*, 196, 212, 268
   colours 74
   dissection of 86
Eden, Sir Robert 62
Egerton, Judy 78
Eglinton, Alexander, 10th Earl of 57, 58, 251
Egremont, George, 3rd Earl of 72
Elizabeth I 14, 15, 17, 19, 21–2
Elizabeth II 138, *138–9*, 140, 141, 166
Erratt family 311
Essex, Robert, 2nd Earl of 22
Evelyn, John 267
Exning *3*, 14–15, 121, *232–3*, 232, 313, 314, *316*

Fagg, Sir Robert 5, 7, 287
Fairfax, Thomas, 3rd Lord 23, 27, 230–1
Fairhaven, Ailwyn, 3rd Lord 166
Fallon, Kieren *165*
Falmouth, Evelyn, 6th Viscount *70*, 106
Farnham, Robert 1st Earl of 222
Feilden, Sir Randle *146*, 147
Fellowes, Robert 150, 159, 166
Fenwick, Edward 39
Ferneley, John 95
   Training at Newmarket 259, 260, *261*
Finch Mason, George *108*
fires 31, *31*, 234, 267, 293, 294

Firth, Pat 147, 150
Fitzroy, Reverend Henry 90
Flatman, John 171–2, 178, *179*, 270
Flatman, Nat *88*, 91, *92*, 110
Fletcher, James 56–8, 59
Fordham, Charlie *110*
Fordham, George 91, *92*, 110
Foster, Christopher 157
Fountain, Sir Andrew 294–5
Four-Mile Stables *74*, 75, 193, 196, *198–9*, *202–3*, 205
Frampton, Tregonwell 31, 32, 35, *36*, 37, 41, 276–7, 279, 288
France 65–6, 107, 129, 236
Freer, Geoffrey 143, 150
Frost, James 224, *229*
Fuller, John 224, *227*

Gainsborough, Thomas, *Thomas Panton 45*
gallops 243–8, 313
General Stud Book (GSB) 41, 69–70, 120, 157
George I *38*, 39, 277
George II 39, 41
George VI 133, 239, 240
Giles, G.D., *Tommy v Toddy at Newmarket 116*
Gillespie, Edward 159
Gillum, John 58
Gilpin, Sawrey, *Duke of Cumberland inspecting his stud, The 55*, *61*
Gittus, William 246
Glasgow, James, 5th Earl of 95, *261*, *261*
Godolphin, Francis, 2nd Earl of 42, *42*, 45, 46, 279, 280, *282*,*283*, 289
Gorton, Major Hugh 142
Gosden, John *151*, 164
Gosling, Captain Miles 158

Grafton, Augustus, 3rd Duke of 90, 258
Grafton, George, 4th Duke of 90, 118
Granby, John, Marquis of 59, 268–9
grandstands *see* stands
Gray, Colonel Douglas 240
Gray, Colonel Nicol 142, 150
Greer, Captain Harry (later Sir Henry) 124, *125*, 126, 237, 239
Greeves, Paul 157
Greville, Charles 93, 180
Grosvenor, Sir Richard (later 1st Earl Grosvenor) 52, 68–9, *69*, 70, 73, 82, 284
Gwyn, Nell 267

Haggas, William 139
Haigh, A.G.,
   Bahram 130
   Blue Peter 131
Hall, Harry 96
   George Fordham 92
   July Course buildings 172–3, *172*
   Nat Flatman 88, *92*
Hambro, Jocelyn 150
Hamilton of Dalzell, Gavin, 2nd Lord *128*, 133, 162, 191
Hammond, John 9
Hancock, Lisa 159, 191
Harding, Field Marshall Lord 147, 148
Harrison, Elizabeth 47
Harrison, Leslie 147
Hartington, Lord *see* Devonshire, Peregrine, 12th Duke of
Hathaway, Alan 246
Havell, E., *Derby Trial, The 9*
Hawker, Thomas, *Charles II 28*
Hawley, Sir Joseph 178, 248
Hayhoe, Joseph 106, 270

Haynes, Christopher 157
Hayter, Sir George, *Captain the Hon. Henry Rous 97*
Healy, John 56
heat racing 117, 279, 299
Heath House 32, 106, 107, 110, *110*
Heber, Reginald 58, 302–3
Henderson, Johnny 148, 150, 158
Henry VIII 14, 19
Herring, J. F., senior 8, 86, 96
   Bay Middleton 215
   Four-Mile Stables 193, 196, *199*
Hervey, Augustus 56
Hillyard, David 158
Hirsch, Baron Maurice de 114
Hobbs, Bruce 150, 151, 271
Hodge, Marcus, *John Taylor 247*
Hogarth, William, Plate 6 from Rake's Progress *293*, 294
Holcroft, Thomas 262–3, *264*, 265
Holland-Martin, Ruby 148
Home of Horseracing Trust (HOHT) 271
Hopkins, W.H., *Derby Trial, The 9*
horse-breeding 17, 19–20, 22, 234
   see also National Stud
horseboxes 96
Horsemen's Group 45
Horseracing Advisory Council 153, 156
horses,
   Affirmed 152
   Aggressor 151
   Aiming High 240
   Ambush 111
   Amerigo 147
   Ascham 62, 68, 78, *80*
   Atlas 263, 264
   Aureole 138, 140, *234*
   The Axe 214
   Bahram *130*
   The Bard 110

Index

Baronet 86, *87*, 212
Bartlet's Childers 35
Bay Bolton 35, *35*
Bay Malton 68, *68*, *79*, *80*, 99, 276
Bay Middleton 214, *215*
Bay Turrell/Bay Tarrall 22, 23, 210
Be My Chief 237
Big Game 237, 239, 240
Blandford 127
Blue Peter 128, 129, *131*, 132
Bonny Boy 52
Boreas 82
Brigadier Gerard 146
Bucephalus 74
Bulle Rock 65
Byerley Turk 33, *33*
Cadland 312
Caergwrle 137
Camilla 281
Carbine 108
Cardinal Puff 82
Careless 262, 263, *264*
Carrozza 139, 237, 240
Catch-'em-Alive 178
Chamossaire 134, 237, 240
Champion 96
Charlottown 140, 141
Chaunter 10
Cherry Lass 238
Cheshire Dick 82
Cicero *113*, 116
Colorado *184*
Come to Daddy 249
Common 311
Conductor 222, *223*
Conqueror 272–3, 295
Coriander 217
Crab 56
Crazy 55
Crepe de Chine 240

Crepello 141
Cresta Run *184*
Crucifix 93
Cyllene *185*
Cypron 62
Dante 108, 134
Darley Arabian *34*, 35, 42, 62
Daylami *154*
Diamond 93, *101–3*, 196
Diamond Jubilee 111, *112*, 113, 114
Diesis 147
Diligence 240
Donovan 214
Dragon 37
Drumator 217
Dunfermline 139, 141
Eagle 224, *225–6*, *228–9*
Eleanor 224, *225–6*, 229
Elephant 265
Elis 96, *97*
Emilius 214
Escape *6*, 66, 70, *70*–1, *70*, 71, 73, 213
Estimate 139
Euston 77, *77*
Fille de l'Air 107
Firetail 222
Florizel II 114
Flying Childers *10*, 34, 35, 43, 44, 269, 281
The Flying Dutchman 95
Flying Fox 69, *112*, *188*
Forester 265
Foxhall 108
Frankel 150, *163*, 164
Gallinule 125
Gay Crusader 126
Gibsoutski 213
Gimcrack *5*, 20, 62, *66*, 68, 69, 74, 75, 82, *83*, 171, 196, 207
Godolphin Arabian *41*, 42, 62, 296

Golden Horn 151
Grand Lodge 147
Grey Diomed 70, *100*
Grey Windham 52
Gudgeon 285
Hackler's Pride 132
Hambletonian 86, 93, 98–9, *101–3*, 196
Herod 62, 65, 78, *81*, 269
Highclere 139
Highflyer 65, *65*
Hollyhock 222
Hyperion 118, *129*, 133
Ile de Bourbon 214
Isinglass 108, *112*
Julia 217
Kingcraft 107
Kisber 270
Kris 147
La Flèche 114, *114*, 196, 214
Ladas *112*
Lady Elizabeth 106
Lamprey 285
Laura 222
Lilian 206
Looby *272–3*, 295
Macaroni 89, 106, 270
Maccabeus 94
Mackerel 22
Mambrino 222
Marske 62
Masaka 240
Matchem *4*, 39, 212
Meld *140*
Melton 110
Merry Andrew 295
Mill Reef 146, 240
Minoru 111, 114, 238
Minting 109, 110
Miss Hen 52
Miss Whip 261

Molly 43, 45
Monarque 107
Moorcock 55
Nearco 133, 234, 240
Never Say Die 128, 240
Nijinsky 146, 151
Noble 56
Northern Dancer 134
Ocean Swell 131
Oncidium 147
Orme 110, 114
Ormonde 69, 109, 110, *110*, 116
Oxo 129
Pall Mall 139
Park Top 156
Parthia 141
Perdita II 111
Persian Wheel 240
Persimmon 111, *112*, 114, 270
Phalaris 118, 127, *127*, 129
Pharis II 129, 131
Pharos 118
Pinza 138, 140, *140*
Pocahontas 224
Polar Star 238
Pont L'Eveque 234, *234*
Pretender 108–9
Priam 91, 95, 214, *215*
Prince 210
Prince Palatine 238
Pyrrhus 222
Queen Bertha 106
Ragstone 149
Rock Sand *113*, 116
Rocket 82
Roxana 42
Royal Lancer 240
Royal Palace *136*, 141, *141*, 146, 151, 240
Running Rein 92, 94
St Amant *113*
St Blaise 311

335

St Gatien 9
St Simon 109, *109–10*, 110, 124
Sanlinea 147
Scotia 90, 217
Shag 52
Shirley Heights 214
Short Sentence 240
Sir Bevys 270
Sir Ivor 141, 146, 151
Sir Peter Teazle 65
Sir Visto *112*
Skylark 70
Sleeping Partner 151
Slip Anchor 147
Sloven 52
Smiling Ball 280
The Soarer 237, 238
Spearmint *113*, 116
Spiletta 62
St Simon *109*, 110
Stray Shot 206
Sun Chariot 133, 237, 239, *239*
Surplice 96
Surprise 224
Sweet Lips 22
Swynford 118
Tadmor 216
Taffolet Barb *33*
Thumps 27, 28, 210
Tiresias 312
Trajan *4*
Traveller *100*
Trentham 196, *222, 223*
Trimmer 56, 62
Tudor Melody 240
Turf 78, *80*
Valoris 151
Vatican 216
West Australian 95
Whipper Snapper 285

Whiskey 217
Wolver Hollow 150
Zinc 214
Zinganee *91*
see also Eclipse
Howard de Walden, John, 9th Lord 143, 147–8, *147*, 153, 156, 166
Hughes, Rob 160, 241
Humphrey, W., *Sir Charles Bunbury* 71
Hunting Towers 22
Huntingdon, William 139
Hutton, John 55, 62

Ilchester, Giles, 6th Earl of 133
Implementation Committee 142
Ireland 39, 107, 211
    and the National Stud 236, 238–40

Jackson, Mr 245, *246*
James I 14, *16*, 19, 210
James II 30–1, 35, 275
Jarvis, Sir Jack 128, 131, 132, 135, 151, 270
Jarvis, William 147
Jennings, Henry 107
Jennings, Tom 107, 108, 248
Jensen, Peter 166
'Jersey Act' 120
Jersey, George, 8th Earl of 126
Jewitt, James 108, *112*
Jockey Club 105, 156, 164
    acquisition of the land 158–9, 243, 246, 311–15, *316–17*
    after World War II 141–2
    and Bentinck 93
    and the BHB 157, 160
    Calendars 42, 69

and the Deards family 46
founding/early history 8–9, 11, 39, *40*, 46–7, 274–91
and Jumping 114–15
and photography 171
and Prentice 57–8
and the Prince of Wales 70–1
and the programme 93
races for three-year-olds 65
and the RHT 149, 153
and Rous 105
and the Royal Charter 149
and the Royal Commission on Gambling 153
rules 82, 95, 105, 109, 119
and the Weatherbys 157
and World War I 124, 126
Jockey Club Racecourses (JCR) 133, 158–9, 246
Jockey Club Rooms 46, 116, 121, *186*, 212, 268, 284, 287, 289
jockeys 7, 66, 68, 164
    American style *113*, 115, 116
    colours 43
    licensing of 109
    see also *individual names*
Joel, Jim 141
Johnson, Ben 74
Johnson, Doctor Samuel 37
Johnson, Noble 237, 239
Jones, Herbert *112*, 113
Jones, Inigo 266, *267*
Jones, Peter 162
judges 290
Judge's Box *222, 223*
July Course (formerly Round Course) *4*, 6, 27, 52, 126, 127, 185, 200–1, *204–5*, 206–7
    buildings *172*, 187–91, *188–90, 192–5*

concerts 162
    Saturday fixtures 142–3
    World War I 124
    World War II 133, 232–3, 234
Jumping 114–15, *115*, 126, 129, 132, 148, 207

Keene, Foxhall 108
Keene, James 108
Keeper of the Match Book 69, 157
Keeper of the Running Horses 32, 43, 45, 46, 71, 276, 279
Kent, John 93
Kérouaille, Louise de 31
Khalid bin Abdullah, Prince *162, 163*, 164, 260
King's Plates 32, 56, 304
King's Stables (Rubbing House) *5, 49, 52*, 86, *114*, 189, 196, *197, 203, 205, 209*

Lagrange, Count Frédéric de 107
Lake, Warwick 70
Lambton, F.W. 124
Lambton, Hon. George *118*, 119, 125, 127, 128, 129, 130, 135
Lambton, Teddy 118
Larkin, James and John 83
Lawson, Joe 128
Leach, Felix 179
Lees, Captain Nick 150, 159
Lefevre, Charles 107
legends of the Heath 249
Levy Board 143–4, 147, 149, 153, 157, 158, 161–2
    and the Millennium Stand 159
    and the National Stud 240–1
    and the RHT 149
Levy System 160
licensing of courses 109

Index

Limekilns 244, 313, 315, *317*
Lloyd George, Major Gwilym 144
Loates, Sam *112*
Loates, Tommy *112*, *116*
Lockwood, Sir Frank, *Oliver Cromwell* 8
Lonsdale, Henry, 3rd Viscount 277, 283, 284
Lonsdale, Hugh, 5th Earl of 128, 191, 240

McCalmont, Colonel Harry 115, 127, 207, 270, 315
MacDonald, Rory 166
Macdonald-Buchanan, Captain John 159
Machell, Captain James 107, *108*, 111, 114
Macready, Sir Nevil 156
Magalotti, Count Lorenzo 30
Maher, Danny *113*, 115, 116
Al Maktoum, Sheikh Mohammed bin Rashid and family *162*, 164, 244
March, Lord (later 4th Duke of Queensberry) 43, 57, 59, *60*, 72, 73, 249, 265, 303–4, *303*, 304
Marlow, William, *Duke of Cumberland inspecting his stud, The* 55, *61*
Marriott, Cecil 115, 119, 126, 128, 134, *135*, 191, 315
Marsh, Marcus 125
Marsh, Richard 111, *112*, 114
Marshall, Ben 8, 86, 90, 96
  Finish—Eagle beating Eleanor, The 224, *226*
  James Frost and Richard Prince 229

  John Fuller 227
  Samuel Betts 227
  Start—Eagle and Eleanor at the Post, The 224, *225*
Match Book 42, 43, 46, 47, 210, 278
match racing 252, 291, 298
Merriott, Sam 74, 76
Millais, J.E., *Archibald, 5th Earl of Rosebery* 122
Monmouth, James, Duke of 30, 31, 267, 275, *275*, 278
Moody, William 58
Moore, Ryan *165*
Moore, Sir John 7
Muddle family 158
Muir, J.B. 275
  'Ye Olde New-Markitt Calendar' 210
Munnings, Sir Alfred 8, 114, 194
  Aureole with owner and trainer 138, *234*
  Sun Chariot 239
Murless, Sir Noel 137, *137*, 140, 141, 143, 147
Muybridge experiments 86
Mytens, Daniel, *James I* 16, *17*
Mytton, John 117

National Horseracing Museum (NHRM) 21, 26, 156, 166, 186, 271
National Hunt 115, 146, 148, 207, *209*
National Stud 11, 133, 146, 148, 159, 236–40
Neale, Frank 70, 90
Newmarket Bank 292–5
Newmarket (engraving) 30
'Newmarket, or an Essay on the Turf' (Parsons) 62, 306–9
Norfolk, Bernard, 16th Duke of 148, *149*, 185, 218

O'Brien, Vincent 151
Ogilvy, Charles 222
O'Kelly, Andrew 73
O'Kelly, Colonel Dennis 62, 64–5, *64*, 73, 74
O'Kelly family 212
Old Cambridgeshire Course, buildings 173, 178
Old Red Weighing House 178
Opie, John, *Thomas Holcroft* 264
Ordinance of the Rump Parliament 22
O'Rourke, Brian 241
Orton, John 96
ownership of courses 133
OWS, *Fred Archer* 111
Oxley, John 146

paddocks 185
  July Course 188, *188*
  Rowley Mile 173, 182, 185–6, *186*
Palace 17, *18*, 20, *30*, 31, *40*, 59, 121, 267–71
  after World War II 234
  in the Civil War 230–1
Panton, Thomas, senior 43, *45*, 46, 52, 68, 71, 82, 279, 283
Parsons, Philip 62, 73, 288, 306–9, *307*
Pattern Scheme 20, 32–3, 149, 157, 167, 211, 214, 220–1
Patton, Nick 245
Paul, George 159, 166
Peat Marwick & Co. 157
Penfold, Major-General Bernard 156

Peppiatt, Sir Leslie 147
Persse, Atty 138
Philipps, Jim 143, 148, 150
Philo-Hippos 58, 301–5
photography 8, 171
Pick, William 96, 299
Piggott, Lester 91, 141, 150–2, *152*, 164
Player, Peter 159
Plummer, Sir Desmond (later Lord Plummer) 148, 160
poisoning 90–1
Pond, John 10, 47, 58, 249, 302–5
Pope, Alexander 28, 73
Porter, John 110, *110*, 111, 114
Portland, William, 4th Duke of *312*, 313
Portland, William, 6th Duke of 124
Portmore, Charles, 3rd Earl of *5*, *12–13*, 43, 283, 285, 287
Pratt, John 74, *75*, 82, 83, *83–5*, 90
Prentice, George 55–8, 62, 95, 304
Prescott, Sir Mark vii–viii, *viii*, 137, 179, 248
Prince, Richard 90–1, 224, *228–9*
prizes 32–3, *32*, 42, 60, 62, 109, 167, 275, 279
programmes, comparison of 120–1
prohibition of racing 22, *22*
Prosser, Mike 159
pulling of horses 93–4

Queally, Tom 163

Race Planning Committee 143

Racecourse Holdings Trust (RHT) 148–50, 153, 157–8, 161, 246
Racecourse Side *2*
racecourses *see under* courses
races 210–21
   1,000 Guineas 90, *184*, 213
   1,200 Guineas Stakes 59, 62, 68, 291
   2,000 Guineas 90, 110, 125, *142*, *143*, *184*, 213, 214
   Ascot Gold Cup *139*
   Boudoir Stakes 217
   Breeders Cup 282
   Bretby Stakes 217
   Cambridgeshire 213, 214, 216
   Cesarewitch 213, 214, 216
   Challenge Cup 212
   Champion Stakes 216
   Cheveley Park 216
   Claret Stakes 213
   Craven Stakes 212, 224
   Criterion Stakes 216
   Derby 65, 94, 110, 124, 145–6, *234*
   Dewhurst 216
   Earl of Sefton Stakes 206
   Grand Duke Michael Stakes 214
   Grand National 111, 126, 129
   Great Stakes 47, 211, 279, 283, 302, 304
   Great Subscription 51, 264, 299, 303
   Heathorn Stakes 214
   Hopeful Stakes 216–17
   Jockey Club Cup 216
   Jockey Club Stakes 216
   July Cup 216, 220
   July Stakes 65, 213
   Leger, World War II 134
   Middle Park 216
   Newmarket Challenge Whip *4*, 211–12, *212*
   Newmarket Handicap 216
   Newmarket October Handicap 216
   Newmarket Stakes 214
   Newmarket Town Plate *27*, *27*, 30, 200, 201, *208–9*, 210, 211, 219, 289
   Noblemen and Gentlemen's Contribution Stakes 52, 211, 278, 279, 283
   Oaks 65, 106, 145–6, 258
   Oatlands/Oatlands Stakes 212–13
   October Stakes 211, 278, 283
   Port Stakes 213
   Prince of Wales Stakes 141
   Prince's Stakes 212, 214
   Princess of Wales Stakes 216, 221
   Riddlesworth Stakes 214
   Royal Plates 32, 41, 42, 55, 201, 211, 299, 302
   Rubbish Stakes 217
   St Leger 65, 114, 124, 129, 131, 32, 133, 211, 258
   September Stakes 124
   Town Plate 30, 210, 211, 219
   Triple Crown 95, 111, 124
   Virgin 217
Racing Reorganisation Committee 133
Racing Welfare 94
railway 96, 105, 134
Raymond, Sir Stanley 148
Red Betting Post 179, *179*, 180, 205
Red Weighing House 173, 180, *180*
Reiff brothers 115
Renton, Ian 159
Reynolds, Sir Joshua, *Charles, 2nd Marquis of Rockingham* 276
Richards, Sir Gordon 92, 129, *140*, 141
Richardson, Sir Albert 121
Richmond-Watson, Julian 159, 166
Ricketts, Sir Tristram 157, 160
Roberts, Michael 165
Robinson, James (Jem) 91, *91*, 92
Robson, Robert 90, *90*
Rockingham, Charles, 2nd Marquis of 43, 68, *68*, 73, *276*
Rosebery, Archibald, 5th Earl of 116, *122*, 124, 126
Rosebery, Harry, 6th Earl of 128, 131, *132*, 134, 142, 144, 191
Rothschild, Baron Meyer de and family 106, 268, 269, 270, 271
Rous, Admiral the Hon. Henry 82, 89, 95–6, *97*, 105, 106–7, 120, 214, 217, *310*, 313
   and the Birdcage 182
   'Proposal for the amelioration' 180–1
   and weighing disaster 178
Routh, Dolly 55
Rowlandson, Thomas 71
   Jockey Club, or Newmarket Meeting 72
   Turfites 64
Rowley Mile 1, *1*, *4*, *9*, *50*, 124, 127, 134, 142, *143*, 162, *208–9*
   buildings 148, 159, 173, 180–7, *180*, *183–4*, *187*, 209
   paddocks 173
   topography 249
   in war times 231, *232*, *232*

Royal Boxes 190
Royal Charter 149
Royal Studs 14, 15, 19, 23
Rubbing House *see* King's Stables
Rubens, Peter Paul *19*, 23
Rutland, Charles, 6th Duke of 244
Rutland, John, 2nd Duke of 10, 44, 277
Rutland, John, 5th Duke of 180, 270, *312*, 313, 314
Rye House Plot 28, 30–1, 32, 267, 275, 284

St Bel, Charles Vial de 86
St Leger, John 56–7
St Quintin, Sir William 62
Salisbury (city) 15, 21–2, *21*, 133
Salisbury, William, 2nd Lord 19, 210
Sangster, Ben 241
Sartorius, Francis,
   Bay Malton, Turf, Herod, and Ascham 80, *196*
   Careless 264
Sartorius, J.N., *Grey Diomed beating Traveller* 100
Sassoon, Sir Victor 140, 141
Saturday fixtures 142–3
Saunders, Seb 165
Savill, Peter 160
Scott, John 90, 95, 106, 107
Scrope, Bunty 147
Sefton, Hugh, 7th Earl of 134, 143, 206
Seymour, James 3, 8, 47, 51, 288
   Bay Bolton 35
   Carriage Match 303, 304
   Conqueror beating Looby 272–3
   Flying Childers 10, 43, 44

Grey horse leaping a sheep 50
Sir Robert Fagg and the cherry girl 7
Shafto, Jenison 60, 68, 73, 193, 258
Sharpe, Harry 239
silks 74, 82
Siltzer, Captain Frank 179
Singleton, John 68, 79, *79*
Site of Special Scientific Interest 248–9
Sloan, Tod 113, 115, *116*, 145
Smith, Doug 151
Smith, Eph *138*
Smith, T., *Finished Horses* 1, *4*
Somerset, Charles, 6th Duke of 52, 268, 283, 311
Sparrow, Sir John 158, 241
Spence, Christopher 241
sponsorship 32–3, 216
stables 173, 192–4, 193, *193*, 258
  see also King's Stables
Standish, Sir Frank 224
stands 6, *9*, 22–3, 172, 173–8, *174*, 203, 205, 207
  Astley Stand *9*, 181, 182, *183*
  Beacon/Old Cambridgeshire Course 98–9, *100–1*, 173–9, *174–7*
  Duke of Portland's Stand 100, 173, 175, *175*, *177*, 178, 203, 205, 207
  Duke's Stand (New Stand) 1, *4*, 175, *176*, 181, 192, 196, *197*, 200, 203, 207
  Head-On Stand *183*, 184–5, 185–6, 186, 191
  Jockey Club Stand 182, *184*, *184*, 189, 205
  July Course 127, 189–90,

189–90, 191, *192–3*, 209
King's Stand 5, *10*, 82, 87, 99, *101*–2, 173–5, *174*, 196, *197*, 207, 222
Ladies Stand 190
Links *115*
Millennium Stand 159, 187, *187*, 222
New Stand *see* Duke's Stand
Private Stand 181
Public Stand, Rowley Mile *9*, 181
Rowley Mile 127, 159, 180–2, *183*–5, 184–5, 207, *209*
Silver Ring Stand 185, *190*
Steeplechasing 114
Stephenson, Willie 129
Stone Reeves, R., *Royal Palace* 136, *141*
stopping horses *117*, 119
Stoute, Sir Michael 137, 139, 150, 151
Stubbs, George *4*, 8, *63*, 69, 73, 74, 96
  Baronet 86, *87*
  Bay Malton and John Singleton 68, *79*
  Conductor 223
  Eclipse at Four-Mile Stables 76
  Euston 77
  Four-Mile Stables 193, *198*
  Gimcrack at Four-Mile Stables 66, *75*
  Gimcrack's Trial 83, *84–5*
  Hambletonian after his match with Diamond 102
  Herod 81
  King's Stables 98, 196, *197*
  Study of the King's Stables 170, 192, *197*

Trentham 223
subscription races 47, 56, 58–9, 62, 68, 276, 282–3, 292–3, 301
  1,200 Guineas Stakes 59, 62, 68
  New Grand Subscription 301, 303
Suffolk, James, 3rd Earl of 27
surfaces, preparation of 244–6, 255
Swain, J. *177*, 183
Swannell, Major David 166
Sweeney, Tony 39

Tattersall, George 180
Tattersall, Richard 65
Tattersalls 69, 164, 166
Tattersalls Sales Pavilion 121
Tattersalls Stand *190*
tax, betting 161
Taylor, Alec, junior 114, 128
Taylor, John 245, *247*
Ten Broek, Richard 108
Tharp family 127, 313, 315
Thomond, Earl of 27, 210
Thomson Jones, Harry 148, 150
thoroughbreds 8, *10*, 33, 35, 42, 43, 62, 236
Tillemans, Peter 5, 47, 288–9
  Waiting to start on the Round Course 49
Tompkins, Mark 248
topography of the Heath 242–9, 245
Tote 119, 128, 133, 144, 153, 161, 162, 186
  building 191
  and the Cesarewitch 216
Townshend, A.L. *Heath Foreman on Donkey* 246

Heath House string at exercise 110, *168–9*
St Simon 109
trade in horses 19–20, *24, 26*, 33, 42, 65
Trafford, Sir Humphrey de *138*, 141
trainers 7, 66, 68, 89–90, 109, 151, 164
  after World War II 137, 141
  licensing of 109
  see also individual names
training 243, 250–8
trials 82
Tsui, Christopher 164
Tully (Ireland) 236, 238–40
Turf Board 146
Turf Club 39
Tuting, William 47
types of horses 20

United Racecourses (UR) 158

Van Dyck, Sir Anthony
  Charles I 20, *23*
Van Geest family 216
Vane-Tempest, Sir Harry 98–9
Vernon, Richard 57, 59, 60, 73, 82, 258, 263, 313
veterinary field 155, 166
Victoria, Queen 268
Villiers, Barbara 31
Vyner, Robert 109

Wales, Edward (later Edward VII), Prince of *104, 111*, 114, 270
Wales, Frederick, Prince of 52, 282, 287

Wales, George (later George II), Prince of 288
Wales, Prince of (later Charles I) 266, 267
Wales, Prince of (later George IV) *2, 6*, 60, *60*, 70, *72*, 86, 114, 164, 212, 224, 258, 268, 269
Waley-Cohen, Robert 159
Walker, John Reid 191
Walker, William Hall (later 1st Lord Wavertree) 125, 236, 237, 239
Wallasey Stakes 47, 279, 283
Wallis, Colonel Tommy 150, 158
Wallis, Stephen 159
Walpole, Horace 45, 73, 306
Ward, James 96, 224
   Hambletonian beating Diamond 103
Warden, Colonel Dick 164
Warren Hill 1, *2, 3*, 244, *317*
wartime,
   Civil War 230–1, 266
   World War I 123–4, 126, 231
   World War II 126, 129, 133–4, 145, 231–4, *232–4*, 240
Wastell, John 90, 217

Watson, John 263, 265, 270
Watts, Jack *112*, 192
Waugh, Jack 147
Wavertree, Lord *see* Walker, William Hall
Weatherby family 69, 157
Weatherbys 41, 69, 157, 278
Webb, *William, Euphrates with trainer and jockey 117*
Weigall, Henry, *Admiral the Hon. Henry Rous 311*
Weighing Rooms 175, 178–9, *178*, 181–2, *182*, 186, 231
   July Course *188–90*, 191
Wernher, Lady Zia 140, *141*
West, Benjamin, *Richard, 1st Earl Grosvenor 69*
Westminster, Hugh, 1st Duke of 110, 114
Wharton, Thomas 276, 278
Whessell, John, *Richard Prince and Eagle 228*
Wigg, Lord George 148–9, 187
Wildman, William 62, *63*, 74, 82
William Hill 144, 161
William III 32, 35, 268, 276
Williams, Roger 42, 46, 47, 284–6, 287, 288, 295, 305

Willoughby de Broke, John, 20th Earl of 144, 153
Wilson, Christopher 96
Wilson, J.C., *Lord George Bentinck 94*
Wood, Charlie 110, 119
Woodcock, John 263
Wootton, Frank 111
Wootton, John 8, 26, 47, 51, 277, 285
   Byerley Turk with the Golden Horn in the background, The 33
   Charles Collyer, 2nd Earl of Portmore, watching his string 5, 12–13
   George I at Newmarket in 1717 38, 40, 288
   Godolphin Arabian, The 41
   race on the Round Course, A 52, 53
   Tregonwell Frampton in old age 36, 288
   Trip 194, *195*
World War I 123–4, 126, 231
World War II 126, 129, 133–4, 145, 231–4, *232–4*, 240, 271
Wragg, Geoffrey 132, 141
Wragg, Harry 129, 132, *132*
Wyatt, Major Michael 149

Wyck, Jan 26
   Round Course 48, 187, 189
   Taffolet Barb(?) 33
Wyvill, Sir Marmaduke 39

'Ye Olde New-Markitt Calendar' (Muir) 210
York, James, Duke of 206
Yorkshire, studs 7–8, 15

Picture Credits

Numerals refer to Figure numbers

4, 132, Endpapers
© British Library Board

10 © Devonshire Collection, Chatsworth. Reproduced by permission of Chatsworth Settlement Trustees.

182 © The Trustees of the British Library

113 Age Fotostock, Spain

160 Alan Grundy

52 Art Archive/Private Collection

123 Charles Church

23, 24, 36, 37, 159, 187 Christie's, London

166 Courtesy National Museum of Racing and Hall of Fame, and National Sporting Library & Museum

1, 3, 27, 28, 32, 38, 42, 43, 44, 46, 53, 65, 66, 72, 128, 162, 163, 192, 193 David Oldrey

41, 58, 79, 129 Earl of Halifax

93 Earl of Rosebery

49 Fitzwilliam Museum, Cambridge

21 Florence, Laurentian Library, Ms. Med. Palat. 123/2, c.42a '-By permission of the MiBACT'

26 George Winn Darley

102 Getty Images

175 Getty Images/Stanley Sherrman

pviii, 8, 9, 18, 31, 33, 45, 48, 50, 55, 59, 61, 63, 74, 77, 78, 80, 81, 82, 83, 84, 85, 86, 87, 97, 98, 99, 109, 111, 133, 156, 161, 178, 180, 181, 183, 185, 189, 194, 195, 196 Jockey Club

145, 146, 153 Jockey Club Racecourses

112, 114, 115, 116, 117, 118, 119, 120, 121, 122, 124, 125, 126 John Crofts

172, 173 John F Hamlin

127 Lowell Libson Ltd, London

130, 131, 134, 135, 136, 137, 154, 155 Martin and the late Gay Slater

106 Max Mumby/Indigo/Getty Images

11, 14 National Gallery, London/ Bridgeman Images

15, 17, 47, 60, 107, 138, 167 National Horseracing Museum

19, 75, 96, 184, 188 National Portrait Gallery, London

67, 68 National Trust

22 Nicholas Reed Herbert

20, 147, 62 Private Collection / Bridgeman Images

30 Private Collection / Photo © Christie's Images / Bridgeman Images

191 Private Collection / Photo © Peter Nahum at The Leicester Galleries, London / Bridgeman Images'

105 Royal Collection Trust. All Rights Reserved

6, 39, 56, 76 Royal Collection Trust/ © Her Majesty Queen Elizabeth II 2015

54 Sir Edward Cazalet

190 Sir John Soane's Museum

73 Sir Mark Prescott

2, 7, 25, 34 Sotheby's, London

12 Stephen Conlin

157, 171 Tate Images

13 The Art Archive / British Museum / Eileen Tweedy

40 The Baltimore Museum of Art: William Woodward Collection, BMA 1956.282

16, 89, 186 Timothy Cox

5, 29, 35, 57, 64, 90, 158 Yale Center for British Art, Paul Mellon Collection

51, 164, 165 Yale University Press, London

Course Meeting begins always a fortnight before the
Spring Meeting is the first Monday in Easter Week
Kings Plate is run for on Thursday following
Second Spring Meeting is always a
fortnight after the first
July Meeting the 2d and 3d of July
First October Meeting the Kings Plate
is run for, on the first Thursday in Oct.
Second October Meeting is one Week
after the first